Small Business in a Global Economy

Small Business in a Global Economy

Creating and Managing Successful Organizations

Volume 2

Scott L. Newbert, Editor

 PRAEGER™

An Imprint of ABC-CLIO, LLC

Santa Barbara, California • Denver, Colorado

Library of Congress Cataloging-in-Publication Data

Small business in a global economy : creating and managing successful organizations / Scott L. Newbert, editor.

   volumes cm

  Includes bibliographical references.

  ISBN 978-1-4408-3015-0 (print : alk. paper) — ISBN 978-1-4408-3016-7 (e-book)

1. Small business. 2. Small business—Management. I. Newbert, Scott L.

  HD2341.S5727 2015

 658.02'2—dc23   2014035888

ISBN: 978-1-4408-3015-0
EISBN: 978-1-4408-3016-7

19 18 17 16 15   1 2 3 4 5

This book is also available on the World Wide Web as an eBook.
Visit www.abc-clio.com for details.

Praeger
An Imprint of ABC-CLIO, LLC

ABC-CLIO, LLC
130 Cremona Drive, P.O. Box 1911
Santa Barbara, California 93116-1911

This book is printed on acid-free paper ∞

Manufactured in the United States of America

Contents

Preface

This two-volume set takes an ambitious agenda by seeking to provide a holistic source of information to scholars, students, practitioners, and policy makers interested in understanding the behavior and decision-making of owners and managers of small businesses; the operational and strategic challenges they face and the strategies they implement in response to them; the environmental constraints on their businesses' ability to emerge, grow, and survive; and the role their businesses play in the larger economy. As idiosyncratic as the small businesses that they investigate, the chapters in this set represent an intentionally eclectic mix of styles, approaches, and contexts in the hopes of triangulating on what is known about the challenges and opportunities faced by would-be and practicing small business owners and managers. As the chapter authors include leading small business researchers from across the globe, each topic is explored in rigorous, scholarly fashion; thus, due attention is given to breadth and depth.

The two volumes view small business through distinct lenses. Volume 1 takes a somewhat microview of the small business phenomenon, focusing mainly on the small business owner. To set the stage for the chapters to follow, this volume begins by assessing the impact of the small business sector on the economic landscape. With the importance of small business established, this volume then proceeds to analyze issues pertaining to the creation and ownership of small businesses of various types. In so doing, it seeks to answer such questions as why and how do individuals seek to start small businesses and how is this decision influenced by characteristics of the owner(s)? This volume then investigates how, once the decision is made to start a small business, the focal opportunity is identified and exploited. Broad questions answered in this vein of research include: how do would-be small business owners navigate their environments in the pursuit of the resources needed to create their businesses, and how does the timing of those actions matter?

Volume 2 widens the level of analysis by viewing the small business phenomenon from both a mesolevel and macrolevel perspective, focusing on both the operational concerns of and the environmental factors impacting small business. Volume 2 begins by exploring the effectiveness of a variety of strategies used by small business owners, answering questions such as how can small business owners successfully manage stakeholders, exploit technological capabilities, leverage networks, implement human resource systems, internationalize, balance economic and social goals, and exit the market? Volume 2 concludes by investigating the various contexts that affect and are affected by small businesses. In so doing, these chapters seek answers to questions that include, to what extent are small businesses influenced by the geographic, institutional, and political environments in which they operate?

Ultimately, this two-volume set is intended to serve as a window into the various and unique dynamics that unfold in small businesses. Thus, it is my hope that multiple constituencies may benefit from its contents, each in their own way. In particular, students may gain a better appreciation of the importance and vitality of the small businesses sector and, in turn, consider careers either as owners or managers of small businesses or as academics who study them. These volumes may also expose current scholars to new theoretical and empirical relationships that will spur their thinking toward proposing and seeking answers to new research questions. Current and would-be owners and managers of small businesses may gain new insights into the internal and external constraints facing their businesses as well as the strategies with which they may respond to them. Finally, the chapters in this set may broaden policy makers' understanding of how extant regulations impact small businesses and facilitate the consideration and development of new programs that may support and promote the small business sector. Given the substantive contributions that small businesses have made throughout history, and continue to make to this day, to virtually every economy on earth, to the extent that this two-volume set achieves the above objectives it may contribute in some small way to global prosperity.

ACKNOWLEDGMENTS

This work could not have come to fruition without the help of many people who deserve special recognition. First and foremost, I would like to thank each of the authors included in these volumes for preparing chapters that seek to provide thoughtful answers to important questions concerning small business. I would also like to thank Mike Maiale for his extensive copyediting assistance. Finally, I would like to thank Harry Halloran for his financial support of this project.

Introduction

Scott L. Newbert

As noted in the introduction to volume 1 of this book set, small businesses are widespread across the globe. Yet, in addition to their mere presence and, by extension, their providing the majority of employment opportunities in most countries, small businesses also contribute in other meaningful ways to the economy. At first glance, it would seem that, because of their advantage in resource endowment and slack, large businesses would benefit accordingly from their innovative investments, just as Schumpeter predicted.[1] However, a good deal of research suggests that scale economies do not seem to benefit large businesses when it comes to innovation. In fact, research shows that small businesses innovate at a greater rate and earn disproportionately greater returns from their R&D investments than large businesses.[2] For these and similar reasons, small businesses have long been identified as the true agents of economic growth and development.

While this is all good news for small businesses, it nevertheless begs the question, how are small businesses able to succeed despite their limited resources? While the chapters in volume 1 provide microlevel explanations for small businesses' ability to grow productively, it is worthwhile to investigate the extent to which meso- and macro-level explanations exist as well. Specifically, to the extent that the implementation of certain strategies may enable small businesses to succeed in the marketplace, a worthy agenda would involve adopting an operational view of small business and seeking to understand how success may be a function of meso-level factors internal to the business. Of course, success may also derive, at least in part, by factors that are beyond the reach of the small business. Thus, a final relevant line of inquiry would involve widening the level of analysis still further so as to understand how the macro-level geographic, institutional, and political factors in which the small business operates also affect success.

In the spirit of these issues, the goal of this volume is to explore small business ownership at the meso- and macro-levels. In so doing, it seeks to provide academics, students, practicing managers, and policy makers greater insights into strategies that may be successful in the small business sector as well as the contextual factors that support (and inhibit) small business on a regional scale.

Volume 2 begins with several chapters dedicated to strategies by which small business owners may create value. In chapter 1, Bosse investigates the dynamic interplay between the small business owner and the market in the pursuit of growth. He contends that conventional wisdom regarding value creation, whereby value is maximized by minimizing transaction costs, is flawed. In contrast, he proposes that small business owners can create more value by attending to the interests and well-being of their stakeholders. Drawing on stakeholder theory, he reasons that stakeholders represent a valuable source of information about the value of the opportunities facing small businesses and that by testing their hypotheses about these opportunities with their stakeholders, small business owners can learn how to improve their value propositions to increase their profit potential.

Building off of the notion of value creation, Tribble, Drnevich, and Ha argue that innovation, defined as the creation, improvement, or implementation of new ideas or activities that may take the form of services, products, structures, or plans, is one of the main drivers of value creation in small firms. In exploring innovation in the small business context, the authors pay particular attention to the role that information technology may play in enhancing and enabling innovation activities in small businesses, how the environment may influence the contributions of technology to innovation, and how small businesses may create and appropriate the value they create from their technological innovations. Based on their analysis, Tribble, Drnevich, and Ha provide strategic advice to small business owners seeking to leverage information technology to drive innovation.

Continuing the focus on innovation, Clark and Newbert drill down more deeply into the topic by investigating the effects of top management team (TMT) networks on the innovation output of small technology businesses in chapter 3. They argue that a TMT network, or the set of individuals with whom TMT members have relationships, can be an important contributor to a business's innovativeness as it tends to be a primary conduit through which the business gains access to resources critical to this task. Given that small businesses tend to be, by definition, resource-poor, such a process is especially important to them. Unfortunately, resource gatekeepers often perceive a business's size to be indicative of its potential for future performance and growth, and, thus, are often unwilling to provide small businesses access to resources from which they may be unlikely to receive a desirable return. In light of these factors, Clark and Newbert note an inherent paradox facing small businesses: they require resources to innovate, but resource gatekeepers are reluctant to provide them. The authors proceed to explore the effects of various network dimensions on the innovative performance of a sample of 70 high-tech firms and find that small businesses do indeed benefit less from their TMT networks than their larger counterparts. They conclude by identifying strategies managers of small businesses can employ to develop the sorts of networks critical for overcoming the liability of smallness.

In chapter 4, Patel takes a slightly different approach to the innovation issue by exploring how high-performance work systems (HPWS) create value for small, innovative businesses. He argues that a HPWS constitutes a bundle of human resource practices that can play a key role in enhancing employee productivity, which may lead to a competitive advantage. Although HPWSs can be important to the success and survival of small businesses, particularly those pursuing an innovation strategy, Patel notes that they require significant investments, which tend to be in short supply in small businesses. Moreover, small businesses often find it difficult to accrue economies of scale and scope from HPWS practices. Thus, Patel seeks to both review the literature on human resource practices in small firms and assess the role of costs and benefits in the implementation of HPWS in small businesses. By analyzing data on innovative firms in the United Kingdom and Japan, he concludes that certain strategic and institutional factors play a role in the degree of effectiveness of HPWS practices.

Taking a somewhat different approach to understanding value creation in the small business context, Eberhard and Craig begin chapter 5 by noting that the global economic landscape is dominated by family-controlled businesses, the overwhelming majority of which are small. Notwithstanding the ubiquitous presence of these small family businesses, the authors note that there is little understanding of the strategies family businesses employ as they seek to expand internationally, which they argue to be important for survival and longevity, and suspect that because small, family businesses often seek to create not only financial, but also, and perhaps more importantly, "socioemotional" value, the strategies they use and the effects of those strategies may be rather idiosyncratic. The authors confirm this suspicion in an exhaustive review of the family business internationalization literature and offer practical advice to owners of small family businesses regarding the importance of non-family ownership, a seamless succession strategy that includes an international mind-set, and networks by which they may collaborate with other family businesses.

Building off the notion in the prior chapter that multiple forms of value may be important to small business owners, Gras, Lumpkin, and Nason explore in chapter 6 the tensions small business owners face when seeking to create financial and social value. Drawing upon dialectical theory, the authors propose that early in the founding process, small business owners pursuing both social and economic goals will confirm the plausibility of the goals' coexistence and the processes to accomplish both goals, resulting in a steadfast commitment to both social and financial goals. They continue by arguing that as these businesses emerge, tension between the goals and logics of their social and business stakeholders will emerge. Given that this tension will arise when the small business owner needs their support the most, their strategic priorities are likely to be highly volatile during this phase. The authors conclude their theorizing by arguing that, over time, either one stakeholder group will dominate the strategic agenda or multiple stakeholders will agree to a compromise as to the strategic priorities, thereby reducing the tension and abating the strategic volatility. They test their assumptions on a sample of newly created businesses and find evidence that strategizing by small businesses seeking to create social and financial value is indeed erratic early on, but that this tension subsides over time.

Bringing the discussion on value creation to a close, DeTienne and Wennberg focus on the phenomenon of exit, or the process by which founders remove themselves from the ownership of the businesses they have created, in chapter 7. The authors note that exit can occur for many reasons (i.e., capture the value created by a high-performing business, minimize the value destroyed by a poor-performing business) and at multiple levels of analysis (i.e., the owner may exit the business while the business remains an ongoing entity or the small business may exit the market altogether). Given this understanding, DeTienne and Wennberg conduct an in-depth review of research on small business exit over the past three decades and summarize it according to three pervasive theoretical perspectives: career choice economics, entrepreneurship, and strategy and organizational theory. Based on their interpretation of this literature, they identify five major themes—further delineation of the exit/failure constructs, exit and performance, exit strategy and exit routes, post-exit implications and concerns, and macro- and regional implications of firm exit—that research on exit should leverage to improve our understanding of the phenomenon.

The remaining chapters in volume 2 highlight the importance of context as the environment in which a small business operates affects the opportunities that are available to it, the means by which it exploits them, and its ability to create and capture value as a result. Leading off this line of inquiry in chapter 8, Gilbert and Kusar explore how industry clustering and knowledge spillovers impact product innovations in small high-technology ventures. The authors acknowledge that geographic regions with large concentrations of same industry firms are widely believed to lead to flows of knowledge between firms, thereby leading to improved innovativeness. However, they note that this broad view omits an understanding of some important nuances about the nature of innovation. Thus, they offer an assessment of the pros and cons of operating within or outside of cluster regions by considering how cluster dynamics affect small firm innovation behavior, with particular attention to the type of innovation pursued. Analyzing data from 128 software firms, they conclude that knowledge flows within clusters do provide resources that enhance innovation capabilities, but that the resulting innovations tend to center around existing products at the expense of new products. In turn, they advise managers at small innovative firms to decrease their use of regional knowledge to avoid becoming trapped in a cycle whereby attention is given to existing products at the expense of new products.

LiPuma and Prange expand the discussion of context in chapter 9 to compare regional support for small business on a global scale. They argue that a country's institutional environment, which encompasses the system of formal laws, regulations, and procedures as well as informal conventions, customs, and norms, affects both the nature of strategies employed by businesses and the ability of those strategies to improve performance. At the same time, they note that although emerging market economies have seen improvements in institutional quality in recent years, they still lag behind developed economies in this regard. Therefore, these authors investigate the extent to which the institutional environment has affected small businesses' performance in emerging versus developed economies. They focus their investigation on exporting as it creates value for both the business, by improving productive capacity, enhancing financial performance, and providing a foundation for future international expansion, and the country at large, by enhancing foreign exchange reserves, improving employment levels and productivity, and driving economic growth. Analyzing data on 7,989 businesses operating in 56 countries collected by the World Bank, the authors conclude that institutional quality is an important antecedent to the export performance of all businesses and that it has a unique effect on small (versus large) businesses. Based on their findings, the authors provide strategic advice to small business owners seeking to navigate institutional frameworks in emerging and developed countries.

In chapter 10, Hasan, Wang, and Zhou delve more deeply into the climate for business in countries not classified as "developed" by exploring the regional banking development in China and its effect on the level of growth of small business activity. The authors begin by noting that the development of a vibrant financial sector is particularly important to small businesses given that they tend to be highly dependent on bank credit for their survival and growth initiatives. They go on to describe the nuances of the Chinese context and argue that the growth of small business will be affected by the type of bank, the duration of the loan, and the overall level of bank concentration. From their analysis of data on small businesses from 30 Chinese provinces, the authors find evidence to suggest that the complex hierarchies in large banks increase the cost of relationship loans and, in turn, result in organizational diseconomies associated with small business lending; thus, in regions where large banks are dominant, loans to small businesses are fewer and on shorter terms, resulting in an unfavorable environment for small business growth. Yet, the authors also find that in highly concentrated markets, large banks are able to help finance small firms because they can subsidize and lock in small businesses and that lending activities by rural credit unions greatly facilitate to the growth of small businesses.

Continuing on with the analysis of small business viability in non-Western countries, Smallbone explores in chapter 11 the broad challenges and opportunities facing small businesses in transition economies, or those countries whose economies have recently emerged from central planning. What is unique about this context is that prior to their transition stage, private business in these countries was actually an illegal activity; thus, they present a unique challenge to individuals seeking to operate small businesses in them. Because not all transition economies are alike, Smallbone develops a typology to analyze the distinct ways in which they have evolved over time: countries that are republics of the former Soviet Union, countries that previously operated under central planning but are now members of the European Union (EU), and China. The author then draws on a series of case studies to illustrate the distinctiveness of the operating environment for small business across the three transition contexts. He concludes with a discussion of the role that government policy can play in improving the level of small business activity and the environment for small business.

In chapter 12, Chavez, Linton, Stinnett, and Walsh extend the discussion on the link between regional influences on small business and public policy by arguing that the commercialization of emerging, and often disruptive, technology by small businesses is the key element in the generation of new Schumpeterian cycles of economic development. In other words, by displacing the current technology competencies required to produce an industry standard product or by creating a new technology-product paradigm for a new industry, small businesses creatively destroy existing industries and create new ones. They contend that each wave of Schumpeterian creative destruction required new types of technological and business training and highlight two such programs focused on supporting the commercialization of products based on microtechnology (micro), nanotechnology (nano) and the Internet of Things (IoT). Based on a case study of these programs, the authors offer a model for emerging technology-based regional economic development that includes mentorship, infrastructure development, and regional policy supporting emerging technology-based activity.

Dennis concludes the discussion of policy in chapter 13 by highlighting the various public policies at the federal level that purposefully assist small business in the United States. The author focuses on policies designed to support small businesses, such as by directly or indirectly subsidizing individual small businesses or small business owners, as well as those intended to reduce impediments to small businesses, such as by eliminating barriers to competition. Based on this review, he proposes a typology characterizing the relative degree of supports and impediments in a jurisdiction that results in four broad policy blends that create a varying set of climates for small businesses: *limiting*, characterized by high impediments and few supports, making it relatively difficult to enter and successfully operate; *competing*, characterized by a hands-off approach to encourage competition, not just among small businesses but among all competitors; *compensating*, characterized by policy to selectively lift a limited number of small businesses (generally incumbents) over the hurdles created; and *nurturing*, characterized by few barriers and many supports to raise affected firms over the minimal impediment, which is the most favorable to small business. Dennis concludes by acknowledging that because relocating to more locations with more favorable policy climates is generally not practical, small business owners may nevertheless improve the existing regulatory climate through involvement in the political process.

Taken together, the chapters contained in this volume are intended to shed new light on the dynamics facing the small business owner. By providing insights as to what types of strategies and what types of environments contribute to small firm success, these chapters may prove a valuable source of information for academics and students interested in meso- and macro-level perspectives of small business as well as individuals currently managing or seeking to manage small businesses. Moreover, by emphasizing the delicate interaction between government regulation and small business, this volume may also aid in decisions by policy makers seeking to support this vibrant sector of the economy.

In total, the rigorous and insightful work of the authors in this volume is intended to inform the collective understanding of small business in the following ways. First, by approaching timely issues with an eye on academic and practical relevance, the chapters convey the current thinking on some of the most important challenges facing today's small business owners. Second, by speaking to a wide variety of audiences, including academics, students, practitioners, and policy makers, the chapters provide insights and action agendas that may improve the current approach to small business theory and practice. At the very least, given the importance that small businesses continue to play in the economy, coupled with the inherent challenges their owners face, the chapters in this volume may add some degree of richness to the ongoing discussion regarding the importance of small business.

NOTES

1. Joseph A. Schumpeter, *Capitalism, Socialism and Democracy*, 3rd ed. (New York: Harper & Row, 1950).

2. The Futures Group, "Characterization of Innovations Introduced on the U.S. Market in 1982" (a report prepared for the U.S. Small Business Administration, Office of Advocacy, Washington, D.C., 1984); Alok K. Chakrabarti, "Industry Characteristics Influencing the Technical Output: A Case of Small and Medium-sized Firms in the U.S.," *R&D Management* 21, 2 (1990): 139–152; Frederic M. Scherer, *Innovation and Growth: Schumpeterian Perspectives* (Cambridge, MA: The MIT Press, 1984).

1

Managing the Small Firm for Growth: Cocreating Stakeholder Value Propositions

Douglas A. Bosse

Some of the primary activities of small business managers include forming and managing value-creating relationships with other parties, such as customers, suppliers, and employees. This set of activities involves everything from selecting the other party, to negotiating about what each side will contribute to the joint effort and how the resulting value will be distributed among them, to determining how conflicts will be resolved when they inevitably arise. As these activities are so important for small business success, business scholars focus substantial research efforts on more fully understanding and explaining how small firm managers work with key stakeholders to create value.

This phenomenon is difficult to fully explain because anytime two or more parties engage to create value, they have mixed motives: each party wants to benefit while also allowing the other party to capture at least enough benefit to stay engaged in the relationship. It is easy to suggest that the more powerful party dictates how this plays out. Differences in bargaining power are, in many situations, the easiest relationship characteristics to explain. However, the behaviors of both parties are *also* affected by multiple decisions about relationship formation and management. These decisions, in addition to bargaining power, drive the value two parties can create together. One perspective through which scholars have worked to make sense of this complicated process is stakeholder theory.

This chapter suggests that stakeholder theory is particularly effective for explaining the process of value creation at small firms. While the broadest definition of a stakeholder is "any individual or group who can affect or is affected by the achievement of the organization's objectives," it is most helpful for the purpose of this chapter to narrow the focus to the small firm's primary stakeholders: the customers, employees, and suppliers whose continuing participation is required for the firm's survival. [1] The core proposition of stakeholder theory is that firms create more economic value by allocating more value than absolutely necessary to their primary stakeholders.[2] How and why this works will be explained shortly.

My approach to explaining stakeholder theory in this chapter includes contrasting it with another theory, transaction cost economics (TCE), which seeks to describe the same phenomenon. This contrast exposes the pivot points of both theories so that their underlying logic can be assessed by the reader. TCE is a theory that offers a range of insights about how firms choose to organize their transactions to maximize value by minimizing certain costs. In sum, TCE provides a helpful foundation for distinguishing stakeholder theory in the context of small firm value creation.

The chapter proceeds as follows: First, I provide overviews of TCE and stakeholder theory with respect to how small firm managers approach day-to-day interactions with stakeholders. Then, using the lenses provided by these two theories, I examine their implications for how and where small firm managers become aware of new value-creating business opportunities. I next provide a brief overview of opportunity formation, followed by a summary of the literature on value cocreation with customers. Throughout the chapter, studies in management, marketing, and negotiation are used to provide reasoning and support for understanding various aspects of the small business opportunity creation phenomenon. And, overall, I derive a new argument by extending the literature on customer cocreation of value to all stakeholders in this setting. I refine additional arguments to suggest that perspective taking, which is a cognitive capability, represents a condition that moderates cocreation activities and outcomes. The chapter concludes with a discussion about the actions that small business managers take to shape value propositions with each stakeholder and how the small firm's overall collection of stakeholder relationships becomes interdependent as this process leads to feasible market opportunities.

TRANSACTION COST ECONOMICS

TCE explains how a small firm and any other party that come together to create value can design their transaction in a way that is most efficient. All economic value is created through transactions, and TCE takes this most basic concept as its unit of analysis. The design of a transaction is referred to among scholars as "governance," and it consists of mechanisms and instruments that influence the behaviors of the parties involved. These mechanisms and instruments might include such formal things as contractual clauses and managerial authority or even less formal mechanisms such as trust and group norms. While TCE focuses on the use of formal mechanisms, it suggests they be used sparingly because devising and implementing formal governance can be costly. For instance, the cost of writing a complex contract that accounts for many future contingencies is one type of cost that is avoided by conducting the transaction without a contract in an anonymous spot market.[3]

At this point, it is important to discuss the assumptions that hold TCE together. A theory is a simplified model of the world that helps to explain some phenomenon. Simplifying what is really an extremely complex world requires theory builders to make assumptions. Two main assumptions used in TCE include bounded rationality and opportunism. Bounded rationality as used in TCE means actors do not have the cognitive capability to accurately predict how all the components of their transaction will influence the future outcome of their transaction. This is a more realistic assumption than the alternative—that actors are certain about how the future will play out.[4] Bounded rationality manifests itself as an inability to fully control the behavior of the other party in the transaction. The implication is that even complex contracts are necessarily incomplete: they cannot be written in a way that accounts for every possible future contingency. Still, in this theory, managers seek to craft contracts as explicitly and as completely as possible so they account for all foreseeable contingencies.

Opportunism is an assumption that extends the common behavioral assumption used in most economics theories that actors are purely self-interested. Theories that are grounded in economics, such as TCE, typically assume that individuals have their own tastes, are very good at perceiving and evaluating risks, and doggedly pursue their own maximum happiness in every possible transaction. TCE goes a little further by assuming that some people will lie, cheat, or steal in pursuit of their self-interest.[5] In this theory, this behavior is called *opportunism*. An opportunistic actor is not torn by mixed motives. He seeks to maximize his own outcomes from the transaction at the expense of the other party.

It is important not to confuse opportunism, or being opportunistic, in the TCE sense, with the decidedly productive entrepreneurial behavior of looking for and attempting to exploit market opportunities to create value. This model of humankind used in such traditional economic theories as TCE, called *homo economicus*, is a distinct idealized species that has emerged through decades of theorizing about group behavior in markets. While most economists agree that this model of human being has helped describe many aggregate market behaviors, when pressed, they also agree that *homo economicus* is not an accurate description of any individual person. In explaining small business management behaviors and their outcomes, stakeholder theorists (described below) argue that altogether different assumptions about human behavior generate a more accurate theoretical model.

Given these two assumptions of bounded rationality and opportunism, TCE suggests the small firm manager's transaction design objective is to assemble the lowest-cost combination of governance devices that adequately addresses such transaction-organizing tasks as establishing, structuring, monitoring, adapting, and enforcing the exchange.[6] Again, these are the activities that a small firm must engage in with stakeholders to create economic value. The costs in TCE arise from conflicting incentives among the parties. The logic follows that because one cannot accurately determine whether a given stakeholder is opportunistic by nature, it is safest to assume every stakeholder will act opportunistically when the characteristics of the transaction itself are amenable. Thus, TCE suggests that the optimal governance choice for reducing incentive conflicts can be determined from attributes of the transaction rather than attributes of the stakeholders.[7] A basic argument of TCE is that governance designs differ in substantive ways and are chosen based on their ability to address these organizing tasks at the lowest total transaction cost. That is, collaborating parties decide which governance devices to include based on their expectations regarding the particular hazards most likely to occur in their transaction.

The main attribute of a transaction to watch out for is asset specificity. The party that makes a larger investment that is specific to the transaction is at greater risk of opportunism. By definition, an asset (or investment) that is specific to a particular transaction has less value in a transaction with any other stakeholder. Thus, if a small firm owner is aware that her supplier has a transaction-specific asset and if that supplier has not inserted the appropriate safeguards in its transaction governance design, then the small firm owner can opportunistically renegotiate the terms of the transaction in his or her own favor. Once the supplier has made its specific investment, it has lost bargaining power to resist the small firm owner.

Consider, for example, a loan transaction between a small firm and its primary bank. In return for a loan, the bank is entitled to a stream of future principal and interest payments. However, there is a risk that the small firm may default on these payments. Moreover, once the small firm manager invests the loan amount in noncash assets (e.g., facilities, equipment, R&D), it is likely to become difficult to redeploy. As a result, absent governance features to protect the bank, the bank is at risk of an opportunistic small firm manager deferring repayment. To prevent this outcome, the supplier (bank) in this example should design the governance upfront in such a way that it has more authority to adjust the transaction later, if the need arises—perhaps by repossessing collateral under certain conditions.

A Practical Boundary of TCE

TCE implies that both parties assess and agree on the governance design for their transaction. Thus, studies of TCE often assume that when two parties enter a transaction, they have equal influence on—and mutual satisfaction with—how the transaction will be organized. However, it is unlikely any two parties will have their underlying interests perfectly aligned. The outcome of the resulting negotiation over governance structure is likely to depend, in part, on the relative bargaining power of the parties involved. Bargaining power, or "the ability of one party to a contract to be able to influence the terms and conditions of that contract or subsequent contracts in its own favor," represents a rarely explored boundary condition of TCE for small firm managers.[8]

The interplay between bargaining power and the negotiations over governance features is of particular interest to small business scholars and practitioners. Small firms often enter transactions with larger firm partners—whether suppliers, customers, or alliance partners.[9] In some transactions, the small firm possesses less bargaining power relative to their large firm partners. For instance, in transactions involving small biotechnology and larger pharmaceutical firms, the relative bargaining power of the small firm may depend on the "shadow of the future" it is able to cast regarding its development of future valuable drugs.

I argue that understanding the extent to which their governance interests are addressed in transactions with large firm partners is important for small firm managers because it provides insight regarding the degree to which they may be burdened by excess transaction costs. For an extreme example, consider a monopolistic supplier. Its small firm customer has no alternatives and no substitutes, so it must accept the monopolist's take-it-or-leave-it offer. There is no negotiation regarding the transaction governance design. Even if the small firm manager does not believe he or she is adequately protected from hazards that may arise in the transaction, he or she must agree to the monopolist's terms—terms that are unlikely to protect the small firm against the threat of opportunism on behalf of the monopolist. The result is that some small firm managers do not see their governance interests reflected in the ultimate agreement with a larger firm stakeholder.[10]

Although TCE does not claim to explain governance choice in transactions characterized by significant *ex ante* (or pretransaction) bargaining power asymmetries, it has been acknowledged that market power can play a role in governance choice.[11] Argyres and Liebeskind state that "in the current version of TCE, firms are generally assumed to operate in a highly competitive environment, in which sources of inefficiency, such as differences in bargaining power, are competed away relatively rapidly. As a result, there are relatively few instances in which the firm's selection of governance arrangements is constrained by bargaining power."[12] Bowles and Gintis argue that less powerful stakeholders (whether individuals or firms) routinely engage in transactions with more powerful firms because they are better off taking the risk than doing without the transaction altogether. They quote Joan Robinson here: "The only thing worse than being exploited by a capitalist is to be exploited by no one at all."[13]

Such arguments provide little guidance for small firm managers seeking to better understand how to create value with stakeholders. Drawing on anecdotes from the airline industry, the trucking industry, and franchising, Argyes and Liebeskind suggest bargaining power differences may be more important and pervasive than TCE admits, and they suggest how changes in bargaining power over the life of a transaction may affect later governance choices.[14]

TCE and Stakeholders

One perspective on TCE is that it argues for managing value-creation activities by treating stakeholders with indifference. That is, because the decision of how to design transaction governance to maximize value is based on characteristics of the transaction itself, it is largely independent of the particular stakeholder on the other end of the transaction. Furthermore, the division of value among the parties seems to be driven by the party with the most bargaining power. The less powerful party—the smaller firm in many cases—is prescribed to be allocated only that level of benefit that is equal to their next best alternative.

As stated previously, all theories are, by necessity, simplifications of the natural world. The simplified world constructed by TCE is generally useful for explaining how large firms—and sometimes small firms—choose to structure their transactions. However, many who wish to understand how value is created by actual managers find TCE's explanation unsatisfying. Managers have lots of reasons for behaving the way they do in their economic relationships that go beyond minimizing transaction costs. The key features of TCE applied to value creation at small firms are used in the remainder of this chapter to help distinguish stakeholder theory.

STAKEHOLDER THEORY

Whereas TCE holds that small firm managers maximize value by structuring transactions according to their own self-interests, stakeholder theory provides a different perspective on the central challenge of forming and nurturing value-creating relationships. To begin with, a fundamental difference between TCE and stakeholder theory is that stakeholder theory explicitly acknowledges that businesspeople do not and cannot make decisions independent of moral norms and values. All business decisions have implications for people, so all business decisions have implications for moral norms and values.[15] While it might seem cleaner to assume away ethical considerations when developing a parsimonious management theory, it might be still more productive to model managerial decision making in ways that accommodate realistic concern for individuals and responsibilities.

This distinction makes stakeholder theory more appropriate for focusing on economic *relationships* as the unit of analysis, whereas TCE primarily focuses on *transactions* as its unit of analysis. This distinction adds realism to explanations of relationship management phenomena, and this chapter suggests it provides more practical guidance for practicing small firm managers.

Bounded Self-Interest Assumption

As explained above, TCE is built upon the assumption that actors are motivated by pure self-interest. While this assumption has provided a wealth of productive theorizing about macro-level phenomena, contemporary research based on a more nuanced behavioral assumption may support new explanatory and predictive management theories. Scholars in a wide variety of fields (including strategy, organizational behavior, economics, political science, philosophy, biology, sociology, psychology, and social psychology) are now arguing that people are *boundedly* self-interested, rather than purely self-interested.[16] Bounded self-interest means that people evaluate others on the basis of fairness and then reciprocate by either rewarding those who are perceived as acting fairly or punishing those perceived as acting unfairly. That is, all actors are self-interested, but the extent to which they will go to maximize their self-interest in a given situation is bounded by perceived norms of fairness. The seemingly small adjustment to acknowledge other-regarding norms of enforcing fairness makes surprisingly large changes to the logical insights provided by a theory.

Bounded self-interest provides an assumption that helps to explain why stakeholder theory's main proposition works. Managers appreciate that how people interact with one another is largely motivated by how they perceive they and others have been treated. People do want what is best for themselves, but they also care enough about how others are treated that they willingly incur costs to enforce what they perceive as important principles of justice and fairness.[17] Behavior, then, can appear very friendly in response to friendly actions and very unfriendly in response to unfriendly actions. The former is called *positive reciprocity*, and the latter is called *negative reciprocity*.[18]

The most common alternative assumption about human behavior, pure self-interest, does not account for such principle-driven behavior. Principle-driven behavior can generate material costs for a party perceived as acting unfairly in the case of negative reciprocity or can result in benefit sharing (with a party perceived as acting with exceptional fairness) by the more powerful party in the case of positive reciprocity.

Bounded self-interest is so prevalent across time and cultures that it is among a very small set of phenomena classified as *hypernorms*. A hypernorm is a basic moral principle so pervasive across time and cultures that it helps people to evaluate other moral norms.[19] The use of bounded self-interest in stakeholder theory is supported by a wealth of exploratory, descriptive, and confirmatory research on this behavior in other fields, including behavioral economics, philosophy, sociology, psychology, social psychology, and even biology.[20] To distinguish this model of behavior from *homo economicus*, it has been labeled *homo reciprocans*.[21]

This brings us to another fundamental difference between TCE and stakeholder theory. Stakeholder theory argues that more value is created by giving attention to the interests and well-being of primary stakeholders as opposed to exploiting those stakeholders as a means to an end. Thus, firms that are managed for their stakeholders maximize value creation.[22] The introduction of other-regarding behaviors, while still showing concern for self, makes stakeholder theory unique among small firm strategy theories. Giving attention to stakeholder interests includes a range of activities, such as seeking to understand the nuances of stakeholders' underlying material interests, including them in decision-making processes that affect their outcomes, and treating them with dignity and respect.[23] The resulting stakeholder behavior is typically positively reciprocal toward the small firm. This is the crucial implication of boundedly self-interested behavior as it relates to small firms. A stakeholder who positively reciprocates toward a small firm acts in ways that contribute more to the small firm's value-creation scheme. This is particularly important for small firm managers who need all the help they can get because they lack the resources to maximize value in more traditional ways (i.e., market power and bargaining power). The value created is then (ideally) distributed among the firm and stakeholders according to a norm of meritocracy that accounts for relative contribution, costs, and risks.[24] In contrast, TCE logic draws attention away from the stakeholder in favor of prioritizing characteristics that signal potential for opportunistic behavior in the transaction.

Unit of Analysis

Another key distinction between TCE and stakeholder theory is their unit of analysis. By focusing on the transaction as its unit of analysis, TCE views value creation as a one-time game. Each transaction initiates its own governance assessment and negotiation as though the transaction could be legitimately isolated from all other transactions. Stakeholder theory, on the other hand, views value creation as a repeated game. Most managers realize that value-creation activities often involve familiar stakeholders. Rarely is the anonymous or one-time transaction partner at the core of a coordinated set of activities representing a business model for value creation. Small firms, especially, tend to sell to the same customer many times, buy from the same supplier many times, and benefit from the contributions of the same employee many times.

Stakeholder Selection and Treatment

In this section, I differentiate TCE and stakeholder theory in terms of stakeholder selection and treatment. Stakeholder selection is not a primary consideration in TCE analysis, which focuses on the inanimate characteristics of a proposed transaction. In contrast, selecting particular stakeholders is quite important in the logic of stakeholder theory, which emphasizes the expectations and behaviors of the other party. Stakeholder theory suggests that small firms create more value when they choose to form trading relationships with stakeholders whose expectations of fairness norms are complementary to their own.[25] Complementary fairness norms create an environment where both the small firm and the stakeholder believe that the other party is behaving in an appropriate and fair way.

How the small firm treats the other party (stakeholder) as it attempts to create value is also understood differently in these two theories. According to stakeholder theory, small firms create more value by allocating more value to stakeholders than is minimally required. Stakeholders who recognize this tend to positively reciprocate toward the small firm by providing some combination of more effort, more information, and more material value back to the small firm. In aggregate, this pattern is so powerful that it even compensates for those few stakeholders who behave opportunistically by only serving themselves and the even more costly ones who might perceive the small firm's actions as unfair and therefore choose to negatively reciprocate.

Harrison and Bosse explain why the optimal amount of material value that a small firm should allocate to a given stakeholder can be difficult to determine.[26] Allocating an amount equal to the stakeholder's next best alternative is only enough to keep that stakeholder engaged, but not enough to stimulate positively reciprocal behavior that would benefit the small firm. Allocating too much material value to a stakeholder can deplete the small firm's resources so dramatically that insufficient value remains to retain the services of the other required stakeholders. The optimal level, then, is to allocate just enough material value that the stakeholder is triggered to positively reciprocate because they appreciate the marginal benefit of working with that small firm. A similar set of arguments explains how much voice small firms should provide a stakeholder in its decision-making processes. The aim is to involve a particular stakeholder in those decisions that affect his or her outcomes and to do so at a level that produces informational advantages about the stakeholder's interests without simultaneously underinvolving other relevant stakeholders in the decision. For example, a business customer who seeks trade credit can be asked to share information about the business's operations cycle, and that information can potentially teach the small firm about how its product or service could be adjusted in value-adding ways for this and similar customers.

In sum, stakeholder theory posits a more cooperative approach to value creation, whereas TCE suggests a more competitive approach. However, it is important to note that, though stakeholder theory seeks to explain how firms create and enjoy more value, it is decidedly not a theory of altruism or exclusively other-regarding behaviors. Bounded self-interest is still self-interest first; it only veers from pure self-interest at the boundary delineated by ethical norms of justice. In an explicit departure from *homo economicus*, people do not necessarily have fixed preferences according to stakeholder theory. Instead, their preferences change, often in reaction to the preferences and behaviors of other people with whom they interact. This further illustrates the challenges of managing a small firm: a small firm's strategy is always surrounded by imperfect information and incomplete knowledge. As managers learn through day-to-day interactions with stakeholders, they acquire better information and knowledge about the situation in which they are operating. Thus, managers are never finished looking for new value-creation opportunities.

Having juxtaposed the critical components of stakeholder theory and TCE, I now proceed with extending stakeholder theory to explain the value-creation process at small firms. Relevant research on customer value cocreation provides a foundation for these arguments.

WHERE DO VALUE-CREATION OPPORTUNITIES COME FROM?

Thus far, the focus has been on relationship management activities that small firm managers perform to create value. Another critical challenge is to better understand the *source* of value-creation opportunities at small firms.

Opportunities are the core ideas about how to organize land, labor, and capital in ways that will be valued by stakeholders. Opportunities do not just lead to the radical breakthrough innovations that transform a small firm; they are also critical to the more common actions that small business managers take to better serve stakeholders on a day-to-day basis. Small businesses win when their preferred stakeholders willingly choose to stay engaged with them. Given that the set of available alternatives for most stakeholders is constantly in flux, small business managers have to constantly look for opportunities to create value for their stakeholders.

A business opportunity can be viewed as a small business manager's hypothesis about the existence of some unserved or underserved stakeholder. Where do value-creation opportunities come from? Some scholars believe opportunities exist in the natural world and only certain people (i.e., heroic entrepreneurs) see and exploit them. Call this the *exogenous* (from outside the model) opportunity perspective. Other scholars take the position that opportunities do not exist until managers create them by interacting with current and prospective stakeholders and learning about their interests and priorities. Call this the *endogenous* (from within the model) opportunity perspective.

Stakeholder theory can help us to understand the generalized processes through which endogenous opportunities are created. The profit potential of an opportunity is the expected surplus value after all of the stakeholders who are necessary to exploit the opportunity have received at least the minimum compensation that they require to participate in the opportunity.[27] A *feasible* opportunity, then, is a combination of value propositions that are superior to the relevant alternatives available to each of the stakeholders necessary to create the profit or surplus. Accordingly, small business managers analyze the feasibility of opportunities by engaging potential stakeholders and inquiring about the appeal of the value proposition they would receive from the small business. Findings from the feasibility analysis often inform the small business manager that some of the value propositions should be modified to make the opportunity more valuable to one or more stakeholders. Any surplus value created this way can be allocated among the small business and its stakeholders.

I suggest that the process through which a small business manager tests hypotheses and learns from stakeholders about the value of each hypothesized opportunity influences the opportunity itself in predictable ways. The tradition in much of the management and economics literature is to regard some stakeholders outside the firm (e.g., customers) as *operand* resources (i.e., upon which operations are performed). As described above, TCE argues that the small business manager assesses the characteristics of a transaction when determining how to create value from it. The stakeholder in this perspective is taken as he or she comes, and his or her idiosyncrasies are not central to the theory. In contrast, stakeholder theory suggests that the small firm manager creates more value by attending to the interests and well-being of stakeholders. This perspective views stakeholders as *operant* resources (i.e., that operate to produce an effect).[28]

Through the process of testing a hypothesized opportunity one value proposition at a time with each required stakeholder, small business managers learn *with* these operant resources how to modify the combination of value propositions to increase their profit potential. The logic presented in this chapter argues that when a small business manager engages potential stakeholders in a collaborative value proposition design process, rather than employing arm's-length hypothesis testing techniques with the market, they develop superior value propositions. This occurs because the small business manager's endogenously forming opportunity interacts with and feeds potential stakeholders' endogenously forming beliefs about the value of the opportunity. This complex, social process raises the probability that the stakeholders' expectations of justice will be complementary to the small business manager's expectations.

The value that is cocreated during this process is likely conditional upon a range of factors, however. Recognizing this process as a form of negotiation suggests that the research on negotiation may provide a logical source for insights about such conditions. Accordingly, the conditions proposed in this chapter to influence the collaborative value proposition design process are ones that are well established in the negotiation realm.[29]

CREATING VALUE ENDOGENOUSLY WITH CUSTOMERS

Recent research on how value is endogenously cocreated with customers provides insight into the actions that managers might take with *all* of their potential stakeholders to favorably influence their opportunities. An argument that new offerings (i.e., products and services) are more valuable when they are cocreated with customers is rapidly spreading across the literature in fields such as strategy, marketing, innovation, and design. This section provides a brief review of this work and links it to the opportunity hypothesis testing phenomenon.

Common among much of this work is the distinction between *use value* and *exchange value*. Use value arises from relieving a beneficiary from the burden of carrying out an activity for itself and from enabling that party to perform the activity better, faster, or cheaper than it could otherwise.[30] More succinctly, use value is the subjective valuation of consumption benefits enjoyed.[31] Exchange value is the amount actually paid for an offering (i.e., product or service).[32]

Marketing scholars have been exploring how use value, as a concept, changes our understanding of the relationship between a firm and its customers. The "service-dominant logic" emphasizes customers' responsibility for cocreating the value that they receive from any product or service based on how they use it.[33] From this perspective, firms can only make value propositions to customers; they do not create value through the act of exchange because each customer determines the value that they receive when they consume the benefits enabled by a product or service. The use value of a new car, for example, is not embedded in the car itself but depends on how often it is driven, what it is used to transport, where it is driven, and how well the user maintains it. This concept is also beginning to find an audience in strategic management. Priem focuses on the role of end consumers in establishing the value created in an industry and reasons that firms get better performance by helping consumers maximize the use value that they experience at the point of consumption.[34]

Identifying customers' use value can be a significant challenge, however, because of its subjectivity.[35] Still, managers seeking to make value-informed decisions about their offerings need some method of learning the target users' subjective valuations. This task becomes even more difficult as the offering becomes more novel. The reason, according to innovation researchers, is that customers often find it hard to understand how they will benefit from truly novel offerings.[36] Managers engaged in analyzing the feasibility of new opportunities are likely to experience these same difficulties in learning their target users' subjective valuations.

Traditional market research techniques are often inadequate in this setting. Eliashberg, Lilien, and Rao find that such traditional market research techniques as customer surveys do not provide firms with a contextual understanding of their target users' subjective assessments of use value.[37] The traditional approaches involve sequentially researching customer needs and responding with new products. The firm is typically responsible for generating the new ideas for how the offering can be of greater use value to customers. As a result, new offerings that are analyzed with these techniques are associated with only marginal changes to existing products and services. Market research methods that involve interactive collaboration with customers, however, tend to result in more novel and profitable opportunities.[38] Interacting with target customers in a collaborative way, where both parties are actively seeking to solve a common set of problems, reveals richer, more context-specific data than arm's-length research techniques.[39]

Findings in the innovation literature suggest the use of the "lead user method" for collaborating with customers to understand how they subjectively value an offering.[40] Von Hippel argues that firms can improve their value propositions to a wider group of customers by incorporating what they learn from their lead users. Lead users are those customers who are already using or modifying a firm's products and services to make them more useful in ways that the firm never expected. Firms using the lead user method host workshops at which their personnel work closely with their lead users to improve new product concepts or cocreate entirely new product concepts. Research has shown that the new offerings resulting from this approach in markets, such as printed circuit boards, industrial pipe hangers, and personal computers and software, are more preferred by potential users than offerings resulting from less customer-interactive methods.[41] A critical challenge to small firm managers who wish to employ this method of fostering cocreation is that they may not have any lead users yet—either because they are analyzing hypotheses about a de novo offering or because no users who are applying an existing offering in unexpected ways can be found.

Bendapudi and Leone review several empirical studies, finding evidence that firms can influence the use value perceived by their customers by actively engaging customers in other activities, too.[42] For example, Goldenberg, Lehmann, and Mazursky show that when customers help a firm identify solutions to particular customer problems, the new products that result generate substantially more positive financial results than products developed by inventors with little market stimulus.[43] Bendapudi and Leone show that when customers are given a choice to participate in the production and delivery of a service, they take more responsibility for the value created, and that when service delivery is interrupted, customers who participate in the service recovery process perceive greater value.[44] The endogeneity of customers' perceptions of value and firms' efforts to create value is explicit in the "service-dominant logic" of marketing. According to this philosophy, "value is always co-created, jointly and reciprocally, in interactions among providers and beneficiaries through the integration of resources and the application of competencies."[45]

Extending this philosophy backward to the opportunity hypothesis testing process suggests that managers may be able to act in ways that improve the profit potential of their opportunity. The insight is that under the assumption of endogeneity, better opportunities are created by managers who engage their target customers in the design of the value proposition rather than those who independently structure the value proposition and then ask prospective customers to indicate whether they would find it acceptable. Engaging the customer in a collaborative effort enables the manager to better understand how the offering may create use value for a specific customer in a specific context. Having a target customer explain how he or she would intend to use a given offering and how the offering could be modified to enhance the customer's value-in-use leverages customers as operant resources. This process maps directly to stakeholder theory: by enhancing use value, small firm managers are creating more overall value and then sharing it with stakeholders (in this case, customers).

The next section expands this reasoning from the customer-focused context to include all of the stakeholders necessary to create and exploit an opportunity.

EXTENDING COCREATION TO OTHER STAKEHOLDERS

The manager's task when testing the feasibility of an opportunity is to design and test a comprehensive set of value propositions to *all* of the stakeholders required to exploit a market opportunity. While customers are certainly a critical stakeholder group in this context, they are not the only stakeholders. Managers typically also need to attract the participation of other types of stakeholders. Which other stakeholders are needed depends on the specific opportunity the small business is seeking to exploit. Some opportunities, for example, will require that value propositions are developed for employees, and others might require a special value proposition for a specific supplier. Each of these stakeholders faces alternatives to entering an exchange or a relationship with the small firm. Therefore, the small firm manager's value proposition to each stakeholder must be superior to the stakeholder's next best alternative to secure the stakeholder's participation.

The concept of use value has, almost exclusively, been applied to customers. Exchanges, however, must provide the promise of value for all of the parties involved. For example, when a potential employee is evaluating a job offer to join a small business (a value proposition from the manager), she considers many aspects of the offer beyond the price (i.e., the fixed compensation). She considers how each day at work will be spent, including such issues as the job duties, quality of colleagues, amount of travel, and opportunities for personal and professional growth. All of these are benefits that she will get as she "consumes" her job, and she subjectively values them just like customers do when they consume the services enabled by a firm's offering. The employee is a potential beneficiary of the job offer value proposition. Engaging potential employees to help to collaboratively design the offer improves their subjective valuation of the value proposition, just like in the case of target customers described above. Indeed, employees are more satisfied when they participate in designing their own jobs.[46]

The reciprocal nature of exchanges means that the small business is also a potential beneficiary in this example. The manager must expect to benefit—experience use value—from the proposed exchange for it to be a superior value proposition. These benefits depend on the specific duties that need to be performed to exploit the market opportunity and that this potential employee will relieve the small firm from doing. The potential employee may even help to cocreate the specific duties that need to be performed as the opportunity evolves and new stakeholder-value propositions form. The manager, therefore, also subjectively values these benefits as they are "consumed." In the opportunity hypothesis testing process, both the potential employee and the small business manager subjectively assess the use value that they anticipate from each value proposition that they discuss. This process is especially salient for small businesses to the extent that they are encumbered by comparatively less bureaucratic decision processes.

The main assertion of the customer-focused literature reviewed above arguably applies to other nonemployee stakeholders as well because all stakeholders are beneficiaries of the firm.[47] Stakeholder theorists explain why all stakeholder exchanges with a firm are incompletely specified ex ante.[48] It follows that all stakeholders subjectively evaluate the use value that they expect to get from a firm over time. Potential suppliers, financiers, and host communities can serve as operant resources in the opportunity creation process if small business managers ask them about their needs, the reasons underlying those needs, and the relative importance of the needs.[49]

When a small business manager collaborates on value proposition design, they can also share information regarding their own needs. This helps both parties to identify more of the differences in their subjective valuations of a proposed exchange. These differences in beliefs provide a foundation for cocreating value propositions that expand the potential gains from trade. Every aspect of a value proposition that is valued differently by the relevant parties represents potential for expanding the benefits to both parties.[50] Thus, small business managers performing a feasibility analysis are likely to develop superior value propositions for stakeholders when they collaborate with those stakeholders to codesign their value propositions.

Conditions Moderating the Collaborative Proposition Design Process

As an extension to stakeholder theory, the discussion above implies that the market against which small business managers test their hypothesized opportunities (i.e., the stakeholders perceived to be critical to the opportunity) is just as endogenous as the opportunities that they are testing. That is, the market knowledge created by a small business manager through the collaborative value proposition design process is (1) small business context specific and (2) stakeholder context specific. Small business managers and stakeholders, however, are not all equally proficient at envisioning how to modify a value proposition to make it superior to alternatives. This section explores one cognitive capability—perspective taking—that has been shown to influence the outcomes of collaborative efforts.

The collaborative value proposition design process, as suggested above, is like a negotiation in that two parties are engaged in an effort to structure a potential exchange.[51] A negotiator's capability to obtain the best outcome for themselves often depends on their understanding of the other party's interests.[52] In more successful negotiations, both parties attempt to determine (1) what they want out of the potential exchange and (2) what they think the other party would want.[53] This information serves as the basis upon which each party attempts to creatively envision alternative value propositions. The ability to accurately understand both parties' perspectives facilitates the identification of similarities and differences among their interests that signify potential for additional gain through exchange.

Perspective taking refers to the cognitive capability to understand what the other party is thinking, including their interests in the situation.[54] Perspective taking occurs when one party stands in the other party's shoes in an effort to predict how they may behave in certain contexts.[55] This cognitive capability enables people to balance their own self-interests with the interests of another party by stepping outside their own biased frame of reference.[56] The perspective-taking capability, therefore, is common among a population of boundedly self-interested actors. When one party errs on the side of self-ishness to the extent that it violates perceived norms, other actors negatively reciprocate in subsequent negotiations. A negotiator who errs in the other direction by focusing exclusively on the other party's interests ends up making excessive concessions. Only with a balance of attention to oneself and the other party are negotiators able to facilitate creative problem solving in an integrative fashion.[57]

Galinsky, Maddux, Gilin, and White report findings of three behavioral experiments that indicate perspective taking is associated with more profitable negotiated outcomes.[58] They find that perspective takers are better than nonperspective takers at generating creative solutions that generate more gains for the perspective takers. They conclude that perspective taking enhances negotiators' outcomes because it enables them to understand the motives of their opponents and, therefore, to uncover potential agreements that would otherwise remain hidden.

The value created through perspective taking is not limited to those with perspective-taking capability. In all three of the studies reported by Galinsky et al., negotiators who had perspective-taking partners enjoyed greater collective gains, too. Thus, it pays to have a partner who takes your perspective.

The nature of the manipulations employed by Galinsky et al. in their experiments show that perspective taking is a learnable skill. With instructions and encouragement, people are able to remove themselves from their typical self-centered frame of reference to explore how the other party in their negotiation sees the context of their negotiation. This suggests another layer in the endogeneity of opportunity creation; the profit potential of an opportunity is not only a function of which potential stakeholders are included in hypothesis testing and of how the hypothesis-testing process is conducted, but also on the ability of each party to see the context from another's perspective.

The advantages of perspective taking suggest that when small business managers and their potential stakeholders both educate and learn from each other they tend to create superior negotiation outcomes. Small businesses are typically well positioned to do this because they are often, out of necessity, closer—both interpersonally and geographically—to their stakeholders. A small business manager who takes the perspective of a stakeholder when collaboratively designing a value proposition with that stakeholder is likely to generate a superior value proposition. The same is true of the stakeholder in this process. A stakeholder who takes the perspective of the small business manager is likely to contribute to the creation of a superior value proposition. Thus, when small business managers take the perspective of their potential stakeholders, their collaborative value proposition design process has more influence on the creation of superior value propositions. The effect is also stronger when potential stakeholders take the perspective of small business managers.

CONCLUSION

This chapter explores choices and actions of small business managers that affect the opportunities that they attempt to exploit under the assumption that opportunities are formed endogenously. The approach taken in this chapter is to link logically related arguments from other fields of study to derive new arguments regarding how small business managers can actively leverage the endogeneity of their opportunities in an effort to improve the economic potential of those opportunities. Key arguments are taken from other fields because the marketing, management, and innovation literatures have already begun examining implications of the endogeneity assumption on firm-customer interactions. Applying those insights to the opportunity-creation context requires extending their application to all stakeholders.

Relevant arguments from the negotiation literature are also applied. The negotiation literature examines how perspective-taking capabilities positively influence the gains created by a small firm manager trying to structure a potential exchange with a stakeholder. Extending these insights simply requires the recognition that small business managers and potential stakeholders who are engaged in collaborative value proposition design activities are, in fact, in a negotiation. In sum, via this negotiation, small business managers can cocreate superior value propositions with each potential stakeholder, thereby creating a superior opportunity—one that is more likely to be feasible because it is acceptable to all of the required stakeholders.

The endogeneity implied by this perspective is not limited to small business managers' influence on opportunities. The behaviors of stakeholders are equally important as the behaviors of the small business manager. If stakeholders refuse to participate in a collaborative value proposition design process, for example, the manager may not be able to create a feasible opportunity. Exclusively self-interested stakeholders can also have a negative influence on the opportunity creation process.

The value that any stakeholder can create with the small business is also interdependent on the value that other stakeholders can create with that small business. Given that profit is the surplus after all of the necessary stakeholders receive just enough compensation to secure their participation in an opportunity, there is a minimum total collective value that the small business and the network of stakeholders needs to create. Improving the value proposition for one stakeholder beyond its minimum threshold can lower the value proposition threshold for other parts of the network (i.e., other small business manager/stakeholder dyads). For example, if the small business manager and suppliers can collaboratively squeeze out costs upstream, the manager can presumably split a portion of this benefit with the supplier and perhaps even decrease the price downstream. Thus, cocreating a superior value proposition with suppliers can also improve the value proposition for customers.

Furthermore, the subjective assessment of a value proposition to a particular stakeholder is often enhanced when the small business already has other value propositions deemed acceptable by other stakeholders. For example, when a small business manager, or owner, approaches an angel investor in search of capital, the potential investor is more likely to find the value proposition appealing when the small business already has talented employees, a valuable and defendable technology, an efficient location, and satisfied pilot customers. Thus, the value proposition formed by a small business manager with one stakeholder is often contingent on the value propositions he forms with his other stakeholders. This adds to the interdependency linking the benefits of stakeholder A to the benefits of stakeholder B. Additional promising insights into this process may be found by integrating stakeholder theory with key arguments from institutional theory (perhaps regarding the institutional legitimacy of a small firm's potential stakeholders) and network theory (regarding how the small firm structures its network of stakeholder relationships).

This chapter provides a starting point for empirical examinations of the opportunity creation process by specifying theoretical constructs of stakeholder theory and proposing how they are related. Examining the nuances of this phenomenon might initially call for the richness of qualitative study methodologies. This work will contribute to small business scholarship by predicting distinct relationships between the nature of an opportunity and the stakeholder management approach that small firms are most likely to employ. It will also contribute to stakeholder theory by adding a contingent argument regarding when managing for stakeholders is most likely to maximize small firm performance. Finally, this work will contribute to small firm management by providing practical distinctions that may help guide investment decisions regarding time, effort, and money.

NOTES

1. R. Edward Freeman, *Strategic Management: A Stakeholder Approach* (Boston: Pitman Publishing Inc., 1984), 46; Max B. E. Clarkson, "A Stakeholder Framework for Analyzing and Evaluating Corporate Social Performance," *Academy of Management Review* 20, 1 (1995): 92–117.

2. Jeffrey S. Harrison, Douglas A. Bosse, and Robert A. Phillips, "Managing for Stakeholders, Stakeholder Utility Functions and Competitive Advantage," *Strategic Management Journal* 31, 1 (2010): 58–74.

3. Oliver E. Williamson, *The Economic Institutions of Capitalism* (New York: Free Press, 1985).

4. Herbert A. Simon, *Models of Man* (New York: Wiley, 1957).

5. Williamson, *The Economic Institutions of Capitalism.*

6. Ronald H. Coase, "The Nature of the Firm," *Econometrica* 4, 1 (1937): 386–405; Williamson, *The Economic Institutions of Capitalism*; Oliver E. Williamson, *Markets and Hierarchies: Analysis and Antitrust Implications* (New York: Free Press, 1975).

7. Williamson, *The Economic Institutions of Capitalism.*

8. Nicholas S. Argyres and Julia Porter Liebeskind, "Contractual Commitments, Bargaining Power, and Governance Inseparability: Incorporating History into Transaction Cost Theory," *Academy of Management Review* 24, 1 (1999): 49–63.

9. Frank T. Rothaermel and David L. Deeds, "Exploration and Exploitation Alliances in Biotechnology: A System of New Product Development," *Strategic Management Journal* 25 (2004): 201–221.

10. Mani R. Subramani and N. Venkatraman, "Safeguarding Investments in Asymmetric Interorganizational Relationships: Theory and Evidence," *Academy of Management Journal* 46, 1 (2003): 46–62.

11. Williamson, *The Economic Institutions of Capitalism.*

12. Argyres and Liebeskind, "Contractual Commitments," 58.

13. Samuel Bowles and Herbert Gintis, "The Revenge of Homo Economicus: Contested Exchange and the Revival of Political Economy," *Journal of Economic Perspectives* 7, 1 (1993): 83–102 (see p. 88).

14. Argyres and Liebeskind, "Contractual Commitments."

15. Jared D. Harris and R. Edward Freeman, "The Impossibility of the Separation Thesis," *Business Ethics Quarterly* 18, 4 (2008): 541–548.

16. Christine Jolls, Cass R. Sunstein, and Richard H. Thaler, "A Behavioral Approach to Law and Economics," *Stanford Law Review* 50 (1998): 1471–1550.

17. Douglas A. Bosse, Robert A. Phillips, and Jeffrey S. Harrison, "Stakeholders, Reciprocity, and Firm Performance," *Strategic Management Journal* 30, 4 (2009): 447–456.

18. Ernst Fehr and Simon Gächter, "Fairness and Retaliation: The Economics of Reciprocity," *Journal of Economic Perspectives* 14, 3 (2000): 159–181.

19. Thomas Donaldson and Thomas W. Dunfee, "Toward a Unified Conception of Business Ethics: Integrative Social Contracts Theory," *Academy of Management Review* 19, 2 (1994): 252–284.

20. Fehr and Gächter, "Fairness and Retaliation"; John Rawls, "Justice as Reciprocity," in *John Rawls: Collected Papers*, ed. Samuel Freeman (Cambridge, MA: Harvard University Press, 1971); Lawrence Becker, *Reciprocity* (Chicago: University of Chicago Press, 1986); Russell Cropanzano and Marie S. Mitchell, "Social Exchange Theory: An Interdisciplinary Review," *Journal of Management* 31, 6 (2005): 874–900; Matthew Rabin, "Psychology and Economics," *Journal of Economic Literature* 36, 1 (1998): 11–46; Robert B. Cialdini, *Influence: The Psychology of Persuasion*, (New York: William Morrow and Company, 1984); Robert L. Trivers, "The Evolution of Reciprocal Altruism," *The Quarterly Review of Biology* 46, 1 (1971): 35–57.

21. Bowles and Gintis, "The Revenge of Homo Economicus."

22. Robert Phillips, R. Edward Freeman, and Andrew C. Wicks, "What Stakeholder Theory Is Not," *Business Ethics Quarterly* 13, 4 (2003): 479–502.

23. Bosse, Phillips, and Harrison, "Stakeholders, Reciprocity, and Firm Performance."

24. Phillips, Freeman, and Wicks, "What Stakeholder Theory Is Not."

25. Douglas A. Bosse and Jeffrey S. Harrison, "Stakeholders, Entrepreneurial Rent, and Bounded Self Interest," in *Stakeholder Theory: Impact and Prospects*, ed. Robert Phillips (Cheltenham, U.K.: Edward Elgar Publishing, 2011): 193–211.

26. Jeffrey S. Harrison and Douglas A. Bosse, "How Much Is Too Much?: The Limits to Generous Treatment of Stakeholders," *Business Horizons* 56, 3 (2013): 313–322.

27. Russell W. Coff, "When Competitive Advantage Doesn't Lead to Performance: The Resource-based View and Stakeholder Bargaining Power," *Organization Science* 10, 2 (1999): 119–133.

28. Robert F. Lusch and Stephen L. Vargo, *The Service-dominant Logic of Marketing: Dialog, Debate, and Directions* (Armonk, NY: ME Sharpe, 2006).

29. Roger Fisher, William L. Ury, and Bruce M. Patton, *Getting to Yes: Negotiating Agreement without Giving In*, 2nd ed. (New York: Penguin, 1991).

30. Richard Normann and Rafael Ramirez, "From Value Chain to Value Constellation: Designing Interactive Strategy," *Harvard Business Review* 71 (1993): 65–77.

31. Cliff Bowman and Véronique Ambrosini, "Value Creation versus Value Capture: Towards a Coherent Definition of Value in Strategy," *British Journal of Management* 11, 1 (2000): 1–15.

32. Richard L. Priem, "A Consumer Perspective on Value Creation," *Academy of Management Review* 32, 1 (2007): 219–235.

33. Stephen L. Vargo and Robert F. Lusch, "Evolving to a New Dominant Logic for Marketing," *Journal of Marketing* 68, 1 (2004): 1–17.

34. Priem, "A Consumer Perspective on Value Creation."

35. David P. Lepak, Ken G. Smith, and M. Susan Taylor, "Value Creation and Value Capture: A Multilevel Perspective," *Academy of Management Review* 32, 1 (2007): 180–194.

36. Kim B. Clark, "The Interaction of Design Hierarchies and Market Concepts in Technological Evolution," *Research Policy* 14, 5 (1985): 235–251; Dorothy Leonard-Barton, *Wellsprings of Knowledge: Building and Sustaining the Sources of Innovation* (Boston: Harvard Business School Press, 1995); Eric Von Hippel, "Lead Users: A Source of Novel Product Concepts," *Management Science* 32, 7 (1986): 791–805.

37. Joshua Eliashberg, Gary L. Lilien, and Vithala Rao, "Minimizing Technological Oversights: A Marketing Research Perspective," in *Technological Innovation: Oversights and Foresights*, ed. Raghu Garud, Praveen Rattan Nayyar, Praveen Rattah, and Zur Baruch Shapira (New York: Cambridge University Press, 1997): 214–230.

38. Jacob Goldenberg, Donald R. Lehmann, and David Mazursky, "The Idea Itself and the Circumstances of Its Emergence as Predictors of New Product Success," *Management Science* 47, 1 (2001): 69–84.

39. Stan Maklan, Simon Knox, and Lynette Ryals, "New Trends in Innovation and Customer Relationship Management," *International Journal of Market Research* 50, 2 (2008): 221–240.

40. Von Hippel, "Lead Users."

41. Glen L. Urban and Eric von Hippel, "Lead User Analyses for the Development of New Industrial Products," *Management Science* 34, 5 (1988): 569–582; Cornelius Herstatt and Eric von Hippel, "From Experience: Developing New Product Concepts via the Lead User Method: A Case Study in a 'Low Tech' Field," *Journal of Product Innovation Management* 9, 3 (1992): 213–221; Erik L. Olson and Geir Bakke, "Implementing the Lead User Method in a High Technology Firm: A Longitudinal Study of Intentions versus Actions," *Journal of Product Innovation Management* 18, 6 (2001): 388–395.

42. Neeli Bendapudi and Robert P. Leone, "Psychological Implications of Customer Participation in Co-production," *Journal of Marketing* 67, 1 (2003): 14–28.

43. Goldenberg, Lehmann, and Mazursky, "The Idea Itself and the Circumstances of Its Emergence as Predictors of New Product Success."

44. Beibei Dong, Kenneth R. Evans, and Shaoming Zou, "The Effects of Customer Participation in Co-created Service Recovery," *Journal of the Academy of Marketing Science* 36, 1 (2008): 123–137.

45. Stephen L. Vargo, Paul P. Maglio, and Melissa Archpru Akaka, "On Value and Value Co-creation: A Service Systems and Service Logic Perspective," *European Management Journal* 26, 3 (2008): 145–152 (see p. 146).

46. J. Richard Hackman and Greg R. Oldham, "Motivation through the Design of Work: Test of a Theory," *Organizational Behavior and Human Performance* 16, 2 (1976): 250–279.

47. Freeman, *Strategic Management*.

48. Cheryl Carleton Asher, Joseph Mahoney, and James Mahoney, "Towards a Property Rights Foundation for a Stakeholder Theory of the Firm," *Journal of Management and Governance* 9, 1 (2005): 5–32; Margaret M. Blair, *Ownership and Control: Rethinking Corporate Governance for the Twenty First Century* (Washington, D.C.: The Brookings Institution, 1995).

49. Max H. Bazerman and Margaret A. Neale, *Negotiating Rationally* (New York: Free Press, 1992).

50. David A. Lax and James K. Sebenius, *The Manager as Negotiator: Bargaining for Cooperation and Competitive Gain* (New York: Free Press, 1986).

51. Leigh Thompson, *The Mind and Heart of the Negotiator*, 3rd ed. (Upper Saddle River, NJ: Pearson Prentice Hall, 2005).

52. Fisher, Ury, and Patton, *Getting to Yes*; Leigh Thompson, "Negotiation Behavior and Outcomes: Empirical Evidence and Theoretical Issues," *Psychological Bulletin* 108, 3 (1990): 515–532.

53. Thompson, *The Mind and Heart of the Negotiator*.

54. Adam D. Galinsky, William W. Maddux, Debra Gilin, and Judith B. White, "Why It Pays to Get Inside the Head of Your Opponent: The Differential Effects of Perspective Taking and Empathy in Negotiations," *Psychological Science* 19, 4 (2008): 378–384.

55. Mark H. Davis, "Measuring Individual Differences in Empathy: Evidence for a Multidimensional Approach," *Journal of Personality and Social Psychology* 44, 1 (1983): 113–126.

56. Don A. Moore, "Myopic Biases in Strategic Social Prediction: Why Deadlines Put Everyone under More Pressure Than Everyone Else," *Personality and Social Psychology Bulletin* 31, 5 (2005): 668–679.

57. Dean Pruitt and Jeffrey Z. Rubin, *Social Conflict: Escalation, Stalemate, and Settlement* (New York: McGraw-Hill, 1986).

58. Galinsky, Maddux, Gilin, and White, "Why It Pays to Get Inside the Head of Your Opponent."

2

Technology-Driven Innovation: Roles and Implications of Technology Capabilities and the Environment for the Success and Survival of Small Businesses

Larry Tribble, Paul Drnevich, and James Ha

Innovation is the creation, improvement, or implementation of new ideas or activities that may take the form of services, products, structures, or plans.[1] Innovation influences the formation, performance, survival, and success or failure of small businesses as well as the growth of new industries. Innovation and the capability to innovate are important competitive factors, particularly for small businesses who suffer from resource constraints as well as the liabilities of newness and smallness. Innovation is often the mechanism that allows small businesses to create value and challenge and disrupt larger and more resource-rich incumbents. Indeed, apart from innovative products, processes, or services, it is difficult to imagine how a small business could compete effectively in any market with large, entrenched incumbents or could develop new markets to avoid such competition. Innovation, in features that differentiate products to increase sales, in processes to reduce costs or increase quality, and in development of services to meet customer needs, is truly the lifeblood of competition and thus a primary driver of success for small businesses. In this chapter, we examine how small businesses may more effectively leverage technology in general, and information technology in particular, to drive innovation.

If there is one defining feature of the early 21st century, it is the rise of information technology to central prominence in the economy. *Homo faber,* "man the toolmaker," continues his work through technology-based tools that increasingly define our modern culture. Information technology has changed both social and business culture in ways that we cannot yet measure. There is currently significant discussion regarding the digital divide between those individuals, communities, organizations, and nations who have embraced modern information technology and those who have not.[2] Another current

technology issue is the concept of big data, where businesses (and governments) are collecting far more data (both ethically/legally and unethically/
illegally in some cases) than they know how to use effectively. This vast
amount of collected data is challenging some of the very definitions of information and knowledge as well as traditional notions and theories within a
number of fields.[3]

Such new and improved technological tools come about as we innovate,
both as individuals and as firms. A small business that produces an innovation, improves a process, or provides a new service may become the next
great firm because of such a technological advance. An innovation may also
provide the foundation for the competitiveness of small businesses or help
to create a new market niche that a small business can exploit. So, what is
the connection between innovation and technology? Is the key to success
merely a matter of luck or inspiration, discovering the right opportunity at
the right time? Alternatively, is there a skill set that an individual utilizes or
an organizational capability that a small business brings to bear in addressing
a problem or pursuing an opportunity for innovation? Regardless of whether
inspiration or capability is the source for innovation, its performance implications and competitive outcomes may be similar. However, it is this latter case
of innovation as a systematic, ongoing process or set of capabilities within the
firm that information technology may best support.

Through this chapter, we analyze the role of information technology as a
driver of innovation in small business. In the following sections, we offer an
overview of the current understanding of innovation; its roles within small
business performance, success, and survival; and the roles that information
technology may play in enhancing and enabling innovation activities in
small businesses. We also consider the external environment in which small
businesses exist and operate and how the environment may influence the
contributions of technology to innovation. Finally, we briefly review how
small businesses may create and appropriate value from technological innovation. We conclude by offering some suggestions, implications, and notes of
caution for small business owners and managers for using information technology to drive innovation.

SMALL BUSINESSES AND INNOVATION

Several decades ago, strategy scholars considered scale efficiency to be an
overwhelming advantage for innovation in large incumbent firms, an advantage with which small businesses simply could not compete. Such scale efficiencies occur because of, among other reasons, the ability of large firms to
diversify the high risk of innovation over a larger number of projects and

to gather a critical mass of highly paid scientists to generate ideas. Schumpeter hypothesized that large monopolistic firms would dominate innovation because of their ability to deploy excess or slack resources, generated from their above-average profits.[4] These considerations led to the notion that small firms only exist as embryonic large firms and can only survive through growth.

However, over time, scholars noticed that, despite their supposed scale disadvantage in innovation, small businesses continued to enter markets successfully—in some cases growing into medium-sized or large-sized firms, while in other cases continuing to be small and profitable in niches within industries dominated by large firms. This observation countered the previous view of growth or death as the only options for small businesses. For this reason, scholars began to reflect on the advantages of small businesses in several areas of performance, including innovation. These considerations resulted in a broader view of small businesses. When compared to large firms, small businesses may be more nimble and less constrained by both history and the relatively tight organization typically required for control of a large firm or business unit. Small businesses may have better capabilities to focus, with smaller firm size allowing for easier unification under the direction of the owner or manager. While all firms, regardless of size, should benefit from innovation in the face of Schumpeterian creative destruction, small businesses, in particular, may use these advantages to attract customers away from existing competitors in an industry.[5] Therefore, we suggest that innovation is of significant importance to small business and that small business in turn plays a pivotal role in innovation.

Evidence and debate in prior literature indicate that the relationship between firm size and innovation is at worst inconclusive and at best slightly in favor of large firms, depending on how size and innovation are measured. Scholars generally make such arguments in favor of large firms along the following lines: large firms are more innovative because they have larger resource and knowledge bases, better abilities to raise capital, greater capabilities, and greater diversification and capacity to sustain risky endeavors. Conversely, scholars generally make such arguments in favor of small businesses along the following lines: small businesses are more innovative because they (are perceived to) have more flexibility, greater responsiveness, less bureaucracy, and less difficulty in accepting and implementing change. However, small businesses lack the size and scale to diversify risk that large firms (presumably) enjoy, and thus failed innovation attempts may be disastrous for a small business as they are more likely to affect survival. The arguments in favor of greater innovativeness for small businesses, along with the importance of innovation to small businesses, may lead managers to make the dangerous assumption that just because a firm is small it is innovative. However, empirical evidence in the literature tends to indicate that small businesses are not implicitly favored by size alone and thus have to work at innovation.[6] In the next section, we offer an overview of the types of innovation (product versus process) and the management and orientation of innovation within small businesses. Following this overview, we introduce the implications of technology as a driver of innovation in small business.

Product versus Process Innovation

Another major factor to consider for small businesses, beyond the role of firm size in innovation, is the type of innovation itself, that is, whether it is a product or process innovation. Product innovations meet external user needs, while process innovations focus on a firm's internal operations. From this perspective, scholars often argue that small businesses should be introducing product innovations when entering new markets and therefore should develop and possess stronger capabilities for product innovation. Similarly, larger firms often respond to competitive challenges (from smaller rivals) by improving their processes for increased efficiency (for existing products) and therefore should develop and possess stronger capabilities for process innovation. However, past research is also inconclusive as to observable differences in the relationship among type of innovation produced, firm size, and performance.[7]

One could reason then, that the lack of evidence of the effect of firm size on innovation, along with the lack of evidence of other differences in the two types, is an indication that the underlying capability supporting either type of innovation may be similar. This argument may also be extended to suggest that both product and process innovation may be necessary for a firm to have an innovation-based competitive advantage. For example, while an innovative product may create value (for a consumer), if the firm cannot innovate a production process that quickly and reliably produces a sufficient quantity of the product innovation and innovate marketing processes to sell the product innovation, it is unlikely to capture a sufficient share of that value. Such notions of the conjoined relationship of value creation and value appropriation from innovation capabilities are also similar to concepts of dynamic capabilities.[8]

Product and Process Innovation in Small Business

One view of small business considers the owner/manager as more critical to the performance of the organization than is typical in large firms. This criticality is because of the wide number of tasks that are performed by the owner/manager, the centrality of the owner/manager to strategy orchestration, and the owner/manager's role as the sole or primary authority on the allocation of resources. Therefore, small businesses may have an advantage over larger firms in the sense that the product innovator and the process innovator may be positioned more closely (organizationally speaking) than the product and process management functions in larger firms.[9] In this view, a small business's product and process innovations may develop in tandem, with better information exchange, and such development may add to the advantage of innovation.[10] Therefore, the small business and the owner/manager may have a strong innovation orientation and may be better than a larger firm at efficiently appropriating value from innovation.

Innovation Process Management and Innovation Orientation

Scholars have studied two basic views of the innovation phenomenon: innovation process management and innovation orientation.[11] The innovation process management paradigm considers a more mechanistic relationship between innovation inputs such as R&D spending, individuals involved in innovation, and innovation outputs such as patents and new services. On the other hand, the innovation orientation view proposes an organizational capability of engaging in and supporting experimentation and creative processes that lead to innovations in both product and process; such an innovation orientation creates a pervasive innovation culture throughout the firm. Research on innovation and firm performance indicates that innovation outputs are more strongly associated with performance than innovation inputs and that innovation orientation more strongly predicts performance than innovation outputs.[12] This evidence supports the case for the effectiveness of innovation efforts that focus on an innovation orientation rather than simply mechanistically increasing spending on innovation inputs. Such notions may also reflect similarities between innovation approaches and dynamic capabilities (discussed in more detail later in the chapter).

Innovation Process Management and Innovation Orientation in Small Business

So, what are the implications of innovation process management and innovation orientation for small businesses? Our argument is that small businesses can appropriate more value from product and process orientation by developing an innovation orientation. Such an orientation refers to ambitious goals, a challenging culture, and effective risk taking. The benefits of an innovation orientation, along with the advantages that small businesses enjoy in establishing and changing their culture, may serve as another strength for small businesses. For example, the small business that can more readily establish and sustain an innovation-oriented culture should more fully appropriate the value created by their innovation activities.

Summary: Innovation in Small Business

While there is no clear evidence that small businesses have an innovation advantage over large firms, there is evidence that some of the particular strengths of small businesses may better support innovation. In particular, small businesses may leverage advantages based on their smaller size to support innovation in two ways. The first is utilization of the close relationships among members of the small business to engage in simultaneous process and product innovation. The second is utilization of the capability in small businesses to establish and sustain an organizational culture that promotes an innovation orientation, rather than mechanistically increasing innovation inputs, such as R&D spending, in hopes of increasing innovation.

TECHNOLOGY: EVOLVING, PURPOSEFUL, AND PROCESS ORIENTED

To more firmly ground the notion of technology as a driver of innovation (i.e., technology-based innovation capabilities), we must first understand what we mean by the term *technology*. We begin our definition by noting that technology harnesses principles of nature discovered by scientific (or less formal) observation of natural phenomena. As knowledge of the natural principles underlying those phenomena increases, engineers and innovators apply that knowledge to cause or manipulate phenomena and attain desired outcomes. In this way, growth of scientific knowledge supports growth of technology. Further, not only does technology build on hard science, it also builds upon itself. For example, until the technology of glass making (based on the principle of the behavior of melted sand) produced reasonably reliable glass lenses, the technology of telescopes, binoculars, microscopes, and eyeglasses (based on the principles of light moving through transparent media) was simply impossible. Another similar example involves the development of atomic energy—a manipulation that could not have come about accidentally but only occurred through scientific discovery. Scientists needed to understand atoms and the principle that energy would be produced if a large atom were split into two smaller ones. This understanding built on previous knowledge of radioactivity and nuclear physics; in fact, a whole chain of hard science developed into the inspired notion that energy could be produced in such a way. Once scientific theory demonstrated that such a thing was possible, a significant amount of technology had to be developed to enable experiments in nuclear fission, and even more technology had to be developed to control fission in such a way as to make it useful in energy production. In this way, technology is based on the understanding and application of natural principles.

We can also observe the application of such logic in small business practices today, such as in the case of Clinical Data, a small business that introduced the fastest blood analyzer to the market through its use of technology developed by Melet Schloesing Laboratories. Melet's proprietary technology allows a five-part differential cell count measure similar in cost to the conventional three-part differential analyzers traditionally used. Melet's technology is based on electronically detecting the different sizes of blood cells and thus incorporates natural principles discovered in the hard sciences: the understanding that different cells are different sizes and the understanding that measurement of cell size can be performed electronically.[13] Clinical Data is an example of a small business that understood the science and built technology based on the application of natural principles.

Second, we note that technology usually develops in the service of some human purpose. Without the desire to amplify or improve the sense of sight, the lens-based technologies in our earlier example would not have attracted meaningful development efforts. There are technologies that, when developed (or discovered accidentally), appeared to serve no practical purpose, yet later, when applied to human purposes, they were found to be quite useful innovations. However, an overwhelming majority of technological development evolves from applied research, which is driven by a desired outcome or purpose. Such technologies (and their applications) help businesses to manipulate their environment, suiting it to their specific purposes.

Third, technology involves a process. In fact, some of the more prominent technologies simply harness processes, speeding up, slowing down, or otherwise controlling a natural process that would occur without human intervention. As an example, most liquids will evaporate at normal temperatures, some quickly, others more slowly, but all evaporation absorbs heat. To control the amount of heat absorbed by evaporation, technology exists to control the rate and amount of evaporation; doing so results in the technology of refrigeration. All technologies involve processes in one way or another: the process of developing the technology, the process of controlling the technology, or the process of utilizing the technology.

Finally, we also note that, despite our use of the singular term *technology*, as if it were a discrete asset that could be obtained in isolation, technology is an ephemeral concept. Let us consider an example to illustrate this idea. Asius, a small business in Colorado, produces innovative in-ear hearing devices for both hearing-impaired and non-hearing-impaired customers. A hearing aid is a discrete asset; it is purchased as a unit and normally perceived and utilized as a unit, and *audio technology* (singular) is a commonly used term. Nevertheless, it represents several partially individualized technologies that have developed more or less symbiotically, but not only within the hearing device industry. Speaker technology is utilized in particular ways in hearing devices, but it is also developed and utilized independently in other markets. Miniaturized circuit technology has reached its highest levels in computer manufacturing, but it is also applied in hearing technology. The Asius device is a bundle of otherwise independent technologies applied to a human purpose: better hearing. As such, technologies are usually bundled together in meaningful ways in an asset.

The Asius example highlights another facet of technology: assets intended for a particular and relatively narrow purpose (i.e., aids for hearing-impaired customers) can be modified to suit other, more or less similar, purposes. Asius recognized that the technology that helps hearing-impaired customers could also be applied to other specialized listening environments, such as, in this case, noisy environments. In addition to aids for hearing-impaired customers, Asius also markets noise-canceling listening devices for non-hearing-impaired customers based on its core technology.[14] Asius represents the adaption of technology to purposes that were not directly considered by other technology producers.

Summary: Technology in Small Business

We argue for and utilize a recent definition of technology as a process based on a natural principle that serves some purpose.[15] As we depicted through the examples above, technology is often embodied in an artifact or asset, so the acquisition of the technology is often achieved through the acquisition of an asset. Further, we see that technology builds upon itself, utilizing previous technologies and scientific findings of natural principles to serve new purposes. Finally, *a* technology is not a discrete, limited set of principles, but a combination of applications that can be aggregated or disaggregated to address different purposes.

Technology and Adaptation in Business Processes

Our consideration above of the relationship between a technological asset and the purpose it serves aids a discussion of another feature of technology. The organizational assets that typically embody technologies and serve human purposes may or may not serve those purposes well. Further, they may also be pressed into service for other purposes that were never intended by the developers of the technology. In these ways, a technology may or may not fit well with the other processes involved in the purpose. In some circumstances, the fit between the available technology and the specific purpose may not be as precise as the user would like. Such a situation presents two basic options: modify the asset in ways that make it fit better or modify the remaining processes to align with the technology. From the Asius example offered earlier, in hindsight, it may be apparent that technology purposed for hearing-impaired customers could be applicable to other listening situations, but that realization and implementation required insight and some modification of the original technology to fit the additional purpose. Small businesses often own the instance of the technology embodied in the asset and have rights, in most circumstances, to modify the asset as they see fit. Similarly, they have every right to change the process to suit the technology. This process of tailoring the process or the asset to more precisely produce the desired result is similar to the notion of *bricolage*, or organizational improvisation, and is a fundamental act of innovation using technology assets.[16]

Absorptive Capacity and Technology

Technology builds on itself similarly to the ways that knowledge builds on itself, often described as *absorptive capacity*.[17] Scholars consider absorptive capacity to be the capability of the firm to acquire and utilize new knowledge from outside the firm as an extension of previous or existing knowledge.[18] The absorptive capacity view asserts that new knowledge allows firms to do new things, in comparison to learning by doing, which allows firms to get better at things that they already do.[19] Absorptive capacity is considered one means for the firm to acquire knowledge, which may be the firm's most valuable resource. However, absorptive capacity encompasses not only the acquisition of knowledge but also the exploitation and use of knowledge in practical ways, such as innovation. A strong tie exists between the definition of technology as the embodiment of knowledge about natural principles and of absorptive capacity as understanding the use of technology-based knowledge and building extensions to that technology through new knowledge.

In fact, the early recognition of absorptive capacity developed from studying the process of R&D in firms.[20] Absorptive capacity research fully embraces technology in finding that absorptive capacity not only allows the firm to use new knowledge but also enables it to better predict or envision the nature of technological advancements. We posit that a new technology fills a similar function to new knowledge in the absorptive capacity view in the sense that the ability to incorporate a new technology involves extending previous or existing technology use and enabling the firm to envision new advancements in technology.

INFORMATION TECHNOLOGY AND SMALL BUSINESS

Information technology, as we see it, is a subdomain of (general) technology. As such, it shares the general properties of technology that we discussed previously. Therefore, for our purposes, information technology is a set of processes based on natural principles that serve a human purpose; it derives its domain from the natural principles and purposes of information and the techniques of digital information creation and processing. Information technology is embedded in assets such as hardware and software and is difficult to completely isolate from the assets and from other technological domains. Further, information technology relates to absorptive capacity in ways similar to technology generally and has the capability to modify business processes to suit existing business processes. Information technology also has specific features that influence its use in small businesses and its relationship to innovation in the firm. We explore some of these aspects and features of information technology for small business in this section.

Information technology is currently driving significant change in small businesses and in society and consumer markets as a whole. Growth in the speed and power of information technology and in its breadth of application is causing many small businesses to assume that spending on information technology is a requirement for competitiveness in modern business. In addition, growth and change in information technology offers opportunities for establishing and growing small businesses. However, given the relentless pace of change, small businesses are hard pressed to continually devote scarce resources in an effort to keep up with competitors, and opportunities in the technology whirlwind seem to disappear as quickly as they appear, overwhelmed by the next opportunities. Nevertheless, managers fear that some specific new information technology or the accumulation of small information technology changes will produce a competitiveness gap, and this fear continues to drive information technology investment in many small businesses.

These contrary visions of the importance of information technology to small business continue to present a conundrum to business scholars over the value of information technology. On the one hand, scholars are accumulating evidence that suggests that information technology directly and indirectly contributes to firm performance.[21] Proponents of a direct link consider information technology a competitive competency that facilitates greater communication, knowledge accumulation, and flexibility. Proponents of an indirect link argue that information technology aids in translating strategies into greater firm performance via similar mechanisms, but that the mechanisms themselves do not directly influence firm performance.

On the other hand, scholars find that information technology is too commonly available to allow any firm to use it in a way that differentiates one firm from another or supports a competitive advantage. Evidence supporting this view is also readily available in the extensive, expensive, and well-documented failures of information technology implementations and in the lack of direct measurable value of information technology.[22] As a powerful and malleable tool, the implications of information technology are widespread, as are its contributions to firm performance. Therefore, directly measuring the value or information technology is difficult. Nevertheless, scholars continue to assert that information technology is valuable to the firm through many streams, such as return on investment in information technology projects, process measurement and improvement, and data collection and availability.[23]

Scholars have also addressed the relationship between information technology investment and innovation, finding that synergies exist between these elements of the organizational system—that doing more of one increases the returns of doing more of the other. Such complementary relationships include the flexibility associated with both innovation success and information technology and the collaborative structures and creative processes to solve problems that occur in innovation efforts and in information technology implementation and application.[24]

The malleability of information technology is worthy of specific note as it concerns the small business. A computer is a multipurpose tool, encompassing such functions as communications (e.g., e-mail, voice, video); entertainment (e.g., audio, video, gaming, social); computation (e.g., bookkeeping, robotics, CAD/CAM); business process support; and more. The many uses of such an information technology component demonstrate one dimension of malleability. But information technology is also malleable in the sense that it can be modified with relative ease by a relatively large proportion of the population, both in modifying the way that specific functions operate (e.g., changing a Web site) and in modifying the combinations of functions so that they operate in a desired way (e.g., integrating an online data source into the firm's bookkeeping). As such, information technology seems to invite modification and to be an exploratory platform for innovation. As we have observed, large firms may have the resources to create innovation labs for such exploration in other domains, but the cost of a computational lab is within the reach of any size firm. This may be the reason that a disproportionate number of the giant information technology firms of the current generation began as small businesses in garages, basements, and dorm rooms.

TECHNOLOGY AND ORGANIZATIONAL CAPABILITIES

The concept of organizational capabilities (and scholars' understanding of them) is an outgrowth of the resource-based view (RBV) of the firm.[25] The RBV defines resources as assets that can be exchanged among firms and considers the firm to be a bundle of resources that are combined to create a competitive advantage upon which a firm may earn *rents*, or profits. The firm can sustain performance or profit emanating from the competitive advantage if the underlying resource is rare, valuable, inimitable, and unique.[26] However, because a firm is more than simply the bundle of resources that it controls, the RBV also recognizes capabilities as attributes that are internal to the firm and cannot be exchanged apart from acquiring the entire firm. In this way, firm capabilities are analogous to skills in individuals. A small business with a particular capability will likely utilize certain resources in a more productive manner than a business without that capability.

While a complete taxonomy of firm capabilities has yet to be defined (nor likely could it be), various capabilities have been defined in extant research. Current literature relates innovation to technological capability but considers different conceptualizations of technological capability, such as "a firm's ability to employ various technologies,"[27] "[the firm's] ability to use [technological] resources . . . to offer products,"[28] and "a firm's internal technology resource base."[29] We conceptualize such a technological capability as an attribute of the firm that supports technology as a driver of innovation. As we have argued previously, technology cannot be conceptualized in a "black box" manner in which one technology seamlessly replaces another; it often requires innovative adaptations of existing physical or organizational processes within the business.[30] We argue that this adaptation in the application and use of technology represents the technological capability that supports innovation.

Technological Capability and Adaptation/Absorptive Capacity

Absorptive capacity is fundamental to technological capability. Such a relationship is positive for small business because absorptive capacity can be strengthened through use. Absorptive capacity, as the building of knowledge on knowledge, technology on technology, is strengthened by means similar to bricolage, where innovation is based on available resources and is brought about by tinkering with technology and processes to produce results.[31] Managers can improve absorptive capacity by changing how the knowledge-based assets of the firm are used, in a sense similar to a dynamic capability. Dynamic capabilities are considered a means to configure other capabilities, such as technological capability.[32] As absorptive capacity builds, technological capability is likely to be strengthened, which may lead to a virtuous cycle in which greater technological capability increases technological knowledge, leading to greater innovation that, in turn, further strengthens absorptive capacity. We argue that such a cycle is a means by which dynamic capabilities, such as absorptive capacity, influence innovation and, in turn, performance in small businesses.[33]

Summary: Technological Capability and Small Business

The strong linkage between technological capability and innovation and the importance of innovation to small businesses indicates that technological capability may be particularly important to small businesses. One view of the small business considers the owner/manager as more critical to performance of the organization than is typical in large firms, as we outlined earlier. In this sense, it is likely that the small business's technological capability is more highly influenced by, or solely exists in, the owner/manager. In addition, unlike large firms, the small business is less likely to support a large technology infrastructure with devoted R&D and technology specialists. For these reasons, we expect the small business to have a more focused technological capability than a large firm does. This focus could have a positive effect on innovation in the sense that there is limited distraction and greater capability in a smaller technological area, but it could also have a negative effect in the sense that insights into combinations of technologies from different domains often produce innovation.

However, research finds that small businesses are more likely to engage in "coopetition" with other small businesses, which may provide additional technological insights from other specific technological domains and, thus, provide a greater breadth of technological capability to balance the potential negative effects of more focused internal technological capability.[34] In this way, two strengths of small businesses can work in tandem to support innovation. In the next section, we consider the external environment in which small businesses exist and how the environment may influence the contributions of technology to innovation, the application of strengths of small businesses, and the ability of small businesses to capture value from innovation.

Dimensions of the External Environment and Implications for Small Business

The external environment may affect all of a small business's functions and activities. For instance, devoting resources to the development of innovations is a strategic decision that may only produce value in the long term. A firm that is in an environment with scarce resources is likely unable to allocate resources away from short-term survival to support long-term goals. Small businesses have a hierarchy of needs and, given the choice, will likely satisfy needs for survival before concerning themselves with growth and innovation. Thus, in this section, we first classify the environment in which small businesses operate according to well-used measures from Dess and Beard, and then we turn our attention to how the environment may affect the contributions of technology to innovation in the small business context.[35]

Dess and Beard surveyed the literature on the environment of the firm, compared it to literature on the natural environment, and developed a view of the environment that consists of three dimensions: *complexity*, *dynamism*, and *munificence*.[36] These dimensions operate at the industry level and are more or less independent, although some combinations are more common than others.

Complexity concerns the heterogeneity of the environment as reflected in the breadth of issues, inputs, competitors, and products with which the firm interacts. With a large number of interactions, the environment can be considered complex, even if the number of interactions is stable and the individual interactions exhibit low levels of variability. Among other effects, managers in a firm facing a complex environment will have greater information processing needs and perceive greater uncertainty. As an example, a highly regulated industry may be complex as managers must track many instances in which they may conflict with a restriction on behavior or a reporting requirement, but the regulations themselves may change slowly. In this way, environmental complexity does not depend on the frequency or magnitude of change in the interactions, nor does it depend on a change in the nature or number of interactions.

Dynamism is the level of instability in the environment also viewed as the unpredictability of environmental change or turbulence in the environment. In this view, dynamism considers whether managers in the firm can comfortably predict the scope and variability of interactions or environmental variables that the firm must consider. A large number of known variables constitutes complexity, while dynamism represents a relatively smaller number of highly uncertain variables or the potential of a sudden change in the number or set of variables. Dynamism, therefore, represents the notion of chaos in the environment. As an example, developing industries can be highly dynamic. As competitors and suppliers enter and exit the industry and new customer groups help to define the products and features that meet their needs, owner/managers may not know where to look for information on suppliers, competitors, and new customer bases.

Munificence considers the level of resources available in the firm's environment. In natural environments, a rainforest would be considered more munificent than a desert. In the same way, a munificent environment would permit organizational growth and stability through a ready supply of resources. A high level of munificence does not guarantee resources to any particular firm, but indicates that resources are available to gather relatively easily. As an example, Fab.com, in an echo of the e-commerce boom of the early 2000s, recently capitalized on a munificent environment to acquire $150 million in new funding (which resulted in a valuation of over $1 billion, despite not yet having achieved profitability).[37] This start-up was created as a social network in 2010; however, instead of allowing other brands to market to its social network, Fab.com decided to shift to merchandising to leverage its brand and its 14 million currently registered members.[38] The munificence of the environment provided the resources for this change in competitive strategy.

Effects of the Environment on Innovation for Small Businesses

We now consider the effect of each dimension on small business innovation. Firms operate and make decisions within the constraints of an environment that likely will not change, short of the firm exiting the industry. Therefore, owner/managers need to understand the nature of the environment that the business faces and its impact on strategic decisions. In this way, small businesses will be better able to determine methods of innovation that fit with the combination of environmental dimensions that they face.

In a complex environment, a firm has to develop awareness of many different interactions with, for example, stakeholders, governmental agencies, competitors, and clients. Therefore, complex environments provide large amounts of input, data, and information to the firm. Small businesses in complex environments can develop broad informational networks among other participants in the industry. These networks enable the business to feed on multiple sets of ideas and approaches, which likely provide broad knowledge that can be an input to the innovation process. In addition, complexity can be managed through the use of tools and rule-based processes. In this sense, complexity provides the motivation and rewards for innovation: if innovation in processes and tools makes managing in a complex environment easier, firms are likely to engage in innovation. For these reasons, we expect small businesses in complex environments to have higher levels of innovation.

In a dynamic environment, small businesses should develop a certain flexibility and speed of response as the environment presents previously unforeseen challenges through continual unexpected change. In one way, dynamism could support innovation hand-in-hand with flexibility; if for no other reason, a firm in a dynamic environment would need short-term, problem-solving innovativeness because it likely is not able to predict in advance the internal and external problems that it may need to solve. Viewed from another perspective, dynamism could make successful innovation difficult because there would likely be little time for the trial and error or experimentation that is ordinarily needed to find candidate solutions to a problem and test them to select the best option. As an example of small business innovation in a dynamic environment, let us consider atom42, a digital marketing agency founded in 2007, just in time to confront the dynamism of the online media environment. This business found time to innovate internally through experimentation with cloud-based information technology infrastructure that allowed its staff to work remotely. Now atom42 is completely reliant on the cloud, having innovated internal processes to manage staff without physical colocation. Such innovation shows that a dynamic environment may not completely eliminate opportunities for innovation.

A munificent environment provides a higher general level of resources through such things as industry-wide sales growth. Environmental munificence also presents an equivocal effect on innovation. A munificent environment is likely to provide slack resources that could support innovation. However, a munificent environment is unlikely to provide the motivation for the effort required to innovate. Small businesses are considered to have a greater need to innovate to survive, particularly when compared to large firms who have other survival mechanisms such as market power and economies of scale. However, munificent environments may provide a level of resources that allows a noninnovative small business to subsist. Therefore, managers of small businesses in a munificent environment may be content and, therefore, may not attempt to build an innovation capability.

TECHNOLOGY, INNOVATION, AND VALUE IN THE SMALL BUSINESS CONTEXT

As Peter Drucker noted, the purpose of a business is to create customers.[39] Small businesses create customers by offering products (and services) that meet potential customer needs (and purposes), both felt and unfelt. Potential customers find value in having their needs met and become actual customers by purchasing a product at a price to meet a need and realize that value. Different mechanisms exist for deciding the price (negotiation, auction, market pricing, etc.), but pricing by negotiation will suffice for our purposes in describing the value capture process. Customers capture value from the transaction to the degree that the price paid for the product is lower than the value that they receive. The creation of customer value may be fundamental to business success.[40] Value creation and capture are central concerns for strategic management research.[41] In a way similar to customers, small businesses capture value from the transaction as profit, the difference between the cost of producing the product and the price the customer pays, based on the customer's perception of value. This value-price-cost model shows how value created by the transaction is divided between the business and the customer based on price.[42]

As we argue and illustrate above, existing technologies can be reconfigured, recombined, and reimagined by small businesses into innovative products that meet customer needs in new or different ways. Customers likely perceive differential value in these products, as compared to existing products. An innovative product, incorporating new or existing technology in new ways, may have a greater perceived value to customers through better meeting their needs. This greater value may support a higher price relative to the product that the customer had formerly acquired, based on the relative bargaining power of the customer and the business. In this way, technology embodied in innovative products relates to value created and value captured by the customer and the small business. Small businesses that innovate and offer differential technology may be in a superior position to create and capture value and therefore to successfully compete.

CONCLUSION

In this chapter, we have argued that technology may be used as a driver of innovation in small businesses, which may, in turn, create value that can be appropriated and influence performance and survival. In this sense, we posit that the use of technology in the firm's processes (information technology or otherwise) likely demands adjustments to the technology or the processes that exercise absorptive capacity. Strong absorptive capacity allows the firm to strengthen technological capability through more deeply understanding technology currently in use or more quickly gaining knowledge of prospective technologies. Strong technological capability supports both product and process innovation and allows for an innovation orientation, all of which have been shown to improve the value created and appropriated from innovation.

In addition, we have argued that information technology will likely serve well as a technology to apply to the firm's processes to begin the process of strengthening the firm's absorptive capacity. The advantages of information technology for this type of use are that information technology can be applied to the firm fairly economically; information technology is malleable, allowing the kind of adjustment in technology and processes that exercise absorptive capability and build technological capability; and, perhaps most importantly, information technology can be used without significant disruption of the core technology uses in the firm.

Summary: Technology-Driven Innovation in the Small Business

Small businesses compete with large firms through innovation by using the particular strengths that smallness often conveys. Because product and process innovation are advantageous when performed in tandem, small businesses are likely better able to keep the two innovation streams in sync because of the cohesiveness of smallness. In addition, because innovation orientation is linked to organizational performance, small businesses are likely able to leverage their strength in creating and maintaining culture to support an innovation orientation. Small businesses are able to use the malleability of information technology to develop innovation labs on a scale that is commensurate with their smaller budgets and to utilize information technology in business processes to maintain and exercise the absorptive capacity that we argue underlies technological and innovative capabilities. Finally, small businesses often have closer relationships to and cooperation with other small businesses; these strengths can be used to guard against the danger of having a too-narrow focus on a particular technological knowledge set.

Further, we argue that the environment is a fundamental consideration in the small business's efforts to innovate with technology, exercise its technological capabilities, and strengthen its absorptive capacity. The environment is of particular interest to small businesses as they are less likely to possess the slack resources, market strength, and resource generation that large firms use to manage through environmental circumstances.

Parting Thoughts: Perils of Ignoring Technology

We conclude with a final note of both caution and optimism in considering the role of technology in the innovation of two firms, Kodak and Instagram. The Kodak information technology outsourcing decision of the late 1980s was widely reported and triggered the spread of the trend of information technology outsourcing among firms.[43] Kodak was one the first organizations to entirely outsource their information technology operations. Subsequently, Kodak developed the technology for digital photography, but it did not develop a commercial product from this early innovation until much later, following a long period of licensing it to competitors who successfully created and captured value from the radical innovation. Around 2010, the growth in digital photography at the expense of film photography (Kodak's original core technology-based competitive advantage) had completely eroded Kodak's sales, and the firm filed for bankruptcy protection in early 2012.[44] As part of the bankruptcy settlement, Kodak sold 1,100 digital-imaging patents, technological innovations that the firm held but had never developed into commercially viable product innovations. Additionally, they also sold cash-generating branded film, digital camera, and picture-printing kiosk businesses to other firms, foregoing longer-term revenue streams for short-term cash infusions. We expect that, over time, this case (and other similar stories) will result in a significant amount of research into the likely cause and effect of such events. However, we speculate, based on the arguments put forth in this chapter, that Kodak may have lost its ability to develop products, despite the development of innovations, as attested by the digital photography patents that it sold.

Contrast the large firm example of Kodak above with the recent small business example of Instagram, a formerly small firm acquired by Facebook in 2012.[45] Instagram embraced digital Web-based photo technology by deemphasizing the printing of photographs. The innovative service allows photograph sharing via its Web site, with the world or a selected set of users. Through reimagining the use of photographs and recognizing that many uses are available via mobile devices rather than through print, Instagram attracted more than 150 million users.[46]

In conclusion, we can only wonder whether the lack of availability of internal technology adoption projects because of the outsourcing decision and the possible concomitant decrease in technological capability were contributing factors in Kodak's decline. A more technologically well-informed Kodak might have envisioned an Instagram-like service to be combined with its (formerly) powerful photography brand. However, the small business utilized the strengths of smallness along with a technology capability to innovate in ways that allowed it to thrive in a niche between Kodak and Facebook.

Such innovation, based in technological capability, absorptive capacity, and environmental awareness, allowed Instagram to create customers by producing a valuable service, to appropriate a significant share of that value, and to become a significant part of a larger firm.

NOTES

1. Fariborz Damanpour, "Organizational Innovation: A Meta-analysis of Effects of Determinants and Moderators," *The Academy of Management Journal* 34, 3 (1991): 555–590.

2. Jan van Dijk and Kenneth Hacker, "The Digital Divide as a Complex and Dynamic Phenomenon," *The Information Society* 19, 4 (2003): 315–326.

3. Philip Delves Broughton, "Big Data Hasn't Changed Everything," *Wall Street Journal*, July 2, 2013: A.11.

4. Joseph Schumpeter, *Capitalism, Socialism and Democracy* (New York: Harper and Row, 1942).

5. Philippe Aghion and Peter Howitt, "A Model of Growth through Creative Destruction," *Econometrica* 60, 2 (1992): 323–351; Schumpeter, *Capitalism, Socialism and Democracy*.

6. Fariborz Damanpour, "An Integration of Research Findings of Effects of Firm Size and Market Competition on Product and Process Innovations," *British Journal of Management* 21, 4 (2010): 996–1010; Andrea Vaona and Mario Pianta, "Firm Size and Innovation in European Manufacturing," *Small Business Economics* 30, 3 (2008): 283–299; Jose Pla-Barber and Joaquin Alegre, "Analysing the Link between Export Intensity, Innovation and Firm Size in a Science-based Industry," *International Business Review* 16, 3 (2007), 275–293.

7. Damanpour, "An Integration of Research Findings"; Vaona and Pianta, "Firm Size and Innovation"; Pla-Barber and Alegre, "Analysing the Link."

8. Damanpour, "An Integration of Research Findings."

9. Athanasios Hadjimanolis, "A Resource-based View of Innovativeness in Small Firms," *Technology Analysis & Strategic Management* 12, 2 (2000): 263–281.

10. Damanpour, "An Integration of Research Findings."

11. Nina Rosenbusch, Jan Brinckmann, and Andreas Bausch, "Is Innovation Always Beneficial? A Meta-analysis of the Relationship between Innovation and Performance in SMEs," *Journal of Business Venturing* 26, 4 (2011): 441–457.

12. Rosenbusch, Brinckmann, and Bausch, "Is Innovation Always Beneficial?"

13. "Clinical Data Obtains Exclusive Distribution Rights for Melet Schloesing Laboratoires' Line of Hematology Analyzer and Reagents," last modified February 1, 2005, accessed March 15, 2013, http://www.businesswire.com/news/home/20050201005799/en/Clinical-Data-Obtains-Exclusive-Distribution-Rights-Melet#.VKMctSvF8lI.

14. Juhi Desai, "Asius Makes the Quiet Audible: Startup's Devices Help the Hearing-impaired, Others Listen to Low-volume Sound," *Wall Street Journal Online*, last modified October 16, 2013, accessed October 17, 2013, http://online.wsj.com/news/articles/SB10001424052702304384104579139853429820312.

15. W. Brian Arthur, *The Nature of Technology: What It Is and How It Evolves* (New York: Simon and Schuster, 2009).

16. Ted Baker and Reed E. Nelson, "Creating Something from Nothing: Resource Construction through Entrepreneurial Bricolage," *Administrative Science Quarterly* 50, 3 (2005): 329–366; Claude Levi-Strauss, *The Savage Mind* (Chicago: University of Chicago Press, 1967).

17. Shacker A. Zahra and Gerard George, "Absorptive Capacity: A Review, Reconceptualization, and Extension," *Academy of Management Review* 27, 2 (2002): 185–203.

18. Wesley M. Cohen and Daniel A. Levinthal, "Absorptive Capacity: A New Perspective on Learning and Innovation," *Administrative Science Quarterly* 35, 1 (1990): 128–152.

19. Peter J. Lane, Balaji R. Koka, and Seemantini Pathak, "The Reification of Absorptive Capacity: A Critical Review and Rejuvenation of the Construct," *Academy of Management Review* 31, 4 (2006): 833–863.

20. Cohen and Levinthal, "Absorptive Capacity."

21. Paul L. Drnevich and David C. Croson, "Information Technology and Business-level Strategy: Toward an Integrated Theoretical Perspective," *Management Information Systems Quarterly* 37, 2 (2013): 483–509; Rajiv Kohli and Sarv Devaraj, "Measuring Information Technology Payoff: A Meta-analysis of Structural Variables in Firm-level Empirical Research," *Information Systems Research* 14, 2 (2003): 127–145.

22. Chris Kanaracus, "10 Biggest ERP Software Failures of 2011," *PCWorld*, last modified December 20, 2011, accessed October 15, 2012, www.pcworld.com/article/246647/10_biggest_erp_software_failures_of_2011.html; Nicholas G Carr, "IT Doesn't Matter," *Harvard Business Review* 81, 5 (May 2003): 41–49.

23. Rajiv Kohli and Varun Grover, "Business Value of IT: An Essay on Expanding Research Directions to Keep Up with the Times," *Journal of the Association for Information Systems* 9, 1 (2008): 23–39; Anitesh Barua, Prabhudev Konana, Andrew B. Whinston, and Fang Yin, "An Empirical Investigation of Net-enabled Business Value," *MIS Quarterly* 28, 4 (2004): 585–620.

24. Clay Dibrell, Peter S. Davis, and Justin Craig, "Fueling Innovation through Information Technology in SMEs," *Journal of Small Business Management* 46, 2 (2008): 203–218.

25. Jay Barney, "Firm Resources and Sustained Competitive Advantage," *Journal of Management* 17, 1 (1991): 99–120.

26. Barney, "Firm Resources and Sustained Competitive Advantage."

27. Kevin Zheng Zhou and Fang Wu, "Technological Capability, Strategic Flexibility, and Product Innovation," *Strategic Management Journal* 31, 5 (2010): 547–561. Quotation on p. 548.

28. Allan Afuah, "Mapping Technological Capabilities into Product Markets and Competitive Advantage: The Case of Cholesterol Drugs," *Strategic Management Journal* 23, 2 (2002): 171–179. Quotation on p. 172.

29. Richard L. Priem, Sali Li, and Jon C. Carr, "Insights and New Directions from Demand-side Approaches to Technology Innovation, Entrepreneurship, and Strategic Management Research," *Journal of Management* 38, 1, (2012): 346–374. Quotation on p. 349.

30. Ingemar Dierickx and Karel Cool, "Asset Stock Accumulation and Sustainability of Competitive Advantage," *Management Science* 35, 12 (1989): 1504–1511.

31. Baker and Nelson, "Creating Something from Nothing."

32. Zahra and George, "Absorptive Capacity."

33. Paul L. Drnevich and Aldas P. Kriauciunas, "Clarifying the Conditions and Limits of the Contributions of Ordinary and Dynamic Capabilities to Relative Firm Performance," *Strategic Management Journal* 32, 3 (2011): 254–279.

34. Devi R. Gnyawali and Byung-Jin Robert Park, "Co-opetition and Technological Innovation in Small and Medium-sized Enterprises: A Multilevel Conceptual Model," *Journal of Small Business Management* 47, 3 (2009): 308–330.

35. Gregory G. Dess and Donald W Beard, "Dimensions of Organizational Task Environments," *Administrative Science Quarterly* 29, 1 (1984): 52–73.

36. Dess and Beard, "Dimensions of Organizational Task Environments."

37. Spencer Ante, "New Funding Values Fab at Over $1 Billion," *Wall Street Journal*, June 19, 2013: B. 4.

38. Ante, "New Funding Values Fab at Over $1 Billion."

39. Peter Drucker, *The Practice of Management* (New York: Harper Brothers, 1954).

40. Richard L. Priem, "A Consumer Perspective on Value Creation," *Academy of Management Review* 32, 1 (2007): 219–235.

41. David P. Lepak, Ken G. Smith, and M. Susan Taylor, "Value Creation and Value Capture: A Multilevel Perspective," *Academy of Management Review* 32, 1 (2007): 180–194.

42. Adam M. Brandenburger and Harborne W. Stuart, "Value-based Business Strategy," *Journal of Economics & Management Strategy* 5, 1 (1996): 5–24.

43. Lawrence Loh and N. Venkatraman, "Diffusion of Information Technology Outsourcing: Influence Sources and the Kodak Effect," *Information Systems Research* 3, 4 (1992): 334–358.

44. Julie Creswell, "Kodak's Fuzzy Future," *New York Times*, May 4, 2013, B1.

45. Shayndi Raice and Spencer E. Ante, "Facebook's New Instagram Playbook," *Wall Street Journal*, April 11, 2012: B.4.

46. Reed Albergotti, "Facebook Brings 'Natural' Ads to Instagram," *Wall Street Journal*, last modified October 3, 2013, accessed October 17, 2013, http://blogs.wsj.com/digits/2013/10/03/facebook-brings-natural-ads-to-instagram.

3

The Effect of Top Management Team Networks on Innovation: A Comparison of Large and Small Organizations

Kevin D. Clark and Scott L. Newbert

The importance of networks in the acquisition of resources emerged in the mainstream management field more than 30 years ago. Beginning with Granovetter's seminal paper on tie strength,[1] much of the early theoretical work on networks focused on their structure, defined as the set of and linkages among individuals or organizations, typically conceptualized as the size, centrality, tie strength, locus, connectedness, and absence of structural holes within the network. Since then, research in the area has expanded to include the network's content or the ability to access needed resources and information from the network.[2] In essence, network theory suggests that the more attractive the network's structure and the greater the access to it, the more likely the focal actor, group, or organization is to outperform those with less well-developed and less well-accessed networks.

Over the past three decades, a considerable body of empirical research has been conducted in the management field to test these hypothesized relationships. While not unanimous, particularly with regard to tie strength, the majority of this research stands in support of network theory.[3] Because of the strength of such results, the dimensions of network structure and content that are most important to individual-, group-, and organization-level performance are generally understood and accepted among management scholars.

Perhaps in response to the success that network theory has received in the management field, Hoang and Antoncic report that a similar interest in networks has arisen in the entrepreneurship field over the past two decades.[4] Indeed, the emergence of network theory as a powerful tool in understanding organizational performance is particularly attractive to entrepreneurship scholars as it helps reconcile a conundrum faced by managers of small firms. Because small organizations are generally resource-poor, they must attract and direct resources that are not within their immediate control to grow.[5] However, primarily because of their limited resource endowments and lack of history, small organizations generally lack the collateral or other insurance against default in any exchanges in which they are provided resources.[6] This liability of smallness ultimately manifests in a lack of legitimacy, or credibility, for the organization, which undermines its attractiveness in the eyes of external parties. Unfortunately for small organizations, "[a] resource holder's decision to support an entrepreneurial enterprise depends on his or her appraisal of the attractiveness of the opportunity identified by an entrepreneur."[7]

Given the challenges associated with a lack of legitimacy, many scholars argue that social networks may provide the means by which small organizations can attain, or build, the legitimacy necessary to encourage resource gatekeepers to engage in transactions with them.[8] Specifically, by associating with a large, diverse group of individuals and organizations, small organizations inevitably increase their opportunities both to build relationships with important resource gatekeepers and, more importantly, to be perceived by them as trustworthy enough to afford them access to these resources.

Despite the fact that networks seem to be of tremendous importance to small organizations, Hoang and Antoncic find that empirical results concerning the importance of network structure and content to their performance is largely mixed.[9] Indeed, these authors report that among several structural dimensions of a new and small organization's social network, only the hypothesized positive relationship between the absence of structural holes and performance has received consistent support, though because of the diversity of measures used to test this hypothesis, even this relationship is far from conclusive.[10] In the years since Hoang and Antoncic's review, little has changed.[11] Not only have only a handful of the many network-based studies that have been conducted explored their importance to small organizations, but the results of these studies provide less than compelling support for network theory.

In terms of network structure, Lechner, Dowling, and Welpe conclude that it is not the size of the network that matters to the development of an organization, as network theorists might suggest, but rather the type (reputational, social, cooperative, or competitive) of network that is leveraged.[12] Similarly, Leung et al. find that organizational growth is enhanced by leveraging different subsets of the network.[13] In terms of network content, Lei et al. find that organizational growth is a function of the degree to which their network partners actually support the organization, which they argue to be a function of the trust that exists between them.[14] Finally, Zhang et al. find that based on the characteristics of the lead entrepreneur, network ties may be less likely to generate financial investment than traditional market-based methods, thereby questioning the relevance of using networks at all.[15]

It seems then that in contrast to the overwhelming support for network effects in large, established organizations, evidence of the value of networks to small organizations is less than compelling. We speculate that this lack of consistent support is a function of the contextual differences among large and small organizations. Thus, while we accept that the liability of small-ness makes small organizations reliant on social networks, we contend that (1) small organizations may be less able than large organizations to establish relationships with individuals and organizations that control valuable resources, and (2) even in cases where they are able to do so, they may still lack the ability to leverage them as effectively as large organizations. Indeed, we believe that the small organization's lack of legitimacy results in a network that is either unable or unwilling to contribute resources to the organization. In other words, because small organizations lack the credibility of their larger, more established counterparts, their top management teams (TMTs) are unlikely to have connections to gatekeepers of critical resources, and, even if they do, these gatekeepers are unlikely to provide these non-credible organizations access to these resources.

Interestingly, no research has been conducted to date examining the moderating effect of organizational size on the network-performance relationship. In response to this gap, we test the contingent effect of organization size on the relationship between a variety of dimensions of TMT network structure and content on innovation performance. We examine innovativeness as a performance measure because innovation is a resource-dependent process that requires organizations of all sizes to gain access to a multitude of resources (both tangible and intangible) that lie beyond their immediate control.[16] Network theorists have long studied the link between networks and innovation, thus we focus our analysis on an important measure of innovation performance, namely, the level of innovation output.[17]

From our empirical analysis, we find that while network structure and content are important to innovation output, they are more important for large than for small organizations. Based on these results, we conclude that although small organizations should benefit more than large organizations from their networks, they do not. Following Hoang and Antoncic's plea for inductive research to better understand findings on entrepreneurial networks and introduce new theoretical ideas on the matter, we then examine the data at a more qualitative level in an attempt to reconcile this conclusion. Based on our theorizing, we propose that one possible solution to this apparent paradox might be the implementation of specific networking strategies that facilitate the development of more effective networks.

NETWORKS AND INNOVATIVENESS

According to Galbraith, top-level decision-makers need to be able to find and collect information, process it, and make decisions (act) to counter environmental threats.[18] Because much salient information exists beyond the boundaries of the organization, members of the top management team (TMT) must often span the boundaries of the organization to gain access to it.[19] This ability to obtain information is particularly important for highly innovative organizations, as the innovation task requires a significant amount of information collection, evaluation, and processing.[20]

Powell, Koput, and Smith-Doerr contend that one means by which such information and knowledge can be obtained is the TMT's network.[21] Networks have been defined as "as set of nodes (persons, organizations) linked by a set of social relationships (friendship, transfer of funds, overlapping membership) of a specified type."[22] Networks can provide innovation benefits to organizations in a variety of ways. Ahuja describes how networks can be used to learn about important innovation successes and failures in the industry and environment as well as how networks potentially serve as "an information-processing mechanism, absorbing, sifting, and classifying new technological development in a manner that goes well beyond the information processing capabilities of a single organization."[23] In addition, key developments in the industry and related fields can be brought to the attention of decision-makers through their network connections.[24] Finally, networks can be used to solve innovation problems in different ways, for example, by gathering specific information or by influencing other critical stakeholders associated with an innovation.

Given the benefits that a network can offer innovative organizations, it is widely believed that studying TMTs with different network characteristics should help us to understand and predict who will be able to make better decisions regarding innovation.[25] In other words, different network characteristics of the TMT will have implications for the amount, type, and quality of information that is available to facilitate innovation output. However, we believe that any advantages that networks might offer to organizations will be a function of the organization's size, primarily because of the liabilities that small organizations face.

NETWORK STRUCTURE

Tie Strength

The strength of the ties in the TMT's network is a key dimension of network theory, as strong ties provide for trust and reciprocity.[26] Although networks potentially link organizations to all types of resources, we mainly focus here on information resources critical to innovation efforts that may be the most critical to the knowledge creation process.[27] Moreover, while weak ties may provide certain efficiency benefits, especially where the meaning of information is not problematic,[28] strong ties involving frequent communication and relationships of long duration will be critical when the information is uncertain and ambiguous.[29] There is significant evidence that when ties or relationships are long lasting or strong, individuals will be more willing to exchange information and cooperate for mutual benefit.[30] We expect TMT members that have relationships of long duration and frequent communication to be able to garner richer knowledge and information and to be more confident in that information than will TMTs with relationships that are more short term with less frequent communication. Moreover, the richer and more accurate information gleaned from strong ties will be important to speedy development of successful innovations.

> Hypothesis 1a: TMT network tie strength will be positively associated with an organization's innovation output.

Redundancy

Redundancy represents the extent to which more than one member of the TMT has a link to the same stakeholder. Highly redundant networks are those in which nearly every team member is connected to the same stakeholders. In contrast, a non-redundant network entails no overlap in connections: each team member is connected to different sets of alters. In network theory, highly redundant networks are considered inefficient. According to the weak ties argument, the TMT should maximize the number of ties, and this is facilitated by the utilization of weak ties, which are less costly to develop and maintain.[31] Therefore, from a weak ties perspective, redundancy in TMT networks is suboptimal because it will make innovation search and discovery repetitive and inefficient. However, another view is that extensive redundancy among actors can facilitate shared norms, increased trust, and greater collaboration.[32] Indeed, when resource gatekeepers have multiple connections to an organization, they may be more willing to provide access to critical inputs. The shared norms associated with such networks can lead to clearer expectations and mutual support, which will assist knowledge sharing.[33] Redundant ties can also lessen opportunism in a network as information on one actor's abnormal behavior will spread quickly through the system and sanctions for such behavior can quickly be imposed.[34] Finally, redundant networks allow team members to quickly validate new information brought to the innovation process, ultimately lowering search costs.

Hypothesis 2a: TMT network redundancy will be positively associated with an organization's innovation output.

Locus of Orientation and Connectedness to Core

Locus of orientation refers to the proportion of TMT direct ties that are connected externally versus internally. A TMT may concentrate its ties within the organization and/or may attempt to build extensive ties with external actors. Though not included in many network studies, the locus of orientation is relevant to the study of TMTs because it reflects the extent to which the team is focused on the external environment (e.g., boundary-spanning and buffering activities) versus internal actors (e.g., coordination and control).[35]

March uses the concepts of exploration and exploitation to describe two ways in which organizations search, discover, and learn.[36] Exploration refers to search and discovery related to adaptation and innovation. In contrast, exploitation refers to refinement, production, efficiency, selection, implementation, and execution. Following Ancona and Caldwell's related discussion of internal and external activity in small groups, we would expect to see differences in the innovation performance of internally versus externally oriented TMTs.[37] Internally oriented TMT networks should be related to increased efficiency and would not have the external contacts to search for and discover new information. In contrast, externally oriented TMT networks would reflect an open systems orientation toward innovation and adaptation. Boeker's work on the relationship between the hiring of outsiders into the TMT and subsequent product market innovations also supports our expectation that external networks will be critical for innovation.[38] Although Boeker investigated the "direct transmission of relevant information between organizations" through hiring, we anticipate that top manager contacts to external parties should also result in identification and absorption of new information and ideas that may result in innovation.[39] Bouty further highlights the potential importance for innovation of external contacts of R&D employees because the information that they access is "neither in the scientist's employing organization nor in any intermediate formal arrangement (such as an alliance or R&D consortium)."[40]

Although external boundary-spanning links are critical to innovation, the ability of the management team to understand the information needs of the organizational core is a prerequisite for effective information search. Simply put, for the TMT to be an effective information-gathering mechanism, team members must understand what information gaps exist in the ongoing innovation efforts located within the organization. Thus, we expect that some level of connection to internal constituencies will provide an adequate understanding of what is required and will facilitate the information search that is so critical to innovation output.

> Hypothesis 3a: TMT network external locus of orientation will be positively associated with an organization's innovation output.
>
> Hypothesis 4a: TMT network connectedness to the core will be positively associated with an organization's innovation output.

NETWORK CONTENT

Utilization

The mere existence of networks does not say anything about the extent to which they are actually used. Indeed, network research implicitly assumes a rational actor model whereby all actors have an equal probability to use their connections to further some purpose.[41] For example, structuralist approaches routinely assume that those positioned as bridges will leverage their brokerage positions to gain information or power.[42] Adler and Kwon suggest that network scholars need to explicitly study the extent to which networks are actually used.[43] In fact, they contend that the value of networks will depreciate with lack of use, noting that networks need to be "renewed and reconfirmed" or they will drop in value. Most recently, scholars such as Reagans and McEvily and Tsai have examined the extent to which structural networks actually lead to the transfer of information and knowledge.[44] We contribute to this emerging area of interest by directly examining the extent to which networks are utilized for information gathering and for influencing others.

Gathering information is defined as the extent to which the network is used for purposes of assembling new information and knowledge. The ability to gather information and knowledge can be a key source of competitive advantage.[45] Moreover, in the knowledge-based view of the firm, organizations are treated as knowledge systems, specializing in creating and transferring information and knowledge.[46] Reagans and McEvily contend that scholars have only inferred that networks are used for information and knowledge-transfer purposes.[47] Hargadon and Sutton describe how engineers learned about potential new technologies through organizational contacts with clients.[48] They describe how the organization's network position made contacts possible, but that it was up to designers to individually exploit this position to gather necessary information and knowledge and then to utilize this information and knowledge for creative purposes.

Influencing others is defined as the extent to which a TMT member uses his or her network for purposes of power and control. Information and knowledge transfer is a discretionary activity.[49] Members of networks are presented with many opportunities to share and exchange knowledge, even though not all prospects are seized. One way in which members of a network may decide to reveal information and knowledge is through power and coercion. Although Hansen focuses on the importance of strong ties in providing the ability to transfer complex knowledge, he acknowledges that even where there is transferability, one party may not be willing to do so.[50] Bouty also recognizes that whether knowledge is transferred between R&D scientists employed by different organizations rests in part on the willingness of the holder of the knowledge to enact the transfer.[51] Although strong ties may be one motivating mechanism, we expect that for the transfer of certain types of sensitive or proprietary knowledge to occur, it may be necessary for the requester to be able and willing to influence the holder.

We combine the use of networks for information gathering and influencing others into one measure of network utilization. As has been stated above, information and influence can be critical to the innovation process. Thus, we propose that the greater the utilization of TMT networks in pursuit of information and influence, the greater the innovation output.

Hypothesis 5a: TMT network utilization will be positively associated with an organization's innovation output.

THE CONTINGENT EFFECT OF ORGANIZATION SIZE

According to Suchman, organizations that are perceived to be attractive, credible, or legitimate are considered to be more meaningful, more predictable, and more trustworthy.[52] Such perceptions (whether warranted or not) are important, given that one factor that motivates organizational stakeholders to provide the organization access to their resources is their belief that the organization is legitimate.[53] Thus, it follows that the more legitimate the organization, the more likely it will be to gain access to the resources held by its network members.[54]

Unfortunately, such logic is a challenge for small organizations. As noted above, small organizations face what is known as the "liability of smallness." According to this view, potential resource-exchange partners assume prior success to be an indicator of future success. More specifically, Hannan and Freeman suggest that the inertial forces within a large organization convey a sense of reliability, or legitimacy, to external parties.[55] Because an organization's size is often perceived to be indicative of its potential for future performance and growth, small organizations are often assumed to lack legitimacy and thus are believed to be more vulnerable to failure than large organizations.

It seems then that small organizations are faced with a paradox: they often require resources to innovate, but resource gatekeepers are reluctant to engage in exchanges with them because of their lack of legitimacy. This conundrum tends to manifest in an inability to obtain needed resources, either at all or at a competitive cost. For example, Aldrich and Auster attribute the difficulty that small organizations have in raising capital, recruiting quality employees, and keeping administrative costs down to this liability of smallness.[56] This scenario is particularly concerning as these factors have been found to negatively affect the innovation process.[57]

Given these liabilities faced by small organizations, one might assume that their dependence on networks for innovation success should be significantly stronger than for large organizations. However, we believe that the network-performance relationship will be stronger for large organizations because they are not subject to the liabilities faced by their smaller counterparts.

As noted above, organizational size is perceived to be indicative of an organization's potential for future performance and growth.[58] As such, resource gatekeepers often use size as a decision criterion when determining whether to invest in a given organization. This is a key point because strong ties are likely to provide access to resources solely on the basis of the trust upon which the relationship is built. Because weak ties lack that trust by definition, they are likely to provide access to their resources only to those organizations with a proven track record or an asset base that is sizable enough to serve as collateral. In support of this logic, Jack finds that all of the ties used among a sample of small organizations were strong.[59]

Unfortunately for small organizations, maintaining a network of strong ties, where relationships are long-standing and exercised frequently, is very expensive. Executives in large organizations may experience a form of prestige centrality whereby potential contacts seek them out and endeavor to preserve relationships once they are established. The attractiveness associated with being an executive in a large, powerful organization lowers the cost of developing and maintaining strong ties. Moreover, managers from large organizations will be more able to extract from strong ties and exploit the information necessary for innovation because the size of their organizations reflects greater commitment and reliability to the network relationship.

> Hypothesis 1b: The positive relationship between network tie strength and innovativeness will be stronger for large organizations than for small organizations.

One alternative mechanism by which small organizations might offset a potentially insufficient number of strong ties could be to simply increase the number of TMT members with ties (either strong or weak) to each network member. In so doing, small organizations could establish stronger connections to and increase trust with important resource gatekeepers. However, as with developing strong ties, developing redundant ties is very expensive. Because small organizations possess less slack than their larger counterparts, they will be comparatively less successful in developing and maintaining multiple ties to resource gatekeepers (e.g., administrative staff and budgets for networking). In sum, while strong and redundant ties could enable small organizations to overcome some of the liabilities associated with their size, they are likely to be less able than large organizations to establish them in a way that would prove cost-effective because they are in relatively short supply of slack resources.

Hypothesis 2b: The positive relationship between network redundancy and innovativeness will be stronger for large organizations than for small organizations.

Because large organizations are perceived as more legitimate than their smaller counterparts, resource gatekeepers may actively seek out large organizations and volunteer access to their resources, as such an alliance may in turn legitimize these network members (e.g., prestige centrality).[60] Consider, for example, that small organizations, by definition, are likely to possess a smaller stock of resources (such as knowledge) than their larger counterparts. Thus, large organizations may well be able to innovate successfully by relying on the diversity of knowledge that exists within the boundaries of the organization. Perhaps because of the lack of knowledge diversity inside small organizations, innovation in small organizations has been found to require the absorption of new information and ideas.[61] However, although large organizations are likely to hold greater amounts of knowledge internally than smaller organizations do, it is also true that the executives of larger, more prestigious organizations may be better able to develop relationships with actors who hold important information that the organization could use. Thus, while external networks may be critically important for smaller organizations (who have limited internal knowledge resources), the quality of the external contacts held by executives of larger, better-known organizations may provide an information advantage. The larger and more differentiated an organization grows, the greater the risk that management will become detached or uncoupled from the core.[62] One key integrating mechanism that provides information on organizational activities is the internal network. Though we expect some level of connectedness between the TMT and the core to be important for effective boundary spanning, we believe that it will be particularly true for larger organizations.

> Hypothesis 3b: The positive relationship between network external locus of orientation and innovation output will be stronger for large organizations than for small organizations.
> Hypothesis 4b: The positive relationship between network connectedness to the core and innovation output will be stronger for large organizations than for small organizations.

Furthermore, once TMT members of large organizations have developed these external and internal connections, they are unlikely to need to resort to coercion to gain access to needed resources precisely because they are perceived as legitimate and unlikely to default in such exchanges. Small organizations, on the other hand, lack this perceived legitimacy and thus often need to persuade outsiders to provide access to needed resources when they might otherwise not do so. In fact, Tornikoski and Newbert find that several types of proactive behavior often build legitimacy and facilitate exchanges between resource gatekeepers and organizations.[63]

Yet, because larger organizations benefit even more from the networks of their executives, it is even more critical for these executives to actually use their networks for information and for influencing. Indeed, because relationships are often asymmetrical with respect to power, we expect the executives of large organizations, which possess both market power and legitimacy, to be better able to leverage their connections to exert influence and enact information transfers.

> Hypothesis 5b: The positive relationship between network utilization and innovation output will be stronger for large organizations than for small organizations.

METHOD

Sample

Field data were collected using on-site, structured interviews with each organization's CEO and in-depth questionnaires completed by the CEO and members of the organization's TMT. It is important to note that this approach results in a network that extends the analysis beyond the personal network of the owner (i.e., CEO), characteristic of much of the recent work on networks of new and small organizations, to the network of the entire TMT. The sample was selected according to two criteria.[64] First, given the intensive nature of the data-collection process, all organizations had to be headquartered within driving distance of the researchers. Second, to ensure that the organizations faced similar competitive environments (to have a focused sample), the companies had to conform to the definition of high-technology organizations. Milkovich defined high-technology industries as being populated by "organizations that emphasize invention and innovation in their business strategy, deploy a significant percentage of their financial resources to R&D, employ a relatively high percentage of scientists and engineers in their workforce, and compete in worldwide, short-life-cycle product markets."[65]

Two hundred thirteen organizations were identified as meeting the study criteria. Initially, an introductory packet consisting of a letter from the research team and three endorsees (the dean of the business school, the director of the university's Center for Entrepreneurship, and the editor of a technology-based trade publication) was mailed to the CEO of each identified organization. The research team then phoned each CEO to provide additional information regarding the study, to answer any specific questions or concerns of the CEO, to ask for the organization's participation, and to schedule a time for an initial site visit and interview.

Of the 213 organizations contacted, 85 companies agreed to be interviewed, yielding an initial participation rate of 39 percent. Each CEO or president was interviewed for approximately one hour. There were three main purposes for the on-site CEO interview. First, the interview enabled us to gain the CEO's support for the study. Second, the interview was used to collect information on the level of innovation within each organization and other background information. Finally, CEOs were asked to identify the members of their top management team. As part of this interview, each CEO was asked to sign a letter encouraging identified team members to complete questionnaires and to identify an internal contact that could help the research team distribute and collect surveys.

Of the 85 organizations that were interviewed, we obtained complete sets of data on 70 organizations (participation rate = 33 percent). The average number of top management team members responding to the study was 3, for an intra-TMT response rate of 59 percent. Approximately 57 percent of the organizations in this sample were publicly traded. The companies that agreed to participate were not significantly different from those not participating in terms of reported sales ($t = 1.364$, $p > 0.05$) or number of employees ($t = 1.695$, $p > 0.05$). The sample was composed of organizations from multiple high-technology industries, including computer software, semiconductor equipment, information technology and integration services, engineering services, and communications, and it included organizations ranging in size from \$320,000 to \$8.4 billion in sales revenues (mean = \$362 million).

Dependent Variable

During the pilot testing of the instrument, it became clear that organizations innovate in a variety of ways. In keeping with the findings of Damanpour, innovation is operationalized as the number of new innovations (e.g., products, services, markets, processes) developed by an organization during the last year.[66] Our definition is similar to what Bantel and Jackson referred to as technical innovation.[67] As the composition of this innovation measure deviates slightly from Damanpour (only new products and services), construct validity was assessed by comparing this measure to Damanpour's and to organization R&D spending. Both the simpler new product and services count measure ($r = 0.885, p < 0.01$) and R&D spending ($r = 0.644, p < 0.01$) were strongly correlated with the measure used in this research. Innovation was collected from CEO interviews and R&D spending from annual reports.

Independent Variables

TMT relational networks were assessed through questionnaires distributed to each team member. The questionnaire was extensively pretested with (a) several MBA students who had extensive experience working in technology-intensive organizations, and (b) four CEOs from organizations that were not part of the study. Consistent with Adler and Kwon's conceptualization of networks as properties of both individuals and organizations, the relational network measures were collected at the individual level and then aggregated to the group level of analysis.[68]

Most network studies focus either on the set of relations that an actor has within the organization or on the network relationships between organizations. With few exceptions, researchers have not collected primary network data on a large sample of top-level managers.[69] Moreover, when researchers have included both internal and external networks, the external network is artificially constrained through the use of a roster methodology.[70] The advantage of such approaches is that the researcher is able to collect data for the entire set of relationships. The serious shortcoming is that the network boundary is difficult to properly define, and yet doing so is critical to the generalizability of results.[71] An alternative to roster methods is the egocentric approach whereby a respondent is asked to list out contacts based on specific criteria (e.g., "those you rely on for advice concerning technology issues").

In this research, we developed a roster of thirteen categories of potential contacts based on extensive pretesting. However, as in egocentric research, respondents were able to self-determine which contacts were most important and responded by rating their relationship with these contacts. The advantage of our primary data collection approach is that we were able to collect data on the networks of a large set of top-level managers in an efficient manner while minimizing the risk of arbitrarily constraining the network.

Most research on TMT networks focuses on board interlocks or links to financial institutions; however, several researchers have advocated the inclusion of a broader set of potential contact types.[72] In this study, TMT members were asked about the relationships that they had with actors from nine general external categories (e.g., financial institutions, suppliers, customers, competitors, alliance partners, government agencies, trade associations, boards of directors, and other) and four general internal categories (e.g., operations, marketing/sales, research and development, and other) of actors. From the responses, we calculated each respondent's mean frequency of contacts, duration of relationships, locus of orientation, connectedness to core, and to what extent they used their ties for information and influence. Respondents' network scores were then aggregated to the group level, and the redundancy across individual networks within the TMT was also calculated. The specific network items are described next.

Tie Strength

Bouty found that long-standing ties were important for information networks among R&D scientists.[73] Tie duration is the average amount of time in months that the TMT has known actors in its network. Granovetter suggests that frequent interaction may also indicate a stronger tie.[74] Hansen underscores the importance that strong ties may have for facilitating the transfer of complex knowledge.[75] Interaction frequency is measured as the average number of times per month that contact is made between TMT members and other actors.

Redundancy

A fully redundant network is one in which the networks of each TMT member are identical, that is, where the contacts that one executive has with different types of contacts mirror those of the other executives on the TMT. In a nonredundant network, some executives would have unique ties or could serve as structural bridges.[76] Our measure captures the extent to which TMT members are linked to the same stakeholder categories. Specifically, the measure of redundancy used in this research is the proportion of categories to which at least two members of the TMT are linked to the total possible number of categories (13).

Network Locus

Network locus has not been a key area of research in network theory; however, a review of information theory suggests that this may be an important factor in TMT functioning.[77] Network locus refers to whether the network tends to be composed of connections to actors inside the company or of connections to actors outside of the company. First, the number of external contacts listed by TMT members was summed. Second, the total number of contacts (external plus internal) listed by TMT members was summed. The measure was the ratio of the number of external ties to the total number of ties. Thus, a locus score of greater than 0.50 indicates an externally-oriented TMT network.

Connectedness to Core

Though the literature on boundary spanning suggests that external relations may be important for innovation, TMTs may also need to maintain adequate linkages to the organization's core as well. We measure connectedness as the number of TMT ties to internal actors divided by the total number of employees (possible internal ties). This measure is essentially the density of the internal network, except calculated for an ego-centered network.

Utilization

We measured network utilization in terms of the extent to which each respondent's network was used for gathering information or influencing others. TMT members were asked to respond to the following two items: "I use these contacts to gain access to information" and "I use these contacts for influencing," using a five-point Likert scale where $1 =$ not at all and $5 =$ a great deal. Individual responses were aggregated and averaged across the two measures to create a group network utilization measure ($I = 0.905$).

Control Variables

Organization Size

Because larger organizations may have more resources (financial capital, organizational slack, etc.) to devote to innovation efforts, organizational size was controlled in the analysis.[78] Organizational size was measured as the logarithm of the number of employees, which was collected from the CompuStat database, annual reports, and, for private organizations, during CEO interviews.

Environmental Dynamism

Organizations facing high rates of environmental change need to adapt to be successful. Innovation is a key adaptive mechanism that organizations display in response to environmental uncertainty. Thus, we control for the rate of change in each organization's environment. During the CEO interview, CEOs responded to the following item: "How quickly do things change in your industry?" on a scale from 1 (slowly, if at all) to 5 (very rapidly).

TMT Experience

Hargadon and Sutton point to prior experience as a key source of new ideas that could lead to innovation.[79] Becker found that years of experience in a job or industry represented specific knowledge of an individual.[80] Based on the findings of Wiersema and Bantel, years of experience is an index of mean TMT tenure in the team, tenure with the employer, and tenure in the industry.[81] First, the individual years of experience were standardized. A linear additive index measure was then constructed for each individual in the TMT. Finally, the aggregation to the group level of analysis was accomplished by computing the group mean.

TMT Education

Following Becker, years of education is used as the measure of the general knowledge residing in the TMT.[82] Education has also been used as a proxy for cognitive complexity.[83] Respondents were asked how many years of post–high school education they had completed. The aggregation to the group level of analysis was accomplished by computing the mean years of education for TMT members.

Network Size

As a measure of network structure, the number of direct ties refers to the number of straight contacts between TMT members and a set of alters.[84] Numerous weak ties, while subject to unreliability and uncertainty, can provide members with tremendous access to valuable resources to which they might not otherwise have access. Podolny and Baron find that network size significantly predicts grade advancement,[85] while Uzzi finds empirical support suggesting that network size is a significant predictor of increasing access to and decreasing costs of capital.[86] Because prior research has connected the number of ties to innovation, we used the number of direct ties as a control in this research.[87] The number of direct ties is the mean number of direct contacts represented by the combined networks of the TMT members.[88]

ANALYSIS AND RESULTS

Table 3.1 is the correlation matrix of all variables used in the analysis. Hierarchical regression analysis (table 3.2) with forced forward selection of blocks of variables was used to ascertain the relative contribution of the network block of variables in explaining variance in organizational innovation when controlled for organization size, rate of environmental change, TMT demography, and TMT network size. Consistent with our expectations, TMT networks do affect organizational innovation when controlled for organization size, environmental change, TMT demography, and network size ($R^2 = 0.302, p < 0.001$). Hypotheses 1a, 2a, 3a, 4a, and 5a concern the directional impact of specific characteristics of the network on innovation output. The test for each hypothesis is a significant beta (one-tailed t-test) in the predicted direction in the regression containing all of the measures; it can be found in column one of table 3.2.

Hypothesis 1a stated that strong ties would be related to innovation output. We found that TMT networks of long duration are associated with increased innovation output ($\beta = 0.502, p < 0.001$); however, interaction frequency was not ($\beta = -0.005$, n.s.). Thus, only certain aspects of tie strength appear to be important for innovation. Redundancy (Hypothesis 2a) was not found to be associated with increased innovation ($\beta = 0.085$, n.s.). The research did find that external ties were important for innovation ($\beta = 0.229$, p < 0.05), thus Hypothesis 3a was supported. However, Hypothesis 4a was also supported ($\beta = 0.496$, p < 0.001). Thus, while an external locus is important, it appears that some level of connectedness to the core is also critical for innovation. Finally, the research shows that actual utilization of executive networks is positively related to innovation (H5a, $\beta = 0.262$, p < 0.01).

Hypotheses 1b, 2b, 3b, 4b, and 5b investigate whether larger organizations benefit more from the networks of their TMT than smaller organizations. As reported in table 3.2, we found that for three of the six network variables, the relationship between networks and innovation was moderated by the size of the organization. For all three of these relationships, the direction of the interaction was the same and consistent with our expectations. Specifically, long-standing ties ($\beta = 1.473$, $p < 0.001$), redundant ties ($\beta = 0.265$, p < 0.001), and externally oriented networks ($\beta = 0.315$, p < 0.001) were found to be even more strongly associated with increased innovation for

TABLE 3.1 Descriptive Statistics and Bivariate Correlations

Variable	Mean	Std. Dev.	1	2	3	4	5	6	7	8	9	10	11
1. Innovation	15.40	24.91											
2. Firm size	1198	2773	0.607**										
3. Environmental dynamism	2.85	0.90	0.208*	0.247*									
4. TMT experience	113.79	55.77	0.097	0.095	−0.011								
5. TMT education	5.73	1.56	0.480**	0.420**	0.087	0.190							
6. Network size	112.36	79.20	0.086	0.337**	0.191	0.120	0.051						
7. Duration	44.95	38.63	0.562**	0.266*	−0.002	0.273*	0.343**	0.090					
8. Frequency	8.71	6.83	−0.154	−0.280**	−0.211*	−0.119	−0.287**	−0.115	−0.068				
9. Redundancy	0.75	0.17	0.016	−0.155	0.118	0.127	−0.101	−0.015	−0.284**	0.055			
10. External locus	0.65	0.15	−0.319***	−0.505**	−0.200*	−0.049	−0.351**	−0.030	−0.163	0.316**	−0.041		
11. Connectedness to core	0.17	0.20	−0.305***	−0.627**	−0.135	0.157	−0.331**	0.105	−0.190	0.065	0.318**	0.127	
12. Utilization	2.28	0.69	0.247*	0.293***	0.038	0.042	0.261*	0.156	0.428**	0.365**	−0.455**	−0.186	−0.208*

* $p < 0.05$, ** $p < 0.01$, *** $p < 0.001$

TABLE 3.2 OLS Regression Results: Innovation

	β	t
Control variables: (F = 10.143***, adjusted R^2 = 0.402)		
Organizational size	0.847***	6.246
Environmental dynamism	0.133	1.856
TMT experience	−0.157*	−2.097
TMT education	0.282**	3.441
Network size	−0.301**	−3.508
Main effects: (F = 15.671***, adjusted R^2 = 0.704,		
ΔR^2 = 0.302***)		
Tie strength—duration	0.502***	6.664
Tie strength—frequency	−0.005	−0.071
Redundancy	0.085	1.091
Network locus	0.229*	2.443
Connectedness to core	0.496***	4.101
Utilization	0.262**	3.569
Interaction terms:		
Organizational size *Tie strength—duration	1.473***	3.823
Organizational size *Tie strength—frequency	−0.419	−1.725
Organizational size * redundancy	0.265***	3.928
Organizational size * Network locus	0.315***	4.198
Organizational size * Connectedness to core	−0.067	−0.285
Organizational size * Utilization	−0.291	−0.655

N = 70, * $p < 0.05$, ** $p < 0.01$, *** $p < 0.001$; one-tailed tests for directional hypotheses.

large organizations than for small organizations. Thus, we conclude support for Hypotheses 1b, 2b, and 3b.

DISCUSSION

This research is important because it shows that TMT networks are strongly associated with innovation output in technology organizations. Though prior research has touted the informational and other advantages that networks provide organizations, this research focuses in a fine-grained way on the specific characteristics of the networks of top-level managers, who are in a position to perform critical boundary-spanning tasks that facilitate the innovation capability of the organization. Importantly, we find that both structure and content of the networks are important. Strong externally focused networks of executives who are connected to the organizational core provide the organization with an information advantage that manifests through increased innovation output. Having the right network, however, is not enough; executive teams must be able and willing to use their networks to gather information and to influence the holders of such information.

We included network size as a control in this study; however, our results suggest that smaller networks are related to innovation. In the context of our other results, we believe that the network size finding suggests that tradeoffs that must be made in any network tend to favor the building of strong ties with the right set of contacts (external resource gatekeepers). In discussing the issue of tie strength, Granovetter argues that "the fewer indirect contacts one has the more encapsulated he will be in terms of knowledge of the world beyond his own friendship circle."[89] Aldrich adds that network size is less important among strong ties than among weak ties.[90] Though this result should be considered preliminary, managers should approach the development of relationships in a purposeful way and must pay particular attention not only to whether to establish a relationship but also with whom relationships should be established and what level of investment should be made in any single contact. Our results suggest that external resource gatekeepers are promising targets but that maintaining good-quality links to important internal actors is also required.

The central question posed in this research was whether TMT network benefits accrue equally to large and small organizations. The literature has long recognized the liability of smallness that smaller organizations face but has suggested that the development and use of networks to access resources outside the boundary of the organization is one critical strategy for overcoming such weaknesses.[91] Our results demonstrate a fundamental flaw in the logic of such an argument: networks are also subject to the liability of smallness. Because smaller organizations may have a more difficult time developing and maintaining the right sorts of contacts and at a sufficient level of tie strength, their actualized networks will often be insufficient to overcome the liability of smallness. This result, while robust, is not deterministic. Three of the six tested interactions were significant (all demonstrating the disadvantage of smaller organizations). Still, our findings suggest that the ability of smaller organizations to develop this critical network resource should result in improved innovation performance—a key success factor for technology firms. In light of this conundrum, we believe that strategy and entrepreneurship research should move beyond the current debate on whether networks can help to overcome the liability of smallness (they do) and focus instead on how smaller organizations can employ strategies to develop the right sorts of networks. It is to this task that we now turn.

Post-hoc Analysis

In this study, networks explain about one-third of the variance in the dependent variable, though it is clear that other factors aside from networks contribute to an organization's ability to innovate. It is likely for this reason that the small organizations in our sample were still able to innovate, even with less effective networks or capabilities to leverage them than their larger counterparts. However, given that networks *do* appear to play an important role in an organization's innovative performance, we conducted the following post-hoc outlier analysis to explore various outliers in our sample in an attempt to better understand how small organizations might create or use networks to their advantage.

To begin, we identified the most and least innovative small organizations in the sample. To do so, we determined which of the small organizations, defined as those with fewer than 500 employees,[92] were in the top quartile on the innovativeness dimension (12 or more new innovations developed during the last year) and which were in the bottom quartile on the innovativeness dimension (1 or fewer new innovations developed during the last year). This process led to the identification of four highly innovative small organizations and nine non-innovative small organizations.

Next, we identified the small organizations with the most and least effective networks by rank, ordering each of the highly innovative and non-innovative organizations according to their scores for each of the network variables that were found to be significant and positive in the main effect model of table 3.2 and then comparing those scores to the median score for all organizations in the sample. The organization with the most effective network scored above the median on three of the four network dimensions (namely, tie duration, connectedness to the core, and utilization). Incidentally, this organization produced 15 new innovations during the last year (the most for any of the small organizations in the sample). The organization with the least effective network scored below the median on all four dimensions. Not surprisingly, this organization produced only one new innovation during the last year (the second fewest for all organizations in the sample).

Having identified these two outlier organizations, we then attempted to identify from a descriptive analysis of our data what fundamental differences lead to such a disparate ability to develop the types of networks that contribute to an organization's ability to innovate. Consistent with Collins and Clark, we examined the degree to which these organizations implemented strategies specifically designed to enable TMT members to build networks.[93] From this analysis, we found that the highly innovative small organization placed far more emphasis than the non-innovative small organization on three broad categories of network-building strategies: those intended to create an environment in which potential network members could be cultivated, those intended to provide tangible resources to facilitate the cultivation of potential network members, and those intended to provide intangible resources to facilitate the cultivation of potential network members.

With respect to the creation of an effective network-building environment, the highly innovative organization hosted private events (i.e., golf outings) at which potential network members were expected to be cultivated and attended civic events at which potential network members were expected to be in attendance more frequently than when the non-innovative organization held such events. We believe that such strategies are effective as they provide TMT members with a forum in which to form and later develop rich relationships with internal and external stakeholders. As such, it is not surprising that an organization that creates opportunities for TMT members to cultivate their networks would have an effective network.

With respect to the provision of tangible resources, the highly innovative organization had larger expense accounts, designed to facilitate the cultivation of potential network members, and provided greater incentives for the successful cultivation of these relationships than the non-innovative organization. We believe such resources are important, as extrinsic rewards have long been argued to be effective in motivating desired behavior.[94] Thus, it is likely that providing money and other incentives to support and reward networking behavior would encourage TMT members to seek to develop networks.

With respect to the provision of intangible resources, the highly innovative organization placed far more emphasis on employees mentoring one another on how to successfully develop relationships with potential network members in the form of shared best practices, guidance, formal training, and mentorship programs than the non-innovative organization did. We believe that such a strategy is effective, as it develops a shared understanding of the importance of networking behavior to the organization. Because research shows that employees often take cues from an organization's culture when determining their behavior, it is likely that strategies that seek to infuse a culture that supports networking activity will lead to the development of effective networks.[95]

The trends that emerge from this outlier analysis, while by no means conclusive, at the very least suggest that managers of small organizations can develop effective networks through focused strategic action. Though we cannot assess causality from this analysis, it is possible that the non-innovative small organization's failure to innovate may have been because of its failure to implement strategic action to build an effective network. To the extent that such logic is plausible, it seems that, because networks appear to be important for innovation and because the small organizations in our sample do not appear to be benefiting from their networks in this manner, managers in small organizations may wish to implement strategies specifically geared toward creating an environment in which potential network members could be cultivated, providing tangible and intangible resources to facilitate the cultivation of potential network members.

CONCLUSIONS

In this chapter we have sought to understand whether and how networks contribute to organizational innovation. In so doing, we have investigated a largely untested area within this stream by comparing the extent to which large and small organizations benefit in this regard. Furthermore, following the calls of prior scholars to conduct inductive research to better understand findings on networks, we have performed a post-hoc analysis on the network-building practices of the outliers in the sample.[96]

While we believe that the above approach is sound—and that the use of multiple TMT-level respondents per firm, a focused sample from a vital and emerging portion of the economy, and multiple sources for the data (interviews, questionnaires, and secondary sources) are significant strengths of the study—we acknowledge that it also has limitations. First, to control for industry and environmental effects, we focused on technology-intensive firms in a geographically restricted region. An apparent path for future research is to explore the role of TMT networks with a broader sample of firms and industries.

Second, and consistent with Coleman and with Nahapiet and Ghoshal, we treated networks as a property of teams.[97] Our research suggests that networks can be a property of teams or organizations and also of individuals. In addition, it suggests that organizations may have an important role in the management and creation of social networks. Both the study of the unit of analysis and management of social networks are good candidates for future research.

Finally, in defining the networks in our study, we chose to focus solely on the TMTs' direct ties for two reasons. From a practical perspective, because of the time constraints of the top managers who participated in our study, we sought to keep the surveys relatively concise. From a theoretical perspective, as discussed under the rubric of exchange motivation, and consistent with Hansen, where information is scarce and valuable or where sources of information may also have competitive use of such information, we focused on direct ties given our expectation that they would be more important to the organization than indirect ties.[98] At the same time, we recognize that the information content garnered through direct ties might be different than that achieved through the use of indirect ties.[99] Thus, scholars extending this stream of research may wish to explore more fully defined networks.

Notwithstanding these limitations, we believe that our findings add richness to what we know about networks. While our finding that networks matter to organizational innovation is not new, our finding that small organizations do not seem to benefit from them in the same way that large organizations do in the absence of strategic network-building practices is new. Although our results must be considered preliminary given the lack of similar research exploring the contingent effect of organizational size on the network-innovation relationship, we are hopeful that this study will lead others to explore the nuances of TMT networks on this and similar organizational outcomes.

NOTES

1. Mark Granovetter, "The Strength of Weak Ties," *American Journal of Sociology* 78 (1973): 1360–1380.

2. Daniel J. Brass, "Power in Organizations: A Social Network Perspective," in *Research in Politics and Society*, ed. Gwen Moore and J. Allen Whitt (Greenwich, CT: JAI Press, 1992): 295–323; Ha Hoang and Bostjan Antoncic, "Network-based Research in Entrepreneurship," *Journal of Business Venturing* 18, 2 (2003): 165–187.

3. Gautam Ahuja, "Collaboration Networks, Structural Holes, and Innovation: A Longitudinal Study," *Administrative Science Quarterly* 45 (2000): 425–455; Morten Hansen, "The Search-transfer Problem: The Role of Weak Ties in Sharing Knowledge across Organizational Subunits," *Administrative Science Quarterly* 44 (1999): 82–111.

4. Hoang and Antoncic, "Network-based Research in Entrepreneurship."

5. Howard E. Aldrich, *Organizations Evolving* (London: Sage Publications, 2000); Amar V. Bhide, *The Origin and Evolution of New Businesses* (New York: Oxford University Press, 2000); Howard H. Stevenson, Michael J. Roberts, and H. Irving Grousbeck, *New Business Ventures and the Entrepreneur*, 3rd ed. (New York: Irwin, 1989).

6. Howard E. Aldrich and Ellen R. Auster, "Even Dwarfs Started Small: Liabilities of Age and Size and Their Strategic Implications," *Research in Organizational Behavior* 8 (1986): 165–98.

7. Scott Shane and Toby E. Stuart, "Organizational Endowments and the Performance of University Start-ups," *Management Science* 48, 1 (2002): 154–170.

8. Mark C. Suchman, "Managing Legitimacy: Strategic and Institutional Approaches," *Academy of Management Review* 20, 3 (1995): 571–610.

9. Hoang and Antoncic, "Network-based Research in Entrepreneurship."

10. Ibid.

11. Ibid.

12. Christian Lechner, Michael Dowling, and Isabell Welpe, "Firm Networks and Firm Development: The Role of the Relational Mix," *Journal of Business Venturing* 21, 4 (2006): 514–540.

13. Aegean Leung, Jing Zhang, Poh Kam Wong, and Maw Der Foo, "The Use of Networks in Human Resource Acquisition for Entrepreneurial Firms: Multiple 'Fit' Considerations," *Journal of Business Venturing* 21, 5 (2006): 664–686.

14. Lei-Yu Wu, Chun-Ju Wang, Cheng-Ping Chen, and Lee-Yun Pan, "Internal Resources, External Networks, and Competitiveness during the Growth Stage: A Study of Taiwanese High-tech Ventures," *Entrepreneurship Theory and Practice* 32, 3 (2008): 529–549.

15. Jing Zhang, Vangelis Souitaris, Pek-hooi Soh, and Poh-kam Wong, "A Contingent Model of Network Utilization in Early Financing of Technology Ventures," *Entrepreneurship Theory and Practice* 32, 4 (2008): 593–613.

16. John Hagedoorn and Nadine Roijakkers, "Small Entrepreneurial Firms and Large Companies in Interfirm R&D Networks—The International Biotechnology Industry," in *Strategic Entrepreneurship: Creating a New Mindset*, ed. Michael A. Hitt, R. Duane Ireland, S. Michael Camp, and Donald Sexton ((Oxford, U.K.: Blackwell Publishers, 2002): 223–252.

17. John R. Kimberley and Michael J. Evanisko, "Organizational Innovation: The Influence of Individual, Organizational, and Contextual Factors on Hospital Adoption of Technological and Administrative Innovations," *Academy of Management Journal* 24, 4 (1981): 689–713; Ahuja, "Collaboration Networks, Structural Holes, and Innovation"; Fariborz Damanpour, "Organizational Innovation: A Meta-analysis of Effects of Determinants and Moderators," *Academy of Management Journal* 34, 3 (1991): 555–590.

18. Hoang and Antoncic, "Network-Based Research in Entrepreneurship"; Jay R. Galbraith, *Designing Complex Organizations* (Reading, MA: Addison-Wesley, 1973).

19. John P. Kotter, *The General Managers* (New York: Free Press, 1982); Fred Luthans, Richard M. Hodgetts, and Stuart A. Rosenkrantz, *Real Managers* (Cambridge, MA: Harper & Row, 1988); James D. Thompson, *Organizations in Action* (New York: McGraw-Hill, 1967).

20. Ahuja, "Collaboration Networks, Structural Holes, and Innovation."

21. Walter W. Powell, Kenneth W. Koput, and Laurel Smith-Doerr, "Interorganizational Collaboration and the Locus of Innovation: Networks of Learning in Biotechnology," *Administrative Science Quarterly* 41, 1 (1996): 116–145.

22. Edward O. Laumann, Joseph Galaskiewicz, and Peter V. Marsden, "Community Structure as Interorganizational Linkages," *Annual Review of Sociology* 4 (1978): 455–484.

23. Ahuja, "Collaboration Networks, Structural Holes, and Innovation," 430.

24. David B. Jemison, "The Importance of Boundary-spanning Roles in Strategic Decision-making," *Journal of Management Studies* 21, 2 (1984): 131–152.

25. Avner M. Porat and John A. Haas, "Information Effects on Decision Making," *Behavioral Science* 14, 2 (1969): 98–104; Thompson, *Organizations in Action*.

26. Granovetter, "The Strength of Weak Ties"; David Krackhardt, "The Strength of Strong Ties: The Importance of Philos in Organizations," in *Networks and Organizations: Structure, Form, and Action*, ed. Nitin Nohria and Robert G. Eccles (Cambridge, MA: Harvard University Press, 1992): 216–239.

27. Ken G. Smith, Christopher J. Collins, and Kevin D. Clark, "Existing Knowledge, Knowledge Creation Capability and the Rate of New Product Introduction in High Technology Firms," *Academy of Management Journal* 48, 2 (2005): 346–357.

28. Janine Nahapiet and Sumantra Ghoshal, "Social Capital, Intellectual Capital, and the Organizational Advantage," *Academy of Management Review* 23, 2 (1998): 242–266.

29. Hansen, "The Search-transfer Problem."

30. Aneil K. Mishira, "Organizational Responses to Crisis: The Centrality of Trust," in *Trust in Organizations*, ed. Roderick M. Kramer and Tom R. Tyler (Thousand Oaks, CA: Sage, 1996): 261–287.

31. Granovetter, "The Strength of Weak Ties."

32. Brian Uzzi, "Social Structure and Competition in Interfirm Networks: The Paradox of Embeddedness," *Administrative Science Quarterly* 42, 1 (1997): 35–67; Gordon Walker, Bruce Kogut, and Weijan Shan, "Social Capital, Structural Holes and the Formation of an Industry Network," *Organization Science* 8, 2 (1997): 109–125.

33. Uzzi, "Social Structure and Competition in Interfirm Networks."

34. Walker, Kogut, and Shan, "Social Capital, Structural Holes and the Formation of an Industry Network."

35. Thompson, *Organizations in Action*.

36. James G. March, "Exploration and Exploitation in Organizational Learning," *Organization Science* 2, 1 (1991): 71–87.

37. Deborah G. Ancona and David F. Caldwell, "Bridging the Boundary: External Activity and Performance in Organizational Teams," *Administrative Science Quarterly* 37, 4 (1992): 634–665.

38. Warren Boeker, "Executive Migration and Strategic Change: The Effect of Top Manager Movement on Product-market Entry," *Administrative Science Quarterly* 42, 2 (1997): 213–236.

39. Ibid., 216.

40. Isabelle Bouty, "Interpersonal and Interaction Influences on Informal Resource Exchanges between R&D Researchers across Organizational Boundaries," *Academy of Management Journal* 43, 1 (2000): 50–65.

41. Paul S. Adler and Seok-Woo Kwon, "Social Capital: Prospects for a New Concept," *Academy of Management Review* 27, 1 (2002): 17–40.

42. Ronald S. Burt, *Structural Holes* (Cambridge, MA: Harvard University Press, 1992).

43. Adler and Kwon, "Social Capital."

44. Wenpin Tsai, "Knowledge Transfer in Intraorganizational Networks: Effects of Network Position and Absorptive Capacity on Business Unit Innovation and Performance," *Academy of Management Journal* 44, 5 (2001): 996–1004.

45. Bruce Kogut and Udo Zander, "Knowledge of the Firm, Combinative Capacities, and the Replication of Technology," *Organization Science* 3 (1992): 383–397.

46. Bruce Kogut and Udo Zander, "What Firms Do?: Coordination, Identity, and Learning," *Organization Science* 7, 5 (1996): 502–518.

47. Ray Reagans and William McEvily, "Network Structure and Knowledge Transfer: The Effects of Cohesion and Range," *Administrative Science Quarterly* 48, 2 (2003): 240–267.

48. Andrew Hargadon and Robert I. Sutton, "Technology Brokering and Innovation in a Product Development Firm," *Administrative Science Quarterly* 42, 4 (1997): 716–749.

49. Daniel A. Levinthal and James G. March, "The Myopia of Learning," *Strategic Management Journal* 14 (1993): 95–114.

50. Hansen, "The Search-transfer Problem."

51. Bouty, "Interpersonal and Interaction Influences on Informal Resource Exchanges between R&D Researchers across Organizational Boundaries."

52. Suchman, "Managing Legitimacy."

53. Monica A. Zimmerman and Gerald J. Zeitz, "Beyond Survival: Achieving New Venture Growth by Building Legitimacy," *Academy of Management Review* 27, 3 (2002): 414–431.

54. Joel A. C. Baum and Christine Oliver, "Institutional Linkages and Organizational Mortality," *Administrative Science Quarterly* 36, 2 (1991): 187–219.

55. Michael T. Hannan and John Freeman, "Structural Inertia and Organizational Change," *American Sociological Review* 49, 2 (1984): 149–164.

56. Aldrich and Auster, "Even Dwarfs Started Small."

57. Andrew H. Van de Ven and Everett M. Rodgers, "Innovations and Organizations: Critical Perspectives," *Communication Research* 15, 5 (1988): 632–651.

58. Hannan and Freeman, "Structural Inertia and Organizational Change."

59. Sarah L. Jack, "The Role, Use and Activation of Strong and Weak Network Ties: A Qualitative Analysis," *Journal of Management Studies* 42, 6 (2005): 1233–1259.

60. Suchman, "Managing Legitimacy."

61. Boeker, "Executive Migration and Strategic Change."

62. Paul R. Lawrence and Jay William Lorsch, *Organization and Environment* (Homewood, IL: Irwin, 1967).

63. Erno T. Tornikoski and Scott L. Newbert, "Exploring the Determinants of Organizational Emergence: A Legitimacy Perspective," *Journal of Business Venturing* 22, 2 (2007): 311–335.

64. E.g., Arent Greve and Janet W. Salaff, "Social Networks and Entrepreneurship," *Entrepreneurship: Theory and Practice* 28, 1 (2003): 1–22; Lechner, Dowling, and Welpe, "Firm Networks and Firm Development"; Eren Ozgen and Robert A. Baron, "Social Sources of Information in Opportunity Recognition: Effects of Mentors, Industry Networks, and Professional Forums," *Journal of Business Venturing* 22, 2 (2007): 174–192.

65. George T. Milkovich, "Compensation Systems in High Technology Companies," in *New Perspectives on Compensation*, ed. David B. Balkin and Luis R. Gomez-Mejia (Englewood Cliffs, NJ: Prentice-Hall, 1987): 80.

66. Damanpour, "Organizational Innovation."

67. Karen A. Bantel and Susan E. Jackson, "Top Management and Innovations in Banking: Does the Composition of the Top Team Make a Difference?" *Strategic Management Journal* 10, S1 (1989): 107–124.

68. Adler and Kwon, "Social Capital."

69. Michael L. McDonald and James D. Westphal, "Getting by with the Advice of Their Friends: CEO's Advice Networks and Firms' Strategic Responses to Poor Performance," *Administrative Science Quarterly* 48, 1 (2003): 1–32.

70. Glenn R. Carroll and Albert C. Teo, "On the Social Networks of Managers," *Academy of Management Journal* 39, 2 (1996): 421–440.

71. Ibid.

72. Pamela R. Haunschild, "Interorganizational Imitation: The Impact of Interlocks on Corporate Acquisition Activity," *Administrative Science Quarterly* 38, 4 (1993): 564–592.

73. Bouty, "Interpersonal and Interaction Influences on Informal Resource Exchanges between R&D Researchers across Organizational Boundaries."

74. Granovetter, "The Strength of Weak Ties."

75. Hansen, "The Search-transfer Problem."

76. Burt, *Structural Holes*.

77. Thompson, *Organizations in Action*; Galbraith, *Designing Complex Organizations*; Henry Mintzberg, *The Nature of Managerial Work* (New York: Harper and Row, 1973).

78. Bantel and Jackson, "Top Management and Innovations in Banking"; Wesley M. Cohen and Richard C. Levin, "Empirical Studies of Innovation and Market Structure," in *Handbook of Industrial Organization*, ed. Richard Schmalensee and Robert Wilig (New York: North-Holland, 1989): 1059–1107.

79. Hargadon and Sutton, "Technology Brokering and Innovation in a Product Development Firm."

80. Marshall H. Becker, "Factors Affecting the Diffusion of Innovations among Health Professionals," *American Journal of Public Health* 60, 2 (1970): 294–304.

81. Margarethe F. Wiersema and Karen A. Bantel, "Top Management Team Demography and Corporate Change," *Academy of Management Journal* 35, 1 (1992): 91–121.

82. Becker, "Factors Affecting the Diffusion of Innovations among Health Professionals."

83. Wiersema and Bantel, "Top Management Team Demography and Corporate Change."

84. John G. Scott, *Social Network Analysis: A Handbook* (London: Sage, 1991); Carroll and Teo, "On the Social Networks of Managers."

85. Joel M. Podolny and James N. Baron, "Resources and Relationships: Social Networks and Mobility in the Workplace," *American Sociological Review* 62, 5 (1997): 673–693.

86. Brian Uzzi, "Embeddedness in the Making of Financial Capital: How Social Relations and Networks Benefit Organizations Seeking Financing," *American Sociological Review* 64, 4 (1999): 481–505.

87. Ahuja, "Collaboration Networks, Structural Holes, and Innovation"; Smith, Collins, and Clark, "Existing Knowledge, Knowledge Creation Capability and the Rate of New Product Introduction in High Technology Firms."

88. Carroll and Teo, "On the Social Networks of Managers."

89. Granovetter, "The Strength of Weak Ties," 1371.

90. Aldrich, *Organizations Evolving*.

91. Aldrich and Auster, "Even Dwarfs Started Small."

92. Donald F. Kuratko, "The Emergence of Entrepreneurship Education: Development, Trends, and Challenges," *Entrepreneurship: Theory and Practice* 29, 5 (2005): 577–597.

93. Christopher J. Collins and Kevin D. Clark, "Strategic Human Resource Practices, Top Management Team Social Networks, and Firm Performance: The Role of Human Resource Practices in Creating Organizational Competitive Advantage," *Academy of Management Journal* 46, 6 (2003): 740–751.

94. Albert Bandura, *Social Learning Theory* (Englewood Cliffs, NJ: Prentice-Hall, 1976).

95. Miriam Erez and P. Christopher Earley, *Culture, Self-identity and Work* (New York: Oxford University Press, 1993).

96. Hoang and Antoncic, "Network-based Research in Entrepreneurship."

97. Nahapiet and Ghoshal, "Social Capital, Intellectual Capital, and the Organizational Advantage."

98. Hansen, "The Search-transfer Problem."

99. Ahuja, "Collaboration Networks, Structural Holes, and Innovation."

4

Balancing Institutional Forces and Strategic Demands in Adopting HPWS Practices in Small Innovative Firms: An Overview and Empirical Analysis

Pankaj C. Patel*

The relationship between firms' investments in high-performance work systems (HPWS) to enhance human capital and overall firm performance is well documented in large firms.[1] HPWS constitute a bundle of human resource practices that play a key role in enhancing the contribution of employees to a firm's competitive advantage. Adopting HPWS is even more important for a small firm than for a large one because small firms are disproportionately more labor intensive than larger firms.[2] Employees play a key role in enhancing a small firm's competitive advantage. Yet, compared to large firms, because of liabilities of smallness, small firms may not necessarily experience a net benefit from implementing HPWS.[3] HPWS practices require significant direct investments (such as incentives, training, participation, and procedures, among others) and indirect investments (such as developing conducive organizational climate for employee participation, fostering trust in management, or ensuring inclusivity of employees across the firm). Because of their smaller size, small firms may not accrue economies of scale and economies of scope from HPWS practices.

*The author thanks H. Whittaker and T. Quince for generously sharing the data on the U.K. Data Archive. The bibliographic citation for the data file is: Whittaker, H., and T. Quince, *Cambridge Centre for Business Research Survey of British and Japanese Entrepreneurs and their Businesses, 2000–2002* [computer file]. Colchester, Essex: UK Data Archive [distributor], September 2006. SN: 5458, http://dx.doi.org/10.5255/UKDA-SN-5458-1. The original data collectors, the funders, or the UK Data Archive UK Data Archive bear no responsibility for their further analysis or interpretation. The data are Crown copyright.

While the literature on HPWS practices in small firms is relatively sparse, findings on the value of HPWS practices remain mixed.[4] Small firms face duality in implementing HPWS practices as they have limited resources and capabilities to implement and exploit HPWS practices, and yet, HPWS practices are critical to deriving competitive advantage in small firms. The purpose of this chapter is to provide a brief overview of findings on HPWS practices in small firms and introduce the role of institutional factors in deriving gains from HPWS practices. The empirical component of the chapter focuses on the extent to which small firms have a choice in implementing HPWS practices and the extent to which they are bound by external constraints.

In addition to firm strategy that may affect net benefits from HPWS practices, institutional factors could also affect the nature of human resource practices adopted, receptivity of human resource practices among employees, and the ease of implementation of certain human resource practices over others. Drawing on contingency theory, firm strategy may play a central role in increasing benefits and reducing costs from HPWS practices.[5] While much of the literature on human resources in small firms focuses on the gains and benefits resulting from the internal fit of HPWS practices with strategic goals, societal institutions may also act as a lubricant in the adoption and implementation of HPWS practices by affecting benefits and costs of these practices.[6] A country's culture may affect organizational routines, systems, and processes, which in turn may affect the effectiveness of HPWS practices. For example, higher levels of collectivism in a cultural setting require fewer extrinsic incentives to motivate employees as employees are intrinsically motivated to work.[7] Reduced interaction and coordination costs emanating from collectivistic cultures further reduce the cost of HPWS practices. Thus, beyond the importance of internal strategic fit, institutional factors may significantly affect the costs and benefits of HPWS practices in small firms.[8] However, from a strategic standpoint, strictly relying on institutional factors in choosing HPWS practices may not benefit a firm either. As firms represent heterogeneous bundles of resources, maintaining strategic and institutional fit could be necessary to improve performance.

The chapter has two goals. First, it provides a brief overview of past literature on human resource practices in small firms. Second, this literature is extended by an empirical study exploring the need for balancing strategic and institutional priorities. Drawing on contingency theory, I assess the effect of fit between firm strategy and HPWS practices on firm performance in the context of two institutional settings: the United Kingdom and Japan.[9]

Accounting for the joint effects of strategic and institutional factors on the effectiveness of HPWS practices is important for many reasons. First, much of the strategic human resource management literature has exclusively focused on strategic dimensions of HPWS practices.[10] However, appeals for accounting for institutional factors in HPWS remain unanswered. Second, by leveraging institutional factors, small firms who are short in resources may optimize their investments in HPWS practices. Institutional factors could increase the costs of using certain HPWS practices but also increase benefits from certain practices. For example, promoting practices that increase intrinsic motivation without addressing extrinsic motivation may be problematic in small firms located in Western institutional settings. Alternatively, institutional factors could promote certain employee behaviors, and hence firms may not derive added benefits from using HPWS practices that also lead to such behavior. Thus, by assessing relative benefits and costs derived from institutional factors on HPWS practices, small firms could effectively channel scarce resources within the firm. Third, by examining samples from two different institutional settings, one can reliably assess the relative effects of balancing strategic and institutional requirements in the adoption of HPWS practices as well as its effects on firm performance.

HPWS PRACTICES AND SMALL FIRM PERFORMANCE

A resource-based view explains how internal resources contribute to enhancing the competitive advantage of a firm.[11] A firm's human capital may be a source of competitive advantage.[12] HPWS practices are a key source of enhancing the effectiveness of human capital. Scholars have found that the benefits of such HPWS practices extend to smaller firms as well as larger ones. In small firms, HPWS practices lead to better performance[13] and are an important means of attaining a sustainable competitive advantage.[14] Recently, researchers have taken a closer look at whether such advantages accrue uniformly in smaller firms. Cardon and Stevens suggest that firm age and firm size may be significant factors in affecting returns to HPWS practices.[15] Extending the argument of costs and benefits of HPWS, Sels, De Winne, Maes, Delmotte, Faems, and Forrier, assess how increases in personnel costs may reduce the glamour of adopting HPWS practices.[16] The key argument is that while benefits of HPWS may be possible, the additional costs—direct and indirect—may not result in a net benefit for a firm.

The varying levels of costs and benefits for small firms are a result of the fundamental characteristics of the small firms. Small firms may not be able to realize larger benefits from the implementation of HPWS for many reasons. First, smaller firms may lack the routines, structures, and systems to fully exploit the benefits of increased human capital.[17] Although HPWS practices enhance human capital, a lack of factors that may enhance the effectiveness of human capital may result in lower benefits. Lack of knowledge-sharing routines, limited economies of scope across departments, and limited avenues for knowledge sharing are a few factors that limit the exploitation of the full potential of a firm's human resources. Second, environmental conditions may limit the full value that can be harnessed from less developed human capital in small firms.[18] As scholars have explained, contingency fit may be becoming increasingly important in realizing the advantages of HPWS practices. Firms operating in more dynamic, uncertain environments where human capital is central to creating appropriate environmental responses may benefit the most from HPWS practices. Small firms typically operate in small niches on or near the margins of the market and could draw on human capital to improve performance.[19] Third, increasing levels of HPWS practices may result in diminished returns.

While uniformity in HPWS practices in the six key areas, (a) selection, (b) training, (c) career advancement, (d) appraisal, (e) compensation, and (f) participation, may result in increased returns, gains from adding more practices under each category may result in diminished returns after a certain level. Diminished returns are a result of the increased costs of managing and implementing multiple practices. Overall, small firms may not be able to fully harness human capital enhancements because of their internal structures and routines, external environments, and overall diminishing returns from HPWS practices.[20]

Small firms may face limited avenues to harness value from HPWS practices, and such practices may significantly increase a firm's expenses. The costs associated with HPWS practices are direct and indirect. Direct costs are associated with the actual expenses a company must incur to facilitate HPWS practices. For example, increased monetary incentives, training costs, and recruiting are a few examples of such direct costs. Indirect costs are associated with work intensification, stress, job strain, and fostering cooperation and coordination among employees at multiple levels in the firm.

While empirical research on increased costs is sparse, support exists that increased costs may negate the value added. Cooke found that while union membership increased employee payoffs, it did not increase value added from HPWS practices.[21] Cappelli and Neumark found that while HPWS practices increased productivity marginally, increased labor costs offset these gains.[22] Furthermore, while HPWS practices may result in lower turnover, they may not result in increased productivity.[23] More recently, Sels et al. explicitly modeled gains in productivity and increased personnel costs from HPWS practices and found that gains in productivity are offset by increased personnel costs.[24] If one adds the indirect costs associated with stress, work intensification, and burnout, the benefits from HPWS practices are obviously questionable. Furthermore, the labor-intensive nature of small firms may further increase the indirect costs of HPWS practices.

Overall, a considerable number of studies have found positive effects in HPWS practices,[25] while others have taken a closer look at the costs and benefits of HPWS practices and found that such practices may add a very limited value to a firm once all factors are considered.

Despite the evidence that these practices add limited value to a small firm, small firms continue choosing to implement such practices. This approach may explain the conflicted findings on the effects of HPWS practices on small firm performance. It takes into consideration that although some amount of HPWS practices are important, at higher levels of such practices, direct and indirect costs may not justify increased levels of HPWS practices. The degree of implementation must be determined using a cost-benefit assessment to find the optimal level of HPWS practices. HPWS practices could be added until the marginal gains equal marginal costs.

> Hypothesis 1: Increased adoption of HPWS practices will have an inverted-U relationship with productivity.

ENHANCING THE EFFECTIVENESS OF HPWS ADOPTION

Although smaller firms may face disadvantages in implementing HPWS practices, because of reduced marginal benefits and increasing costs, the importance of HPWS practices to enhancing competitive advantage remains no less important. What factors may play a role in further understanding the effectiveness of HPWS practices in small firms? Some factors may enhance a firm's marginal benefits or reduce its marginal costs, or both. Such effects may enhance the degree of adoption of HPWS practices and hence productivity gains. Compared to a universalistic approach in which increasing HPWS practices leads to linear returns, in the case of small firms, a contingency approach may be important.

A contingency approach may be especially relevant for small firms. The contingency approach explains how organizations achieving a "vertical fit" between HPWS choices, strategic options, and environmental features will outperform other organizations.[26] Attaining this fit is even more important for small firms than for larger ones. First, smaller firms have limited resources. Judicious use of resources may be important to achieve fit while expending the fewest firm resources. Second, small firms are more susceptible to liabilities of smallness.[27] Achieving such fit may be important for surviving in hostile environments. Thus, strategic and environmental factors may play a key role in enhancing the effectiveness of HPWS practices. Matching the amount and nature of HPWS practices may enhance marginal gains and reduce marginal costs. While small firms that match strategy and HPWS practices may experience greater gains from HPWS practices, institutional factors may play a key role in affecting the fit between strategy and HPWS practices.

Small firms matching their HPWS practices with other strategies may create a better fit for enhancing their productivity. However, HPWS literature has typically focused on the strategic choices of firms. Paauwe and Boselie, among others, have challenged the resource-based view's (RBV) assumptions of strategic human resource management (SHRM) as being overly rational and systems oriented, proposing instead a larger role for institutional forces in design, implementation, and effectiveness of HPWS strategy.[28] Small firms must meet their strategic goals to survive. They must also weather the challenges of liabilities of smallness and newness from external forces to ensure legitimacy and thus survival.[29] Therefore, balancing a firm's strategic goals with institutional pressures appears critical for the firm's survival and growth.[30] In conforming to institutional demands, small firms may be able to increase legitimacy and thus acquire resources with favorable terms, recruit and retain employees, and gain support from stakeholders. At the same time, firms cannot grow or survive unless they make choices that help them create and sustain a competitive advantage. In other words, they must differentiate themselves from other firms to win customers.

The support for each of these incongruent approaches in the literature of the field presents a paradox for small businesses, particularly innovative ones,[31] suggesting that small firms must balance institutional pressures to conform to the strategic necessity of differentiation. In the adoption and implementation of HPWS practices, wider cultural institutions may play a significant role. For example, small firms in cultures with greater power distance may find it easy to implement participation-based HPWS, thus reducing direct implementation costs.

While regulatory, normative, and cognitive institutions at the industry level may be important, the effects of cultural institutions in a country may play an important role in enhancing the marginal returns and marginal costs of HPWS adoption. The role of national culture is important in explaining the differences for three reasons. First, the key hurdle for small firms in experiencing the benefits of HPWS practices is the increased direct and indirect costs involved. National culture may play an important role in reducing explicit and implicit costs in the implementation of HPWS practices. For example, in Eastern cultures, greater collectivism may promote greater levels of cooperation and sharing.[32] Such cultural dispositions may reduce the increased costs and stress on employees because expectations do not have to be generated artificially but are culturally embedded. Second, marginal gains may be greater as well. In cultures with greater feministic orientations, employees may tend to share knowledge and be more open to cooperation.[33] Thus, cultural dispositions may strengthen the marginal gains of a firm because the firm may not have to invest in developing such dispositions. Finally, the joint effects of increased marginal gains and reduced marginal costs may simultaneously enhance the effectiveness of HPWS practices in small firms. I will first discuss the role of ensuring a proper fit between strategy and HPWS practices within small firms, and a discussion on how institutional factors affect the fit will follow.

ROLE OF STRATEGY

I extend earlier findings on differentiation strategy leading to higher returns in comparison to using HPWS practices with greater levels of cost leadership by assessing its relevance in decreasing returns from HPWS practices.[34] Porter differentiates between cost leadership and differentiation strategy.[35] A firm pursuing a cost-leadership strategy gains a competitive advantage by becoming the lowest cost producer in the market. Firms pursuing a differentiation strategy, on the other hand, differentiate their products or services from their competitors' on the basis of factors such as quality or innovation. Differentiation strategy has been consistently shown to increase returns to HPWS practices.[36] In this chapter, I focus on increasing marginal benefits and reducing marginal costs based on differentiation strategy.

Differentiation of products and services on the basis of quality or innovation requires a highly skilled and motivated workforce. Developing and enhancing products requires that employees proactively identify and solve problems in the environment. Furthermore, employees must be able to interact and exchange knowledge to create economies of scope. Such sharing of knowledge facilitates a greater ability and speed with which to respond to market needs.[37] Employees working under cost-leadership regimes focus on firm efficiency. In firms following greater levels of cost leadership, the production factor, labor, has much less significance than capital.[38] This may result in lower levels of returns for cost-leadership strategy. Thus, a greater level of human capital that may have been developed through HPWS practices may lead to reduced returns. By helping employees in firms that follow differentiation strategy to develop greater levels of competence and adaptability, firms may experience increased returns because employees may show higher levels of personal initiative than the employees of competing firms. Firms using differentiation strategies benefit significantly from HPWS practices that provide enriched team-based jobs and investments in comprehensive selection, induction, training, performance appraisal, and compensation systems. In contrast, cost-leadership strategy requires an increase in managerial control through introducing systems, processes, and technologies that enhance efficiency. Increased managerial control limits the possible differences in knowledge; skill and motivation enhance a firm's productivity.[39] Overall, compared to small firms that are focused on cost reductions, firms focused on differentiation strategy may experience greater marginal gains from adopting HPWS practices.

Alternatively, on the marginal cost dimension, firms following differentiation strategy adapt their production and organizational processes to meet market demand. Constant adaptation may mean that the direct costs of HPWS practices are much higher.[40] In other words, incentive schemes, training, and selection costs may be significantly higher in firms following a differentiation strategy. Cost leaders may not incur such increased direct costs. On the dimension of indirect costs associated with increased workload and stress, a differentiation strategy will lead to greater levels of indirect employee costs. Employees working in firms using differentiation strategy have jobs that are more complex and varied, requiring broader skill sets as well as the ability and the will to succeed in more challenging and varied circumstances.[41] While differentiation will probably magnify the value of high-performance practices, it may also considerably increase the direct and indirect costs of HPWS practices. However, it may still increase the overall productivity by increasing the net-productivity levels. In other words, increases in both marginal costs and marginal benefits may cause optimization to occur only when HPWS practices are used at much higher levels. To offset the costs of HPWS practices, the scope and scale of HPWS practices must be increased to realize a net benefit.

> Hypothesis 2: Differentiation strategy moderates the nonlinear relationship between HPWS practices and firm productivity, positively affecting labor productivity.

ROLE OF CULTURAL INSTITUTIONS IN AFFECTING HPWS PRACTICE AND STRATEGY FIT

More importantly, the effectiveness of the vertical fit between strategy and HPWS practices may be significantly affected by institutional settings. Institutional theory explains how economic exchanges, organizational structures and systems, and individual behavior are influenced by institutional factors.[42] Formal institutions include social, political, and regulatory institutions, whereas informal institutions include culture and norms of social exchange. Institutional norms and rules result in socially constructed behavior templates created and maintained through ongoing social interactions.[43] Institutional forces limit the role of rational decision making by imposing demands and actions that can result in inefficiencies. Institutional norms and prescriptions impel individuals and firms to pursue goals within institutional constraints. Institutions may affect firms at different levels: employee norms of behavior,[44] culture,[45] strategic choice and resource choice,[46] and organizational structures and systems.[47] National cultural institutions play a more important role in increasing marginal gains and reducing marginal costs than firm-level factors.

Employee behavior is influenced by normative institutions such as national culture. Studies over the last decade have consistently shown the critical role of culture in entrepreneurial processes at the national, individual, and small firm level.[48] Normative institutions reinforce social norms, values, beliefs, and assumptions about behaviors.[49] Normative institutions determine which processes are legitimate. One of the most widely used models of culture is Hofstede's four dimensions of culture:[50] (1) individualism-collectivism, (2) power distance, (3) masculinity-femininity, and (4) uncertainty avoidance.[51]

Cultural factors in a specific country may provide behavioral infrastructure that may facilitate the effective implementation of HPWS practices. As suggested above, culture plays an important role in facilitating differentiation strategy. Firms in Eastern cultures may be more amenable to realizing increased gains from HPWS adoption beyond those provided by national culture in general. In other words, the relevant institutional environment may affect the differentiation capability. Still, implementation of HPWS practices seems to further enhance labor productivity. Thus, HPWS practices may significantly affect labor productivity beyond the cultural factors. However, cultural factors may increase marginal benefits and reduce marginal costs. Cultural dimensions may increase marginal gains by promoting the employee behavior that leads to realization of differentiation strategy. More specifically, cultural factors may enhance sharing, cooperation, and group behavior in general among employees, which would aid in adequately meeting market demands.

In individualistic cultures, experimentation through innovation and risk taking is encouraged,[52] and curiosity, creativity, and broadmindedness are valued.[53] Individualism and collectivism affect group membership,[54] communication styles,[55] and wealth creation.[56] Individualistic cultures respond better to formal mechanisms through which the requirements for integration are explicitly stated.[57] Members of such cultures will be less inclined to work in teams and other decentralized structures. However, individualism helps small firms to implement role flexibility mechanisms, which challenge and enhance individual task objectives by seeking knowledge from all organizational areas. Similarly, such cultures promote incremental innovation while building on existing routines and skills.[58]

In cultures emphasizing power distance, firms must engage in increased buy-in of certain HPWS practices at the firm level because many HPWS practices focus on enhancing communication and promoting flatter hierarchies that could be unconventional in such cultural settings.[59] Greater power distance increases loyalty and cohesion.[60] National culture plays a key role in successful innovation activities.[61] Culture appears to significantly affect managerial behavior, the interaction among units, and reward structures.

Masculinity helps individuals to become more assertive and goal directed, as opposed to emphasizing warm social relationships.[62] Purposefulness and formalization, related to masculinity, result in greater task orientation and formalization, which reduces group conflicts, confusion, redundancy, and overlapping authority.[63] In feminine societies, members tend to have greater trust, communication, and team spirit as well as low instances of conflict. Thus, in highly uncertain environments, a feminine culture may facilitate product innovation.[64]

Uncertainty avoidance reduces an employee's ability to deal with unstructured situations, which are often unpredicted and different from those normally encountered in everyday life.[65] Greater uncertainty avoidance reduces flexibility and promotes the use of centralization and formalization mechanisms.

Overall, culture plays a key role in increasing marginal benefits and reducing marginal costs for firms using HPWS practices. An increase in productivity resulting from HPWS practices may therefore be much higher for small firms in Eastern cultures than for those in Western cultures. In other words, in Eastern cultures, small firms may gain more from implementing HPWS practices and face lower marginal costs for such implementation. Both direct and indirect marginal costs may be reduced.

Alternatively, greater willingness to cooperate, along with greater cohesion, may reduce turnover, which in turn reduces staffing costs. In individualistic cultures, firms must implement direct incentives that may significantly increase direct costs. The indirect costs may be less because the cooperative and communal nature of firms may reduce significant employee communication and coordination costs as well as stress while promoting better work-life balance. Small firms in Eastern cultures realize greater levels of productivity gains than small firms in Western cultures. Given the facilitation provided by cultural values, small firms in the East will enjoy greater productivity, ceteris paribus.

Hypothesis 3: Eastern cultural institutions enhance the implementation of strategic and HPWS practices more positively than Western cultural institutions do.

DATA

The data for this study is from Whittaker and Quince (2002). In additional to providing a brief overview of the literature on the effects of HPWS practices on performance in small firms, this second part of the chapter conducts empirical testing of the hypotheses proposed above. To test the hypotheses, I used data based on two surveys of small firms that were conducted in Japan and Britain. The surveys were carried out from December 2000 to January 2001 in Britain and from February to March 2002 in Japan.[66] To create a comparable matching sample for both countries, only businesses in high-tech industries were targeted. The sample for the British survey was composed of single-site, independent businesses listed by Dun & Bradstreet in January 1998. For the Japanese survey, the sampling frame ensured the businesses were limited to those with SIC activities comparable to the high–tech activities found in the British study. Japanese businesses were added to the survey from Toyo Keizai's *Nihon no kaisha 78000* (Japanese Companies, 78000).

The postal survey yielded 236 responses (a 34.2 percent response rate) from Great Britain and 343 responses (a 9.4 percent response rate) from Japan. The surveys focused on the chief executive officers of high-technology small businesses and their entrepreneurial behavior. Additionally, its purpose was to explore the interplay of the widely recognized entrepreneurial drive for independence with the various forms of interdependence. For the purposes of the current study, the survey provides an ideal way to examine institutional factors from two very distinct institutional environments: those of the United Kingdom and Japan. The questionnaire covered the following topics: business development, personnel management, and strategic goals. For institutional data, I used measures from meta-analyses of HPWS practices across the countries.[67]

MEASURES

Dependent Variable

Labor Productivity

Past work has proposed that labor productivity is the most important indicator of workforce performance.[68] Samuelson and Nordhaus define labor productivity as total output divided by labor input.[69] More importantly, the relationship between HPWS and firm outcome (labor productivity) is a more proximal and direct outcome of HPWS than firm profits. Guest suggests that the effects of HPWS become increasingly weaker as other firm factors intervene.[70] Furthermore, as a proxy for firm success, labor productivity has a greater face validity than other contributing factors.[71]

Prior research measured productivity as a logarithm of the ratio of firm sales to the number of employees.[72] However, this measure does not account for the increase in costs that results from increased revenues. In the context of the current study, one must account for such costs to realize the true effects of marginal benefits and marginal costs in HPWS implementation. Labor productivity is calculated here as the following: where p represents the pretax profits before interest and depreciation, ppi represents the producer price index, n represents the number of employees, and sp represents the sector productivity. This equation was adopted from Neal, West, and Patterson.[73] By normalizing the equation with the producer price index and the sector productivity, firm-level labor productivity is normalized by sector-level productivity.

Independent Variables

HPWS Index

Compared to large firms that have formalized and enduring HPWS, small firms may not have such sophisticated measures. As an alternate measure, the HPWS index provides a more conservative measure that operationalizes key HPWS practices.[74] Data were collected on a set of 15 HPWS practices, with the goal of measuring the extent of HPWS practices in a firm. The items were related to effects of managing *competencies* (knowledge, skills, and abilities of employees); *behaviors* (prompted by offering intrinsic and extrinsic rewards); and *empowerment* practices (allowing employees to exert influence) on labor productivity.[75] Each HPWS variable was a scaled composite of multiple items that were either dichotomous responses (1 = yes; 0 = no) indicating the existence of a practice, management reports of the proportion of nonmanagerial employees covered by the practice, or management attitudes toward the practice's effectiveness (scale of 1–5 for level of importance of a specific practice; 1 = not important to 5 = crucial).

Drawing on previous research, a systems-level measurement is appropriate for determining the extent of HPWS practices in a firm.[76] It must be noted that a single index results in a parsimonious model that leads to fewer interaction terms. The HPWS index was created by standardizing the six variables described and averaging the standard scores. Such an index assumes that a low score on any one variable can be compensated for by a high score on any other. A multiplicative index may not be appropriate because an extreme score on any one variable would exert a disproportionate influence on the index as a whole.[77] More importantly, because no basis exists for predicting a priori whether the items within the index are substitutes or complements, an additive index provides a more conservative measurement. Becker and Huselid and Delery provide further discussion regarding the strengths and weaknesses of using an additive approach to create a unitary index in HPWS research.

I created an HPWS index using a second-order latent factor model.[78] First, an exploratory factor analysis showed three distinct factors related to competency, behaviors, and empowerment practices. In the second step, a second-order factor model was created to combine the three factors that showed adequate fit, and a model with three separate factors showed inadequate fit.

Differentiation Strategy

The items on business-level differentiation strategy were based on an 11-item scale from Dess and Davis; Jácome, Lisboa, and Yasin; Ward and Duray; and Zahra and Bogner.[79] The scaled items ranged from 1 (not impor-tant) to 5 (crucial). These items were assessed by the degree to which a firm has a competitive advantage in the following areas: (1) technologi-cal/scientific expertise, (2) price/cost advantages (which were reverse coded), (3) marketing and promotion, (4) speed of service, (5) established reputation, (6) design of product/service, (7) quality of product/service, (8) specialized product/service, (9) range of products/services, (10) personal attention and responsiveness to client needs, and (11) being first in the market with new products. The mean of all 11 items is an indicator of degree of differentiation. The scale reliability was 0.84 for the United King-dom and 0.81 for Japan.

The polynomial regression approach allows one to measure the fit between two similar yet distinct constructs while retaining the underlying values of the individual variables,[80] which in this case are HPWS index and differentiation strategy. To test the proposed framework, we use polyno-mial regression. The fit between two predictors (x and y) is assessed to pre-dict effects on the outcome (z). If fit increases performance, then the joint increase in x and y must lead to higher z, and if misfit leads to lower perfor-mance, then increasing x but decreasing y (or, increasing y but decreasing x) leads to lower z.

Polynomial regression model:

Labor Productivity $= b_0 + b_1$(HPWS Index) $+ b_2$(Differentiation Strategy) $+ b_3$(HPWS Index)^2 $+ b_4$(HPWS Index)(Differentiation Strategy) $+ b_5$(Differentiation Strategy)^2 $+ b_n$Controls$_n + e$

Control Variables

Six control variables were included in the analyses to study how potential industry differences in productivity may significantly affect labor productivity. In the *technology sector*, dummy codes represent categories in the technology industry. The data represented nine unique categories. More importantly, sector dummies serve as controls for studying the significant effects of regulatory, cognitive, and normative cultural institutions. *Capital intensity* differences among industries may introduce possible differences in labor productivity because of different manufacturing and service requirements in labor-intensive and capital-intensive small firms.[81] This variable is measured by the ratio of the value of the fixed assets to the total assets of an average firm in a given sector. The effectiveness of HPWS intensity, as well as the level of turnover and productivity, may differ between companies with 10 employees and those with 99 employees. The likeliness of using HPWS may increase with company size.[82] Larger firms may provide better internal labor market opportunities, which may lead to lower levels of voluntary turnover. Therefore, *firm size* (shown as the natural logarithm of the number of employees) is included as a control variable. (The fact that the narrow sampling frame consists only of small firms with 10–100 employees may partially mitigate this issue.) The *age* of a firm (number of years since start-up) was included as a control to study the time available for developing HPWS practices and the possible learning-curve effects on productivity.[83] Finally, we used self-report measures of *employee growth* and *sales growth* on a 3-point scale (low-average-high).[84] If a particular HPWS practice leads to growth, then this profitability might provide incentives to further develop this practice, or even to introduce new practices.[85]

The term *technological intensity* relates to the degree to which HPWS are similar in relevant industries. With higher levels of innovation, small firms might mimic commonly accepted structures and systems to manage, share, and exploit knowledge among employees.[86] To operationalize cognitive institutions within an industry, country-specific science and technology indicators have been aggregated at the SIC code level. Indicators were drawn from the OECD dataset for the respective survey years. The indicators are (a) sector R&D intensity, (b) number of researchers per 1,000 people in a labor force, (c) percentage of researchers in a sector as a percentage of national total, and (d) patents per thousand employees in an industry. I calculated standardized values for the four factors and added them. The combination of sector dummies and industry-level indicators serves as a control for overall industry-based institutional effects in the hypothesized model.

Robustness Checks

Hult, Ketchen, Griffith, Finnegan, Gonzalez-Padron, Harmancioglu, Huang, Talay, and Cavusgil explain the necessity of ensuring measurement equivalence across dimensions of construct equivalence, measurement equivalence, and data-collection equivalence.[87] To remove some of the effects of multicollinearity, the measures have been centered. Beyond the expected high correlations between HPWS practices and institutions, the correlations between other variables were low (table 4.1). The correlation of *technological intensity* with other factors shows how industry practices may significantly affect the proposed model. This finding further affirms that this experiment is significantly controlling for industry-based institutions. In addition, sector dummies may control for industry-based institutions as well. To assess whether multicollinearity was a significant problem at the firm level, I calculated the variance inflation factors (VIF) and condition index. Multicollinearity was not a significant issue in this study because all VIF values were below 10 (VIF = 3.01), and the condition index was below 30 (condition index = 20.04) for firms in both the United Kingdom and Japan.[88]

To address common method variance, I followed the recommendations of Podsakoff and Organ.[89] For firms in both samples, Harman's factor analysis resulted in at least six factors, and the first factor explained at least 18.38 percent of the variance. Using external data sources for some of the measures further reduces concerns for common method bias.

To determine construct validity, I ran a confirmatory factor analysis for the two endogenous variables, HPWS index and differentiation strategy. The overall model provided a satisfactory fit. All factor loadings (p < 0.01) were highly significant, and the composite reliabilities of all constructs exceeded the usual benchmark of 0.60.[90] Although I ruled out the possibility of common method variance and confirmed convergent validity of measures, discriminant validity may still be an issue.[91] To measure the degree to which the constructs are distinct, I measured the chi-square difference by constraining a pair of constructs to 1. The results showed that the differences between constrained and unconstrained models were significant

TABLE 4.1 Correlation Tables

United Kingdom

	Mean	SD	1	2	3	4	5	6	7	8	9
1. Labor productivity	1.59	0.18	1								
2. HPWS index	0.68	0.12	0.17*	1							
3. Differentiation strategy	3.68	0.32	0.11*	0.09*	1						
4. Capital intensity	0.29	0.18	−0.08	0.05	0.03	1					
5. Firm size	42.57	17.27	0.12*	0.05	0.08	0.01	1				
6. Firm age	14.58	10.26	0.04	0.03	0.05	0.02	0.05*	1			
7. Employee growth	1.22	0.48	0.04	0.04	0.07	0.05	0.03	0.02	1		
8. Sales growth	1.25	0.46	0.06	0.09	0.02	0.06	0.03	0.03	0.08*	1	
9. Technological intensity	2.54	0.57	0.21*	0.14*	0.16*	0.11*	0.06	0.07	0.05	0.12	1

Japan

	Mean	SD	1	2	3	4	5	6	7	8	9
1. Labor productivity	2.13	0.06	1								
2. HPWS index	0.77	0.15	0.12*	1							
3. Differentiation strategy	3.72	0.26	0.06*	0.08*	1						
4. Capital intensity	0.26	0.20	−0.03	0.03	0.04	1					
5. Firm size	31.23	20.13	0.06	0.01	0.11*	0.03	1				
6. Firm age	17.51	12.44	0.03	0.05	0.04	0.04	0.02	1			
7. Employee growth	1.02	0.31	0.05	0.06	0.06*	0.07	0.04	0.06	1		
8. Sales growth	1.05	0.42	0.08	0.07*	0.02	0.03	0.02	0.05	0.07	1	
9. Technological intensity	2.15	0.51	0.19*	0.14*	0.11*	0.09*	0.07*	0.02	0.07	0.05	1

*$p < 0.05$
Source: U.K. Data Archive.

ANALYTICAL APPROACH AND RESULTS

The results are listed in table 4.2. The polynomial regression model (U.K.: $R^2 = 0.36$, ΔR^2: $p < 0.05$; Japan: $R^2 = 0.31$, ΔR^2: $p < 0.05$) exhibited significantly greater explanatory power. This lends support to my contention that the fit relationship between HPWS index and differentiation strategy is curvilinear in nature, and the hypotheses are best tested using this method.

TABLE 4.2 Regression Results of HPWS Intensity and Differentiation Strategy on Labor Productivity for U.K. and Japanese Ventures

Independent Variables	United Kingdom β	Japan β	z (Difference Test)
Intercept	1.186**	2.198**	
Capital intensity	0.14*	0.13*	
Firm size (# of employees)	0.11	0.09*	
Firm age	0.19*	0.13	
Employee growth	0.22	0.14*	
Sales growth	0.12*	0.25*	
Technological intensity	0.17*	0.18*	
HPWS index (b_1)	0.21**	0.10**	3.527**
Differentiation strategy (b_2)	0.23**	0.17**	2.07*
HPWS index squared (b_3)	−0.09**	−0.05**	−2.137**
HPWS index × Differentiation Strategy (b_4)	0.11**	0.21*	−2.031*
Differentiation strategy squared (b_5)	0.04	0.03	1.431
R^2	0.36***	0.31***	
Along Fit Line			
Linear shape along P = S	$a_1 = b_1 + b_2$ $= 0.44^{**}$	$a_1 = b_1 + b_2$ $= 27^{**}$	1.634
Curvilinear shape along P = S	$a_2 = b_3 + b_4 + b_5$ $= 0.06^{*}$	$a_2 = b_3 + b_4 + b_5$ $= 0.19^{*}$	−3.159**
Along Misfit Line			
Linear shape along P = −S	$x_1 = b_1 - b_2 = -0.02$	$x_1 = b_1 - b_2$ $= -0.07$	−0.533
Curvilinear shape along P = −S	$x_2 = b_3 - b_4 + b_5$ $= -0.16^{*}$	$x_2 = b_3 - b_4 + b_5$ $= -0.23^{*}$	−1.254

Notes: Unstandardized parameter estimates shown; nine sector dummies included in the model, but the parameters are not listed.
Labor productivity = b_0 + b_1(HPWS index) + b_2(Differentiation strategy) + b_3(HPWS index)^2 + b_4(HPWS index)(Differentiation strategy) + b_5(Differentiation strategy)^2.
Source: U.K. Data Archive.

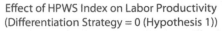

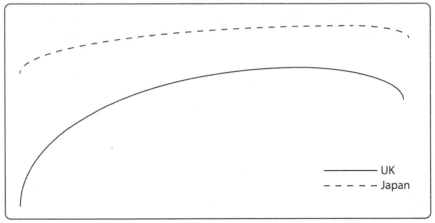

FIGURE 4.1 Effect of HPWS Index on Labor Productivity
Source: Adapted from data available in U.K. Data Archive.

Hypothesis 1 suggested that after a certain point, HPWS practices could lead to decreased returns for small firms. The greater levels of value added may be neutralized by higher costs. For both the United Kingdom ($\beta = -0.09$; $p < 0.01$) and Japan ($\beta = -0.09$; $p < 0.01$), the nonlinear relationships indeed have significance. Figure 4.1 depicts the curvilinear relationship in the absence of differentiation strategy. Returns to HPWS practices are much higher in the United Kingdom (i.e., they have a steeper left side) than in Japan. However, the opposite story holds on the right side of the curves. Japanese firms may not witness a substantial increase in marginal costs; however, U.K. firms may see a faster increase in marginal costs if they introduce more than the optimal number of practices. Overall, depending on the institutional settings, firms may have different degrees of marginal benefits and marginal costs. However, the inverted-U relationship proposed in Hypothesis 1 is supported.

Hypothesis 2 relates to how increasing fit between the HPWS and the differentiation strategy may increasingly enhance marginal benefits and reduce marginal costs. Table 4.1 provides inferential and figure 4.2 visual support for this hypothesis. The fit line (P = S) shows a significant positive linear relationship (U.K.: $a_1 = 0.44$, $p < 0.01$; Japan: $a_1 = 0.27$, $p < 0.01$). Furthermore, the curvilinear relationship along the fit line is positive (i.e., convex). This relationship illustrates that with increasing HPWS practices and greater levels of differentiation strategy, the returns are nonlinear and positive. The

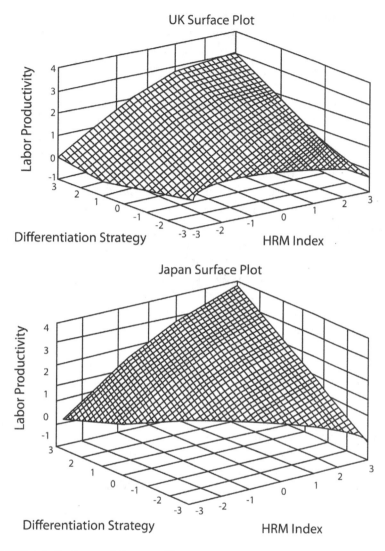

FIGURE 4.2 Surface and Contour Plots
Source: Adapted from data available in U.K. Data Archive.

convex relationship illustrates that the rate of increase in net benefit (marginal benefits − marginal costs) is significant in the presence of differentiation strategy. Given that the relationship between the HPWS index and productivity is expressed as an inverted U, an increase in net benefit suggests that the marginal benefits are increasing and the marginal costs are decreasing, thus explaining the nonlinear rate of change in benefits and costs. The misfit line further corroborates this inference (P $=$ $-$S). Although the linear relationship (x_1) is negative but insignificant for the United Kingdom and Japan, the curvilinear relationship is concave (U.K.: $x_2 = -0.16$, $p < 0.05$; Japan: $x_2 = -0.23$, $p < 0.05$). In other words, firms with a higher HPWS index but low levels of differentiation may experience a rapid deterioration in labor productivity. This trend may be explained by lower marginal benefits being derived from HPWS practices because of lower levels of differentiation and higher costs of implementation. Thus, the evidence supports Hypothesis 2.

Finally, Hypothesis 3 suggests that institutional factors may affect the nature of fit between the HPWS index and differentiation strategy. The surface and contour plots provide visual evidence that the behavior of the fit between the HPWS index and differentiation strategy differs based on institutional settings. The inferences were drawn based on the last column in table 4.2. Based on differences in z-score tests suggested by Cohen and Cohen, all parameters are significantly different between the two institutions.[92] The nonlinear relationship between the HPWS index and labor productivity differs significantly between Japan and the United Kingdom. Figure 4.1 provides a visual depiction of this relationship, which is much steeper in the case of the United Kingdom.

Although the rate of increase in labor productivity in firms with increasing levels of HPWS practices is higher among U.K. firms, Japanese firms have greater labor productivity. The differences in linear and curvilinear parameters along the fit line tell an interesting story. The positive difference in z-score shows that although U.K. firms have greater returns to fit, Japanese firms experience a significant increase in fit. Continuing from Hypothesis 2, this convex difference along the fit line indicates that U.K. firms may experience lower marginal returns and higher marginal costs. Overall, institutional factors play a key role in affecting the relationship between the HPWS index and labor productivity and enhancing the fit between strategy and the HPWS index. Thus, the evidence supports Hypothesis 3.

DISCUSSION AND IMPLICATIONS

The objective of this study was to assess the extent to which returns on HPWS practices are nonlinear for smaller firms. The evidence shows that small firms may maximize their returns to a certain extent by using HPWS practices. The economic argument of marginal benefits and marginal costs discussed earlier may determine the optimal point of use for HPWS practices. Beyond the importance of fit between HPWS practices and strategy, the evidence has demonstrated that fit significantly enhances the marginal benefits and reduces the marginal costs to increase the overall benefits. Most importantly, regarding the role of institutional factors in the effectiveness of HPWS practices, the evidence has shown that Eastern cultural values significantly affect the net benefit from HPWS adoption.

The study has shown that institutional factors play an important role in the degree of effectiveness of HPWS practices. This appears to be one of the few studies that assess the role of costs and benefits in the implementation of HPWS in small firms. While listing both benefits and costs for HPWS practices may be analytically intractable, the overall assessment of the relationship between HPWS practices and productivity supports the nonlinear relationship. While some scholars have suggested that HPWS practices may have overall negative effects on the firm,[93] others have suggested that HPWS practices have overall positive effects on productivity. The findings in this study show that the answer may lie somewhere in between.

Small firms may not categorically avoid HPWS practices, but they may not adopt them disproportionately either. Having a differentiation strategy plays an important role for these firms. More importantly, institutional factors account for much of the overall benefits and costs of HPWS practices. Prior literature on HPWS in small firms focused on firm or environmental factors that affect firm HPWS policies. However, the effectiveness of HPWS is not completely driven by economic motivations that optimize their resources, strategies, and structures; it is also driven by institutional factors. This study explores the role of institutions in affecting such choices. The study indicates that regulatory institutions promoting entrepreneurial growth play a limited role in affecting firms' choices about HPWS and firm performance. By focusing only on high-tech firms with similar characteristics of performance, I drew a reliable understanding of the productivity phenomenon.

In recent years, researchers have increasingly proposed that institutional factors play an important role in HPWS choices.[94] While Datta et al. assessed the degree to which industry dynamics make HPWS practices more or less important, I have moved to a level above the industry to examine whether institutional factors play a significant role.[95] Understanding institutional effects may further aid in understanding the mechanisms of interaction between institutions, industry, and firms. Understanding the differing effectiveness of firms in such contexts may further aid in understanding the relative effects on labor productivity. Scholars in human resource literature have traditionally considered HPWS to be an endogenous choice. The findings from this study indicate that institutions, beyond those within the industry, play a very important role in determining whether small firms adopt HPWS practices.

Paauwe laments that much of the human resource literature focuses on North American HPWS practices while others have focused on HPWS practices in different countries.[96] This appears to be one of the first studies to compare the relative differences among firms' HPWS practices and the effectiveness of these practices in two different cultural contexts. The "quasi-natural" experimental setting with a matched sampling frame provided a unique opportunity to test the relative effects of institutional factors. HPWS literature may potentially benefit from such "experimental settings."

This study contributes to the literature on HPWS in small firms in some important ways. First, it addresses the key question of whether small firms lack resources, ability, or motivation to implement sophisticated HPWS. Most of the previous studies have focused on the voluntary choices of entre-preneurs to grow, acquire certain resources, develop strategies, and develop structures and systems that accommodate growth.[97] The literature review has also revealed that scholars have pointed to human, financial, and out-side resources as being important factors in new firm performance, yet these studies fail to acknowledge how the resources a venture requires depend on the decisions the entrepreneurs have already made for how growth is to be realized. Whereas heterogeneity among firms remains critical for competitive advantage,[98] the results of this study indicate that similarities among firms are crucial as well.[99]

The effectiveness of compensation systems in small firms is contingent upon the institutional environment. Compensation schemes in small firms have become an area of increased interest in recent years.[100] While financial components such as pay level and promotion structures that focus on intrinsic motivations of employees have importance, this study has found that extrin-sic motivations hold equal importance. High-performance work practices are critical in enhancing firm performance and employee growth.[101] However, beyond these previous studies, this study's findings suggest that institutions could play a significant role in the implementation and success of such high-performance work systems (HPWS).

The results indicate that the ability of firms to adopt and exploit HPWS is not independent of institutional demands. Institutional factors ease or make it difficult to implement HPWS practices. Additionally, the results suggest that Japanese firms not only tend to choose greater levels of HPWS, ceteris paribus, but are also able to enhance firm performance. This might be par-tially explained by the fact that implementation of such systems is largely contingent on institutional forces that may facilitate implementation and effectiveness of these systems. For example, in Japanese culture, higher col-lectivism, low focus on masculinity, and a tendency to focus on the long-term are prevalent. Clearly, these factors may significantly enhance firm structures and systems, thereby facilitating innovation.

Managerial Implications

In making decisions on adopting, implementing, and leveraging HPWS practices, the findings provide a few guidelines. In deciding to adopt HPWS practices, small firms must first ask the relevance of human capital in meeting their strategic goals. As small firms with cost leadership may rely less on human capital, the number and scope of human resource practices in these firms should be much lower than in small firms pursuing differentiation strategy.

Next, with greater possibilities of returns from HPWS practices under differentiation strategy, managers in small firms must pick HPWS practices that cannot be subsidized by the institutional environment. By focusing on practices not conducive under specific institutional conditions, small firms can manage and control requisite HPWS practices with limited resources. Finally, because of decreasing scale and scope economies from increasing HPWS, small firms must not aggressively invest in HPWS, as it has decreasing returns under increasing differentiation.

Limitations

This study does have certain limitations. First, because of the nature of self-reported data, issues of key informant bias and common method bias should not be neglected. However, greater levels of reliability and assured confidentiality in the survey reduce the effects of conflated responses. In addition, I also conducted Harman's one-factor analysis, which showed no evidence for the presence of one common factor. Alternatively, institutional data came from different sources, thus reducing the effects of possible common method bias. Second, despite the support for the majority of the hypotheses, the measures might not completely capture the essence of such constructs as institutions, resources, strategies, structures, and systems. More importantly, I did not consider the interrelations between different institutional factors. Future studies could further enhance these measurements. Third, the data employed in this study were cross-sectional in nature. Future longitudinal research should empirically establish the causal claim of this model. More importantly, the effects of mediated moderation through industry-level variables could be useful. Fourth, the study data were limited to two countries, and similar institutional factors may have different effects in other contexts.

Polynomial regression and the response surface methodology approach used here have certain drawbacks. As an extension of multiple regression analysis, polynomial regression assumes that independent variables can be measured without error. When measurements have significant errors, coefficient estimates are negatively affected. In tests with higher order terms, measurement error reduces statistical power. Additionally, this approach requires a priori specification of relationships, which are difficult to foresee, and therefore smaller effects in the data for which there was no existing theoretical basis are likely to arise.

Future Research Directions

The present study provides several directions for future research. Future research may explore the specific mediating roles of components of firms, such as the organizational forms, incentive systems, cultures, different types of resources, and strategic processes in multiple institutional environments. While this research explored the *why* of small firm performance and growth through HPWS practices, future studies may examine the interactive and individual processes of individual HPWS. Other institutional factors, such as country-level culture, may help to explain the distal effects of such institutions on more proximal HPWS institutions within a country. Finally, future research could also extend the current framework by focusing on multilevel models—institutions, industries, and firms—to draw better inferences on HPWS effectiveness.

CONCLUSION

Small firms face very different conditions than larger firms when adopting HPWS practices. How can firms balance increasing benefits with increasing costs when implementing HPWS practices? Do institutional factors play a role in the effectiveness of HPWS practices on firm productivity? The quasi-natural experimental setting showed that although fit between strategy and HPWS practices is obviously critical, irrespective of the institutional setting, cultural institutions play a central role in affecting such fit. Specifically, in the case of small firms in which returns to HPWS practices may not be strictly linear, institutional factors play a key role in affecting the net benefit of labor productivity, beyond that resulting from internal fit.

NOTES

1. Mark A. Huselid, Susan E. Jackson, and Randall S. Schuler, "Technical and Strategic Human Resource Management and Effectiveness as Determinants of Firm Performance," *Academy of Management Journal* 40, 1 (1995): 171–188; Sean A.

Way, "High Performance Work Systems and Intermediate Indicators of Firm Performance within the US Small Business Sector," *Journal of Management* 28, 6 (2002): 765–785.

2. José Wynne, "Wealth as a Determinant of Comparative Advantage," *American Economic Review* 95, 1 (2005): 226–254.

3. Luc Sels, S. De Winne, J. Delmotte, J. Maes, D Faems, and A. Forrier, "Linking HRM and Small Business Performance: An Examination of the Impact of HRM Intensity on the Productivity and Financial Performance of Small Businesses," *Small Business Economics* 26, 1 (2006): 83–101.

4. Ibid.; Melissa S. Cardon and Christopher E. Stevens, "Managing Human Resources in Small Organizations: What Do We Know?" *Human Resource Management Review* 14, 3 (2004): 295–323.

5. Huselid, Jackson, and Schuler, "Technical and Strategic Human Resource Management."

6. Jaap Paauwe and Paul Boselie, "Challenging 'Strategic HRM' and the Relevance of the Institutional Setting," *Human Resource Management Journal* 13, 3 (2003): 56–70.

7. Tahira M. Probst and John Lawler, "Cultural Values as Moderators of Employee Reactions to Job Insecurity: The Role of Individualism and Collectivism," *Applied Psychology* 55, 2 (2006): 234–254.

8. Christine Oliver, "Sustainable Competitive Advantage: Combining Institutional and Resource-based Views," *Strategic Management Journal* 18, 9 (1997): 697–713.

9. Hugh Whittaker and Thelma Quince, *Cambridge Centre for Business Research Survey of British and Japanese Entrepreneurs and Their Businesses, 2000–2002*, [computer file], (Colchester, Essex: U.K. Data Archive [distributor], September 2006), SN: 5458, http://dx.doi.org/10.5255/UKDA-SN-5458-1.

10. Paauwe and Boselie, "Challenging 'Strategic HRM.'"

11. Jay B. Barney and Asli M. Arikan, "The Resource-based View: Origins and Implications," in *The Blackwell Handbook of Strategic Management*, ed. Michael A. Hit, R. Edward Freeman, and Jeffrey S. Harrison (Maiden, MA: Blackwell Publishers, Inc., 2001), 124–188.

12. Patrick M. Wright, "Strategy-HR Fit: Does It Really Matter?" *Human Resource Planning* 21, 4 (1998): 56–57.

13. Damodar Y. Golhar and Satish P. Deshpande, "HRM Practices of Large and Small Canadian Manufacturing Firms," *Journal of Small Business Management* 35, 3 (1997): 23–34; Donald F. Kuratko, John C. Goodale, and Jeffrey S. Hornsby, "Quality Practices for a Competitive Advantage in Smaller Firms," *Journal of Small Business Management* 39, 4 (2001): 293–311; Glenn M. McEvoy, "Small Business Personnel Practices," *Journal of Small Business Management* 22, 4 (1984): 1–8.

14. David J. Flanagan and Satish P. Deshpande, "Top Management's Perceptions of Changes in HRM Practices after Union Elections in Small Firms," *Journal of Small Business Management* 34, 4 (1996): 23–34.

15. Cardon and Stevens, "Managing Human Resources in Small Organizations."

16. Sels, et al., "Linking HRM and Small Business Performance."

17. Allan Macpherson and Robin Holt, "Knowledge, Learning and Small Firm Growth: A Systematic Review of the Evidence," *Research Policy* 36, 2 (2007): 172–192.

18. Brian Harney and Tony Dundon, "Capturing Complexity: Developing an Integrated Approach to Analysing HRM in SMEs," *Human Resource Management Journal* 16, 1 (2006): 48–73.

19. Paul Edwards and Monder Ram, "Surviving on the Margins of the Economy: Working Relationships in Small, Low-wage Firms," *Journal of Management Studies* 43, 4 (2006): 895–916.

20. Cardon and Stevens, "Managing Human Resources in Small Organizations"; Sels, et al., "Linking HRM and Small Business Performance."

21. William N. Cooke, "Employee Participation Programs, Group-based Incentives, and Company Performance: A Union-nonunion Comparison," *Industrial and Labor Relations Review* 47, 4 (1994): 594.

22. Peter Cappelli and David Neumark, "External Job Churning and Internal Job Flexibility" (NBER Working Paper Series, Working Paper 8111, National Bureau of Economic Research, Cambridge, MA, February 2001), www.nber.org/papers/w8111.pdf.

23. Way, "High Performance Work Systems and Intermediate Indicators of Firm Performance within the US Small Business Sector."

24. Sels, et al., "Linking HRM and Small Business Performance."

25. Golhar and Deshpande, "HRM Practices of Large and Small Canadian Manufacturing Firms."

26. Lloyd Baird and Ilan Meshoulam, "Managing Two Fits of Strategic Human Resource Management," *Academy of Management Review* 13, 1 (1988): 116–128.

27. Howard E. Aldrich and Ellen Auster, "Even Dwarfs Started Small: Liabilities of Age and Size and Their Strategic Implications," *Research in Organizational Behavior* 8 (1986): 165–198.

28. Howard E. Aldrich and C. Marlene Fiol, "Fools Rush In? The Institutional Context of Industry Creation," *Academy of Management Review* 19, 4 (1994): 645–670; Paauwe and Boselie, "Challenging 'Strategic HRM'"; Mark C. Suchman, "Managing Legitimacy: Strategic and Institutional Approaches," *Academy of Management Review* 20, 3 (1995): 571–610; Patrick M. Wright and Gary C. McMahan, "Theoretical Perspectives for Strategic Human Resource Management," *Journal of Management* 18, 2 (1992): 295.

29. Suchman, "Managing Legitimacy"; Wright and McMahan, "Theoretical Perspectives for Strategic Human Resource Management."

30. David L. Deephouse, "To Be Different, or to Be the Same? It's a Question (and Theory) of Strategic Balance," *Strategic Management Journal* 20, 2 (1999): 147; Oliver, "Sustainable Competitive Advantage."

31. Howard E. Aldrich and Amy L. Kenworthy, "The Accidental Entrepreneur: Campbellian Antinomies and Organizational Foundings," in *Variations in Organization*

Science: In Honor of Donald T. Campbell, ed. Joel A.C. Baum and Bill McKelvey, (Newbury Park, CA: Sage, 1998): 19–33.

32. Chao C. Chen, Xiao-Ping Chen, and James R. Meindl, "How Can Cooperation Be Fostered? The Cultural Effects of Individualism-collectivism," *Academy of Management Review* 23, 2 (1998): 285–304.

33. Anne S. Tsui, Hui Wang, and Katherine R. Xin, "Organizational Culture in China: An Analysis of Culture Dimensions and Culture Types," *Management and Organization Review* 2, 3 (2006): 345–376.

34. Andrew Neal, Michael A. West, and Malcolm G. Patterson, "Do Organizational Climate and Competitive Strategy Moderate the Relationship between Human Resource Management and Productivity?," *Journal of Management* 31, 4 (2005): 492.

35. Michael E. Porter, *Competitive Strategy: Techniques for Analyzing Industries and Competitors* (New York: Free Press, 1980).

36. James P. Guthrie, "High Involvement Work Practices, Turnover and Productivity: Evidence from New Zealand," *Academy of Management Journal* 44, 1 (2001): 180–190; Randall S. Schuler and Susan E. Jackson, "Linking Competitive Strategies with Human Resource Management Practices," *Strategic Human Resource Management* (1999): 159–176; Mark A. Youndt, Scott A. Snell, James W. Dean, Jr., and David P. Lepak, "Human Resource Management, Manufacturing Strategy, and Firm Performance," *Academy of Management Journal* 39, 4 (1996): 836–866.

37. David P. Lepak and Scott A. Snell, "Managing the Human Resource Architecture for Knowledge-based Competition," *Strategic Human Resource Management* (2006): 333.

38. Torstein Nesheim, Karen M. Olsen, and Arne L. Kalleberg, "Externalizing the Core: Firms' Use of Employment Intermediaries in the Information and Communication Technology Industries," *Human Resource Management* 46, 2 (2007): 247–264.

39. B. Michael Arthur and Chris Hendry, "Human Resource Strategy and the Emergent Strategy of Small to Medium Sized Business Units," *The Journal of Human Resource Management* 1, 3 (1990): 235–250; John Paul MacDuffie, "Human Resource Bundles and Manufacturing Performance: Organizational Logic and Flexible Production Systems in the World Auto Industry," *Industrial & Labor Relations Review* 48, 2 (1995): 197–221.

40. Barry A. Colbert, "The Complex Resource-based View: Implications for Theory and Practice in Strategic Human Resource Management I," *Strategic Human Resource Management* (2006): 98.

41. Deepak K. Datta, James P. Guthrie, and Patrick M. Wright, "Human Resource Management and Labor Productivity: Does Industry Matter?" *Academy of Management Journal* 48, 1 (2005): 135–145.

42. Douglass C. North, *Institutions, Institutional Change and Economic Performance* (Cambridge, U.K.: Cambridge University Press, 1990).

43. John W. Meyer and Brian Rowan, "Institutionalized Organizations: Formal Structure as Myth and Ceremony," *The American Journal of Sociology* 83, 2

(1977): 340–363; Lynne G. Zucker, "The Role of Institutionalization in Cultural Persistence," *American Sociological Review* 42, 5 (1977): 726–743.

44. Suchman, "Managing Legitimacy."

45. Gaylen N. Chandler, Chalon Keller, and Douglas W. Lyon, "Unraveling the Determinants and Consequences of an Innovation-supportive Organizational Culture," *Entrepreneurship: Theory and Practice* 25, 1 (2000); Oliver, "Sustainable Competitive Advantage."

46. Ibid.

47. J. Douglas Orton and Karl E. Weick, "Loosely Coupled Systems: A Reconceptualization," *Academy of Management Review* 15, 2 (1990): 203–223; Patrick M. Wright and Wendy R. Boswell, "Desegregating HRM: A Review and Synthesis of Micro and Macro Human Resource Management Research," *Journal of Management* 28, 3 (2002): 247–276.

48. James C. Hayton, "Strategic Human Capital Management in SMEs: An Empirical Study of Entrepreneurial Performance." *Human Resource Management* 42, 4 (2003): 375–391.

49. K Praveen Parboteeah, Martin Hoegl, and John B. Cullen, "Managers' Gender Role Attitudes: A Country Institutional Profile Approach," *Journal of International Business Studies* 39, 5 (2008): 795–813.

50. Geert Hofstede, *Cultures & Consequences* (Thousand Oaks, CA: Sage Publications, 2001).

51. Pankaj Ghemawat, "Semiglobalization and International Business Strategy," *Journal of International Business Studies* 34, 2 (2003): 138–152; Hofstede, *Cultures & Consequences*; Bruce Kogut and Harbir Singh, "The Effect of National Culture on the Choice of Entry Mode," *Journal of International Business Studies* 19, 3 (1988): 411–432; Kwok Leung, et al., "Social Axioms and Values: A Cross-cultural Examination," *European Journal of Personality* 21, 2 (2007).

52. James C. Hayton, Gerard George, and Shaker A. Zahra, "National Culture and Entrepreneurship: A Review of Behavioral Research," *Entrepreneurship: Theory and Practice* 26, 4 (2002): 33–53; P. A. Herbig and J. C. Miller, "Culture and Technology: Does the Traffic Move in Both Directions?" *Journal of Global Marketing* 6, 3 (1992): 75–104; Scott Shane, "Uncertainty Avoidance and the Preference for Innovation Championing Roles," *Journal of International Business Studies* 26, 1 (1995).

53. Shalom H. Schwartz, "A Theory of Cultural Values and Some Implications for Work," *Values and Work: A Special Issue of the Journal Applied Psychology* (1999): 23.

54. Harry C. Triandis, "The Self and Social Behavior in Differing Cultural Contexts," *Psychological Review* 96, 3 (1989): 506–520.

55. Fons Trompenaars and Charles Hampden-Turner, *Riding the Waves of Culture: Understanding Cultural Diversity in Business* (London: Brealey, 1998).

56. Scott Shane, "Cultural Influences on National Rates of Innovation," *Journal of Business Venturing* 8, 1 (1993): 59–73.

57. Cheryl Nakata and K. Sivakumar, "National Culture and New Product Development: An Integrative Review," *The Journal of Marketing* 60, 1 (1996): 61–72.

58. Tom Elfring and Willem Hulsink, "Networks in Entrepreneurship: The Case of High-technology Firms," *Small Business Economics* 21, 4 (2003): 409–422.

59. Scott Shane, S. Venkataraman, and Ian MacMillan, "Cultural Differences in Innovation Championing Strategies," *Journal of Management* 21, 5 (1995): 931.

60. Irene K. H. Chew and Joseph Putti, "Relationship on Work-related Values of Singaporean and Japanese Managers in Singapore," *Human Relations* 48, 10 (1995): 1149; Michael Clugston, Jon P. Howell, and Peter W. Dorfman, "Does Cultural Socialization Predict Multiple Bases and Foci of Commitment?" *Journal of Management* 26, 1 (2000): 5.

61. Nakata and Sivakumar, "National Culture and New Product Development."

62. Hofstede, *Cultures & Consequences*.

63. Peter Smith, Shaun Dugan, and Fons Trompenaars, "National Culture and the Values of Organizational Employees: A Dimensional Analysis across 43 Nations," *Journal of Cross-cultural Psychology* 27, 2 (1996): 231.

64. James R. Detert, Roger G. Schroeder, and John J. Mauriel, "A Framework for Linking Culture and Improvement Initiatives in Organizations," *Academy of Management Review* 25, 4 (2000): 850–863.

65. Victoria Miroshnik, "Culture and International Management: A Review," *Journal of Management Development* 21, 7 (2002): 521–544.

66. Whittaker and Quince, "Cambridge Centre for Business Research Survey of British and Japanese Entrepreneurs and Their Businesses, 2000–2002."

67. Markus Pudelko, "A Comparison of HRM Systems in the USA, Japan and Germany in Their Socio-economic Context," *Human Resource Management Journal* 16, 2 (2006): 123–153.

68. John E. Delery and Jason D. Shaw, "The Strategic Management of People in Work Organizations: Review, Synthesis, and Extension," in *Research in Personnel and Human Resource Management*, ed. Gerald R. Ferris (Stamford, CT: JAI Press, 2001): 167–197.

69. Paul Samuelson and William Nordhaus, *Principles of Economics* (New York: McGraw-Hill, 1989).

70. David E. Guest, "Human Resource Management and Performance: A Review and Research Agenda," *International Journal of Human Resource Management* 8, 3 (1997): 263–276.

71. Lee Dyer and Todd Reeves, "Human Resource Strategies and Firm Performance: What Do We Know and Where Do We Need to Go?," *International Journal of Human Resource Management* 6, 3 (1995): 656–670; Paul Boselie, Graham Dietz, and Corine Boon, "Commonalities and Contradictions in HRM and Performance Research," *Human Resource Management Journal* 15, 3 (2005): 67–94.

72. Guthrie, "High Involvement Work Practices, Turnover and Productivity"; Mark A. Huselid, "The Impact of Human Resource Management Practices on Turnover, Productivity, and Corporate Financial Performance," *Academy of Management Journal* 38 (1995): 635–672; Marianne J. Koch and Rita Gunther McGrath, "Improving Labor Productivity: Human Resource Management Policies Do Matter," *Strategic Management Journal* 17, 5 (1996): 335–354.

73. Neal, West, and Patterson, "Do Organizational Climate and Competitive Strategy Moderate the Relationship between Human Resource Management and Productivity?"

74. Clint Chadwick and Peter Cappelli, "The Performance Effects of Competing Human Resource Systems" (working paper, 2000); Sels, et al., "Linking HRM and Small Business Performance."

75. Delery and Shaw, "The Strategic Management of People in Work Organizations"; Huselid, "The Impact of Human Resource Management Practices on Turnover, Productivity, and Corporate Financial Performance"; Patrick M. Wright and Scott A. Snell, "Toward an Integrative View of Strategic Human Resource Management," *Human Resource Management Review* 1, 3 (1991): 203–225.

76. Brian Becker and Barry Gerhart, "The Impact of Human Resource Management on Organizational Performance: Progress and Prospect," *Academy of Management Journal* 39 (1996): 779–801; John Delery, "Issues of Fit in Strategic Human Resource Management: Implications for Research," *Human Resource Management Review* 8, 3 (1998): 289–309.

77. MacDuffie, "Human Resource Bundles and Manufacturing Performance."

78. Brian E. Becker and Mark A. Huselid, "High Performance Work Systems and Firm Performance: A Synthesis of Research and Managerial Implications," in *Research in Personnel and Human Resource Management*, ed. G. R. Ferris (Stamford, CT: JAI Press, 1998): 53–101; Delery, "Issues of Fit in Strategic Human Resource Management."

79. Gregory G. Dess and Peter S. Davis, "Porter's (1980) Generic Strategies as Determinants of Strategic Group Membership and Organizational Performance," *Academy of Management Journal* 27, 3 (1984): 467–488; Rui Jácome, João Lisboa, and Mahmoud Yasin, "Time-based Differentiation—An Old Strategic Hat or an Effective Strategic Choice: An Empirical Investigation," *European Business Review* 14, 3 (2002): 184–193; Peter T. Ward and Rebecca Duray, "Manufacturing Strategy in Context: Environment, Competitive Strategy and Manufacturing Strategy," *Journal of Operations Management* 18, 2 (2000): 123–138; Shaker A. Zahra and William C. Bogner, "Technology Strategy and Software New Ventures' Performance Exploring the Moderating Effect of the Competitive Environment," *Journal of Business Venturing* 15, 2 (2000): 135–173.

80. Jeffrey R. Edwards and Mark E. Parry, "On the Use of Polynomial Regression Equations as an Alternative to Difference Scores in Organizational Research," *Academy of Management Journal* (1993): 1577–1613.

81. Datta, Guthrie, and Wright, "Human Resource Management and Labor Productivity."

82. Guthrie, "High Involvement Work Practices, Turnover and Productivity."

83. Ibid.; Gedaliahui H. Harel and Shay S. Tzafrir, "The Effect of Human Resource Management Practices on the Perceptions of Organizational and Market Performance of the Firm," *Human Resource Management* 38, 3 (1999): 185–199.

84. Raymond E. Miles and Charles C. Snow, "Designing Strategic Human Resource Systems," *Organizational Dynamics* 13, 1 (1984): 36–52.

85. Johan Maes, Luc Sels, and Filip Roodhooft, "Modelling the Link between Management Practices and Financial Performance: Evidence from Small Construction Companies," *Small Business Economics* 25, 1 (2005): 17–34.

86. Jennifer W. Spencer, "Firms' Knowledge-sharing Strategies in the Global Innovation System: Empirical Evidence from the Flat Panel Display Industry," *Strategic Management Journal* 4, 3 (2003): 217–233.

87. G. Tomas M. Hult, et al., "Data Equivalence in Cross-cultural International Business Research: Assessment and Guidelines," *Journal of International Business Studies* 39, 6 (2008): 1027–1044.

88. Joseph F. Hair, Rolph E. Anderson, Ronald L. Tatham, and William C. Black, *Multivariate Data Analysis* (New York: Prentice Hall, 1998).

89. Phillip M. Podsakoff and Dennis W. Organ, "Self-reports in Organizational Research: Problems and Perspectives," *Journal of Management* 12 (1986): 531–544.

90. Richard P. Bagozzi and Youjae Yi, "On the Evaluation of Structural Equation Models," *Journal of the Academy of Marketing Science* 16, 1 (1988): 74.

91. N. Venkatraman, "Strategic Orientation of Business Enterprises: The Construct, Dimensionality, and Measurement," *Management Science* 35, 8 (1989): 942–962.

92. Jacob Cohen and Patricia Cohen, *Applied Multiple Regression/Correlation Analysis for the Behavioral Sciences* (Hillsdale, NJ.: Lawrence Erlbaum, 1983).

93. Theresa M. Welbourne and Alice O. Andrews, "Predicting the Performance of Initial Public Offerings: Should Human Resource Management Be in the Equation?" *Academy of Management Journal* 39, 4 (1996): 891–919.

94. Paauwe and Boselie, "Challenging 'Strategic HRM.'"

95. Datta, Guthrie, and Wright, "Human Resource Management and Labor Productivity."

96. Paauwe and Boselie, "Challenging 'Strategic HRM'"; Sels, et al., "Linking HRM and Small Business Performance"; Luc Sels, et al., "Unravelling the HRM-performance Link: Value-creating and Cost-increasing Effects of Small Business HRM," *Journal of Management Studies* 43, 2 (2006): 319–342.

97. J. Robert Baum, Edwin A. Locke, and Ken G. Smith, "A Multidimensional Model of Venture Growth," *Academy of Management Journal* 44, 2 (2001): 292–303; Thomas M. Box, Margaret A. White, and Steve H. Barr, "A Contingency Model of New Manufacturing Firm Performance," *Entrepreneurship: Theory and Practice* 18, 2 (1993); James J. Chrisman, Alan Bauerschmidt, and Charles W. Hofer, "The Determinants of New Venture Performance: An Extended Model," *Entrepreneurship: Theory and Practice* 23, 1 (1998): 5–7; Sanjay Prasad Thakur, "Size of Investment, Opportunity Choice and Human Resources in New Venture Growth Some Typologies," *Journal of Business Venturing* 14, 3 (1999): 283–309.

98. Jay Barney, "Firm Resources and Sustained Competitive Advantage," *Journal of Management* 17, 1 (1991): 99–120.

99. Michael T. Hannan and John Freeman, "The Population Ecology of Organizations," *American Sociological Review* 49, 5 (1976): 149–164.

100. Melissa S. Cardon, "Contingent Labor as an Enabler of Entrepreneurial Growth," *Human Resource Management* 42, 4 (2003): 357–373.

101. Bruce R. Barringer, Foard F. Jones, and Pamela S. Lewis, "A Qualitative Study of the Management Practices of Rapid-growth Firms and How Rapid-growth Firms Mitigate the Managerial Capacity Problem," *Journal of Developmental Entrepreneurship* 3, 2 (1998): 97–122; Chandler, Keller, and Lyon, "Unraveling the Determinants and Consequences of an Innovation-supportive Organizational Culture"; Welbourne and Andrews, "Predicting the Performance of Initial Public Offerings."

5

Family Businesses and How They Internationalize: A Review

Manuel Eberhard and Justin B. Craig

The international expansion of family businesses (e.g., through exports and foreign direct investment) emerged as an important topic in the small business literature almost 30 years ago. At the time, because of the increased international exposure of firms worldwide, pioneering scholars began to question whether the internationalization of family businesses was distinct from that of other businesses. The accumulated body of knowledge remained narrow and fragmented in the subsequent years, with a limited number of studies having analyzed the strategic approaches of family businesses and even fewer having examined the internationalization strategies adopted.[1] It is still not clear what factors unique to family businesses distinguish their internationalization behavior and what resources need to be invested to instigate their international venturing.[2]

This chapter's contribution is anchored by the following research question: how does being a family business impact internationalization? While the extant literature indicates that family involvement in the firm matters with respect to internationalization, the precise effect remains unclear and ambivalent.[3] To solve this confusion and address our research question, we review 53 peer-reviewed journal articles, beginning with the publication of the first article in 1991 and ending with articles published in 2013. Following rigorous literature review protocols enables us to present the key constructs that have emerged from the theoretical and empirical work in this area. We structure our findings according to (1) the impact of family management and ownership on internationalization and (2) the internationalization process of family businesses. We identify areas of controversy and formulate questions for further research. This review is timely, given that, along with other streams of family business literature, the internationalization focus has evolved into a significant research area.[4] Publications on the topic have almost tripled in the past five years, indicating the contemporary nature of family business internationalization research and the growing interest in this phenomenon.

Our review is organized as follows: We first highlight the significance of family businesses in today's economy and address definitional challenges. Following this, we provide a brief description of the research methodology employed. We then present our findings according to the above-mentioned key constructs and follow with a discussion of managerial implications and potential future work that can enrich this research area.

SIGNIFICANCE OF FAMILY BUSINESSES AND DEFINITIONAL CHALLENGES

Family businesses dominate the economic landscape in most developed countries,[5] and recently a rising number of researchers have taken an interest in this type of business.[6] Across Europe, family businesses constitute about 70–80 percent of all businesses, conservatively accounting for 40–50 percent of employment.[7] Similarly, in the United States, family businesses constitute around 90 percent of businesses and account for 60 percent of employment. Most of these family enterprises are small businesses, and it is particularly in smaller firms that the family influence becomes most prevalent.[8] However, the complexities associated with managing a family business are not fully addressed by classical management theory.[9] This is because the intertwinement of family and business leads to an extraordinary amount of emotional commitment.[10] Recent studies have aimed to explain this additional complexity by using the concept of socioemotional wealth (SEW), first introduced by Gomez-Mejia et al.[11] In contrast to former approaches that struggle to accommodate the family firm context, these authors emphasize the preservation of SEW, referring to nonfinancial utilities of the business as the most important objective for family business owners. Thus, the preservation of SEW may serve as the predictor of strategic choices in family businesses.[12]

Handler points out that defining a family firm is the first and most important challenge for family business scholars.[13] Litz identified two main approaches to defining family businesses: a structure-based approach and an intention-based approach.[14] The first approach focuses on the structural dimensions of the organization, using the core constructs of ownership and management.[15] As such, family businesses are defined as those owned, controlled, or managed by a family unit. The second approach focuses on intraorganizational aspirations. It considers the preferences of an organization's members toward intraorganizational family-based relatedness.[16] In the literature of family business internationalization, most articles define family businesses through the combination of ownership and management.[17] These studies follow Gallo and Sveen's seminal paper in which a family business is "a firm where the family owns the majority of stock and exercises full management control."[18]

In addition, Chua, Chrisman, and Sharma propose that a company is a family business because it behaves as one and that this behavior is distinct from that of nonfamily businesses.[19] Accordingly, if being a family business is a matter of the behavior of the people, they can only behave as a family business if the people consider their company to be a family business.[20] In this review, we include all articles that focus on family businesses, irrespective of the definition employed. Because of the definitional challenges, however, it is important to recognize that family businesses are heterogeneous and that the interpretation of any results needs to take this into consideration.

METHODOLOGY

The extensive literature collation followed accepted guidelines for a systematic review: (1) planning the review, (2) conducting the review, and (3) reporting and disseminating the results.[21] At the first stage, we identified all relevant family business and internationalization publications by searching for keywords in scientific databases. These included Business Source Complete (EBSCO), ProQuest, ISI Web of Knowledge, Google Scholar, Sage Journals Online, and Science Direct. The relevant keywords were taken from the literature and included combinations of the following terms: *internationalization, entry mode, entry process, international trade, international operation, globalization, family firm, family business, family-owned business, ownership, family involvement,* and *family corporation.*

To ensure high-quality standards, we only considered articles published in peer-reviewed academic journals. In all, we considered 53 articles for the final review. These articles were published in 27 different academic journals. Most articles appeared in the following journals: *Family Business Review* (10), *Journal of International Business Studies* (4), *Entrepreneurship Theory and Practice* (3), *Journal of Small Business Management, Management International Review* (3), and *Journal of Small Business and Enterprise Development* (3). The majority (39 of 53) were published between 2005 and 2012, with a peak of interest between 2008 and 2012.

FINDINGS

This section explores the impact of family on the internationalization of firms. First, as described earlier, most scholars use the constructs of management and ownership to extract the family influence. Consequently, we distill the positive and negative aspects of family involvement in management and ownership on firm internationalization. In addition, several studies examine the influence of sourcing supplementary external capital (e.g., venture capital; private equity) on family businesses' internationalization. Therefore, we continue by examining the effect of external shareholders in the family business. This is followed by the examination of *how* family businesses internationalize. We distinguish this process based on four established theories.

Impact of Family Involvement in Management and Ownership on Internationalization

Management and ownership structures influence the way companies define, coordinate, and address business and family-related objectives[22] and thereby influence internationalization strategy.[23] The concept of family involvement in management is thereby distinct from family involvement in ownership of the firm, given that family-owned companies can be managed by family or nonfamily members.[24] Furthermore, other companies and external shareholders, such as institutional investors and venture capitalists, can hold ownership stakes in the family business and thus influence their international expansion.[25]

Family Involvement in Ownership

The impact of family ownership on internationalization has been a controversial issue. Several studies have revealed that family ownership negatively influences the internationalization of the firm.[26] In their seminal work, Gallo and Sveen identify family ownership as a restraining factor.[27] Fernandez and Nieto draw the same conclusion, using a sample of 6,000 Spanish family businesses.[28] Bhaumik et al. claim that the proportion of a family businesses' assets held overseas declines with higher concentrations of ownership, justified by the higher perceived risk of internationalization with higher shares of family ownership.[29] Family ownership not only hinders the firm's international extent but also limits the geographic diversity of its international activities.[30] The perceived risk of operating in several foreign markets increases with rising family ownership. George, Wiklund, and Zahra confirm the risk-aversion tendency by demonstrating that internationalization declines as the management's ownership in the firm increases.[31]

There is further evidence that businesses with family ownership are less inclined to invest overseas and have a smaller proportion of their assets invested in other countries than nonfamily businesses. If an "average family firm, with its strategic simplicity and attachment to its home business culture, is not given an impetus to invest overseas by factors such as size of the domestic market and availability of resources in the home country, it would be reluctant to undertake outward foreign direct investment (FDI)."[32] The research framed by agency theory shows that firms that are founder owned, as many family businesses are, are less likely to pursue a high-risk entry strategy than firms with more dispersed ownership structures.[33] From the family perspective, committing too many resources to a single venture is associated with high risk and adverse-selection problems.[34]

Conversely, a number of studies have identified a positive relationship between family ownership and internationalization.[35] Puig and Perez point out that family ownership is not in itself an obstacle for growth and internationalization.[36] In fact, family businesses are more likely to search actively for opportunities in the international market space to ensure the sustainability of the business for future generations. Family businesses have a patient outlook to capital, which is linked to their focus on generational sustainability, and are therefore more willing to commit financial resources to such long-term strategies as internationalization.[37] Strange et al. associate high levels of family ownership with FDI locations that offer both high risk and potential reward because of the superior monitoring abilities and longer time horizons of family shareholders in comparison to more diffused shareholders.[38] This is supported by Carr and Bateman, who examined 65 of the world's largest family businesses.[39] They suggest that family-owned businesses are slightly more internationally oriented than non-family-owned businesses.

While extant empirical studies are conflicted regarding the role of family ownership, Sciascia et al.'s study provides possible explanations for these opposing findings.[40] They suggest an inverted U-shaped relationship between family ownership and internationalization, where moderate levels of family ownership are associated with the highest level of internationalization. The stewardship effect of increasing family ownership fosters continuity and stability. However, in cases where family ownership becomes excessive, such negative effects as risk aversion, low resource endowment, and conflicts among family members reduce the positive effects of family ownership predicted by the stewardship perspective.[41]

Raising Capital through External Public and Corporate Ownership

Family businesses were found to be unwilling to access external capital for their growth strategies; self-financing appears to remain the first option.[42] This aspiration is a consequence of the family's long-term commitment to the business and ensures that the family heritage can be passed on to the following generations. This risk-averse behavior, in combination with the objective to maintain total control over the business, restricts family businesses to raise financial capital through loans from lending institutions or by bringing in outside equity.[43] This financial policy, which incorporates low debt and high dependency on self-financing, reduces expansion chances and decreases the probability of using high-level equity modes.[44] Therefore, family businesses are highly dependent on their access to financial resources and the family's willingness to commit those to internationalization-related activities.

Interestingly, studies have shown that family businesses that raise external capital from outside the family circle have an undisputed advantage in their internationalization strategy.[45] This is attributed to three reasons.

First, the corporate investor can help the family business accumulate necessary resources for their intended internationalization. To implement a successful internationalization, several activities are often mandatory, such as hiring new employees, building up a manufacturing plant, and engaging in promotion. A lack of financial resources represents an obstacle to pursuing those and similar activities.

Second, the new shareholders will be keen to introduce formal governance mechanisms aimed at resolving the potential conflicts of interest emerging from the coalescence of family and business systems. The decision making in family businesses is often centralized around the owner-manager.[46] In these situations, control systems are often not in place or are very informal, lines of authority are not always clear, and information systems can be poorly developed.[47] These idiosyncratic communication and decision-making practices facilitate responding to contingencies in family businesses; however, they restrict their ability to pursue a national or international expansion strategy.[48] Therefore, external shareholders may encourage the family business to implement structures and systems best suited to the firm's strategy.[49]

Third, external owners bring in social and professional networks from their previous international ventures that help to establish important relationships with external stakeholders.[50] These networks may stimulate the awareness of foreign market opportunities,[51] trigger firms' initial internationalization intention, and promote credibility in foreign markets.[52]

These three explanations help the family business to create and maintain a sustainable competitive advantage in the international marketplace, which it can leverage through venturing abroad. Furthermore, the risk averseness of family businesses diminishes when other partners are invested in the business, leading to a higher willingness to take risks through internationalization.[53] Hence, with the introduction of institutional investors and venture capitalists to the ownership registry, the international operations increase significantly. It can be claimed, therefore, that corporate (i.e., nonfamily) ownership offsets the partially found unwillingness of family businesses to invest overseas.

Calabro, Torchia, Pukall, and Mussolino have extended this discussion to external foreign investors and, similar to the previous findings, also found a positive effect on the firm's internationalization.[54] Arregle et al. demonstrate that this positive relationship is further moderated by the level of environmental heterogeneity and past performance.[55] In uncertain and complex environments, finding the right external shareholders will be more challenging, and families may be less willing to accept external party ownership. Additionally, in heterogeneous environments, family members are more likely to come into conflict with external shareholders, provoking conflicts that may harm the firm's internationalization. A positive past performance provides the firm with additional resources and eases the demand for external shareholders. Hence, their positive impact on internationalization is weaker in times of firm prosperity.

Family Involvement in Operating Management

Most studies have shown that family involvement in management, often measured as the percentage of family members in management, restricts the number of countries entered by family businesses.[56] Family members approach internationalization with caution, trying to maximize revenues from particular markets rather than targeting a broad range of markets. Studies have shown that family businesses experience the risks connected to internationalization more strongly than nonfamily businesses.[57] In family businesses, the separation between business and personal objectives often becomes blurred.[58] As a result of the mixture of business and personal interests, family businesses may suffer from high agency costs rooted in altruism and self-control.[59] A conflict of interest arises when both family and business objectives need to be addressed while preserving family harmony.[60] This has the potential to lead to management decisions that are beneficial for the family but unfavorable for the business.[61] In addition, many family business owner-managers lack the knowledge of the international market space and the necessary foreign contacts, international experience, or language skills to expand their business across borders.[62] Banalieva and Eddleston show that businesses managed by family members perform worse than businesses managed by nonfamily members when the company has a global strategic focus.[63]

This dilemma is less prominent in family businesses with a nonfamily CEO. Employing nonfamily managers leads to an increase in managerial capabilities, less confusion between personal and business interests, and ultimately lowers the risk aversion.[64] Cerrato and Piva support this notion by showing that employing managers from outside the family positively impacts the firm's choice to enter a foreign market.[65] Despite the positive impact of nonfamily members in management, family businesses were found to have lower levels of qualified managers.[66] They often solely rely on familial ties for their upper-management positions, thereby restricting growth ambitions to the limited pool of resources of their descendants.[67] The difficulties for nonfamily managers to develop a career in competition with family members diminish family businesses' attractiveness.[68] The incentive and promotion systems are strongly biased toward family members.[69] Consequently, they suffer from an adverse-selection problem, making it more difficult to attract qualified, professional managers.[70] This scarcity of qualified people negatively influences the rate at which family businesses grow internationally.[71]

Family businesses also face the challenge of generational succession, an attribute that is often described as being characteristic of family businesses. Succession generally incorporates the transfer of management from the incumbent to the succeeding generation,[72] and it can impact internationalization differently,[73] as each generation brings new management styles, ideas, and objectives into the family business.[74]

Many family businesses aim to offer career opportunities for subsequent generations. As the major management positions are usually already occupied by the incumbent generation, Gallo and Pont have shown that family businesses pursue an internationalization strategy to open work opportunities for their successors.[75] Similarly, successors' ambitions to look for new responsibilities within the family business may initiate the internationalization process.[76] Subsequent generations often have more information and are better prepared and qualified to implement the internationalization process.[77]

However, succession can also restrict internationalization.[78] Following generations perceive internationalization as more risky than previous generations and have a skeptical attitude toward export participation.[79] During the generational transfer process, the search for union and harmony within the family is likely to become a factor that hinders the internationalization process.[80] Okoroafo states that if family businesses do not become involved in foreign markets in the first or second generation, they are unlikely to do so in later generations.[81]

Family Involvement in the Board of Directors

Similar to the findings for operating management, studies support the notion that a board of directors mixed with family and nonfamily members will lead to the highest internationalization outcome. Zahra argues that family members on the firm's board bring in elements of stewardship, which increases identification with the firm and ultimately leads to more internationalization.[82] From our review, we can say that past studies seem to agree that a low to moderate level of family involvement in the board of directors facilitates internationalization; however, a board of directors filled exclusively with members of the family leads to inward thinking and limited access to know-how.[83] This is because nonfamily members provide access to critical resources that are beyond the family members' horizon.[84] Hence, a strong presence of nonfamily members on the board of directors facilitates firm internationalization.[85] In a recent study, Sciascia, Mazzola, Astrachan, and Pieper confirmed this nonlinear relationship.[86] Specifically, a low level of family involvement in the firm's board of directors maximizes the level of firm internationalization.

Summary Observation

In sum, it appears that the majority of studies have found negative impacts of excessive family involvement in operating management, the board of directors, and ownership structures. Moderate levels of family influence have been found to provide some positive stewardship effects on the business as long as family and business interests are in balance and not dominated by either side. It is also worth noting that some studies could not find any persistent difference between family and nonfamily businesses. For example, Graves and Thomas highlight that although the extent of family business internationalization is less than that of nonfamily businesses, the difference was not persistent over time.[87] This implies that the greatest challenge faced by family businesses is initiating the internationalization process.

The Internationalization Process of Family Businesses

The following section examines the family effect on the processes of firm internationalization. This incorporates the *how* to expand internationally, specifically the pattern, pace, and rhythm of internationalization.[88] According to Chandra, Styles, and Wilkinson, we distinguish firm internationalization processes into three approaches: sequential approach, born-global approach, and network approach.[89]

Sequential Model

Most family businesses follow a sequential internationalization process, as stated by the Uppsala School,[90] where firms usually start the process of internationalization in countries that are physically and culturally close to the domestic market.[91] As a result, physical distance appears to be a relevant and salient factor, mainly because of the general cautiousness caused by family presence. Family businesses with a strong stewardship attitude especially prefer to follow the sequential model. This is caused by the family managers' strong sense of duty toward the other family members to grow in a cautious manner.[92]

However, physical distance can be compressed substantially by institutional convergences and mutual benchmarking between societies in an age of globalization. Therefore, not only the physical distance but also the role of institutional compatibility as a strategic factor has influenced family businesses' decisions on locations for foreign expansion.[93] The pace of a family businesses' expansion is slow and gradual, focusing on one market at a time, and tends to be financed out of retained earnings and owner contributions rather than external funding. Family business owner-managers seek to maximize revenues from a selected range of foreign markets instead of aggressively venturing abroad on a more general front.[94] They commonly start with conventional market entry strategies such as direct sales and the use of agents as well as distributors, and their international strategy tends to remain ad hoc, opportunistic, and reactive to particular opportunities. As family businesses gain more experience and confidence in foreign markets, their international commitment increases over time.

Born-Global

Other research suggests that family businesses do not follow a sequential path of international expansion but instead internationalize rapidly to multiple markets concurrently. The revolutionary economic and technological changes taking place in many markets around the world, in conjunction with global-minded managers, propel these firms to operate internationally soon after their inception.[95] These firms have engaged in international operations from the early days of their existence and are described as "born-globals" in the literature.[96]

Lin found that family ownership has a positive influence on the firm's pace of internationalization.[97] Family business managers are more willing to devote time and effort to build new facilities from the ground and screen potential acquisition targets. In addition, and contrary to the sequential approach, Lin argues that family businesses' internationalization behavior does not follow a regular path, but instead responds to economic volatility and resource fluctuations.[98] This behavior can be explained by the flexibility and autonomy that family business owners and leaders enjoy when managing the company. Furthermore, family businesses that only showed a weak or moderate stewardship attitude were often internationalized from the beginning.[99]

Network Internationalization Approach

According to the network perspective, internationalization of the firm means that the firm establishes and develops positions in relation to counterparts in foreign networks.[100] The reliance and composition of networks is one factor that distinguishes family from nonfamily businesses.[101] Family businesses are less involved in networking,[102] which creates a potential drawback for them as the role of networks in the internationalization process is crucial,[103] and the managers' personal networks are considered to be the most significant resource of a firm.[104] Family businesses often have a single dominant owner-manager with centralized authority.[105] These family entrepreneurs are independent in their thinking and dedicated to the survival and prosperity of their firm. As a consequence, they often govern the firm on their own without paying attention to input from others and hence neglect the benefits of network relationships.[106]

Kontinen and Ojala demonstrated that the social capital of family managers is limited to their strong bonding and national social capital. When family businesses internationalize, they generally need to look for new network relationships to collect some bridging social capital.[107] In the case of Finnish family SMEs, they did not make any use of family contacts to exploit international opportunities. This is in line with Ozgen and Baron, who have shown that family contacts do not facilitate firm internationalization.[108] However, in the context of transnational immigrant entrepreneurship, familial ties seem to be a crucial factor in discovering and exploiting international opportunities.[109]

In contrast to those informal contacts, international involvement is also encouraged if the firm has networks with other companies around the world.[110] In comparison to nonfamily businesses, family businesses need fewer socioeconomic networks, are less involved in collaborating with other firms, and make less use of subcontracting. Family businesses are often not aware of networks, such as governmental programs, that would assist them in venturing abroad.[111] It was further shown that the willingness to resort to public entities decreases with the manager's experience in the family business.[112] Family business managers are, in most cases, also the owners of the business and thus more independent from the environment, culture, and macroeconomic situation than managers in nonfamily businesses.[113] As a consequence, they establish fewer joint ventures with other firms.[114]

The lack of knowledge and involvement in networks suggests that family businesses face more problems in internationalizing their operations in comparison to nonfamily businesses. Basly identifies this isolation from other firms as a negative factor for family businesses' internationalization.[115] Based on the relational perspective of internationalization, this might be a reason why family businesses struggle in venturing abroad: they are more inward looking and lack the relationships required to venture abroad.[116] Even if the family business has the same amount of networks available, Eberhard and Craig have shown that they are less capable than nonfamily businesses of exploiting those networks.[117] Family firms have problems building trust with partners in growth and restructuring phases, and these phases are typical during a firm's internationalization process.[118] This hampers the exchange of information between the family firm and nonfamily network actors.

However, family businesses that enter joint ventures with other family-owned businesses may find commonalities that extend across several key areas of business and may share some very important values, even between different cultures. These values, which include trust, loyalty, long-term orientation, and continuation of family, make international joint ventures between family businesses more likely to succeed.[119] If a family business is able to identify these common characteristics in family businesses in other countries and make them common ground, then it can be easier for the family business to form strategic alliances and enter foreign markets.[120] Hence, family businesses prefer to enter psychic distant countries by using joint ventures with other family businesses.[121] This is especially the case for internationally inexperienced family businesses. Kuo, Kao, Chang, and Chiu demonstrated that inexperienced family businesses, compared with inexperienced nonfamily businesses, prefer to enter foreign markets with the help of a partner (JV) instead of going alone (wholly owned subsidiary).[122] Interestingly, this relationship changes as the family business accumulates sufficient experience. Relinquishing control to a partner is no longer necessary, and investing without a partner becomes the better option. This is identical for both family and nonfamily businesses; however, because of the family's socioemotional motives, it is more pronounced in the family business context.

Summary Observation

In summary, the decision to internationalize is increasingly important in many firm strategies. It is a risky and complex path that often runs counter to family businesses' traditional desires to maintain control and avoid risk. But paradoxically, internationalization increases the firm's chance of survival and longevity.[123] Despite its importance for family business scholars and managers, the literature on family business internationalization remains limited.[124] Further work is needed to explore how different types of family businesses may establish collaborative agreements and joint networks as well as the effects that these networks have on international expansion, and this is elaborated upon along with other suggestions below.

PRACTICAL IMPLICATIONS

Our review findings offer some relevant practical implications for family business managers and owners. First, the majority of studies have shown that a moderate level of family involvement is most desirable for firm internationalization. This conclusion applies to ownership stakes as well as to family involvement in operating management and the board of directors. Family influence brings in elements of stewardship, which enables a long-term planning perspective, psychological commitment, and trustworthy behavior, all of which facilitate international expansion. Excessive family control, however, hampers access to necessary resources for growth and limits the firm's risk propensity. Arguing from these findings, it is advisable to open the family business toward nonfamily stakeholders, which bring a new perspective into the business and facilitate access to networks and resources that otherwise would lie beyond the firm's horizon. Indeed, Sciascia et al. argue that allowing nonfamily member participation in the board of directors is the most effective and easiest to implement solution to reach higher levels of internationalization.[125]

Second, succeeding generations should be prepared and educated with an international mind-set. As outlined, the next generation significantly influences the firm's strategic outlook, and the way those successors approach an international strategy is rather heterogeneous. Studies have shown that some family businesses had strong episodes of international growth triggered by new generations, although other businesses have not benefited from new perspectives associated with management succession. An important moderating effect seems to be the harmony among the family members. In cases where the new successor has to settle disputes within the family, less energy can be directed toward international strategies, and the business's growth potential remains suboptimal.

Third, this review conveys to family business managers the essential role of networks on growth and international expansion. Despite the importance of networks, family business managers have not utilized the full potential of their networking capabilities. On the one hand, they are too skeptical and inward looking to fully embrace the positive effects of social and professional networks. They often distrust outsiders and meet new partners with extreme caution and suspicion. On the other hand, they are still foregoing opportunities to leverage collaborative agreements with other family businesses. Family businesses share a common work ethic and culture that nonfamily businesses do not always possess. These characteristics offer the potential for highly successful collaborations that could lead to sustainable competitive advantages when competing with nonfamily businesses.

FUTURE RESEARCH PATHWAYS

This review demonstrates that the knowledge of family businesses' internationalization is still narrow. The number of articles published is growing rapidly, and the majority of existing articles are descriptive, laying nothing more than the foundation for research in the subfield of family business internationalization.[126] This presents significant opportunities, some of which have been identified in the extant literature reviewed in this chapter.

Tolstoy showed that networks not only play a crucial role when first entering a foreign market, but also when firms strive to retain an entrepreneurial and internationally focused mind-set after the initial market entry.[127] Because of the important role of networks, several studies call for more research into the networking relationships of family businesses.[128] They suggest performing studies based on the network theory of internationalization as well as clarifying the kinds of networks that family businesses use when they venture abroad and examining how these networks evolve during internationalization.[129]

Studies that investigate within family firm genre differences could provide a fruitful future research avenue. For example, the number of generations owning the business could be an important driver behind the decision to take the family business international.[130] If views differ generationally, emphasis should be placed on the views of the younger generation.[131] By investigating the role of predecessors and the succession process in future studies, differences between family and nonfamily businesses could be better understood.[132] Also, cultural differences may impact the way family businesses internationalize. Elango and Pattnaik have shown that firms from emerging markets do not necessarily possess the same monopolistic advantages that firms from developed economies enjoy.[133] Although firms from developed markets generally compete based on product differentiation, emerging market firms compete primarily based on cost advantages. Studies that compare those cultural differences and illustrate their impact on family firms' internationalization will further enrich this research arena.

Future research should also investigate the growth path of family businesses and the timing of their internationalization relative to other strategic alternatives.[134] The international business literature highlights the multiplicity of the dimensions of the internationalization construct. Other dimensions include diversity of industries and market segments, dispersion versus integration of international operations, and timing of international entry. Examining these and other dimensions will improve our understanding of the approaches that family businesses use to internationalize their operations.[135]

Another research pathway that has been neglected in previous studies is the relation between international involvement of family businesses and financial results obtained from these strategies.[136] Empirical results outside the family business genre have been mixed and inconclusive, indicating positive, negative, or U-shaped relationships.[137] However, work that examines this relationship in the context of family business internationalization is scarce.

Building upon the resource-based view (RBV) and the framework of resource orchestration, Sirmon et al. argue that to successfully internationalize, the firm's resource portfolio must be structured and subsequently bundled to create the appropriate capabilities to implement this strategy.[138] Specifically, marketing and financial capabilities are pivotal to achieving high growth.[139] Because family businesses often lack the necessary resources to expand internationally, it may be necessary to accumulate these resources (e.g., develop them internally). One pathway for future research could be to examine how family business managers engage in structuring, bundling, and leveraging processes with the goal of effectively utilizing the firm's resources to compete in foreign markets. For example, Holcomb, Holmes, and Connelly have found that managers differ in their resource management abilities and that these differences matter to firm outcomes.[140] In the case of family businesses, this could be further investigated in relation to the different resource management capabilities of the incumbent and successive generation or between family and nonfamily managers.

The evolving technology associated with dramatically changing buying habits opens another research field that has not been investigated. Kim and Lennon noted that the Internet is the fastest growing sales channel and an important vehicle in firms' strategic tool set.[141] This technology not only impacts firms' communication, control, and collaboration processes but also promises accelerated international expansion avenues.[142] Bell, Deans, Ibbotson, and Sinkovics therefore framed the term *internetalization*, which implies selling products over the Internet without an equity-based market presence.[143] While important for firms of all sizes, it is more relevant for smaller firms, which are inherently more resource poor than larger corporations.[144] In the family business literature, there is a lack of research on this topic. Future research may examine how family businesses have adopted the new technological possibilities in the pursuit of international opportunities.

In summary, the knowledge about family business internationalization offers ample future research opportunity pathways. However, like any emerging field, there is a risk that the field is open to opportunistic exploitation. Family business as a field has arguably gained much earned legitimacy,[145] and with this comes increased expectations of a more discerning community. The understanding of the internationalization process in the context of family business will continue to develop through the application of accepted theory.

To date, there has perhaps been an overreliance on RBV and stage theories, and, though appropriate in the early paradigmatic stages, this is not sustainable. An obvious theoretical frame that has not been optimized but that holds promise is that of stakeholder theory. As well, researchers will need to begin to integrate multiple theoretical approaches, and this, as many who have attempted to accomplish this have discovered, is difficult to achieve without being accused of concocting a "theory soup."

Other pathways that have not been explored at length in the context of family businesses to date, and which offer exciting opportunities, include (1) the role of mergers and acquisition in the internationalization process in family firms; (2) licensing intellectual property as an alternative to more traditional internationalization approaches; (3) understanding the internationalization opportunities emanating from the reverse innovation phenomenon; (4) considering the impact of business models, such as one-for-one offers (think, Tom's Shoes) from the social venturing movement; and (5) the impact of technology in reaching previously inaccessible markets.

Additionally, there are multiple methodological options that remain untouched. Multilevel analyses, for example, would be ideally suited for research projects related to family business internationalization.

CONCLUSION

This study contributes by identifying past research findings in the subfield of family business internationalization. It is hoped that multiple academic and practitioner stakeholders will benefit from this endeavor. Additionally, because family businesses play such an essential role in most economies around the world, as a consequence of this review, it is hoped that the ongoing focus on research in this area will prompt policy makers to actively consider ways of sharing knowledge about how best to facilitate the internationalization of this vital business community.

NOTES

1. Tonja Kontinen and Arto Ojala, "The Internationalization of Family Businesses: A Review of Extant Research," *Journal of Family Business Strategy* 1, 2 (2010): 97–107; Guadalupe Fuentes-Lombardo and Rúben Fernandez-Ortiz, "Strategic Alliances in the Internationalization of Family Firms: An Exploratory Study on the Spanish Wine Industry," *Advances in Management* 3, 6 (2010): 45–54.

2. Tonja Kontinen and Arto Ojala, "Internationalization Pathways among Family-owned SMEs," *International Marketing Review* 29, 5 (2012): 496–518; Wen-Ting Lin,

"Family Ownership and Internationalization Processes: Internationalization Pace, Internationalization Scope, and Internationalization Rhythm," *European Management Journal* 30 (2012): 47–56.

3. Jean-Luc Arregle, Lucia Naldi, Mattias Nordqvist and Michael A. Hitt., "Internationalization of Family-controlled Firms: A Study of the Effects of External Involvement in Governance," *Entrepreneurship Theory and Practice* 36, 6 (2012): 1115–1143.

4. Salvatore Sciascia, Pietro Mazzola, Joseph H. Astrachan, Torsten M. Pieper "The Role of Family Ownership in International Entrepreneurship: Exploring Nonlinear Effects," *Small Business Economics* 38, 1 (2012): 15–31.

5. Randall Morck and Bernard Yeung, "Agency Problems in Large Family Business Groups," *Entrepreneurship Theory and Practice* 27, 4 (2003): 367–382; Ernesto J. Poza, *Family Business*, 2nd ed. (Mason, OH: Thomas South-Western, 2007).

6. Justin B. Craig, Ken Moores, Carole Howorth, and Panikkos Poutziouris, "Family Business Research Approaching a Tipping Point Threshold," *Journal of Management and Organization* 15, 3 (2009): 282–293; Justin B. Craig and Carlo Salvato, "The Distinctiveness, Design, and Direction of Family Business Research: Insights from Management Luminaries," *Family Business Review* 25, 1 (2012): 109–116.

7. Irene Mandl, *Overview of Family Business Relevant Issues* (Vienna, AT: Austrian Institute for SME Research, 2008).

8. Melissa Carey Shanker and Joseph H. Astrachan, "Myths and Realities: Family Businesses' Contribution to the US Economy—A Framework for Assessing Family Business Statistics," *Family Business Review* 9, 2 (1996): 107–123.

9. Ronald C. Anderson and David M. Reeb, "Founding-family Ownership and Firm Performance: Evidence from the S&P 500," *The Journal of Finance* 58, 3 (2003): 1301–1327; Peter Davis and Douglas Stern, "Adaption, Survival, and Growth of the Family Business: An Integrated Systems Perspective," *Human Relations* 34, 4 (1980): 207–224; Ken Moores, "Paradigms and Theory Building in the Domain of Business Families," *Family Business Review* 22, 2 (2009): 167–180.

10. Danny Miller, Isabelle Le Breton-Miller, and Barry Scholnick, "Stewardship vs. Stagnation: An Empirical Comparison of Small Family and Non-family Businesses," *Journal of Management Studies* 45, 1 (2008): 51–78.

11. Luis R. Gomez-Mejia, Cristina Cruz, Pascual Berrone, and Julio De Castro, "The Bind That Ties: Socioemotional Wealth Preservation in Family Firms," *Academy of Management Annals* 5, 1 (2011): 653–707.

12. Pascual Berrone, Cristina Cruz, and Luis R. Gomez-Mejia, "Socioemotional Wealth in Family Firms: Theoretical Dimensions, Assessment Approaches, and Agenda for Future Research," *Family Business Review* 25, 3 (2012): 258–279.

13. Wendy C. Handler, "Methodological Issues and Considerations in Studying Family Businesses," *Family Business Review* 2, 3 (1989): 257–276.

14. Reginald A. Litz, "The Family Business: Toward Definitional Clarity," *Family Business Review* 8, 2 (1995): 71–81.

15. Adolf Berle and Gardiner Means, *The Modern Corporation and Private Property* (New York: Harcourt, Brace, and World, 1932).

16. Litz, "The Family Business."

17. Kontinen and Ojala, "The Internationalization of Family Businesses."

18. Miguel Angel Gallo and Jannicke Sveen, "Internationalizing the Family Business: Facilitating and Festraining Factors," *Family Business Review* 4, 2 (1991): 181–190 (see p. 182).

19. Jess H. Chua, James J. Chrisman, and Pramodita Sharma, "Defining the Family Business by Behavior," *Entrepreneurship Theory and Practice* 23, 4 (1999): 19–39.

20. Ibid.

21. David Tranfield, David Denyer, and Palminder Smart, "Towards a Methodology for Developing Evidence-informed Management Knowledge by Means of Systematic Review," *British Journal of Management* 14 (2003): 207–222.

22. Guido Corbetta and Daniela Montemerlo, "Ownership, Governance, and Management Issues in Small and Medium-size Family Businesses: A Comparison of Italy and the United States," *Family Business Review* 12, 4 (1999): 361–374; Shaker A. Zahra, "Goverance, Ownership, and Corporate Entrepreneurship: The Moderating Impact of Industry Technological Opportunities," *Academy of Management Journal* 39, 6 (1996): 1713–1735.

23. WM. Gerard Sanders and Mason A. Carpenter, "Internationalization and Firm Governance: The Roles of CEO Compensation, Top Team Composition, and Board Structure," *Academy of Management Journal* 41, 2 (1998): 158–178.

24. Corbetta and Montemerlo, "Ownership, Governance, and Management Issues in Small and Medium-size Family Businesses."

25. Zumila Fernández and María J. Nieto, "Internationalization Strategy of Small and Medium-sized Family Businesses: Some Influential Factors," *Family Business Review* 18, 1 (2005): 77–89.

26. Sumon Kumar Bhaumik, Nigel Driffield, and Sarmistha Pal, "Does Ownership Structure of Emerging-market Firms Affect Their Outward FDI? The Case of the Indian Automotive and Pharmaceutical Sectors," *Journal of International Business Studies* 41, 3 (2010): 437–450; Fernández and Nieto, "Internationalization Strategy of Small and Medium-sized Family Businesses"; Zumila Fernández and María J. Nieto, "Impact of Ownership on the International Involvement of SMEs," *Journal of International Business Studies* 37, 3 (2006): 340–351; Gallo and Sveen, "Internationalizing the Family Business."

27. Gallo and Sveen, "Internationalizing the Family Business."

28. Fernández and Nieto, "Internationalization Strategy of Small and Medium-sized Family Businesses"; Fernández and Nieto, "Impact of Ownership on the International Involvement of SMEs."

29. Bhaumik, Driffield, and Pal, "Does Ownership Structure of Emerging-market Firms Affect Their Outward FDI?"; Enrique Claver, Laura Rienda, and Diego Quer, "Family Firms' Risk Perception: Empirical Evidence on the Internationalization Process," *Journal of Small Business and Enterprise Development* 15, 3 (2008): 457–471.

30. Lin, "Family Ownership and Internationalization Processes."

31. Gerard George, Johan Wiklund, and Shaker A. Zahra, "Ownership and the Internationalization of Small Firms," *Journal of Management* 31, 2 (2005): 210–233.

32. Bhaumik, Driffield, and Pal, "Does Ownership Structure of Emerging-market Firms Affect Their Outward FDI?," 440.

33. Michael C. Jensen and William H. Meckling, "Theory of the Firm: Managerial Behavior, Agency Costs and Ownership Structure," *Journal of Financial Economics* 3, 4 (1976): 305–360.

34. Oliver E. Williamson, "The Theory of the Firm as Governance Structure: From Choice to Contract," *The Journal of Economic Perspectives* 16, 3 (2002): 171–195.

35. Nuria Puig and Paloma Fernández Pérez, "A Silent Revolution: The Internationalisation of Large Spanish Family Firms," *Business History* 51, 3 (2009): 462–483; Roger Strange, et al., "Insider Control and the FDI Location Decision: Evidence from Investing Firms in Emerging Markets," *Management International Review* 49 (2009): 433–454; Shaker A. Zahra, "International Expansion of U.S. Manufacturing Family Businesses: The Effect of Ownership and Involvement," *Journal of Business Venturing* 18, 4 (2003): 495–512.

36. Puig and Pérez, "A Silent Revolution."

37. David G. Sirmon and Michael A. Hitt, "Managing Resources: Linking Unique Resources, Management, and Wealth Creation in Family Firms," *Entrepreneurship Theory and Practice* 27, 4 (2003): 339–358.

38. Strange, et al., "Insider Control and the FDI Location Decision."

39. Chris Carr and Suzanne Bateman, "International Strategy Configurations of the World's Top Family Firms," *Management International Review* 49 (2009): 733–758.

40. Salvatore Sciascia, Pietro Mazzola, Joseph H. Astrachan, Torsten M. Pieper "The Role of Family Ownership in International Entrepreneurship."

41. Ibid.

42. William S. Schulze, Michael H. Lubatkin, and Richard N. Dino, "Toward a Theory of Agency and Altruism in Family Firms," *Journal of Business Venturing* 18, 4 (2003): 473–490.

43. Chris Graves and Jill Thomas, "Determinants of the Internationalization Pathways of Family Firms: An Examination of Family Influence," *Family Business Review* 21, 2 (2008): 151–167.

44. Enrique Claver, Laura Rienda, and Diego Quer, "Family Firms' International Commitment," *Family Business Review* 22, 2 (2009): 125–135; Chandra S. Mishra and Daniel L. McConaughy, "Founding Family Control and Capital Structure: The Risk of Loss of Control and the Aversion to Debt," *Entrepreneurship Theory and Practice* 23, 4 (1999): 53–64.

45. Jean-Luc Arregle, Lucia Naldi, Mattias Nordqvist and Michael A. Hitt "Internationalization of Family-controlled Firms"; Bhaumik, Driffield, and Pal, "Does Ownership Structure of Emerging-market Firms Affect Their Outward FDI?"; B Elango and Chinmay Pattnaik, "Building Capabilities for International Operations through Networks: A Study of Indian Firms," *Journal of International Business Studies* 38, 4 (2007): 541–555; Fernández and Nieto, "Internationalization Strategy of Small and Medium-sized Family Businesses."

46. Pramodita Sharma, James J. Chrisman, and Jess H. Chua, "Strategic Management of the Family Business: Past Research and Future Challenges," *Family Business Review* 10, 1 (1997): 1–35.

47. Catherine Daily and Marc J. Dollinger, "Alternative Methodologies for Identifying Family- versus Nonfamily-managed Businesses," *Journal of Small Business*

Management 31, 2 (1993): 79–90; Guy Geeraerts, "The Effect of Ownership on the Organization Structure in Small Firms," *Administrative Science Quarterly* 29, 2 (1984): 232–237.

48. Fernández and Nieto, "Impact of Ownership on the International Involvement of SMEs."

49. Ibid.

50. Jean-Luc Arregle, Lucia Naldi, Mattias Nordqvist, and Michael A. Hitt, "Internationalization of Family-controlled Firms."

51. Yanto Chandra, Chris Styles, and Ian Wilkinson, "The Recognition of First Time International Entrepreneurial Opportunities: Evidence from Firms in Knowledge-based Industries," *International Marketing Review* 26, 1 (2009): 30–61; Paul Ellis, "Social Ties and Foreign Market Entry," *Journal of International Business Studies* 31, 3 (2000): 443–469.

52. Nicole E. Coviello and Hugh J. Munro, "Growing the Entrepreneurial Firm: Networking for International Market Development," *European Journal of Marketing* 29, 7 (1995): 49–61; Sharon Loane and Jim Bell, "Rapid Internationalisation among Entrepreneurial Firms in Australia, Canada, Ireland and New Zealand," *International Marketing Review* 23, 5 (2006): 467–485; Benjamin M. Oviatt and Patricia P. McDougall, "Defining International Entrepreneurship and Modeling the Speed of Internationalization," *Entrepreneurship Theory and Practice* 29, 5 (2005): 537–554.

53. David G. Sirmon, Jean-Luc Arregle, Michael A. Hitt and Justin W. Webb "The Role of Family Influence in Firms' Strategic Responses to Threat of Imitation," *Entrepreneurship Theory and Practice* 32, 6 (2008): 979–998.

54. Andrea Calabrò, Mariateresa Torchia, Thilo Pukall, and Donata Mussolino, "The Influence of Ownership Structure and Board Strategic Involvement on International Sales: The Moderating Effect of Family Involvement," *International Business Review* 22, 3 (2013): 509–523.

55. Jean-Luc Arregle, Lucia Naldi, Mattias Nordqvist, and Michael A. Hitt, "Internationalization of Family-controlled Firms."

56. For example, see, Fernández and Nieto, "Internationalization Strategy of Small and Medium-sized Family Businesses"; Zahra, "International Expansion of U.S. Manufacturing Family Businesses."

57. Claver, Rienda, and Quer, "Family Firms' Risk Perception."

58. John Davis and Renato Tagiuri, "Bivalent Attributes of the Family Firm," in *Family Business Sourcebook*, ed. Craig E. Aronoff and John L. Ward (Detroit, MI: Omnigraphics, 1991): 62–73.

59. Schulze, Lubatkin, and Dino, "Toward a Theory of Agency and Altruism in Family Firms."

60. Davis and Tagiuri, "Bivalent Attributes of the Family Firm"; William Schulze, Michael H. Lubatkin, and Richard N. Dino, "Altruism, Agency, and the Competitiveness of Family Firms," *Managerial and Decision Economics* 23, 4–5 (2002): 247–259.

61. Otto Andersen and Arnt Buvik, "Firms' Internationalization and Alternative Approaches to the International Customer/Market Selection," *International Business Review* 11, 3 (2002): 347–363; Nieto, "Impact of Ownership on the International

Involvement of SMEs"; William S. Schulze, Michael Lubatkin, Richard N. Dino, and Ann K. Buchholtz, "Agency Relationships in Family Firms: Theory and Evidence," *Organization Science* 12, 2 (2001): 99–116.

62. Sam C. Okoroafo, "Internationalization of Family Businesses: Evidence from Northwest Ohio, U.S.A.," *Family Business Review* 12, 2 (1999): 147–158.

63. Elitsa R. Banalieva and Kimberly A. Eddleston, "Home-region Focus and Performance of Family Firms: The Role of Family vs Non-family Leaders," *Journal of International Business Studies* 42 (2011): 1060–1072.

64. Lucia Naldi and Mattias Nordqvist, "Family Firms Venturing into International Markets: A Resource Dependence Perspective," *Frontiers of Entrepreneurship Research* 28, 14 (2008): 1–18.

65. Daniele Cerrato and Mariacristina Piva, "The Internationalization of Small and Medium-sized Enterprises: The Effect of Family Management, Human Capital and Foreign Ownership," *Journal of Management and Governance* 16 (2012): 617–644.

66. Miguel Angel Gallo and Carlos Garcia Pont, "Important Factors in Family Business Internationalization," *Family Business Review* 9, 1 (1996): 45–59.

67. Henry Wai-Chung Yeung, "Limits to the Growth of Family-owned Business? The Case of Chinese Transnational Corporations from Hong Kong," *Family Business Review* 13, 1 (2000): 55–70.

68. Poza, *Family Business*.

69. Harvey S. James, "What Can the Family Contribute to Business? Examining Contractual Relationships," *Family Business Review* 12, 1 (1999): 61–71; Ivan S. Lansberg, "Managing Human Resources in Family Firms: The Problem of Institutional Overlap," *Organizational Dynamics* 12, 1 (1983): 39–46.

70. Schulze, Lubatkin, and Dino, "Toward a Theory of Agency and Altruism in Family Firms."

71. John Child, Sek Hong Ng, and Christine Wong, "Psychic Distance and Internationalization: Evidence from Hong Kong Firms," *International Studies of Management and Organization* 32, 1 (2002): 36–56; Graves and Thomas, "Determinants of the Internationalization Pathways of Family Firms."

72. Khai Sheang Lee, Guan Hua Lim, and Wei Shi Lim, "Family Business Succession: Appropriation Risk and Choice of Successor," *Academy of Management Review* 28, 4 (2003): 657–666.

73. Claver, Rienda, and Quer, "Family Firms' Risk Perception"; Fernández and Nieto, "Impact of Ownership on the International Involvement of SMEs"; Graves and Thomas, "Determinants of the Internationalization Pathways of Family Firms"; Sam C. Okoroafo, "Generational Perspectives of the Export Behavior of Family Businesses," *International Journal of Economics and Finance* 2, 3 (2010): 15–24.

74. Okoroafo, "Internationalization of Family Businesses."

75. Gallo and Pont, "Important Factors in Family Business Internationalization."

76. Ibid.

77. Fernández and Nieto, "Internationalization Strategy of Small and Medium-sized Family Businesses."

78. Graves and Thomas, "Determinants of the Internationalization Pathways of Family Firms."

79. Claver, Rienda, and Quer, "Family Firms' Risk Perception"; Okoroafo, "Internationalization of Family Businesses."

80. Kelin E. Gersick (Ed.)., *Generation to Generation: Life Cycles of the Family Business*, (Boston: Harvard Business School Press, 1997).

81. Okoroafo, "Internationalization of Family Businesses."

82. Zahra, "International Expansion of U.S. Manufacturing Family Businesses."

83. Igor Filatotchev, "FDI by Firms from Newly Industrialised Economies in Emerging Markets: Corporate Governance, Entry Mode and Location," *Journal of International Business Studies* 38, 4 (2007): 556–572.

84. Naldi and Nordqvist, "Family Firms Venturing into International Markets."

85. Andrea Calabrò, Donata Mussolino, and Morten Huse, "The Role of Board of Directors in the Internationalization Process of Small and Medium Sized Family Business," *International Journal of Globalization and Small Business* 3, 4 (2009): 393–411.

86. Salvatore Sciascia, Pietro Mazzola, Joseph H. Astrachan, Torsten M. Pieper, "Family Involvement in the Board of Directors: Effects on Sales Internationalization," *Journal of Small Business Management* 51, 1 (2013): 83–99.

87. Chris Graves and Jill Thomas, "Internationalisation of the Family Business: A Longitudinal Perspective," *International Journal of Globalisation and Small Business* 1, 1 (2004): 7–27.

88. Lin, "Family Ownership and Internationalization Processes."

89. Chandra, Styles, and Wilkinson, "The Recognition of First Time International Entrepreneurial Opportunities."

90. Jan Johanson and Jan-Erik Vahlne, "The Internationalization Process of the Firm—A Model of Knowledge Development and Increasing Foreign Market Commitments," *Journal of International Business Studies* 8, 1 (1977): 23–32; Jan Johanson and Finn Wiedersheim-Paul, "The Internationalisation of the Firm—Four Swedish Cases," *The Journal of Management Studies* 12, 3 (1975): 305–322.

91. Enrique Claver, Laura Rienda, and Diego Quer, "The Internationalisation Process in Family Firms: Choice of Market Entry Strategies," *Journal of General Management* 33, 1 (2007): 1–14.

92. Kontinen and Ojala, "Internationalization Pathways among Family-owned SMEs."

93. Child, "Psychic Distance and Internationalization: Evidence from Hong Kong Firms."

94. Zahra, "International Expansion of U.S. Manufacturing Family Businesses."

95. Gary A. Knight and S. Tamer Cavusgil, "The Born Global Firm: A Challenge to Traditional Internationalization Theory," in *Advances in International Marketing*, ed. S. Tamer Cavusgil and Tage Koed Madsen (Greenwich, CT: JAI Press, 1996): 11–26; Alex Rialp, Josep Rialp, and Gary A. Knight, "The Phenomenon of Early Internationalizing Firms: What Do We Know after a Decade (1993–2003) of Scientific Inquiry?," *International Business Review* 14, 2 (2005): 147–166.

96. Luis E. Lopez, Sumit K. Kundu, and Luciano Ciravegna, "Born Global or Born Regional? Evidence from an Exploratory Study in the Costa Rican Software Industry," *Journal of International Business Studies* 40, 7 (2009): 1228–1238; D. Deo Sharma and Anders Blomstermo, "The Internationalization Process of Born Globals: A Network View," *International Business Review* 12, 6 (2003): 739–753.

97. Lin, "Family Ownership and Internationalization Processes."

98. Ibid.

99. Kontinen and Ojala, "Internationalization Pathways among Family-owned SMEs."

100. Jon Johanson and Lars-Gunnar Mattson, "Internationalization in Industrial Systems—A Network Approach," in *Strategies in Global Competition*, ed. Neil Hood and Jan-Erik Vahlne (New York: Croom Helm, 1988): 287–314; Jan Johanson and Jan-Erik Vahlne, "Business Relationship Learning and Commitment in the Internationalization Process," *Journal of International Entrepreneurship* 1, 1 (2003): 83–101.

101. Jolien Huybrechts, Wim Voordeckers, Badine Lybaert and Sigrid Vandemaele "The Distinctiveness of Family-firm Intangibles: A Review and Suggestions for Future Research," *Journal of Management and Organization* 17, 2 (2011): 268–287.

102. Rik Donckels and Erwin Froehlich, "Are Family Businesses Really Different? European Experiences from STRATOS," *Family Business Review* 4, 2 (1991): 149–160.

103. Tain-Jy Chen, "Network Resources for Internationalization: The Case of Taiwan's Electronics Firms," *Journal of Management Studies* 40, 5 (2003): 1107–1130; Tatiana S. Manolova, Ivan M. Manev, and Bojidar S. Gyoshev, "In Good Company: The Role of Personal and Inter-firm Networks for New-venture Internationalization in a Transition Economy," *Journal of World Business* 45, 3 (2010): 257–265; Oviatt and McDougall, "Defining International Entrepreneurship."

104. Johanson and Mattson, "Internationalization in Industrial Systems."

105. Edgar H. Schein, "The Role of the Founders in Creating Organisational Culture," *Organisational Dynamics* 12, 1 (1983): 13–28; Pramodita Sharma, "An Overview of the Field of Family Business Studies: Current Status and Directions for the Future," *Family Business Review* 17, 1 (2004): 1–36; Ernesto J. Poza, Theodore Alfred, and Anil Maheshwari, "Stakeholder Perceptions of Culture and Management Practices in Family and Family Firms—A Preliminary Report," *Family Business Review* 10, 2 (1997): 135–155.

106. Shaker A. Zahra, "Entrepreneurial Risk Taking in Family Firms," *Family Business Review* 18, 1 (2005): 23–40.

107. Tonja Kontinen and Arto Ojala, "Social Capital in Relation to the Foreign Market Entry and Post-entry Operations of Family SMEs," *Journal of International Entrepreneurship* 9, 2 (2011): 133–151.

108. Eren Ozgen and Robert A. Baron, "Social Sources of Information in Opportunity Recognition: Effects of Mentors, Industry Networks, and Professional Forums," *Journal of Business Venturing* 22, 2 (2007): 174–192.

109. Michael Mustafa and Stephen Chen, "The Strength of Family Networks in Transnational Immigrant Entrepreneurship," *Thunderbird International Business Review* 52, 2 (2010): 97–106.

110. Fernández and Nieto, "Internationalization Strategy of Small and Medium-sized Family Businesses"; Jill Thomas and Chris Graves, "Internationalising the Family Firm as a Demonstration of an Entrepreneurial Culture" (paper presented at the Association for Small Business and Entrepreneurship Annual Conference 2004), retrieved from http://hdl.handle.net/2440/28647.

111. Okoroafo, "Internationalization of Family Businesses."

112. Jose C. Casillas and Francisco J. Acedo, "Internationalisation of Spanish Family SMEs: An Analysis of Family Involvement," *International Journal of Globalisation and Small Businesses* 1, 2 (2005): 134–150.

113. Donckels and Froehlich, "Are Family Businesses Really Different?"

114. Mahamat Abdellatif, Bruno Amann, and Jacques Jaussaud, "Family versus Nonfamily Business: A Comparison of International Strategies," *Journal of Family Business Strategy* 1, 2 (2010): 108–116.

115. Sami Basly, "The Internationalization of Family SME: An Organizational Learning and Knowledge Development Perspective," *Baltic Journal of Management* 2, 2 (2007): 154–180.

116. Graves and Thomas, "Internationalisation of the Family Business."

117. Manuel Eberhard and Justin Craig, "The Evolving Role of Organisational and Personal Networks in International Market Venturing," *Journal of World Business* 48, 3 (2013): 385–397.

118. Linda Wong and Brian Kleiner, "Nepotism," *Work Study* 43, 5 (1994): 10–12.

119. Robert L. Swinth and Karen L. Vinton, "Do Family-owned Businesses Have a Strategic Advantage in International Joint Ventures?," *Family Business Review* 6, 1 (1993): 19–30.

120. Gallo and Sveen, "Internationalizing the Family Business."

121. Dawn Harris, Jon I. Martinez, and John L. Ward, "Is Strategy Different for the Family-owned Business?," *Family Business Review* 7, 2 (1994): 159–174.

122. Anthony Kuo, Ming-Sung Kao, Yi-Chieh Chang, and Chih-Fang Chiu, "The Influence of International Experience on Entry Mode Choice: Difference Between Family and Non-family Firms," *European Management Journal* 30 (2012): 248–263.

123. Regis Coeurderoy, Marc Cowling, Georg Licht, and Gordon Murray, "Young Firm Internationalization and Survival: Empirical Tests on a Panel of 'Adolescent' New Technology-based Firms in Germany and the UK," *International Small Business Journal* 30, 5 (2012): 472–492.

124. Kontinen and Ojala, "The Internationalization of Family Businesses."

125. Sciascia et al., "The Role of Family Ownership in International Entrepreneurship."

126. Kontinen and Ojala, "The Internationalization of Family Businesses."

127. Daniel Tolstoy, "Differentiation in Foreign Business Relationships: A Study on Small and Medium-sized Enterprises after Their Initial Foreign

Market Entry," *International Small Business Journal* (published online, 2012), doi: 10.1177/0266242612456571.

128. Donckels and Froehlich, "Are Family Businesses Really Different?"; Fernández and Nieto, "Impact of Ownership on the International Involvement of SMEs"; Graves and Thomas, "Internationalisation of the Family Business"; Kontinen and Ojala, "The Internationalization of Family Businesses"; Mustafa and Chen, "The Strength of Family Networks in Transnational Immigrant Entrepreneurship."

129. Johanson and Mattson, "Internationalization in Industrial Systems."

130. Mustafa and Chen, "The Strength of Family Networks in Transnational Immigrant Entrepreneurship."

131. Okoroafo, "Generational Perspectives of the Export Behavior of Family Businesses."

132. Ethiopia Segaro, "Internationalization of Family SMEs: The Impact of Ownership, Governance, and Top Management Team," *Journal of Management and Governance* 16 (2012): 147–169.

133. Elango and Pattnaik, "Building Capabilities for International Operations through Networks."

134. Mustafa and Chen, "The Strength of Family Networks in Transnational Immigrant Entrepreneurship."

135. Zahra, "International Expansion of U.S. Manufacturing Family Businesses."

136. Fernández and Nieto, "Internationalization Strategy of Small and Medium-sized Family Businesses."

137. Chen, "Network Resources for Internationalization"; Elango and Pattnaik, "Building Capabilities for International Operations through Networks"; Denice E. Welch and Lawrence S. Welch, "The Internationalization Process and Networks: A Strategic Management Perspective," *Journal of International Marketing* 4, 3 (1996): 11–28; Paul Westhead, Mike Wright, and Deniz Ucbasaran, "The Internationalization of New and Small Firms: A Resource-based View," *Journal of Business Venturing* 16, 4 (2001): 333–358.

138. David G. Sirmon et al., "Resource Orchestration to Create Competitive Advantage: Breadth, Depth, and Life Cycle Effects," *Journal of Management* (published online, November 1, 2010).

139. José L. Barbero, José C. Casillas, and Howard D. Feldman, "Managerial Capabilities and Paths to Growth as Determinants of High-growth Small and Medium-sized Enterprises," *International Small Business Journal* 29, 6 (2011): 671–694.

140. Tim R. Holcomb, R. Michael Holmes Jr., and Brian L. Connelly, "Making the Most of What You Have: Managerial Ability as a Source of Resource Value Creation," *Strategic Management Journal* 30, 5 (2009): 457–485.

141. Minjeong Kim and Sharron Lennon, "The Effects of Visual and Verbal Information on Attitudes and Purchase Intentions in Internet Shopping," *Psychology and Marketing* 25, 2 (2008): 146–178.

142. Ruey-Jer Bryan Jean and Rudolf R. Sinkovics, "Relationship Learning and Performance Enhancement via Advanced Information Technology: The Case of Taiwanese Dragon Electronics Firms," *International Marketing Review* 27, 2 (2010): 200–222;

Rudolf R. Sinkovics and Elfriede Penz, "Empowerment of SME Websites: Development of a Web-empowerment Scale and Preliminary Evidence," *Journal of International Entrepreneurship* 3, 4 (2005): 303–315.

143. Jim Bell, Ken Deans, Pat Ibbotson, and Rudolf R. Sinkovics, "Towards the 'Internetalization' of International Marketing Education," *Marketing Education Review* 11, 3 (2001): 69–79.

144. Noemi Pezderka and Rudolf R. Sinkovics, "A Conceptualization of E-risk Perceptions and Implications for Small Firm Active Online Internationalization," *International Business Review* 20, 4 (2011): 409–422.

145. For comments from leading management scholars related to the state of the field, see Craig and Salvato, "The Distinctiveness, Design, and Direction of Family Business Research."

6

Strategizing by Social Entrepreneurs: A Longitudinal Analysis

David Gras, G. T. Lumpkin, and Robert S. Nason

Owners and operators of small social enterprises often wrestle with a challenge that commercial enterprise owner/operators may not face: how to combine two, often conflicting, objectives—social and financial.[1] These objectives are manifest in the social enterprise's strategic decisions and actions.[2] Ideally, socially oriented strategies ensure that the small business fulfills its core mission and delivers value to its constituents, while financial strategies may enable enterprises to effectively compete with other firms and ensure long-term sustainability. However, recent research reveals the challenges in effectively meeting both of these objectives simultaneously. On the one hand, strategies that are more commercially than socially oriented may compromise the social mission,[3] create conflicting logics and human resource challenges,[4] and distract attention from social-impact initiatives.[5] On the other hand, small businesses that invest too heavily in social goals may forfeit opportunities, sacrifice resources, constrain growth, or limit profitability to such an extent that they stagnate or fail.[6] In attempting to balance competing demands, small social enterprises often find themselves juggling trade-offs between social and financial objectives.

Underlying these trade-offs are a host of stakeholders with competing expectations. Research indicates that, in contrast to commercial enterprises, social enterprises are guided and influenced by a wider variety of stakeholders, some of which have a stronger voice in decision making.[7] While some stakeholders, such as investors, may advocate for one strategic focus, others such as employees or beneficiaries may lobby for different strategies. In this chapter, we suggest that it is the stakeholders of small social enterprises who, to a great extent, determine the degree of focus on either social or financial goals. We also argue that over the life cycle of a social enterprise, different stakeholders will gain or lose precedence and power, and that these shifts will influence the small business owner/operator's strategic priorities.[8]

In this chapter, we investigate how small social enterprises manage the tension between social and financial objectives and use dialectical theory to understand this process. We draw upon established research on the types of strategies used by small commercial enterprises and explore how importance levels assigned to strategies change over time as a result of conflicting strategic goals. Specifically, we argue that the divergent and conflicting issues that small social ventures face will produce an internal dialogue to manage them. To understand how social ventures manage these competing internal strategic tensions over time, we draw on dialectical theory,[9] which provides a strong theoretical basis to understand the process of conflict and change within organizations.[10] Based on dialectical theory, we suggest that early in the organizational founding process, small social enterprise owners will exhibit high variability in importance levels assigned to different types of strategies. However, this conflict should become resolved over time, and, thus, small social enterprise owners will exhibit stability in their strategic profile later in the organizational founding process.

We explore our arguments using real-life small social ventures and employ data from the Panel Study of Entrepreneurial Dynamics II (PSED II). Utilizing a recently formulated method to distinguish social and commercial enterprises within the PSED II sample, we analyze changes in the strategic foci of 94 small social enterprises over five years.[11] The findings suggest that small social enterprises endure dialectical tensions that in turn produce erratic strategic foci. However, we also find evidence that the variability in these tensions subsides over time.

This chapter contributes to the understanding of social enterprises in four ways. First, we discuss and demonstrate the applicability of strategies used by commercial small businesses to social small businesses. In doing so, we provide social small business owners with a typology of business strategies they may employ and a baseline understanding of which strategies other social small business owners utilize. Second, we demonstrate how dialectical theory may inform and predict small social enterprise behaviors and strategy. Based on this work, small social business owners may establish realistic expectations for their organizations and gain insight as to the underlying cause of tensions within small social businesses. Third, our findings advance understanding of the decision processes employed by small social enterprise owners. This has important implications for how operating social enterprises with constrained resources and competing demands can effectively be practiced. Fourth, we establish a link between the demands of stakeholders, which are more diverse in social organizations,[12] and the competitive strategies employed by small social organizations. Prior work on strategy setting has largely focused on the top management of organizations; yet shifting this focus more toward stakeholders may add important nuances to the antecedents of strategy formation.

SOCIAL AND COMMERCIAL ENTERPRISE STRATEGIES

Strategies typically refer to systematic plans of action that businesses use to compete in the marketplace. In contrast to an organization's vision and goals, or its efforts to achieve operational effectiveness, a strategy is the game plan that enables an organization to achieve a distinct competitive position relative to other similar companies.[13] For small business owner/operators, developing and implementing strategic game plans is among their most important activities.

While the term *strategy* has been used to describe a wide range of business activities, an extensive stream of prior research has identified 10 strategic categories or foci that capture a reasonably comprehensive range of strategies used by new and small ventures:

- Lower prices
- Quality products or services
- Serving those missed by others
- Being first to market a new product or service
- Doing a better job of marketing and promotion
- A superior location and customer convenience
- More contemporary, attractive products
- Technical and scientific expertise of the start-up team
- Developing new or advanced product technology or process technology for creating goods and services
- Development of intellectual property such as patents, copyrights, or trademarks[14]

Recent work has shown that these 10 strategic foci are employed by social and commercial enterprises alike.[15]

Although it is important to be able to adapt to changing conditions, prior research suggests that new and small commercial firms benefit from identifying a clear strategic direction and sticking with it until they have advanced past the early stages of organizational development.[16] Because they face many of the same challenges, it stands to reason that small social businesses would also benefit from relying on focused strategies and simple strategizing, especially during the early stages of the organizational life cycle. Researchers have found that it is often beneficial for large or established organizations to adopt multiple strategies, but younger and smaller ventures benefit more from narrowly focusing their strategic efforts to put their limited resource base to more effective use. However, we argue that, because of tensions between social and financial goals within small social enterprises, such stability may not be present or even possible. Social enterprises pursue specific social outcomes in addition to the largely commercial foci listed above. As a result, we argue that the presence of multiple stakeholders with different priorities and likely conflicting goals may cause both social and financial objectives to alternate over time. When this occurs, we would expect that the firm is also likely to strategize differently over time.

As an example, consider an enterprising social businessperson who gathered investors to help create a small organization to sell low-cost eyeglasses in a developing nation. At times, the enterprise may feel the pressure of investors to raise prices to gain a greater profit margin and return on investment while excluding more impoverished people from purchasing the eyeglasses. At other times, the enterprise may be pulled by their socially oriented stakeholders, such as the more impoverished consumers, to lower the cost of the glasses (in turn lowering the profit margins) and make them more accessible to a wider beneficiary base. Thus, tensions between the social and financial stakeholders of a small social enterprise may encourage differing strategies. Importantly, a firm that has only financial goals should not feel such a tension. Instead, a purely commercial firm should set its price at the level that it believes will generate the highest profits and stick with that price over time. We next turn to dialectical theory as a foundation for our expectations with regard to strategic instability.

DIALECTICAL THEORY

The origins of dialectical theory have been attributed to a number of renowned philosophers, including Socrates, Kant, Hegel, and Marx. Organizational scholars most commonly build on the Marxian perspective,[17] which is concerned with the processes through which patterns of interactions between competing forces are produced, maintained, and transformed.[18] Underlying it is the assumption that "developing entities exist in a pluralistic world of colliding events, forces, or contradictory values which compete with each other for domination and control."[19] In organizational settings and among individuals, these oppositions may be either internal because of conflicting goals or external because the organization's goals conflict with conditions in the environment.[20] From this assumption, the central tenet of Marxian dialect is "the 'negation of negation,' which posits that where there is a collision of two opposites, one opposite negates the other and is in turn negated by higher order historical or social processes which allow aspects of both negated positions to be preserved."[21] Said differently, (1) contradictory goals and worldviews naturally arise both within and among people and organizations;

(2) when these players or points of view interact with other incompatible views, it creates tension and conflict; and (3) the reaction to and resolution of the conflict may produce a reconstructed and value-adding paradigm that is shared. The dialectical framework is generally presented in three stages: thesis, antithesis, and synthesis.

The initial thesis stage—sometimes referred to as "social construction"—concerns the social process through which orderly relations between potentially contradictory forces are produced. This process is not necessarily rational or purposive. Instead, patterns of interaction are formed as the forces continually interface. Through ongoing relationships, prior patterns may be modified or replaced as needed. The culmination of this stage may be the establishment of an orderly set of institutional arrangements between forces in the system.

Although the thesis stage displays order and predictable patterns of interactions between the forces, it also invariably contains contradictions, incompatibilities, or "ruptures." Such contradictions may be necessary features of a particular social order. For example, Benson notes that "an integral part of capitalist social formations is that they are antithetical to the interests of labor, yet the functioning system maintains or reproduces this contradiction."[22] Common contradictions within businesses often revolve around reward structures, control structures, and departmental divisions.[23] Moreover, some organizations may be charged with managing multiple contradictory functions. The contradictions inherent in most organizations give rise to the second stage, antithesis—sometimes referred to as "contradiction." During this stage, radical breaks with the present order are possible. As conflicting forces jockey to impose their own "peculiar priorities," tensions may escalate and priorities may oscillate based on the power held by each competing force.[24]

For those relationships that endure through and advance past antithesis, there is a final stage of synthesis—often referred to as "praxis." Synthesis "is the free and creative reconstruction of social patterns on the bases of a reasoned analysis of both the limits and the potentials of present social forms."[25] Synthesis is a second-order change that breaks the current mold and sets forth new, cohesive processes that depart from arrangements established in either of the prior two stages. In short, in its ideal form, synthesis is a win-win situation in which the values of opposing sides are incorporated and built upon. Importantly, synthesis is not an inevitable outcome of antithesis; many organizations or social systems do not construct a new paradigm. Instead, conflict and contradictions may persist, or one force may simply overpower its counterpart and impose its own values upon others.

Such a dialectical framework composed of thesis, antithesis, and synthesis has been an enduring, albeit ancillary, facet of organizational study for decades. Blau and Scott as well as Benson provided seminal arguments for the applicability and value of dialectical theory to the study of organizations.[26] Following these works, a variety of studies have employed dialectical frameworks to study change in firms. Lourenco and Glidwell used a dialectical lens to study conflict over social control between subsidiary organizations and their headquarters.[27] McGuire applied a dialectical framework to the study of interorganizational networks to shed light on the process of network formation and the reconciliation of network tensions.[28] Van de Ven and colleagues identified four types of theories that can be drawn upon to understand strategy processes in organizations, with dialectical theory being one of them.[29]

In a recent study, Di Domenico and colleagues applied dialectical theory to a social enterprise context.[30] These authors studied the collaboration process between corporations and social enterprises, highlighting four sources of tension between these organizations: paradigm commitments (e.g., goals and logic); legitimate structural arrangements (e.g., ownership); constitution (e.g., governance); and organization-environment linkages (e.g., accountability). It was argued that these tensions manifest antithetical partnership dissonance and that those collaborations that endure are characterized by a synthesis via the emergence of a new collaborative state.

Our chapter follows in this tradition. We believe that small social organizations are ideal arenas in which to apply a dialectical framework. This is principally because of the competing logics of financial and social goals inherent in all such enterprises. Regardless of whether a small social organization is in the form of an enterprising nonprofit, a socially oriented for-profit, or a hybrid, the strategies of social enterprises are guided by some manifestation of a double-bottom line. While it has been argued that the interplay of financial and social goals may provide benefits to an organization,[31] it is also well established that conflicts and tensions are likely to manifest where the two goals come in contact.[32] As Firstenberg noted, "Where both nonprofit and profit-making activities coexist within the same enterprise, there is a strong risk of confusion of objectives and operating style between the two components."[33] Moreover, given the fact that small business owners are largely resource constrained,[34] social enterprises may face continual trade-offs concerning allocation decisions surrounding financial or social goals. Although not always the case, this can become a zero-sum game, whereby advancing social aims detracts from a firm's profitability, and vice versa. In such cases, individual or organizational players that prioritize one bottom line may be highly invested in challenging those that prioritize the other bottom line. Issues that give rise to such conflicts in small social businesses may be further augmented by three factors that are especially salient to social enterprises: stakeholder scope, mission drift, and performance measurement.

The broad scope of stakeholders involved with social enterprises may be a source of tension because dialects may be influenced by environmental factors.[35] As noted by Lumpkin et al., social enterprises will interact with the stakeholders that are typical of a commercial venture (e.g., owners, investors, employees, suppliers, and customers), plus others that are common in a social setting (e.g., donors, the community, local authorities, and benefit recipients).[36] With this broader array of stakeholders, more, and often conflicting, demands on the small organization are likely to arise. For example, a local community is likely to push for social goals, while investors are likely to lobby for the advancement of financial goals. Sometimes the social and financial goals are in alignment; for instance, growing business sales and creating additional jobs may benefit both investors and a local community. However, financial and social objectives often run contrary to each other. For instance, announcements of large-scale layoffs are almost a daily occurrence in newspapers around the country of late; the rationale is often based around improving the organizations' financial performance, yet the local community suffers in the process. Importantly, the tensions discussed within this chapter arise only in situations where social and financial goals are in conflict with each other.

In social enterprises, the tension between social and financial goals is often manifest by mission drift. Mission drift is the notion that the presence of business logics can inadvertently shift attention to goals or priorities that vary from the organization's primary purpose. This drift, in the case of social enterprises, tends to be a shift in priorities away from the social and toward the financial.[37] Weisbrod provided a seminal work on the topic, which argued that engagement in commercial activities causes social organizations to devote significant time, energy, and money toward competing in commercial markets.[38] In turn, these resources are diverted from the social mission, resulting in a shift in priorities—a drift from the organization's original mission. This drift is likely to create significant discomfort and tension among those who are deeply connected to the social goals of the organization. Real-world examples of mission drift include charity hospitals that, over time, begin turning away uninsured patients and citing "the bottom line" as the reason, summer camps that shift their target market to children with AIDS to qualify for grant funding, and public broadcasting stations that move away from sponsorship and toward paid commercial announcements.[39]

Because of the uncertainty surrounding social goal attainment, performance measurement can become complicated as small businesses seek to account for both financial and social goal attainment. Whereas indicators of financial performance may be gleaned by simple cost-revenue calculations, there is no widely accepted, standardized measure of social performance. Social performance assessment tools and indicators such as the social return on investment (SROI) and Impact Reporting and Investment Standards (IRIS) are gaining in popularity yet remain far from universal. Young[40] attributes this lack of widely accepted performance measures to five factors, namely, that social value is (1) subjective, (2) negotiated between stakeholders, (3) contingent and open to reappraisal, (4) composed of incommensurable elements that cannot easily be aggregated within a single metric, and (5) inseparable from social activity. Absent the ability to accurately measure social performance, small business owners must often make decisions and resource allocations on mutable gut instinct. This is likely to be a source of tension for proponents of both social and financial goals.

For the aforementioned reasons, dialectical theory, which addresses the nature of the interactions among opposing forces, seems an appropriate framework for theorizing on dynamic processes within young and small social enterprises. We turn next to an application of the three dialectical stages as they pertain to the strategies of social enterprises.

THE THESIS-ANTITHESIS-SYNTHESIS OF SOCIAL ENTERPRISES

Thesis Stage

In applying the three dialectical stages to commercial and social enterprise partnerships, Di Domenico et al. argued that the "initial thesis stage of the collaboration occurs during the early phases of the relationship and involves establishing whether the exchange values of the partners are sufficiently high to justify formally establishing the partnership."[41] We argue that a similar thesis is constructed within the minds of social enterprise owners and within the enterprises themselves during the early stages of organizational founding. That is, when small business owners decide to pursue a venture with both social and economic goals, they establish the plausibility of the goals' coexistence and the processes to accomplish both goals. Should a potential small business owner come to the conclusion that the goals are mutually exclusive or that they cannot both feasibly be encompassed in the organization, they would not engage in establishing a social venture. This logic applies to both for-profit and nonprofit social ventures. Although financial goals often manifest themselves differently in nonprofit ventures—that is, through donations, grants, and the like—they may still conflict with the social goals of the organization. For instance, nonprofit organizations may struggle with the amount of resources (human and financial) they need to devote to donation solicitation, as resources devoted to soliciting donations generally may not be used concurrently to achieve social aims (e.g., an animal charity employee making solicitation phone calls may not care for wounded animals at the same time).

Thus nonprofits, like for-profits, must also reconcile financial and social goals. In sum, in the inception phase of a small social venture, we purport that an orderly arrangement between social and financial goals is established and developed.

Antithesis Stage

Following the thesis stage, the early congruence that the social business owner reached internally may be put to the test once an organization has been formed. In the launch phase, venture founders will engage with stakeholders to gain their support and resources for the organization.[42] The diversity and potentially conflicting goals of these stakeholders will likely be particularly pronounced within organizations that engage with both business and social constituents. The small business owner will be challenged to integrate the contradictory goals and logics of both social and business stakeholders into the venture to gain their support. A simple example of this occurs when the small social business hires employees. As a social organization, the business owner may want to provide for his or her employees above and beyond commercial competitors with such benefits as higher pay, more health care, education scholarships, and so on. However, as small firms are resource constrained, more financially oriented stakeholders, such as investors or managers, may push for fewer employee provisions to buffer the bottom line of the firm.

As more and more decisions are made that require the social enterprise to jockey between the two goals, however, we expect the manifestation of conflicts and tension, which will shift organizations into the antithesis stage. Whereas order was created between the two forces in the thesis stage by the actions of the small business owner, unexpected ruptures and inconsistencies in the relationship are arguably inevitable during the later stages of organizational founding. As the organization grows, as resources are committed, as stakeholders make demands, and as performance is evaluated, frictions are likely to escalate. Actors (e.g., entrepreneurs, employees, stakeholders) may find themselves taking the side of one goal over another, and the power and legitimacy of these actors influences the degree of friction.[43] In short, we argue that social enterprises will find themselves in the midst of a unique dialectical struggle that is rarely experienced by commercial enterprises. Whereas commercial enterprises tend to place primacy on financial goals because of the salience of shareholders and face little ambiguity surrounding performance measurement, social enterprises have competing demands and contradictory goals. In social enterprises, their very raison d'être is often to serve beneficiaries and fulfill a social mission. This creates a unique, salient, and legitimate stakeholder that is often largely absent in commercial ventures. Not only do beneficiaries themselves demand attention, but government, community, and media stakeholders also hold social enterprises to higher levels of social performance requirements than their commercial counterparts. At the same time, small social enterprises still need to satisfy financial supporters and fulfill financial objectives to survive and grow. This creates the potential for conflict between the objectives of a more diverse and broader range of stakeholders in a small social enterprise.

We argue that this unique tension will be manifest in the strategies a firm decides to pursue. Holistically stated, the achievement of different goals generally requires the enactment of different strategies. Notably, this is not necessarily the case, as the financial and social goals of some enterprises may be in alignment. For instance, many microfinance organizations enjoy an alignment between the two types of goals. Microfinance is the provision of small financial services, such as loans, savings accounts, insurance, and fund transfers, to an impoverished clientele. For many microfinance organizations, the whole of their income is derived from the interest and fees that they accrue from providing financial services, and these financial services also comprise their social mission. Thus, in general it may be argued that the more money they make, the greater the social benefit they are providing (assuming the increased revenues are not generated through price gouging or other practices of ill repute). However, this chapter focuses on those situations in which the financial and social goals of an enterprise are not in alignment. Microfinance organizations face such situations as well, for they may also make more money by, for example, raising interest rates on their loans, thereby excluding many potential borrowers and restricting the ability of their impoverished clients to repay loans. In this situation, the financial and social goals of the organization are in conflict. Based on dialectical theory, we argue that, when social and financial goals are in conflict, as they often are within small social organizations, enterprises that prioritize financial goals will likely strategize differently than those that prioritize social goals. Then, as different goals are pursued, firms will vacillate between different strategies as they are perceived to be more or less important.

Importantly, the antithesis stage is commonly characterized by the oscillation of forces. As Van de Ven states, "Organizational transformations and anomie are produced when strong oscillations occur between opposing forces that push the organization out of its equilibrium orbit and produce deconstructions."[44] Thus, we argue that following the decision to pursue a new social venture (the thesis stage), social small business owners will oscillate with respect to their strategic foci. That is, early in the organizational founding process, social enterprises will exhibit erratic changes in the importance levels assigned to different strategic foci.

Synthesis Stage

The conflict between social and economic goals may be a small firm's undoing. Extant work has noted that many organizations do not reconcile the dialectical tensions and therefore do not progress into the third stage of synthesis.[45] This is likely the case with many small social ventures, as conflicting demands decrease the efficiency or effectiveness of the organization to significantly uncompetitive levels. However, those that do break the antithesis mold and accomplish second-order change should display a new, orderly, and more stable relationship between the formerly opposing forces.

More specifically, the oscillation should subside during this phase. The implication for strategy perceptions is that, for those enterprises still in the founding process, strategic foci ratings will oscillate less as time progresses. The rationale here is that priorities will be set straight, likely in one of two ways: either (1) one stakeholder establishes power and dominance over others such that their priorities are given precedence, or (2) previously conflicting stakeholders arrive at a mutually agreed upon compromise as to the strategic priorities. Regarding the former, an example would be if a financier were at odds with the strategic priorities of another stakeholder. If the financier wished to make a power play, he or she may buy a controlling (or more controlling) stake in the firm, in essence, giving the financier more control over the strategic decisions of the firm.

As an example of compromise, consider strategies related to the development of intellectual property, such as patents. It may be the case that more financially oriented stakeholders will prioritize patent acquisition as important to prevent competitors from using similar methods, technologies, or resources. In doing so, the firm may have a competitive advantage and reap higher rents. However, more socially oriented stakeholders may welcome other firms to use similar methods in an effort to help more customers or beneficiaries. Thus, socially oriented stakeholders may view intellectual property development as less important than financially oriented stakeholders. During the antithesis phase, this may lead enterprises to flip-flop as to the importance of intellectual property in an effort to appease multiple stakeholders. However, when a synthesis is reached, whereby stability is gained between formerly conflicting stakeholders, such shifting around may subside. For instance, a synthesis may be established by acquiring a patent on a key technology, yet agreeing to license the property to other firms at reasonable rates. As a result, we suggest that later in the organizational founding process, social enterprises will exhibit stability in the importance levels assigned to strategic foci.

RESEARCH DESIGN AND METHODOLOGY

While theory and logic are a good starting point for explaining real-world phenomena, empirical analysis of actual firms can support or deny suppositions made by extant rationale. As such, given our expectations of how goal conflict occurs when creating small social ventures, we set out to explore our arguments with data on real enterprises.

Sample

Our sample is composed of the Panel Study of Entrepreneurial Dynamics II dataset—a large-scale data collection effort conducted at the University of Michigan and supported by more than 130 scholars and over 30 research centers. The PSED II is a time-series survey of individuals in the process of starting businesses, the vast majority of which are very small. These individuals were identified based on a random digit dialing method of over 30,000 U.S. adults. To be included in the survey, respondents needed to meet several criteria: (1) the individual must have been actively involved in starting a new business within the last 12 months; (2) he or she must have anticipated ownership in this business; (3) the firm must have still been in the start-up phase at the time of the call screening; and (4) the firm must not be majority owned by another business. The screening resulted in the identification of 1,214 nascent entrepreneurs across the country. Five waves of telephone interviews were subsequently conducted on this sample, taking place at roughly one-year intervals. In the analysis that follows, we include all five years of data. To test differences between time periods, we needed to divide the observation window into early and late stages. As there are five time periods, we deem periods 1–3 as the early phase and periods 4–5 as the late phase.

We followed prior studies in identifying social enterprises within the PSED II dataset.[46] Each respondent was asked the following two survey questions: (1) "Why do you want to start this new business?" and (2) "What are the one or two main opportunities that prompted you to start this new business?" Coders recorded both the first and second answers provided to these questions and then classified answers into one of 44 potential responses for the first question and one of 62 for the second. Consistent with prior researchers, we label social respondents as those who answered either of the two questions with the responses "help others; help community" or "aid in economy; economic development" on their first or second response. Examples of other responses that we did not classify as socially oriented are those based on income (e.g., "to make money"; "unlimited income potential"); business opportunities (e.g., "take advantage of opportunity"; "high demand for products"); employment (e.g., "cannot find employment elsewhere"; "more free time"); personal reasons (e.g., "have a talent in the field"; "inheritance"); and life style ("to do more fulfilling work"; "try new career"). This resulted in a final sample of 94 individuals.

Variables

The variables we explore are the individuals' perceptions of the strategic foci critical to competitive performance.[47] Each respondent was asked the following: "[Strategic foci] is important for this business to be an effective competitor. Would you say you strongly agree, agree, neither agree nor disagree, disagree, strongly disagree or is it not relevant as it applies to this (new) business?" The 10 strategic foci that apply to these questions are derived from, and consistent with, those established in previous research on new and young venture strategies: [48]

- "Lower prices"
- "Quality products or services"
- "Serving those missed by others"
- "Being first to market a new product or service"
- "Doing a better job of marketing and promotion"
- "A superior location and customer convenience"
- "More contemporary, attractive products"
- "The technical and scientific expertise of the start-up team"
- "Developing new or advanced product technology or process technology for creating goods and services"
- "Development of intellectual property such as a patent, copyright or trademark"

The answers provided to each of these questions were used in creating our variables of interest. Responses were coded on five-point scales with strongly agree scored as 5 and strongly disagree scored as 1. We took these responses and rank ordered them from 1 to 10, with 1 corresponding to the strategic focus that had the highest score (indicating that is was the most important strategic factor in being an effective competitor) and 10 corresponding to the strategic focus that had the lowest score.

Analyses

Unlike many organizational theories, dialectical theory is difficult to analyze empirically. Models based on dialectical theory have traditionally been composed of theoretical propositions[49] or analyzed via qualitative analysis.[50]

To analyze our data, we graph variations in the importance-level rankings assigned to each focal strategy and employ visual analyses of the figures.[51]

Our first argument predicts that early in the organization-founding process, social enterprises will experience erratic changes in importance levels assigned to strategic foci. To view this, we plot variations in the average importance-level rankings given to each strategic foci during each wave of the PSED II on a radar graph that we can inspect visually. Support for this argument would be gained by identifying large changes in average importance levels as reported in the interviews between the first three waves (i.e., years).

To understand whether the importance attributed to strategies stabilizes over time, we test whether there is less variation later in the organizational founding process when compared with the earlier period. Here we again utilize visual plots and reason that our arguments will be supported if there is less variation in strategy ratings in periods 4–5 than in periods 1–3.

RESULTS

Figure 6.1 presents the radar graphs of average importance-level rankings assigned to each strategic focus for social enterprises over the first

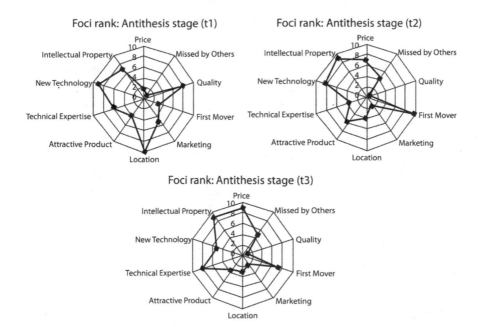

FIGURE 6.1 Strategic Foci Importance Rankings over Antithesis Stage
Source: Adapted from data available in PSED II.

three years—the expected antithesis period described in dialectical theory. Figure 6.2 presents the radar graphs of average importance-level rankings over the final two years—the expected synthesis period described in dialectical theory. A radar graph is a method of displaying multivariate data in two-dimensional space. Each axis on the radar graph illustrates a ranking from 1 to 10 of how important, on average, entrepreneurs in our sample rate the strategy listed on the axis. By examining the change in rankings from year to year, one can better understand the patterns of strategic importance over time.

Our first argument predicts a variant pattern among the founders with large changes in importance levels assigned to the different strategies in the early phase. A visual analysis of the patterns lends support to this line of reasoning. Erratic patterns seem to be particularly prominent for the following strategic foci: "Lower prices," "Being first to market a new product or service," "A superior location and customer convenience," and "The technical and scientific expertise of the start-up team." The prominence of patterns for these strategies may suggest that stakeholders are more involved or focused on these strategies than on the others. As a plausible example, perhaps investors highly support being first to market in an effort to avoid early competition, while employees may feel uncomfortable with the ambiguity and risk that accompanies first movers. As each of these stakeholders vies for decision-making power, the importance level attributed to being first to market may vary. Notably, none of the strategic foci had identical rankings in each of the first three years. In summation, we find some support for our expectation that strategic foci ratings will vary over time.

Our second argument suggests that there will be less variation in strategic foci rankings in later periods, as compared to earlier periods. A visual analysis of the radar graphs in figure 6.2 lends support for this expectation as well.

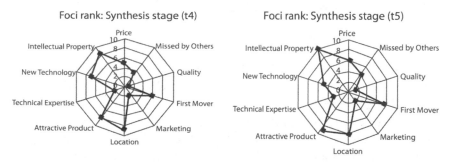

FIGURE 6.2 Strategic Foci Importance Rankings over Synthesis Stage
Source: Adapted from data available in PSED II.

Several of the foci did not change at all in their importance rankings between time periods 4 and 5 (the synthesis stage). Namely, "Serving those missed by others," "Quality products or services," and "Doing a better job of marketing and promotion" maintained identical rankings. Moreover the following strategic foci changed by only one place in the rankings within the synthesis stage: "Lower prices," "Being first to market a new product or service," "A superior location and customer convenience," "More contemporary, attractive products," "The technical and scientific expertise of the start-up team," and "Development of intellectual property such as a patent, copyright or trademark." Taking these findings together, we find support for the notion that although there are erratic changes in strategic foci rankings over time, these changes subside over time.

DISCUSSION

Small, young social enterprises that are pursuing social goals while remaining financially viable often face competing demands and contradictory forces that commercial enterprises rarely encounter. These demands may come from several sources. Among the most important is the influence of multiple stakeholders because of the alternative viewpoints and additional complexity that they introduce to strategic decision-making processes. As a result, the strategic choices that nascent social entrepreneurs need to highlight to be successful are often unclear, especially during the organizational-founding process. In this chapter, we explored the strategies that founding social entrepreneurs focus on and how these change over time. The results of our analyses have yielded several interesting insights with implications for research and practice. In this section, we discuss each of the findings in turn.

Dialectical Tensions in Small Social Enterprises

Through our analysis of strategy dynamics over time, our findings support the applicability of dialectical theory to small social enterprises at the firm level of analysis. Prior social entrepreneurship research has applied dialectical theory to the interfirm level of analysis.[52] But because of the internal tensions between social and financial goals, our chapter indicates that social enterprises may also comprise an ideal arena in which to study, apply, and contribute to dialectical theory. All firms likely experience dialectical tensions; however, the importance of both social and financial performance to the achievement of social enterprise goals, coupled with their potential for conflict, makes the social enterprise an exciting setting for exploring the dialectical change process.

On a more specific level, our results support the argument that the dialectical tensions within social enterprises have implications for the strategies deemed important by the business owners. Because of the competing priorities surrounding social and financial goals, social enterprises frequently change their strategic foci. This strategic dynamism has important implications. For one, a business owner or firm that sticks with the same strategy is likely to enjoy economies of learning. That is, the more they replicate their strategic processes, the more skilled they become at those strategies. Firms with alternating strategies may perpetually reside at the disadvantageous beginning of the learning curve. Further, firms that deploy alternate strategies may be sending mixed messages to their current and potential customers. For instance, establishing a low-price strategy and then switching away from it is likely to disenfranchise certain customers. As a result, strategic dynamism may put the social venture at a disadvantage when competing with commercial firms, assuming that the latter do not experience the same tensions and resulting strategic dynamism. Future work is needed to investigate mechanisms that entrepreneurs can employ to prevent dialectical tensions from impacting strategic perceptions or organizational processes.

Finally, our findings may allow small social enterprise owners/managers to anticipate some problems that may arise in their businesses. Specifically, those practitioners in the very early phase of starting a social enterprise should anticipate and prepare for tensions between stakeholders and differing organizational behaviors based on those tensions. Our results provide evidence that these tensions may be reconciled and that erratic outcomes may be stabilized over time. The sooner that small social enterprise owners are able to recognize the conflicting tensions in their stakeholder demands (and corresponding strategies), the sooner that they can take action to address them. Integrating competing tensions and reaching synthesis sooner will ensure that the organization is not crippled by its dialectic struggle.

Limitations and Conclusions

As is the case with other social enterprise research on the PSED II, our study includes several limitations. First, our study is conducted entirely within the United States. While the PSED II has been acclaimed as a representative sample of the United States,[53] the generalizability of our findings may not include other countries. Future research on the extent of dialectical tensions and variability in firm strategies within social enterprises in other countries may provide substantial theoretical and empirical extensions to this study.

Second, although we used an established method for identifying social enterprises, it is limited in at least one significant way; namely, the measure is dichotomous. Thus, we are unable to capture the extent of social missions or practices within each firm. Importantly, the extent of the social missions and practices is likely directly linked to both the extent of the theoretical tensions and the willingness of the enterprises to solve the tensions. That is, an organization in which a social mission is present yet largely peripheral would likely experience lesser tensions as compared with firms that place social goals on an equal footing with financial goals. Alternatively, an organization that gives primacy to its social mission and relegates its financial mission to secondary status would also likely experience less tension, given that priorities have already been determined. Thus, we expect that the extent of social missions or practices within organizations is a large determinate of the magnitude of tensions.

Third and related, while it is beyond the scope of our study, social enterprise occurs in many forms. For example, nonprofits that engage in sales of goods and services may be classified as social enterprises.[54] It would be interesting to explore the dialectical tensions (or lack thereof) within such enterprises as compared with their for-profit counterparts.

Fourth, although our overall sample size is sufficient for our methodology, the number of social enterprises in the sample is relatively small. Therefore, while the PSED II may be a representative sample of entrepreneurs in the United States, the extent to which these 94 social individuals are representative of all social business owners and enterprises in the United States is unknown. Future research employing larger sample sizes could generate alternative findings or add important nuances to our results.

Fifth, our data is limited to early stage social ventures and only consists of a five-year window. Thus, we may not have a window of observation long enough to capture phenomena such as the reemergence of antithetical issues within organization. An ideal window of observation would capture the entirety of organizational life cycles, from idea inception to the death of a firm. Future studies on dialectical tensions in small social enterprises would benefit from a significantly longer time frame.

CONCLUSION

While prior work has elucidated the notion that small social organizations endure tensions between their social and financial objectives, little research has been conducted on the implications of these tensions across time. We find that strategic dynamism may develop within these organizations yet dissipate with time. In doing so, we hope to illuminate the social enterprise strategy-making process further and open a dialogue around the unique strategic patterns in a social enterprise's life trajectory.

NOTES

1. We use the term *social enterprises* to refer generally to enterprises with a social mission. As such, it can be used interchangeably with terms such as *social venture* and *social business* and is not limited to a specific organizational form that is found in the United Kingdom and elsewhere. Paul Tracey and Nelson Phillips, "The Distinctive Challenge of Educating Social Entrepreneurs: A Postscript and Rejoinder to the Special Issue on Entrepreneurship Education," *Academy of Management Learning & Education* 6, 2 (2007): 264–271.

2. David Gras and G. T. Lumpkin, "Strategic Foci in Social and Commercial Entrepreneurship: A Comparative Analysis," *Journal of Social Entrepreneurship* 3, 1 (2012): 6–23.

3. J. Gregory Dees and Beth Battle Anderson, "For-profit Social Ventures," *International Journal of Entrepreneurship Education* 2, special issue on social entrepreneurship (2003): 1–26.

4. Julie Battilana and Silvia Dorado, "Building Sustainable Hybrid Organizations: The Case of Commercial Microfinance Organizations," *Academy of Management Journal* 53, 6 (2010): 1419–1440.

5. G. T. Lumpkin, Todd W. Moss, David M. Gras, Shoko Kato, and Alejandro S. Amezcua, "Entrepreneurial Processes in Social Contexts: How Are They Different, if at All?," *Small Business Economics* 40, 3 (2013): 761–783.

6. Battilana and Dorado, "Building Sustainable Hybrid Organizations," 1419; David Gras and Karla I. Mendoza-Abarca, "Risky Business? The Survival Implications of Exploiting Commercial Opportunities by Nonprofits," *Journal of Business Venturing* 29, 3: 392–404.

7. Lumpkin et al., "Entrepreneurial Processes in Social Contexts," 761.

8. Gras and Lumpkin, "Strategic Foci in Social and Commercial Entrepreneurship," 6.

9. J. Kenneth Benson, "Organizations: A Dialectical View," *Administrative Science Quarterly* 22, 1 (1977): 1–21; Myeong-Gu Seo and W. E. Douglas Creed, "Institutional Contradictions, Praxis, and Institutional Change: A Dialectical Perspective," *Academy of Management Review* 27, 2 (2002): 222–247.

10. Andrew H. Van de Ven and Marshall Scott Poole, "Explaining Development and Change in Organizations," *Academy of Management Review* 20, 3 (1995): 510–540.

11. Scott Newbert, Kevin Clark, and Narda Quigley, "Why They Do What They Do: Comparing the Personal Characteristics and Motivations of Social and Commercial Entrepreneurs" (paper presented at the 2010 NYU Satter Conference on Social Entrepreneurship), November 5, 2010, New York.

12. Lumpkin et al., "Entrepreneurial Processes in Social Contexts," 761.

13. Michael Porter, "What Is Strategy?" *Harvard Business Review* 6, November (1996): 61–78.

14. Nancy M. Carter, Timothy M. Stearns, Paul D. Reynolds, and Brenda A. Miller, "New Venture Strategies: Theory Development with an Empirical Base," *Strategic Management Journal* 15, 1 (1994): 21–41.

15. Gras and Lumpkin, "Strategic Foci in Social and Commercial Entrepreneurship," 6.

16. G. T. Lumpkin and Gregory G. Dess, "Simplicity as a Strategy-making Process: The Effects of Stage of Organizational Development and Environment on Performance," *Academy of Management Journal* 38, 5 (1995): 1386–1407; Danny Miller, "The Architecture of Simplicity," *Academy of Management Review* 18, 1 (1993): 116–138.

17. Maria Laura Di Domenico, Paul Tracey, and Helen Haugh, "The Dialectic of Social Exchange: Theorizing Corporate-Social Enterprise Collaboration," *Organization Studies* 30, 8 (2009): 887–907.

18. Benson, "Organizations," 1.

19. Andrew H. Van de Ven, "Suggestions for Studying Strategy Process: A Research Note," *Strategic Management Journal* 13 (1992): 178.

20. Klaus F. Riegel, "Toward a Dialectical Theory of Development," *Human Development* 18, 1-2 (1975): 50–64.

21. Benson, "Organizations," 3.

22. Ibid., 5.

23. Ibid.

24. Ibid., 14.

25. Seo and Creed, "Institutional Contradictions," 225.

26. Peter Michael Blau and William Richard Scott, *Formal Organizations: A Comparative Approach* (Stanford, CA: Stanford University Press, 1962); Benson, "Organizations," 1; J. Kenneth Benson, "The Analysis of Bureaucratic-professional Conflict: Functional versus Dialectical Approaches," *The Sociological Quarterly* 14, 3 (1973): 376–394.

27. Susan V. Lourenco and John C. Glidewell, "A Dialectical Analysis of Organizational Conflict," *Administrative Science Quarterly* 20, 4 (1975): 489–508.

28. Jean B. McGuire, "A Dialectical Analysis of Interorganizational Networks," *Journal of Management* 14, 1 (1988): 109–124.

29. Van de Ven, "Suggestions for Studying Strategy Process"; Van de Ven and Poole, "Explaining Development and Change in Organizations."

30. Di Domenico et al., "The Dialectic of Social Exchange," 887.

31. Adalbert Evers, "The Significance of Social Capital in the Multiple Goal and Resource Structure of Social Enterprises," in Carlo Borgaza and Jaques Defourney (eds.) *The Emergence of Social Enterprise* (London: Routledge, 2001): 296–311.

32. James Austin, Howard Stevenson, and Jane Wei-Skillern, "Social and Commercial Entrepreneurship: Same, Different, or Both?" *Entrepreneurship Theory and Practice* 30, 1 (2006): 1–22; Di Domenico et al., "The Dialectic of Social Exchange," 887.

33. Paul B. Firstenberg, *Managing for Profit in the Nonprofit World* (New York: Foundation Center, 1986), 61.

34. Howard Aldrich and Ellen R. Auster, "Even Dwarfs Started Small: Liabilities of Age and Size and Their Strategic Implications," *Research in Organizational Behavior* 8, (1986): 165–198.

35. Van de Ven, "Suggestions for Studying Strategy Process," 169.

36. Lumpkin et al., "Entrepreneurial Processes in Social Contexts," 761.

37. Peter Frumkin, *On Being Nonprofit: A Conceptual and Policy Primer* (Cambridge, MA: Harvard University Press, 2002).

38. Burton Weisbrod, "The Pitfalls of Profits," *Stanford Social Innovation Review* 2 (2004): 40–47.

39. Paul Clarke, "Go! Stay on Target. Be Mission Focused. Nonprofit Resource Center" (2004), http://www.acpl.lib.in.us/docs/default-source/ACPLdocs/mission_focused-1.pdf.

40. Rowena Young, "For What It Is Worth: Social Value and the Future of Social Entrepreneurship," in *Social Entrepreneurship: New Models of Sustainable Social Change*, ed. Alex Nichols (New York: Oxford University Press, 2006): 56–73.

41. Di Domenico et al., "The Dialectic of Social Exchange," 896.

42. Saras D. Sarasvathy, "Causation and Effectuation: Toward a Theoretical Shift from Economic Inevitability to Entrepreneurial Contingency," *Academy of Management Review* 26, 2 (2001): 243–263.

43. Van de Ven, "Suggestions for Studying Strategy Process," 169.

44. Ibid., 179.

45. Di Domenico et al., "The Dialectic of Social Exchange," 887.

46. Gras and Lumpkin, "Strategic Foci in Social and Commercial Entrepreneurship," 6; Newbert et al., "Why They Do What They Do."

47. Gras and Lumpkin, "Strategic Foci in Social and Commercial Entrepreneurship," 6.

48. Carter et al., "New Venture Strategies," 21.

49. Seo and Creed, "Institutional Contradictions," 225.

50. Di Domenico et al., "The Dialectic of Social Exchange," 887.

51. Robert McGill, John W. Tukey, and Wayne A. Larsen, "Variations of Box Plots," *The American Statistician* 32,1 (1978): 12–16.

52. Di Domenico et al., "The Dialectic of Social Exchange," 887.

53. Paul Davidson Reynolds and Richard T. Curtin, *New Firm Creation in the United States: Initial Explorations with the PSED II Data Set* (New York: Springer, 2009).

54. Janelle A. Kerlin, "Social Enterprise in the United States and Europe: Understanding and Learning from the Differences," *Voluntas: International Journal of Voluntary and Nonprofit Organizations* 17, 3 (2006): 246–262.

7

Small Business Exit: Review of Past Research, Theoretical Considerations, and Suggestions for Future Research

Dawn R. DeTienne and Karl Wennberg

Although entrepreneurial exit has recently been defined as "the process by which the founders of privately held firms leave the firm they helped to create; thereby removing themselves, in varying degree, from the primary ownership and decision-making structure of the firm," exit research has a broader foundation.[1] Exit varies on at least two dimensions: small firm exit and small business owner exit. Thus, the current research has examined scenarios wherein both firms and small business owners exit the market. These exits may be the result of either poor or strong performance.[2] That is, poorly performing firms might exit the market through bankruptcy or liquidation because of financial troubles, and strongly performing firms might be acquired and subsumed into an existing organization or broken apart for their assets (e.g., intellectual property).[3] In each of these cases the small business owner also exits entrepreneurial activity (at least with the current firm).

Alternately, the small business owner may exit the firm while the firm remains an ongoing entity, most often through founder succession or harvest.[4] Founder succession may be planned (e.g., family succession)[5] or it may be forced (as could happen through loss of control from equity funding).[6] Harvesting refers to the process of cashing in an investment (in this case, the investment of the entrepreneur's time, money, and energy) and realizing the full value of that investment.[7] This type of exit is most often deliberate on the part of the founder and can be attributed to planned exit strategies, retirement, a desire to pursue different interests, or a better or different use of resources.

Finally, some researchers argue that a small business owner may make the decision to close one firm and open another (entrepreneurial recycling)[8] or close one and focus on another in his or her portfolio of firms.[9] That is, the firm may exit the market while the small business owner remains involved in entrepreneurial activity. Therefore, researchers examining small business exit may engage in several different levels of analysis: the firm, the founder (individual), or a combination of both.

The exit of entrepreneurs and firms may impact other actors and institutions, including competitors, industries, regions, and economies.[10] In small business, this might include family members, friends, the community, and the balance of competition. For example, Mason and Harrisson find that exit triggers a process of entrepreneurial recycling wherein cashed-out entrepreneurs use their new wealth to engage in the creation of other new ventures, equity funding for other local ventures, and philanthropy.[11] Using individual-level data for 24 countries, Hessel et al. show that exit substantially increases the probability of being involved in new entrepreneurial activity.[12] Thus, while researchers employ a single level of analysis, exit has the potential to impact several levels. In the next section, we turn to the different theoretical perspectives employed by exit scholars.

THEORETICAL PERSPECTIVES ON EXIT

Exit can be researched through different theoretical perspectives, such as those posited in economics, sociology, organization studies, or more generally in entrepreneurship research. To some extent, research from each of these perspectives builds on research from the others. Therefore, an important reason for distinguishing among these perspectives is that each adopts different assumptions on, for example, economic or social embeddedness, individual agency and rationality, and level of analysis. For example, studies from a macrosociological perspective have long touched upon different routes of exit, but they tend to equate exit with low organizational performance. And studies in organization and strategic management have investigated the role of financial performance in the exit of new firms, but they seldom address exit as a potentially volitional decision of small business owners.[13] These assumptions have to be taken into account when trying to understand and reconcile the empirical evidence accumulated on small business exit.

Different strands of the literature have tended to focus on one assumption over another; thus, theories focusing solely on a single level of analysis have less explanatory power for the exit phenomenon. Wennberg argues that three theoretical areas are relevant for the study of the entrepreneurial and small business exit: economic career choice theory, strategy and organizational studies, and entrepreneurship research.[14] Table 7.1 briefly summarizes these key theoretical perspectives on exit. We examine each of these in the paragraphs that follow.

TABLE 7.1 Theoretical Perspectives on Exit

Research Area	Level of Analysis	Key Assumptions	Key Contributions
Career choice economics	Individual	Exit is a swift decision; labor can be employed elsewhere.	Entrepreneurship is a **choice** among alternative occupations.
Entrepreneurship	Individual/Firm	Firms are founded by individuals or teams with volitional control of their venture.	The **individual-firm interface** is important.
Strategy and organization theory	Firm	The focus is on exit as failure; organizations are resource-dependent entities.	Exit is often preceded by **failure-avoiding** strategies.

Economic Career Choice Theory and Small Business Exit

A large body of research from labor economics and microeconomics has addressed the choice of entry into, and exit from, entrepreneurship. A characteristic of this research is a focus on the individuals' occupational choices, specifically, the conditions under which they choose to sell their labor on the job market as waged employees or employ themselves by starting a business. As it is assumed that labor can be employed elsewhere, exit from entrepreneurship is most often considered a voluntary decision and not necessarily a sign of failure of the business or of the individual as an entrepreneur and small business owner. This is mirrored by the use of the terms "entry" and "exit," as opposed to "success" and "failure." Compared with entry, there are fewer studies that deal explicitly with exit. One reason might be that most economic studies of entrepreneurial choice (entry and exit) are based on the logic that individuals make choices that maximize their lifetime incomes; thus, determinants of exit become less of an issue because the logic implies that people will switch in and out of entrepreneurship if future income streams change.

One example is the self-employment choice model presented by Evans and Jovanovic.[15] Their influential article examines small business choices under liquidity (capital) constraints. They find that small business owners are limited to capital that is about one and a half times their wealth; thus, because their access to start-up capital is constrained, not all individuals who desire to become a business owner can do so. The wealthier are more inclined to become entrepreneurs and have more opportunities to enter into and exit from entrepreneurship. A large body of work discusses the Evans and Jovanovic model in light of other empirical material and replicates the findings, including articles where wealth is replaced with inheritance[16] or lottery windfalls.[17] Other researchers argue that capital availability is, by and large, a function of an individual's human capital and that the whole question of liquidity constraints is therefore little more than a question of omitted variables.[18]

Van Praag distinguishes between compulsory and voluntary exits and tests her model on the NLSY data used by Evans and Jovanovic.[19] Her results show different predictors of voluntary and compulsory exits, such as that individuals who started their ventures while employed were less likely to exit voluntarily and those who started their ventures while unemployed were more likely to exit compulsorily. In other work related to unemployment and career choice, researchers found that while unemployment might lead to self-employment, the failure rates are higher for those who enter self-employment during periods of unemployment than for those who enter during periods of employment.[20] Additionally, receiving unemployment benefits reduces the likelihood of entering into self-employment.[21] Gianetti and Simonov investigated 61,151 Swedes who had engaged in any type of self-employment activity between 1990 and 1995 and found that economic performance, the individual's age, and local economic conditions were the major determinants of exit from entrepreneurship.[22]

To summarize, career choice economics indicates that individuals have several opportunities wherein to employ their labor and that entrepreneurship is simply one alternative among many occupations; however, as noted above, research has shown that career choice economics has identified some constraints to this logic (e.g., wealth, employment, age). Because individuals will make choices that maximize their lifetime incomes, they may enter and exit entrepreneurship if future income potential changes. Table 7.2 provides additional evidence and more in-depth discussion of economic career choice, organization theory and strategy, and entrepreneurship studies.

Organizational Theory, Strategy, and Small Business Exit

Research from this perspective has tended to focus on why some organizations survive while others are disbanded. To a significant extent, organizational theory overlaps with the more macro-oriented organizational ecology stream of research, an area where exit by entrepreneurs and established firms is of key concern. Although this literature has primarily focused upon the firm as the unit of analysis, in several studies, the individual emerges as important as well. Several researchers have explained how the pertinent question for

TABLE 7.2 Prior Studies on Small Business Exit, from 1984 to 2013

Reference	Primary Topic	Level of Analysis	Findings	Theoretical Perspectives
Kushnir, 1984[1]	Social-psychological factors (equity, mood, evaluation of self and partner, level of agreement) associated with the dissolution of business partnerships.	Individual	Individuals from dissolved businesses have stronger feelings of inequity and anxiety and more disagreement with and aggression toward the partner. Tendency exists to blame ex-partner for failure. Most prominent reasons given for the dissolution were inequity and personality incompatibility.	Entrepreneurship
Ronstadt, 1986[2]	Studies ex-entrepreneurs who have returned to workforce.	Individual	Financial reasons 31%, venture reasons 15%, personal/family reasons 11%. All other exits (41%) were a combination of the above.	Career choice/ Entrepreneurship
Schary, 1991[3]	Probability and type of exit. A firm may leave an industry in at least three ways: through merger, voluntary liquidation, or bankruptcy.	Firm	Results suggest that type of exit is not related to profitability. There is some heterogeneity across forms of exit, and information about firm characteristics alone is not sufficient to predict all forms of exit.	Strategy Organization theory
Bruderl, Preisendörfer, and Ziegler, 1992[4]	Factors that influence the mortality of 1849 new businesses in Germany.	Individual Firm	Both individual and firm characteristics are important determinants of business survival.	Strategy/ Organization theory
Holtz-Eakin, Joulfaian, and Rosen, 1994[5]	Why do some individuals survive as entrepreneurs and others do not? Do liquidity constraints increase failure?	Individual	The effect of an inheritance raises probability of survival by about 1.3% points. For those that survive, an inheritance is associated with nearly 20% increase in sales.	Career choice

(Continued)

TABLE 7.2 Prior Studies on Small Business Exit, from 1984 to 2013 (Continued)

Reference	Primary Topic	Level of Analysis	Findings	Theoretical Perspectives
Gimeno, Folta, Cooper, and Woo, 1997[6]	Why do some firms survive while other firms with equal economic performance do not	Firms Individual	Individuals with low performance thresholds may choose to continue their firms despite comparatively low performance.	Entrepreneurship
Sullivan, Crutchley, and Johnson, 1997[7]	The motives behind managers' choice toward voluntary liquidation.	Individual	Motives toward voluntary liquidation related to firm distress, agency conflicts, and potential for shareholder gain.	Economics/ Strategy/ Career choice
Everett and Watson, 1998[8]	Explores the impact of macroeconomic factors on small business mortality.	Firm	Economic factors are associated with between 30% and 50% of small business failures, depending on the definition of failure. Failure positively associated with interest rates (failure as bankruptcy) and unemployment (failure as discontinuance) lagged employment rates (failure as to prevent further losses) and with current and lagged retail sales.	Strategy/ Organization theory
Harhoff, Stahl, and Woywode, 1998[9]	Relationship between legal form, firm survival, and growth in 11,000 West German firms.	Firms	In all sectors, firms under limited liability have higher growth and higher insolvency. Firms with owners approaching retirement have a high hazard of voluntary liquidation.	Strategy/ Organization theory
Pennings, Lee, and Van Witteloostuij, 1998[10]	Examines the effect of human and social capital on firm dissolution.	Individual Firm	Industry tenure, firm tenure, and social capital all negatively related to firm exit unemployment.	Strategy/ Organization theory
Bates, 1999[11]	A nationwide analysis of U.S. Asian immigrants and their exit from small businesses	Individual	Highly educ. Asian owners are more likely to exit self-employment and exit from retail and personal services are high. Suggests that self-employment is a form of underemployment among Asian immigrants.	Strategy/ Organization Theory/ Entrepreneurship

Study	Topic	Level	Findings	Discipline
Carrasco, 1999[12]	A study of the factors influencing decision to enter into S/E and likelihood of remaining in business.	Individual	Unemployment leads to self-employment but those who enter self-employment while unemployed have higher failure rates. Receiving unemployment benefits reduces the likelihood of entering into self-employment. Better educated and middle-age are more likely to switch.	Economics/Career Choice
Taylor, 1999[13]	Examines voluntary exits and bankruptcies	Individual	Most self-employment exits are voluntary exits and not bankruptcies. Self-employment persistence pos. related to length of work experience, quitting the prior job, and wealth. Negatively related to prior unemployment.	Economics/Career Choice
Bachkaniwala, Wright, and Ram, 2001[14]	Forms of succession (second generation, MBO, trade sale, shutdown) in ethnic minority family business.	Firm Family	Internal factors (preparation of heirs, nature of relationships, planning and control activities) and external factors (alternative employment opportunities for offspring, business growth) affects forms of succession.	Strategy/ Organization theory/ Entrepreneurship
Becchetti and Sierra, 2002[15]	Determinants of bankruptcy.	Firm	The degree of relative firm inefficiency has sig power in predicting bankruptcy. Customers' concentration, strength, and proximity of competitors also contribute to bankruptcy.	Strategy/ Organization theory
Haveman and Khaire, 2002[16]	Does founder succession hurt or help the organization?	Firm Individual	Ideology is a strong moderator between founder succession and organization failure. Ideology conditions the impact of managerial roles and organizational affiliations on failure following founder succession.	Entrepreneurship

(Continued)

TABLE 7.2 Prior Studies on Small Business Exit, from 1984 to 2013 (*Continued*)

Reference	Primary Topic	Level of Analysis	Findings	Theoretical Perspectives
Van Praag, 2003[17]	Quantify the person-specific determinants of survival duration in self-employed white males.	Individual	Age and industry experience are negatively related to exit, both compulsory and voluntary. Occupation experience is negatively related to exit. Starting while employed reduces risk of both exit and voluntary exit. Starting while unemployed is positively related to exit and compulsory exit. Failure is positively related to all exits.	Strategy/ Organization theory/ Entrepreneurship
Bates, 2005[18]	An analysis of U.S. entrepreneurs who made deliberate decisions to close "successful" firms.	Firm Individual	Decisions to discontinue operations are shaped by opportunity costs, switching costs, and availability of alternative opportunities. Alternative opportunities are identified as a key reason for choosing to discontinue successful firms.	Strategy/ Organization theory/ Entrepreneurship
Cefis and Marsili, 2006[19]	The relationship between innovation and the survival of firms in the Netherlands.	Firm	An innovation premium exits. Firm survival is lowest among small, young, noninnovative firms. Among innovative firms, survival of small and young firms is comparable to other size/age classes and higher than for noninnovators.	Strategy/ Organization theory
Harada, 2007[20]	Examines exit behavior of Japanese small firms and their managers.	Firms Individual	Small firm exits occur because of both economic difficulties in their business (economic-forced exit) and non-economic-forced exit. Probability of economically forced exit is higher if the manager is young and male, the firm has loans, and sales are decreasing	Strategy/ Organization theory/ Entrepreneurship

Cumming, 2008[21]	The relationship between European venture capital contracts and exits.	Firm	VC control rights (board control, fight to replace the founder, use of common equity rather than preferred, majority boards) related to type of exit (IPO or acquisition).	Entrepreneurship
Stam, Thurik, and van der Zwan, 2010[22]	Explores exit before start-up (ex-ante) due to market expectations and after start-up (ex-post) due to real market selection processes.	Individual	Entrepreneurs in the U.S. are less likely to exit before actual start-up and more likely to exit from started ventures than entrepreneurs in Europe. Other moderating factors are welfare-state regime, locating in a rural or urban area, and, on the individual level, tolerance of risk and self-employed parents.	Entrepreneurship
Wennberg, Wiklund, DeTienne, and Cardon 2010[23]	Conceptual model and test of entrepreneurial exit routes.	Individual Firm	Entrepreneurs exit from both firms in financial distress and firms performing well. Human capital factors and failure-avoidance strategies differ substantially across the four exit routes.	Entrepreneurship
Hessels, Grilo, Thurik, and van der Zwan, 2011[24]	Whether, how a recent entrepreneurial exit relates to subsequent engagement.	Individual	A recent exit increases the probability of being involved at five levels of entrepreneur engagement. The probability of reengagement in entrepreneurship after exit is higher for males, for persons who know an entrepreneur, and for persons with a low fear of failure.	Entrepreneurship
Balcaen, Manigart, Buyze, and Ooghe, 2012[25]	Firm-level determinants of 6,118 Belgium distress-related exits (firm's revenue cannot cover opportunity expense, debt, or taxes).	Firm	41% of firms exited through a court-driven exit procedure (mainly bankruptcy), 44% were voluntarily liquidated, and 14% were acquired, merged, or split.	Strategy/Organization theory
Buehler, Kaiser, and Jaeger, 2012[26]	Geographic determinants of firm bankruptcy in Switzerland.	Firm	Bankruptcy is lower in the central municipalities and in regions with favorable business conditions (corporate taxes and unemployment are low and public investment is high).	Strategy/Organization theory

(Continued)

TABLE 7.2 Prior Studies on Small Business Exit, from 1984 to 2013 (*Continued*)

Reference	Primary Topic	Level of Analysis	Findings	Theoretical Perspectives
DeTienne and Cardon, 2012[27]	Entrepreneurs' intentions to exit by a range of possible exit paths.	Individual	Entrepreneurs intend to pursue different exit paths based on entrepreneur experience (positively related to IPO, negatively related to industry sale, liquidation), industry experience (positively related to EBO), age (positively related to liquidation), and education (positively related to IPO, acquisition, negatively related to family succession).	Entrepreneurship
Oertel and Walgenbach, 2012[28]	Studies the effect partner exits have on the survival of SMEs, firm size, legal form, industry, and change moderate.	Firm	Partner exits include the mortality risk of organizations. This effect is moderated by size, legal form, and industry affiliation. Harmful effect increases if partner was involved in founding.	Strategy/ Organization theory
Robb and Watson, 2012[29]	Prior studies have reported that females underperform in male-owned firms, but key demographic differences may be a problem.	Individual Firm	Using longitudinal database with more than 4,000 ventures and analyzing 4-year closure rates, return on assets (ROA), and a risk-adjusted measure, there is no difference in the performance of female- and male-owned new ventures.	Strategy/ Organization theory/ Entrepreneurship
Ryan and Power, 2012[30]	What factors influence the business exit choice from the owner-manager's perspective?	Individual	Size, location, sector, gender, exit plan, and intentions affect exit. Actual exits from Ireland and (Scotland): family succession 35% (22%); sales 49% (66%); and shutdown 16% (12%).	Entrepreneurship
DeTienne, McKelvie, and Chandler, 2013[31]	Entrepreneurial exit strategies: model development and an empirical test.	Individual	Strategies are grouped into 3 higher-level categories (i.e., financial harvest, stewardship, and cessation). An initial test indicates differences among the 3 groups.	Entrepreneurship

[1] Kushnir, "Social-Psychological Factors Associated with the Dissolution of Dyadic Business Partnerships."

[2] Ronstadt, "Exit, Stage Left."

[3] Martha A. Schary, "The Probability of Exit," RAND Journal of Economics 22, 3 (1991): 339–353.

[4] Josef Brüderl, Peter Preisendörfer, and Rolf Ziegler, "Survival Chances of Newly Founded Business Organizations," American Sociological Review 52, 2 (1992): 227–242.

[5] Holtz-Eakin, Joulfaian, and Rosen, "Sticking It Out."

[6] Javier Gimeno et al., "Survival of the Fittest? Entrepreneurial Human Capital and the Persistence of Underperforming Firms," Administrative Science Quarterly 42 (1997): 750–783.

[7] Sullivan, Crutchley, and Johnson, "Motivation for Voluntary Corporate Liquidations."

[8] Everett and Watson, "Small Business Failure and External Risk Factors."

[9] Harhoff, Stahl, and Woywode, "Legal Form, Growth and Exit of West German Firms."

[10] Pennings, Lee, and Witteloostuijn, "Human Capital, Social Capital, and Firm Dissolution."

[11] Bates, "Entrepreneur Human Capital and Small Business Longevity."

[12] Carrasco, "Transitions to and from Self-employment in Spain."

[13] Mark P. Taylor, "Survival of the Fittest? An Analysis of Self-employment Duration in Great Britain," Economic Journal 109, 454 (1999): 140–155.

[14] Bachkaniwala, Wright, and Ram, "Succession in South Asian Family Businesses in the U.K."

[15] Becchetti and Sierra, "Bankruptcy Risk and Productive Efficiency in Manufacturing Firms."

[16] Haveman and Khaire, "Survival beyond Succession?"

[17] van Praag, "Business Survival and Success of Young Small Business Owners."

[18] Bates, "Analysis of Young, Small Firms That Have Closed."

[19] Cefis and Marsili, "Survivor."

[20] Harada, "Which Firms Exit and Why?"

[21] Cumming, "Contracts and Exit in Venture Capital Finance."

[22] Erik Stam, Roy Thurik, and Peter van der Zwan, "Entrepreneurial Exit in Real and Imagined Markets," Industrial & Corporate Change 19, 4 (2010): 1109–1139.

[23] Wennberg et al., "Reconceptualizing Entrepreneurial Exit."

[24] Hessels et al., "Entrepreneurial Exit and Entrepreneurial Engagement."

[25] Balcaen et al., "Firm Exit after Distress."

[26] Buehler, Kaiser, and Jaeger, "The Geographic Determinants of Bankruptcy."

[27] DeTienne and Cardon, "Impact of Founder Experience on Exit Intentions."

[28] Oertel and Walgenbach, "The Effect of Partner Exits on Survival Chances of SMEs."

[29] Alicia M. Robb and John Watson, "Gender Differences in Firm Performance: Evidence from New Ventures in the United States," Journal of Business Venturing 27, 5 (2012): 544–558.

[30] Ryan and Power, "Small Business Transfer Decisions."

[31] DeTienne, McKelvie, and Chandler, "The Impact of Motivation, Innovation, and Causation and Effectuation Approaches on Exit Strategies."

organizational theorists—why some organizations survive while others die— can be examined through the decisions and strategic initiatives of key individuals within or outside the organization.[23]

At the firm level, low exit rates have been positively associated with larger initial capital investment,[24] more employees,[25] greater innovativeness,[26] and the presence of growth strategies.[27] Strong and geographically close competitors[28] and founders' having low switching costs[29] are negatively related to low exit rates. For example, Cefis and Marsili demonstrate that an innovation premium exists; that is, firm survival is lowest among small, young, noninnovative firms.[30] Among innovative firms, survival of small and young firms is comparable to other size and age classes and always higher than for noninnovators. There is also ample evidence from the organization theory literature on small business exit that new firm exit rates first rise and then decline, indicating a liability of adolescence. *Liability of adolescence* is a term coined by Bruderl and Schussler to explain their finding that new firms initially survive because of the initial stock of resources that they can draw upon.[31] They argue (in contradiction to Stinchcome who favored a liability of newness) that rather than declining monotonically with age, new firms initially survive and then failure rates climb during adolescence.

In addition, Mitchell investigated 141 new firms and 274 diversifying entrants in seven U.S. medical product markets.[32] Despite the preconception that new firms are more prone to failure, Mitchell found that, ceteris paribus, new firms were no more likely than diversifying entrants to exit, but that they were less likely to sell their firms. Mitchell's findings that entrepreneurs are less likely to sell their firms are interesting in that they suggest that entrepreneurs are attached to their ventures in excess of the economic value that can be earned from divesting them. Cardon et al. also note that entrepreneurs often refer to their venture as their "baby."[33] Consequently, it is possible that less profitable firms can subsist for many years, or that, as in van Witteloostuijn's model of organizational decline, "inefficient firms might outlast efficient rivals."[34] Underperforming, highly persistent firms have been referred to as chronic failures,[35] the living dead,[36] failure-avoidance organizations,[37] and permanently failing organizations.[38] DeTienne et al. (2008) note that reasons for the existence of underperforming, highly persistent firms include how munificent the environment is, the organization's previous track record of success, the firm's collective efficacy, and the founders' personal investment and the other options available to them.[39]

Thus, we note that organization theory and strategy theories provide insights into small business exit. However, the work by the scholars noted just above indicates that organization theory and strategy alone do not provide a complete model of exit, in particular by seldom considering the role and actions of founders. We now turn to the current entrepreneurship literature and explore how entrepreneurship—the examination of the intersection of individuals and opportunities[40]—provides a different perspective on small business exit.

Entrepreneurship Theories and Small Business Exit

A key feature of entrepreneurship theory is that entrepreneurship occurs at the intersection of individuals and opportunities, in that entrepreneurship is generally conceptualized as individuals pursuing entrepreneurial opportunities to create new ventures.[41] Several researchers have explicitly mentioned that, for new ventures, the firm can be considered "an extension" of the small business owner.[42] Yet, a problem in entrepreneurship research has been the lack of distinction between failure and exit, that is, the difference between attempting to keep a business open but failing to do so and the deliberate closure or successful sale of a business.[43] Furthermore, as noted above, exit operates on several levels of analysis: for example, the small business owner may exit while the firm persists (e.g., by selling and leaving the business), signifying exit at the individual but not the firm level, or the small business owner may close the business but continue being a small business owner by starting a new business through serial entrepreneurship.[44]

The recent entrepreneurship literature shows development toward theory-driven models. For example, Shepherd et al. present a microlevel theoretical model that distinguishes between natural (evolutionary) and manageable (strategic) mortality patterns of new firms.[45] According to the model, survival is dependent on the firm's novelty vis-à-vis the market, its product, and its management. Mortality risk decreases as the venture's novelty in each of the three dimensions is eroded by information search and dissemination processes or risk-reduction strategies taken by small business owners.

Another theory-driven approach to new firm survival was Cooper et al.'s study of 2,994 firms belonging to the National Foundation of Independent Businesses.[46] Cooper and colleagues built a theoretical framework through the examination of human and financial capital perspectives. Their work examined how initial human and financial capital impacts three different outcomes: failure, marginal survival, and high growth. General human capital did not differentiate between the outcomes except that women were less likely than men to be involved with a high-growth venture. The number of founding partners impacted growth (but not survival), and having parents who owned a business contributed to survival (but not growth). The amount of initial financial capital contributed to both growth and survival. Dahlqvist et al. later replicated the predictions of Cooper et al. on a representative sample of 7,256 new Swedish firms.[47] Their results confirm the importance of general human capital, management know-how, and industry effects on the probability of continuation among new ventures, as well as the importance of financial and general human capability on the economic performance of new firms.

Headd investigated perceptual measures of success among 12,185 firms in the 1996 Characteristics of Business Owners Survey, a representative sample of all U.S. firms started between 1989 and 1992.[48] He found that after four years in business, half of all businesses had exited; however, one-third of all exiting entrepreneurs considered their firm to be "successful." Headd also found that factors characterizing exiting firms, such as lack of initial resources, having been started by a young entrepreneur, and so on, did not differ between what the entrepreneurs themselves perceived as "successful" or "unsuccessful" exits. A conclusion of the study was that searching for factors associated with firm exit is less meaningful because a high proportion of exiting entrepreneurs seem to consider this a satisfactory outcome. Another conclusion was that entrepreneurs' goals and time horizons at the onset of their firms are likely to diverge: some may want a life-style business, some are trying to build a high-growth firm that they can divest of in a few years, and others desire to avoid unemployment, among other reasons. This interpretation receives support from DeTienne and Cardon's study of exit strategies among 189 entrepreneurs.[49] They found that such common human capital variables as age, education, and experience were related to what specific exit strategy the entrepreneurs envisioned; thereby concluding that entrepreneurs have different motivations and thresholds that impact their exit strategy. Another study by Wennberg et al. followed 4,463 Swedish firms started in 1994 until their culmination, or until 2002, and found that the same human capital variables were also associated with the eventual exit outcome (merger, employee buyout, liquidation, retirement).[50]

Thus, while career choice models adopt an economic perspective and organization theory and strategy primarily adopts a firm-level perspective, the entrepreneurship literature is more likely to adopt a perspective that includes the importance of the owners and how the owners (or individuals) interact with the opportunity. As Pavone and Banerjee note, the destiny of the firm is intimately linked to that of the owners.[51] We are not suggesting that career choice models and organization theory and strategy models are not relevant, but simply that it is difficult to establish a theory of small business exit and not include the owner or founder.

We now return to our sample of 31 published articles on small business exit, which, together, cover each of the three theoretical perspectives, and we examine the current state of the exit literature more closely, propose research to address the gaps, and provide insights for practicing small business owners.

MAJOR THEMES AND FUTURE RESEARCH

In this next section, we identify five major themes. We believe the bulk of research in small firm exit over the next decade will (and should) focus upon these themes and begin to develop a coherent body of knowledge that will not only increase our understanding of the phenomenon but also provide practical guidance. Although much of the extant research has utilized the theories outlined above, scholars will need to expand their theoretical perspectives to address these issues and concerns. In the paragraphs that follow, we propose additional perspectives that will help scholars to better understand small business exit. The five major themes include (1) further delineation of the exit/failure constructs, (2) exit and performance, (3) exit strategy and exit routes, (4) postexit implications and concerns, and (5) macro- and regional implications of firm exit. See table 7.2 for reference, specific level of analyses, and primary topics in the extant literature.

Further Delineation of the Exit/Failure Constructs

There are clear indications in the literature that exit from small business ownership is not the same as failure. Bates and Headd found that about one-third of discontinued business owners characterize their firms as successful at closure.[52] Ucbasaran et al. surveyed a representative sample of 767 entrepreneurs in Great Britain and found that among the entrepreneurs that had closed down a business, close to a third considered their last business to be "a success."[53] In a study of Japanese small firms, Harada found that small firm exits occur because of both economic difficulties and noneconomic issues such as age, gender, and type of funding.[54] Even among distress-related exits, Balcaen et al. noted that only 41 percent of firms exited through a court-driven exit procedure (mainly bankruptcy), 44 percent were voluntarily liquidated, and 14 percent were acquired, merged, or split.[55] The difficulty is in how we categorize these exits. Are voluntary liquidations failures? If one sells the firm or merges with another, are these failures?

Firms may exit because of many factors—some of which are related to failure and some of which are not. For example, Oertel and Walgenbach show that the exit of a partner substantially decreases the survival chances of an organization and that founder exits decrease survival chances of an organization more than partner exits.[56] And clearly firms exit the market for individual-related reasons such as retirement, discovery of new opportunities, death, divorce, declining interest, and so on. For example, Van Praag found that the age and industry experience of the small business owner and employment of the owner when starting the venture reduce the risk of both compulsory and voluntary exit.[57] Starting a venture while unemployed increases the risk of both types of exits. And Harhoff et al.'s study of 11,000 West German firms suggests that firms with owners approaching retirement have high incidence of voluntary exits.[58] These and other findings indicate that failure and exit are two distinct concepts; yet, the guiding assumption in the bulk of the literature is that the disappearance equates with failure.

Through in-depth case studies, qualitative inquiry, and, ultimately, large empirical studies, this area of research is ripe with possibilities for researchers. For small business owners, this research provides a welcome respite from the majority of articles, which have assumed that exit equates with failure. Certainly, exit rates are high in the new or adolescent phase of the venture, but this could be construed as a positive outcome, as many small business owners have voluntarily exited the firm. Greater understanding of the conditions and decisions that lead to failure and exit will be highly beneficial for small business owners.

Exit and Performance

A key finding in our literature review is that initial resources and current performance of a small firm are strong factors that shape the involuntary exit decision. For example, Becchetti and Sierra find the degree of relative firm inefficiency has significant power in predicting bankruptcy.[59] Customers' concentration, strength, and proximity of competitors also contribute to bankruptcy. While this fact is hardly surprising, it does indicate the importance of future work in disentangling the effect of performance from that of other factors. Empirical studies need to control for current earnings if they are to say anything about exit or, preferably, use some type of decomposition analyses or simultaneous estimation technique to ascertain the true determinants of exit.

A study using such a simultaneous technique is the previously noted work of Gimeno et al., which outlined and tested a threshold model of firm continuation.[60] According to this model, a venture is terminated because of a lack of performance below a critical threshold. Gimeno and colleagues point to a number of limitations with their original study that future work should address. As their study was very broad, spanning all types of businesses in all industries all over the United States, the results might have been affected by unobserved heterogeneity. This would be remedied by controlling for more specific institutional or environmental effects. For example, researchers might consider sociogeographic or cultural factors or consider testing the model on a single industry or population of entrepreneurs. In addition, the Gimeno et al. study measured economic performance as money taken out of a firm. This did not allow the study to distinguish between low performance and entrepreneurs that reinvest most of their profit to foster future growth and profitability. Here we have noted a few, of the many, research opportunities regarding entrepreneurs' performance thresholds.

In another study, Wennberg et al. demonstrated that both successful and unsuccessful firms exit the market.[61] However, many questions remain to be answered. For example, Wennberg and Wiklund found in their study of 25,529 Swedish knowledge-intensive firms that 78 percent of sold firms performed above the population average.[62] They termed these seemingly successful sell offs "exit by success." In the literature to date, there are still no investigations of the founders of such firms post–sell off. How does the financial net worth of these individuals compare to their net worth before they started their firms? In subjective terms, do these individuals evaluate their sold firm as a "personal success" or a "personal failure," and what are the factors associated with such evaluations?[63]

Bates suggests that a key reason for choosing to discontinue a successful firm is the availability of alternative opportunities. These might include creation of a new venture, returning to wage employment, returning to education, or a multitude of other potential opportunities. We have very little understanding of these factors and why entrepreneurs might leave a successful venture. Is it simply boredom? The need for a challenge? The need to contribute to society in a different manner? The desire to create rather than to manage? Family issues? Partnership conflict? Or could the reasons be related to such institutional factors (potentially unobserved by the layman) as increasing regulatory impact, globalization, or changes in tax laws?

Exit Strategy and Exit Routes

Several recent studies have examined exit routes. In particular, the literature discusses initial public offering (IPO), acquisition, employee buyout, management buyout, family succession, independent sale, liquidation, and discontinuance.[64] For example, Cumming relates venture capital control rights to two types of exit: IPO and acquisition.[65] The research by Balcaen et al. examines rates of different types of exit, including bankruptcy (41 percent), voluntary liquidation (44 percent), and acquisitions and mergers (14 percent).[66] Ryan and Power examined actual exits in Ireland and Scotland and found that family succession accounts for 35 percent of exits in Ireland and 22 percent in Scotland. Sale of the firm accounts for 49 percent of exits in Ireland and 66 percent in Scotland. And shutdown accounts for 16 percent of firms in Ireland and 12 percent in Scotland.[67]

Clearly, there are country-level differences; however, it is also important that scholars clearly state what is meant by the terms used in the literature. Does the term "shutdown" as used by Ryan and Power have the same meaning as "voluntary liquidation" as used by Balcaen et al.? To do cross-country comparisons, we must, where possible, develop standard terminology. In addition, as the worldwide economic situation changes, new modes of exit (e.g., partial exits, private equity) are emerging.

Furthermore, there has been a call to better understand exit strategies. For example, in their study of U.S. firms in the electrical measurement and surgical medical instruments industries, DeTienne and Cardon examined a range of possible exit strategies, including liquidation, independent sale, family succession, employee buyout, acquisition, and IPO, and found that entrepreneurs have different exit strategies based on previous entrepreneurial experience, industry experience, age, and education level.[68]

DeTienne et al. examined the same exit strategies in their 2013 study of U.S. firms in the plastic products and software industries and found that perceived innovativeness of an opportunity, motivational considerations, decision-making approach, and team size impacts the choice of exit strategies.[69] These studies suffer from single-industry and single-country limitations, but the arguments surrounding the importance of exit strategies as well as their findings that differences exist for individuals and firms with differing exit strategies is interesting. Their argument for studying exit strategies, as opposed to actual exit, revolves around the idea that if an exit strategy develops early in the life of the firm, it may drive future firm development and thus have an impact on the entire entrepreneurial life cycle. The question is, does the exit strategy drive the future development of the firm? Does it impact the accumulation of initial resources, thereby imprinting the firm in such a manner that it is less receptive to change? For example, if the small business owner makes a decision early in the life of the firm that family succession is his or her exit strategy, does that impact other exit possibilities? What if no successor emerges or the intended successor is not interested? Can the firm change exit strategies? What limitations might it encounter? Not only are these questions practical, but they may also have an impact on the entire entrepreneurial process.

Postexit Implications and Concerns

An additional area of research that has had little attention in the literature is the question of what happens after the exit. Although there has been literature that examines the effect of founder exit or succession on the firm, very little of this work has been conducted with the small firm (see Wasserman for an exception),[70] and almost none has examined the impact on the small business owner. These issues can range from personal-identity issues (who am I without the firm, and what do I do now?) to the impact of the small business owner's new wealth (do I reinvest in other start-ups, begin again, share with family members, or invest in other investments?). In their study of how exits relate to subsequent engagement, Hessels et al. found that a recent exit increases the probability of being involved at multiple levels of entrepreneurial engagement.[71] They also found that the probability of reengagement in entrepreneurship after the exit is higher for males, for persons who know an entrepreneur, and for persons with a low fear of failure.

Shepherd's research into grief after failure may provide important theoretical considerations for the exited small business owner as well.[72] Do small business owners who exit their business grieve? How is this grief different than that for a failure? Are there other emotions related to the exit? Kushnir claimed that individuals from dissolved businesses have stronger feelings of inequity and anxiety and more disagreement with and aggression toward the partner.[73] There is a tendency to blame an ex-partner for failure. To further this line of research, scholars might draw upon theoretical perspectives in sociology and psychology, which examine the results of dramatic changes in a person's financial situation (e.g., winning the lottery or receiving an inheritance) to explore exit. Is harvesting a venture different from other inflows of cash? Does it matter that the small business owner has invested time, money, and energy into the venture?

In addition to the implications of firm exit for small business owners, there may also be implications for industry-level (e.g., how does exit of a single firm affect the competitive landscape), macroeconomic-level (e.g., how does exit impact unemployment), and societal-level outcomes (e.g., how does an exit impact philanthropic efforts). We address these issues in this next section.

Macro- and Regional Implications of Firm Exit

Our review suggests that exit rates are strongly tied to overall economic conditions. Everett and Watson explored the impact of macroeconomic factors on small business mortality and found that economic factors are associated with between 30 percent and 50 percent of small business failures, depending on the definition of *failure* used.[74] Failures are positively associated with interest rates (failure as bankruptcy) as well as unemployment (failure as discontinuance). Buehler et al. studied geography and macroeconomic conditions in Switzerland and found that bankruptcy is lower in the central municipalities and in regions with favorable business conditions (lower corporate taxes, lower unemployment, and high public investment).[75] This research has important implications for policy makers and entrepreneurs.

For policy makers, it is important to understand the impact of decisions to incentivize entrepreneurs. Rather than policies that have an impact in the long run (e.g., receiving a tax credit on the next year's tax return), policy makers might be more inclined to develop policies that create new small businesses and allow for small business expansion in the short term (such as lowering corporate taxes or making capital available). For small business owners, this research points out the importance of locating in areas with favorable business climates and in areas with an entrepreneurial infrastructure. While this decision is fairly obvious in a country such as the United States, where each state, and even municipality, has differing tax laws, incentive programs, and infrastructure, this decision is more complicated in countries wherein policy decisions are made by a single governing body. For example, in the United States, an oil-discovery company may choose to locate in Texas, Oklahoma, or North Dakota because of tax laws, incentives, regulation, and entrepreneurial infrastructure rather than in California, Oregon, or Michigan, which likely have oil and gas reserves as well but have significant regulation and high taxes.

However, in the long term, firm exits may also hold implications for societal-level outcomes. Mason and Harrisson studied five successful Scottish entrepreneurs that had used their newly acquired wealth, together with their network and business experience, to engage in other entrepreneurial activities, notably starting new business ventures, investing in other businesses, and engaging in philanthropic efforts.[76] Aviad and Vertinski investigated all Canadian plants in the foodstuffs and manufacturing sectors in 3,908 local census subdivisions (small geographical areas) from 1983 to 1998.[77] They found that the exits of older firms increase entry rates of new firms and that, on average, new entrants were more productive. Although Hoetker and Agarwal find that exit impairs the ability of other firms to draw on knowledge generated by the firm, firm exits provide spillover benefits to other firms.[78] These three initial studies indicate that exit could positively impact new firm creation, funding availability, philanthropic donations, and the competitive landscape. We look forward to similar studies that examine potential positive implications of exit.

CONCLUSIONS

According to PrivCo, a major source for business and financial data on major, non-publicly traded corporations, private worldwide middle-market exits (i.e., those between $2 million and $500 million) reached $805 billion in 2011.[79] In addition, because of a latent supply of baby-boomer businesses coming into the market, the improving economic climate, increased buyer demand because of recovering stock portfolios, and the slowly improving lending situation, there will be a significant increase in the number of exit transactions over the next decade.[80] Yet, as scholars, our understanding of this phenomenon is clearly deficient.

In this chapter, we have outlined different theoretical perspectives on small business exit and described the evidence from various empirical studies. We have argued that exit is a multifaceted phenomenon spanning different levels of analysis. The empirical studies have amassed a number of research findings that seem to be consistent across different countries and contexts. Yet, there are still several inconsistencies in the findings. Many of these could be the result of confusion in the interpretation and specification of the dependent variable of scrutiny (i.e., exit), ad-hoc usage of theoretical predictors from different levels of analyses, and researchers relying on survey data with underreporting biases. Our review points toward several interesting paths for future research, including further delineation of the exit/failure constructs, exit and performance, exit strategy and exit routes, postexit implications and concerns, and macro- and regional implications of firm exit. It is our hope that future research will begin to disentangle the existing research and future scholars will embark on this interesting and timely field of study.

NOTES

1. Dawn R. DeTienne, "Entrepreneurial Exit as a Critical Component of the Entrepreneurial Process: Theoretical Development," *Journal of Business Venturing* 25, 2 (2010): 203–215.

2. Karl Wennberg, Johan Wiklund, Dawn R. DeTienne, and Melissa Cardon, "Reconceptualizing Entrepreneurial Exit: Divergent Exit Routes and Their Drivers," *Journal of Business Venturing* 25, 4 (2010): 361–375.

3. Sofie Balcaen, Sophie Manigart, Jozefien Buyze, and Hubert Ooghe, "Firm Exit after Distress: Differentiating between Bankruptcy, Voluntary Liquidation and M&A," *Small Business Economics* 39, 4 (2012): 949–975; Robert Ronstadt, "Exit, Stage Left: Why Entrepreneurs End Their Entrepreneurial Careers before Retirement," *Journal of Business Venturing* 1, 3 (1986): 323–338.

4. Darshan Bachkaniwala, Mike Wright, and Monder Ram, "Succession in South Asian Family Businesses in the UK," *International Small Business Journal* 19, 4 (2001): 15–27; Heather A. Haveman and Mukti V. Khaire, "Survival beyond Succession? The Contingent Impact of Founder Succession on Organizational Failure," *Journal of Business Venturing* 19, 3 (2002): 437–463; Harvest: James C. Brau, Ninon K. Sutton, and Nile W. Hatch, "Dual-track versus Single-track Sell-outs: An Empirical Analysis of Competing Harvest Strategies," *Journal of Business Venturing* 25, 4 (2010): 389–402;

Colin Mason and Richard Harrisson, "After the Exit: Acquisitions, Entrepreneurial Recycling and Regional Economic Development," *Regional Studies* 40, 1 (2006): 55–73.

5. Carlos Salvato, Francisco Chirico, and Pramodita Sharma, "A Farewell to the Business: Championing Exit and Continuity in Entrepreneurial Family Firms," *Entrepreneurship & Regional Development* 22, 3–4 (2010): 321–348.

6. Garry Bruton, Vance Fried, and Robert D. Hisrich, "Venture Capital and CEO Dismissal," *Entrepreneurship Theory & Practice* 21, 3 (1997): 41–54.

7. Mason and Harrisson, "After the Exit."

8. Mason and Harrisson, "After the Exit."

9. Paul Westhead and Mike Wright, "Contributions of Novice, Portfolio and Serial Founders Located in Rural and Urban Areas," *Regional Studies* 33, 2 (1998): 157–173.

10. DeTienne, "Entrepreneurial Exit."

11. Mason and Harrisson, "After the Exit."

12. Jolanda Hessels, Isabel Grilo, Roy Thurik, and Peter van der Zwan, "Entrepreneurial Exit and Entrepreneurial Engagement," *Journal of Evolutionary Economics* 21, 3 (2011): 447–471.

13. Michael J. Sullivan, Claire E. Crutchley, and Dana J. Johnson, "Motivation for Voluntary Corporate Liquidations: Distress, Agency Conflicts, and Shareholder Gain," *Quarterly Journal of Business and Economics* 36, 2 (1997): 3–18.

14. Karl Wennberg, "Knowledge Combinations and the Survival of Financial Service Ventures," *Journal of Evolutionary Economics* 19, 2 (2009): 259–276.

15. David S. Evans and Boyan Jovanovic, "An Estimated Model of Entrepreneurial Choice under Liquidity Constraints," *The Journal of Political Economy* 97, 4 (1989): 808–827.

16. David G. Blanchflower and Andrew J. Oswald, "What Makes an Entrepreneur?" *Journal of Labor Economics* 16, 1 (1998): 26–60; Douglas Holtz-Eakin, David Joulfaian, and Harvey S. Rosen, "Sticking It Out: Entrepreneurial Survival and Liquidity Constraints," *The Journal of Political Economy* 102, 1 (1994): 53.

17. Thomas Lindh and Henry Ohlsson, "Self-employment and Windfall Gains: Evidence from the Swedish Lottery," *The Economic Journal* 106 (1996): 1515–1526.

18. Timothy Bates, "Entrepreneur Human Capital and Small Business Longevity," *The Review of Economics and Statistics* 72, 4 (1990): 551–559; Robert Cressy, "Are Business Startups Debt Rationed?" *The Economic Journal* 106 (1996): 1253–1270.

19. C. Mirjam van Praag, "Business Survival and Success of Young Small Business Owners," *Small Business Economics* 21, 1 (2003): 1–17.

20. Raquel Carrasco, "Transitions to and from Self-employment in Spain: An Empirical Analysis," *Oxford Bulletin of Economics and Statistics* 61, 3 (1999): 315–341.

21. Ibid.

22. Mariassunta Giannetti and Andrei Simonov, "On the Determinants of Entrepreneurial Activity: Individual Characteristics, Economic Environment, and Social Norms," *Swedish Economic Policy Review* 11, 4 (2004): 269–313.

23. Joseph Brüderl, Peter Preisendörfer, and Rolf Ziegler, "Survival Chances of Newly Founded Business Organizations," *American Sociological Review* 52, 2 (1992): 227–242; Robert A. Burgelman, "Fading Memories: A Process Theory of Strategic Business Exit in Dynamic Environments," *Administrative Science Quarterly* 39, 1 (1994): 24–56; Johannes M. Pennings, Kyungmook Lee, and Arjen van Witteloostuijn, "Human Capital, Social Capital, and Firm Dissolution," *Academy of Management Journal* 41, 4 (1998): 425–440.

24. Bates, "Entrepreneur Human Capital and Small Business Longevity."

25. Frédéric Delmar, Karin Hellerstedt, and Karl Wennberg, "The Evolution of Firms Created by the Science and Technology Labor Force in Sweden, 1990–2000," in *Managing Complexity and Change in SMEs: Frontiers in European Research*, ed. John Ulhöi and Poul R. Christensen (Cheltenham, U.K.: Edward Elgar, 2006): 69–102.

26. Elena Cefis and Orietta Marsili, "Survivor: The Role of Innovation in Firms' Survival," *Research Policy* 35, 5 (2006): 626–641.

27. Brüderl, Preisendörfer, and Ziegler, "Survival Chances of Newly Founded Business Organizations"; Elaine Romanelli, "Organization Birth and Population Variety: A Community Perspective on Origins," *Organizational Behavior* 11 (1989): 211–246.

28. Leonardo Becchetti and Jaime Sierra, "Bankruptcy Risk and Productive Efficiency in Manufacturing Firms," *Journal of Banking & Finance* 27 (2002): 2099–2120.

29. Bates, "Entrepreneur Human Capital and Small Business Longevity."

30. Cefis and Marsili, "Survivor."

31. Josef Bruderl and Rudolf Schussler, "Organizational Mortality: The Liabilities of Newness and Adolescence," *Administrative Science Quarterly* 35, 3 (1990): 530–547.

32. Will Mitchell, "The Dynamics of Evolving Markets: The Effects of Business Sales and Age on Dissolutions and Divestitures," *Administrative Science Quarterly* 39, 4 (1994): 575–602.

33. Melissa Cardon, Joakim Wincent, Jagdip Singh, and Mateja Drnovsek, "A Tale of Passion: New Insights into Entrepreneurship from a Parenthood Metaphor," *Journal of Business Venturing* 20, 1 (2005): 23–46.

34. Arjen van Witteloostuijn, "Bridging Behavioral and Economic Theories of Decline: Organizational Inertia, Strategic Competition, and Chronic Failure," *Management Science* 44, 4 (1998): 501–519.

35. Arjen van Witteloostuijn, "Bridging Behavioral and Economic Theories of Decline."

36. John C. Ruhnka, Howard Feldman, and Thomas Dean, "The 'Living Dead' Phenomenon in Venture Capital Investments," *Journal of Business Venturing* 7, 2 (1992): 137–155.

37. Rita McGrath, "Falling Forward: Real Options Reasoning and Entrepreneurial Failure," *Academy of Management Review* 24, 1 (1999): 13–30.

38. Marshall W. Meyer and Lynne G. Zucker, *Permanently Failing Organizations* (Newbury Park, CA: Sage Publications, 1989).

39. Dawn R. DeTienne, Dean Shepherd, and Julio DeCastro, "The Fallacy of 'Only the Strong Survive': The Effects of Extrinsic Motivation on the Persistence Decisions for Under-performing Firms," *Journal of Business Venturing* 23, 5 (2008): 528–546.

40. Scott Shane and S. Venkataraman, "The Promise of Entrepreneurship as a Field of Research," *Academy of Management Review* 25, 1 (2000): 217–226.

41. William Gartner, "What Are We Talking About When We Talk About Entrepreneurship?," *Journal of Business Venturing* 5, 1 (1990): 15–28.

42. Gaylen Chandler and Steven Hanks, "Market Attractiveness, Resource-based Capabilities, Venture Strategies, and Venture Performance," *Journal of Business Venturing* 9, 4 (1994): 331–349; Margaret Peteraf and Mark Shanley, "Getting to Know You: A Theory of Strategic Group Identity," *Strategic Management Journal* 18, 1 (1997): 165–186.

43. Dean Shepherd and Johan Wiklund, "Entrepreneurial Small Businesses: A Resource-based Perspective," *Foundations and Trends in Entrepreneurship* (forthcoming).

44. Karl Wennberg and Johan Wiklund, "Entrepreneurial Exit" (paper presented at the Academy of Management Meeting, Atlanta, GA, 2006).

45. Dean Shepherd, Evan Douglas, and Mark Shanley, "New Venture Survival: Ignorance, External Shocks, and Risk Reduction Strategies," *Journal of Business Venturing* 15, 5–6 (2000): 393–410.

46. Arnold Cooper, Javier Gimeno-Gascon, and Carolyn Woo, "Initial Human and Financial Capital as Predictors of New Venture Performance," *Journal of Business Venturing* 9, 5 (1994): 371–395.

47. Jonas Dahlqvist, Per Davidsson, and Johan Wiklund, "Initial Conditions as Predictors of New Venture Performance: A Replication and Extension of the Cooper et al. Study," *Enterprise and Innovation Management Studies* 1, 1 (2000): 1–17.

48. Brian Headd, "Redefining Business Success: Distinguishing between Closure and Failure," *Small Business Economics* 21, 1 (2003): 51–61.

49. Dawn R. DeTienne and Melissa Cardon, "Impact of Founder Experience on Exit Intentions," *Small Business Economics* 38, 4 (2012): 351–374.

50. Wennberg et al., "Reconceptualizing Entrepreneurial Exit."

51. Carla Pavone and Sanjay Banerjee, "No Exit: Explaining the Persistence of 'Living Dead' Firms" (paper presented at the Academy of Management Conference, Hawaii, 2005).

52. Timothy Bates, "Analysis of Young, Small Firms That Have Closed: Delineating Successful from Unsuccessful Closures," *Journal of Business Venturing* 20, 3 (2005): 343–358; Headd, "Redefining Business Success."

53. Denis Ucbasaran, Dean Shepherd, Paul Westhead, Mike Wright, and Simon Mosey, "Experiences of Habitual Entrepreneurs: Business Failure, Overconfidence and 'Small Wins'" (paper presented at the Babson-Kauffman Entrepreneurship Conference, Babson College, Wellesley, MA, 2005).

54. Nobuyuki Harada, "Which Firms Exit and Why? An Analysis of Small Firm Exits in Japan," *Small Business Economics* 29 (2007): 401–414.

55. Balcaen et al., "Firm Exit after Distress."

56. Simon Oertel and Peter Walgenbach, "The Effect of Partner Exits on Survival Chances of SMEs," *Journal of Organizational Change Management* 25, 3 (2012): 462–482.

57. Van Praag, "Business Survival and Success of Young Small Business Owners."

58. Dietmar Harhoff, Konrad Stahl, and Michael Woywode, "Legal Form, Growth and Exit of West German Firms—Empirical Results for Manufacturing, Construction, Trade and Service Industries," *The Journal of Industrial Economics* 46, 4 (1998): 453–488.

59. Leonardo Becchetti and Jaime Sierra, "Bankruptcy Risk and Productive Efficiency in Manufacturing Firms."

60. Javier Gimeno, Timothy B. Folta, Arnold C. Cooper, and Carolyn Y. Woo, "Survival of the Fittest? Entrepreneurial Human Capital and the Persistence of Underperforming Firms," *Administrative Science Quarterly* 42, 4 (1997): 750–783.

61. Wennberg et al., "Reconceptualizing Entrepreneurial Exit."

62. Wennberg and Wiklund, "Entrepreneurial Exit."

63. Bates, "Analysis of Young, Small Firms That Have Closed."

64. Balcaen et al., "Firm Exit after Distress"; DeTienne and Cardon, "Impact of Founder Experience on Exit Intentions"; Dawn R. DeTienne, Alexander McKelvie, and Gaylen Chandler, "The Impact of Motivation, Innovation, and Causation and Effectuation Approaches on Exit Strategies" (paper presented at the Academy of Management Annual Meeting, Boston, MA, 2013); Geraldine Ryan and Bernadette Power, "Small Business Transfer Decisions: What Really Matters?" *Irish Journal of Management* 31, 2 (2012).

65. Douglas Cumming, "Contracts and Exit in Venture Capital Finance," *Review of Financial Studies* 21, 5 (2008): 1948–1982.

66. Balcaen et al. "Firm Exit after Distress."

67. Ryan and Power, "Small Business Transfer Decisions."

68. DeTienne and Cardon, "Impact of Founder Experience on Exit Intentions."

69. DeTienne, McKelvie, and Chandler, "The Impact of Motivation."

70. Norm Wasserman, "Founder-CEO Succession and the Paradox of Entrepreneurial Success," *Organization Science* 14, 2 (2003): 149–172.

71. Hessels et al., "Entrepreneurial Exit and Entrepreneurial Engagement."

72. Dean Shepherd, "Lessons from Business Failure: Propositions of Grief Recovery for the Self-employed," *Academy of Management Review* 28, 2 (2003): 318–328.

73. Talma Kushnir, "Social-psychological Factors Associated with the Dissolution of Dyadic Business Partnerships," *The Journal of Social Psychology* 122, 2 (1984): 181–188.

74. Jim Everett and John Watson, "Small Business Failure and External Risk Factors," *Small Business Economics* 11, 4 (1998): 371–390.

75. Stefan Buehler, Christian Kaiser, and Franz Jaeger, "The Geographic Determinants of Bankruptcy: Evidence from Switzerland," *Small Business Economics* 39, 1 (2012): 231–251.

76. Mason and Harrisson, "After the Exit."

77. Aviad Pe'er and Ilan Vertinsky, "Firm Failures as a Determinant of New Entry: Is There Evidence of Local Creative Destruction?," *Journal of Business Venturing* 23, 3 (2008): 280–306.

78. Glenn Hoetker and Rajshree Agarwal, "Death Hurts, but It Isn't Fatal: The Postexit Diffusion of Knowledge Created by Innovative Companies," *Academy of Management Journal* 50, 2 (2007): 446–467.

79. PrivCo: Private Company Financial Intelligence, www.privco.com.

80. BuyBizSell, "Small Business Transactions Continue to Rise," www.bizbuysell. com/news/article092.html; Dawn R. DeTienne and Francesco Chirico, "Exit Strategies in Family Firms: How Socioemotional Wealth Drives the Threshold of Performance," *Entrepreneurship Theory & Practice* 37, (6): 1297–1318.

8

Geographic Cluster Region Influences on Innovation: Outcomes for Small Businesses

Brett Anitra Gilbert and Mika Tatum Kusar

Geographic cluster regions (clusters), which are regions with large concentrations of same industry firms, have received a significant amount of attention in the popular press. Familiar examples of clusters include financial services in New York, medical devices in Boston, biotechnology in the Raleigh-Durham area, and IT in Austin, Texas, and Silicon Valley. The reason for the attention given to clusters is simply that many innovative new firms tend to emerge from these regions. Firms such as Google, Apple, and Intel and many of our most innovative companies around the world operate from clusters. In fact, geographic clusters have an impressive track record for contributing to the innovativeness of their local firms[1] and also to higher levels of start-up activity.[2]

The emergence of clusters has led many to conclude that these regions improve the innovation operations of firms. However, we know very little about the types of innovation activities that cluster firms undertake. In fact, there are reasons to believe that the innovativeness of cluster firms is tied to the improvements that they make to existing products and not the introduction of new products. As a result, many have tried to explain why industry clusters facilitate firm innovation. Some believe it is because of interfirm relationships,[3] the knowledge spillovers firms receive about nearby firms' innovation activities,[4] or the strength of the local labor market, which provides employees with understanding of the technology or market.[5] However, the extent to which cluster firms actually collaborate with other cluster firms has been widely debated, leading researchers to conclude that the impact of clustering on innovation may not be as clear as presumed.[6]

Knowledge spillovers are defined as flows of innovative knowledge between firms. They are generally thought to be regionally bounded[7] and to spillover between two or more innovative firms or organizations.[8] The roles of knowledge spillovers and the strength of the labor market in industry cluster regions are considered conventional wisdom, even though these factors also exist to varying degrees outside of a focal industry's cluster. Therefore, firms operating outside of their industry's geographic cluster have the potential to receive knowledge from firms within their geographic region that may be in the same industry or a different industry. These spillovers may occur to a lesser degree in firms located outside of the regions where the industry is clustered than in firms operating from within the clusters; however, to date, we know little about the direct role of knowledge spillovers for firms within a cluster region relative to knowledge spillovers for firms outside of cluster regions.

Much of the anecdotal evidence about geographic clustering attributes the occurrence of spillovers to the presence of many small innovative firms,[9] yet we lack an understanding of the type of innovative activities in which small, clustered firms engage relative to others outside of the cluster. This gap leads us to wonder, if we measured innovative activities in different ways, would small cluster firms still emerge as more innovative than small firms outside of a cluster?

This question is important because by operating within a cluster region, small firms gain access to specialized resources, knowledge about other firms' activities, and a culture of innovation that relates better to the types of innovations that are being developed by other cluster firms rather than to new forms of innovations.[10] Small firms that operate from cluster regions may also face pressures and competitive dynamics that push them to accelerate their innovation activities around what they already know rather than work to develop new innovations.[11] As a consequence, small cluster firms could be more likely to enhance existing products than they are to introduce new products, which would limit the learning that is needed to generate new innovations.[12]

A focus on enhancing existing products has the potential to increase small firm dependence on one product category or technology and subsequently to limit their ability to adapt to major technological changes.[13] For small technology ventures, an understanding of how industry clustering impacts their innovations is particularly important because these firms commonly introduce innovative products that open up new markets that are characterized by high technological uncertainty (meaning the technology is not proven or well known) and consumer uncertainty (meaning the demand from the consumer is not well established).[14] These early products are often primitive in design[15] and require improvements to resolve design imperfections, which typically make the product-enhancement innovation activities prevalent for small firms in the beginning of their life cycles.[16]

Furthermore, as firms grow with their industry, their focus shifts from innovating around products to innovating around processes,[17] which elevates the importance for small technology ventures to remain relevant in a changing technological context.[18] The extent to which industry cluster regions make it easier or harder for small technology firms to change with the environment means that these regions hold important implications that affect the firm's long-term potential for success.[19]

This chapter seeks to explain how industry clustering and knowledge spillovers impact product innovations in small high-technology ventures. It offers an assessment of the pros and cons of operating within or outside of cluster regions. The theoretical development begins with an understanding of the relationship between industry clusters, new products, and product-enhancement innovations. It continues by discussing the nature of the relationship between knowledge spillovers and product innovations. The theory section concludes with a discussion about the ways in which the product innovations of small technology firms are influenced, depending on whether the firm operates from a cluster *and* receives knowledge spillovers from local firms.

This study is important for two reasons. First, it is important to consider the independent effects of cluster region attributes directly to understand how cluster dynamics affect small firms that operate within them. Second, by examining firm innovation behaviors in terms of new products and product enhancements, we are able to determine that high innovative output of some small cluster firms is in fact not attributable to the new products they introduce but rather to improvements they make to existing products. This story is important for future small business owners to consider as they contemplate growing their technology ventures.

WHY CLUSTER REGIONS MATTER

Scholars have long recognized the influence of geographic clusters on firm outcomes. In research dating back to Marshall, three primary benefits of clusters were identified as (1) specialized labor resulting from industry demand, (2) specialized input providers, and (3) knowledge spillovers.[20] Specialized labor emerges from the critical mass of industries and firms that develops within a geographic region.[21] When a location has a concentration of firms in a particular industry, other industries that require the use of employees with a similar skill set are drawn to the region.[22] Firms in these regions produce workers with competencies and skills that are valuable to the industries represented within the region.[23] In fact, firm labor requirements are argued to make the availability of labor in a geographic region a critical and perhaps even primary driver for the clustering of industries within regions.[24] The colocation of industry activity also fosters the development of such support agencies as attorneys, accountants, venture capitalists, and trade associations who develop expertise in the industries of the region.[25] An industry cluster may be especially beneficial for small firms because they are dependent on their local environment for many resources that are needed to start and grow their operations.[26] The availability of and access to specialized resources makes it possible for entrepreneurs to build their firms with quality inputs and insights for their industry.

Another regional resource with the potential to benefit small ventures to a great extent is access to knowledge spillovers, which provides technological information, competitor information, and information about market or other industry trends, along with operating or management procedures.[27] Firms receive knowledge spillovers without the costs associated with creating the knowledge.[28] When the knowledge differs from what the firm's founders and managers know to be true, it broadens a firm's learning by enabling it to strengthen the innovations that it produces[29] and aligns the firm's technologies to current industry trends.[30] It also suggests that firms operating from regions with industry clustering benefit when there is greater availability of industry-specific knowledge within a geographic region.[31] Extant research confirms that firms receiving knowledge spillovers enhance their innovation performance, for example, by introducing more new products and patenting more.[32] However, we do not know the extent to which firms incorporate the knowledge that they receive into their operations to improve their existing product lines.[33]

Some have found that imitation is a strategy among cluster firms, which has the potential to focus their attention on adapting existing innovations to become more consistent with those of local competitors.[34] Understanding how knowledge spillovers from a cluster region influence a small firm's new product and product-enhancement activities is important because engaging in one form of innovation reduces the resources that are available for another form of innovation.[35] Also, new product and product-enhancement innovations differentially affect firm performance.[36] For example, the financial returns from product-enhancement innovations are usually more certain and closer in time than the returns that come from new product innovations. However, in the long run, focusing on existing products may lead to inertia and outdated capabilities.[37] New product innovations, on the other hand, allow a firm to continue offering products that meet target market demand and are how firms renew their strategic identity to sustain performance advantages.[38] However, a continued focus on new products does not allow the firm to appropriate the full value from their existing innovations.[39] Thus, balancing new product and product-enhancement innovations is important for small firms to succeed in the marketplace.[40]

PREDICTIONS OF CLUSTERING EFFECTS FOR SMALL TECHNOLOGY FIRM INNOVATIONS

Operating from a region with a concentration of industry clustering provides small firms with access to industry-specific human, manufacturing, technological, and financial resources within the local region.[41] However, close proximity to competitors and greater awareness of one another's actions can contribute to imitation behavior among clustered firms,[42] which would motivate the firms to focus their efforts around existing innovations rather than new ones. Moreover, cluster firm operations commonly relate to a focal technology.[43] Therefore, small technology ventures in cluster regions develop their technologies based on the innovations and resources available within the region.[44] Regions provide the resources needed to establish and sustain the architectural knowledge, which is the technological framework that will be used, the system for producing and marketing the product,[45] as well as the framework on which future routines of the organization are built.[46] Once the architectural knowledge is established, firms become less likely to deviate from their routines,[47] which often makes it hard for firms to change course when necessary.

For small technology firms, the necessity to improve their initial product innovations for legitimacy and competitiveness reasons increases as competitors release more innovations.[48] These releases change market preferences and presumably push firms to quickly revise their existing products in response.[49] Because small firm innovations are commonly tied to regional resources,[50] the available resources may relate more to existing technologies, which could cause small cluster firms to focus on their existing products to a greater extent than other small firms. The small firms in regions without industry clustering rely on different forms of regional resources, which, because of the limited concentration of its focal industry resources, may not be industry specific. Thus, while many attributes of cluster regions support new product development for some firms, they are unlikely to have the same effect on small cluster firms. Small cluster firms face the need to improve existing product, and regional peer pressures to innovate; therefore, they are expected to make more product-enhancement innovations and fewer new product innovations than small firms in other regions.

PREDICTIONS OF REGIONAL KNOWLEDGE SPILLOVER EFFECTS FOR SMALL TECHNOLOGY FIRM INNOVATION

Knowledge spillovers are knowledge received into a firm's operations that is sourced from other firms or organizations.[51] Our specific interest is on technological-knowledge spillovers. While technological-knowledge spillovers are transmitted in a variety of ways, they are largely thought to accumulate and spread within constrained geographic boundaries.[52] Regional knowledge spillovers are possible from any innovating firm within the region, not just from those within a firm's same industry,[53] and are thought to increase firm innovation outputs.[54] A firm that receives knowledge spillovers into its operations may be well positioned to get ahead technologically by combining and reconfiguring existing knowledge with newly acquired knowledge to create new forms of products.[55] In fact, Laursen et al. showed that regional differences in innovation existed depending on the regional social capital, which in turn influenced how firms received external knowledge.[56] This characteristic has led some to argue that knowledge spillovers are learning mechanisms that enhance a firm's innovation capabilities,[57] which should ultimately increase a firm's ability to introduce new products.

Knowledge spillovers that differ from a firm's existing knowledge stock are not easily evaluated or applied[58] and may not be directly relevant to the products that the venture currently has on the market. Therefore, some knowledge spillovers may direct firm innovation activities toward new types of products. Consequently, knowledge spillovers in general are expected to influence a small firm's new innovations to a greater extent than its existing innovations. However, knowledge spillovers received by firms within cluster regions may have a different effect than general spillovers that firms receive from regional firms.

Much of the benefit that accrues to cluster firms is because of the proximity to their industry firms, which promotes informal exchanges between regional employees and contributes to knowledge sharing between firms within cluster boundaries. These interactions influence managers' and scientists' recognition, perception, and evaluation of innovation opportunities,[59] which in turn has the potential to influence the innovations that the ventures pursue. In fact, Guo and Guo found that imitation is a common form of knowledge transfer within cluster regions.[60] With a shared way of thinking,[61] cluster firms may have limited access to the diverse knowledge that is needed to create new innovations.[62] Moreover, the tendency for small firms to be dependent on their local environment for the resources they need[63] makes it likely that the regional-knowledge spillovers that a small firm receives from an industry-clustering location are more similar to the firm's technology than is true of the regional-knowledge spillovers received by firms that operate from regions where their focal industry is not clustered.[64] The knowledge similarity combined with the urgency to introduce innovations could increase the tendency for small firms in clusters to use external knowledge for enhancing existing products rather than for creating new product innovations.[65]

Thus knowledge spillovers within clusters may have a stronger influence on existing products than those received by firms in locations with less industry clustering.

By contrast, small firms assimilating less knowledge from an industry cluster may not be as entrenched in the cognitive framework of the cluster environment and may have greater ability to incorporate new knowledge into diverse product applications. Similarly, firms operating from locations where limited industry clustering exists are less influenced by their focal industry and more influenced by other industries in their region. For these firms, assimilating high levels of regional-knowledge spillover means that the firm has the ability to apply knowledge that may be unrelated to their focal-industry knowledge.[66] In these cases, regional-knowledge spillovers should still serve as new forms of knowledge that a small firm can use in new product innovations to a greater extent than in their existing products. Taken together, these arguments suggest that the combination of higher levels of industry clustering and the receipt of high levels of regional-knowledge spillover elevates a small firm's level of product-enhancement innovations while at the same time constraining its level of new product innovations.

TESTING THE PREDICTIONS

Sample

To determine whether our predications about the nature of industry clustering and knowledge spillovers for small firm innovations are true, the research required a sample of small high-technology ventures that engage in both new product and product-enhancement innovation. We identified the software industry as an attractive sample to use for this purpose. As Cottrell and Nault acknowledged, software firms exhibit innovative flexibility in "offering products over different computing platforms . . . [introducing] new products into old or new categories and for old and new platforms," thereby satisfying our innovation-activity criterion.[67] We also found the software industry to be appealing because it exhibits an attractive mix of geographic concentration within a few U.S. locations while also exhibiting geographic presence in locations with very limited concentrations of industry clustering. We selected a sample of young software firms (less than 8 years of age) that had undertaken an initial public offering (IPO). IPO firms have pressures to be innovative before and after the IPO to attract and retain investor attention. By using this group of firms, we were able to test the relationships on a sample of firms engaging in both forms of innovation.

The IPO years that we selected were 1996–2000. This time period is intriguing because Internet technologies surfaced around 1992 and were experiencing unprecedented growth by 1995. Many of the software firms formed immediately before and during this time were founded to exploit the emergence of Internet-based technologies, and a large number of software firms undertook IPOs during this time. We selected a group of firms that compete in the computer programming (SIC 7370–7371), prepackaged software (7372), and systems design and integration (SIC 7373) industry sectors.

We included firms up to eight years of age by the time they undertook their IPO. Age eight is when start-up operations are believed to begin mirroring those of established firms.[68] Each of the 128 firms in our sample was founded as an independent start-up (i.e., without corporate ownership) between the years of 1990 and 2000 and had operated for at least two years after the IPO.

COLLECTING DATA AND CONSTRUCTING VARIABLES

Firms were identified through the Securities Data Corporation (SDC) Platinum New Issues database and matched to the Compustat Financial database, where their financial data and other control-variable information was drawn. We provide detailed information on the operationalizations of our dependent, independent, interactive, and control variables below.

Dependent Variables

Product innovation announcements were obtained from press releases stored in the Lexis-Nexis academic database. *New products* were identified by comparing product announcements from the two years after the IPO to a listing of products we compiled from the firm's prospectus and product announcements from its IPO year. A product was considered "new" if it (1) was not listed in the IPO prospectus nor announced during the year of the IPO or (2) included a product version designation of 1.0. New products represent new categories of products that the venture included in its product portfolio. *Product enhancements* were the total count of post-IPO product enhancements made to the products listed in the prospectus or announced during the IPO year. We counted any product with a designation higher than 1.0 as a product enhancement in this study. Product enhancements not only included updates to existing products but also changes that enabled the software to interoperate with other software systems or to work in different languages.

Independent Variables

Capturing when a knowledge spillover has occurred is difficult,[69] but it has been done effectively through analyses showing when a firm's patented technologies have been influenced by the technologies of other firms.[70] Research has also shown that knowledge spillovers, at least in the short run, are geographically constrained.[71] One reason offered for this finding is that new knowledge tends to be tacit, which requires close interactions between individuals for knowledge to transfer.[72] Proximity between a knowledge-generating actor and others helps to facilitate the flow of knowledge out of one firm and into another for use in its innovation initiatives. For this reason, knowledge spillovers are unique to the region in which they occur.

Following prior research, we operationalized *regional-knowledge spillovers* using a proportion variable that reflects the extent to which technological-knowledge spillovers that assimilated into a firm's patented technologies are from the region in which the venture operates.[73] The proportion variable is important to use because it not only shows how much of the technology may have been influenced by other firms within the region but also the extent to which the technology's foundations were influenced by firms outside of the geographic region. Thus, as measured, this variable shows the extent to which the firms incorporated knowledge from the local region into their innovation process.

Anselin et al. found that knowledge spillovers typically occur within a 50 mile radius of the innovating firm;[74] therefore, we considered a citation to another firm's patent as a regional-knowledge spillover if the cited firm operates within the same economic area as the venture, which is defined by the firm's metropolitan statistical area (MSA) combined with interdependent MSAs and the adjoining counties that do not belong to an MSA. Economic areas are defined by the Office of Management and Budget and represent regions in close enough proximity that individuals commonly commute between them, even daily. This operationalization captures the potential geographic boundaries within which knowledge realistically flows.

To determine the influence of regional-knowledge spillovers, we counted the citations made to patents that were filed within four years of the venture's patent application file date and included citations from patents received through the venture's year of IPO. Our basis for the four-year cutoff point is Moore's Law, which states that the pace of technological change within computer industries results in the performance doubling every 18 months and new technological generations emerging within three years.[75] Given that knowledge loses its economic value within five years[76] and most of the citations for the ventures' patents were between two and six years of the ventures' filing dates, a four-year time period seemed appropriate to ensure the venture had opportunity to assimilate knowledge that was not widely available to firms in more distant locations into its operations.[77] This time period also ensures that the knowledge still had the potential to be of economic value to the firm. Patent data were sourced from the U.S. Patent and Trade Office database.

A growing number of software firms patent their technologies,[78] and in this sample, 60 percent of the firms had patented innovations. Given that the operationalization that we used to represent regional-knowledge spillovers is tied to observable evidence from patent applications,[79] firms that lacked patents during the time period of this study would receive a zero value, as would those that patent their technologies but do not cite firms in their local region. To distinguish between firms for which technological-knowledge spillovers are indeterminate and those that patent but do not rely upon the technologies of regional firms, we added a dummy value of 1 to each patenting firm's proportions of regional-knowledge spillovers. This step was done to preserve sample size. Nonpatenting firms, whose technical-knowledge spillovers are indeterminate, have a value of 0, patenting firms without local spillovers have a value of 1.0, and those receiving local spillovers have a value equal to 1.0 plus the proportion value.

The *industry clustering* variable we used is a location quotient measure, which reflects the extent to which the information technology industry cluster is overly, similarly, or underrepresented in the venture's MSA relative to the United States as a whole. MSAs reflect the traditional political, economic, and social integration of a region and is the most commonly used operationalization of communities.[80] The Cluster Mapping Project of the Institute for Strategy and Competitiveness at the Harvard Business School defines a cluster as interdependent industries that are colocated across geographic space. It determines interdependence by correlating employment levels across industries and then groups industries with high correlations together as a cluster.[81] The project then calculates the employment level for that cluster of industries across several geographic levels of analysis.[82] The measure used in this study reflects the proportion of information technology cluster employment in the venture's MSA relative to the proportion of information technology cluster employment in the United States. This is the formula:

$$\frac{\text{IT cluster employment in MSA/Total employment in MSA}}{\text{IT cluster employment in U.S./Total employment in U.S.}}$$

This measure supports the underlying assumption that firms operating from locations where the IT industry is overrepresented have more industry-relevant resources, customers, suppliers, and knowledge that are important for commercializing innovations than firms operating from regions where industry clustering is less prevalent. We determined the industry cluster quotient for the year in which the firms were founded to ensure that our measure of clustering temporally precedes our regional-knowledge spillovers measure and to ensure the tests for knowledge-spillover effects can be assessed after a venture has assimilated it over a period of time.

Interaction Variable

In addition to the direct effects of our independent variables on the dependent variables, an interaction effect is expected between industry clustering and regional-knowledge spillovers. We created an interaction term that is the multiplicative of the regional-knowledge spillovers and industry-clustering variables, each mean-centered before multiplication. Mean-centering the independent variables prior to their multiplication reduces overlap between the independent variables and interactive term.[83]

Control Variables

We included control variables for several factors that could influence the nature of the relationship between the independent and dependent variables. *Age*, measured as years since founding and recorded at the time of IPO, is included to account for the fact that older firms have greater potential to enlarge their portfolio of products. Older firms may also be more inclined to filter the knowledge they receive through a biased lens, which may influence their orientation toward product-enhancement innovations.[84] We also included a measure for the firm's *size* as of the year of IPO to account for the fact that the higher level of resources within clusters could result in cluster firms being larger and, therefore, more capable of initiating and executing product-development activities. As knowledge spillovers are believed to be transferred through employee mobility,[85] we used the number of employees as of the year of IPO as our measure of size. Our sample is composed of mostly young, high-growth (IPO) firms. Consequently, approximately 28 firms exceeded 500 employees, which is the size typically used to classify small firms. However, these firms, although larger in size, were only three years old at the time of IPO and would share many challenges that small firms have in sustaining innovation. Therefore, the larger firms were retained in the sample. Because we measured the performance of these ventures after they undertook their IPO, we included a control for the innovative capabilities the ventures may have developed, which naturally would influence their innovation performance. We used the *R&D expenditures* to determine the financial commitment that the ventures were making toward their innovation objectives.

Our final set of control variables enabled us to partial out differences due to the industry markets in which the firms competed and the conditions in the economic environment during the time period when the performance measures were drawn. Software firms can produce a variety of products and services that are sold into various markets. The markets from which these ventures operated include e-commerce, Web portals and online communities, information management systems, information technology services, custom software development, Internet service providers, Internet other, and a general other category. Markets were categorized using descriptions provided by an organization called the Gale Group. We found that the SIC categories for Internet service providers, other, and information technology services were the only sectors that differed significantly from the others. Therefore, we used single controls for each of those sectors, a fourth dummy representing e-commerce, Web portals and online communities, and information management systems, and a fifth dummy representing Internet other and custom software development firms. The "other" dummy variable serves as the reference category in all analyses. Dummy variables representing each year of IPO were also used, with 1996 as our reference year.

ANALYZING THE DATA

Before running the analyses, we tested all variables for outliers and found that outliers were present in each of our independent and dependent variables. Without theoretical reasoning to exclude these ventures, we rescaled the outlying values to the top percentile of values within the sample. We used negative binomial regression to test the product-innovation models because this analytical technique relaxes the constraint of equal mean and variance that is required for Poisson regression analyses. Because our dependent variables are tested on the same set of independent variables and firms, it is important to employ estimation techniques that account for the fact that the dependent variables are interdependent. More specifically, when small firms engage in new product or product-enhancement activities, it generally limits their ability to engage in the other form of innovation. Seemingly unrelated estimation (SUEST) allows us to simultaneously estimate our independent variables across the two interdependent dependent variables, which is important because that is how they are occurring. The procedure ensures that the standard errors are adjusted to account for the fact that the innovation activities lack independence of observations. The SUEST procedure also provides estimates for use in post-hoc nonlinear Wald tests that enable us to analyze whether the effect is larger or smaller and therefore more or less important in the new product or product-enhancement models. All analyses were run in Stata 8.1.

WHAT THE DATA SUGGEST

Table 8.1 provides correlations, means, and standard deviations for all dependent and independent variables analyzed in this study. Of interest to note is the significant correlation between new product innovations and product-enhancement innovations. These correlations highlight the inherent need that software firms have to modify their innovations while simultaneously introducing new innovations.[86] Industry clustering and knowledge spillovers are also significantly correlated ($p < 0.001$). The size of the correlation at 0.38 suggests that there is less than 20 percent shared variance between them, which supports our practice of examining these variables separately despite the fact that in extant literature knowledge spillovers are almost conceptualized as a function of industry clusters. The industry cluster variable may represent the potential for knowledge to spillover, but our measure reflects the realized technological-knowledge spillovers from the region that the venture brought into its operations.[87]

Table 8.2 presents the results of the negative binomial regressions by product-innovation type. In Model 1, we present the coefficients for the control variables in each of the models. Model 2 shows the independent effects of industry clustering and knowledge spillovers on innovation. We expected to find that industry clustering would have a stronger positive effect on product-enhancement innovations than on new product innovations. The industry cluster estimate for new product innovations was -1.13 and nonsignificant. The same estimate for product-enhancement innovations was 4.06 and significant ($p < 0.05$). We ran a nonlinear Wald test, which is used to determine whether the obtained estimates are significantly different from each other ($p = 0.05$). Figure 8.1 provides a pictorial representation of the relationship between industry clustering and product innovation. It clearly indicates an increasing trend of firms at higher levels of industry clustering more than firms at lower levels of industry to engage in higher levels of product-enhancement activities. New product innovation activity did not differ significantly based on the industry clustering. This supports our predictions.

TABLE 8.1 Correlations, Means, Standard Deviations

	1	2	3	4	5	6	7	8	9	10	11	12	13	14	15
Means	0.19	3.76	6.59	0.05	0.68	3.79	0.48	0.28	0.60	0.12	0.07	0.14	0.19	0.41	0.13
Stand Dev.	0.27	3.58	6.78	0.04	0.60	1.62	0.47	0.45	0.49	0.32	0.26	0.35	0.40	0.50	0.34
1 SGROWTH	1.00														
2 NEW PRODUCT	0.19*	1.00													
3 PRODUCT ENH	0.03	0.29**	1.00												
4 INDUSCLUS	0.13	0.06	0.26**	1.00											
5 KNOWLEDGE	0.12	0.17†	0.21*	0.38***	1.00										
6 IPOAGE	-0.32***	0.07	0.07	-0.04	0.04	1.00									
7 EMPSIZE	0.33***	0.09	0.00	0.13	-0.05	-0.18*	1.00								
8 SICCPROG	0.27**	-0.14	-0.27**	-0.15†	-0.22*	-0.31***	0.16	1.00							
9 SICSOFT	-0.18*	-0.17†	0.36***	0.17†	0.22*	0.33***	-0.14	-0.77***	1.00						
10 SICSYSDIN	0.11	-0.06	-0.18*	-0.04	-0.02	-0.07	-0.02	-0.23**	-0.44***	1.00					
11 1996IPO	-0.01	-0.16†	-0.02	0.09	0.06	-0.12	0.04	-0.06	-0.06	0.17†	1.00				
12 1997IPO	0.23**	-0.04	0.01	-0.20*	-0.06	-0.05	0.02	0.07	-0.10	0.05	-0.12	1.00			
13 1998IPO	0.07	0.06	-0.03	-0.15†	-0.14	0.05	0.14	0.08	-0.03	-0.06†	-0.14	-0.21*	1.00		
14 1999IPO	-0.05	0.09	-0.08	0.19*	-0.11	0.06	-0.03	0.03	-0.01	-0.03	-0.26**	-0.37***	-0.43***	1.00	
15 2000IPO	-0.23**	-0.02	0.15†	0.04	0.02	0.01	-0.18*	-0.16†	0.20*	-0.08	-0.12	-0.16†	-0.20*	-0.36***	1.00

†$p < 0.10$, *$p < 0.05$, **$p < 0.01$, ***$p < 0.001$
Data sources: Securities Data Corporation (SDC) Platinum New Issues database, Compustat Financial database, Lexis-Nexis academic database, and U.S. Patent and Trade Office database.

TABLE 8.2 Regression Analysis

VARIABLES	New Product Innovations			Product Enhancement Innovations		
	Model 1	Model 2	Model 3	Model 1	Model 2	Model 3
CONTROL						
Age at IPO	0.002	0.003	0.002	−.01	−.003	−0.03
Size (Employees)	0.230	0.250	0.25	0.16	0.07	0.07
Software Sector	.41†	0.360	0.36†	.85***	.73***	0.81***
Systems Design	0.240	0.170	0.17	−.12	−.13	−0.09
1997 IPO	.68†	.76*	0.76†	0.06	0.52	0.59
1998 IPO	.83*	.87*	0.87*	−.17	.24	0.29
1999 IPO	.81*	.85**	0.85*	−.16	.10	0.24
2000 IPO	.70†	.73*	0.73†	0.1	0.39	0.52
INDEPENDENT						
Industry Gustering		−1.13	−1.28		4.06*	1.18
Knowledge Spillovers		.30*	0.31*		0.180	0.25
INTERACTION						
Industry Gustering* Knowledge Spillovers			0.49			9.09*
Pseudo R^2/R^2	0.02	0.02	0.02	0.03	0.04	0.04
Log-Likelihood	−306.71	−304.86	−304.857	−367.97	−364.79	−362.48

WALD TESTS

	chi-square	p-value
β(New_Industry Clustering) = β(Enhancements_Industry Clustering) (Model 2)	4.00	.05*
β(New_Knowledge Spillovers) = β(Enhancements_Knowledge Spillovers) (Model 2)	0.45	0.50
β(New_Interaction) = β(Enhancements_Interaction) (Model 3)	7.06	.01**

†$p < 0.10$, *$p < 0.05$, **$p < 0.01$, ***$p < 0.001$
Data sources: Securities Data Corporation (SDC) Platinum New Issues database, Compustat Financial database, Lexis-Nexis academic database, and U.S. Patent and Trade Office database.

We expected to find that regional-knowledge spillovers would have a stronger positive effect on new product innovations than on product-enhancement innovations. The regional-knowledge spillovers estimate in the new products model was positive and significant ($p < 0.05$). The same estimate in the product-enhancements model was positive but not significant. Counter to our expectations, the nonlinear Wald test revealed no significant difference in the impact of regional-knowledge spillovers on new and enhanced product innovations.

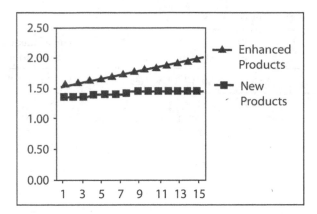

FIGURE 8.1 The Effects of Industry Clustering by Type of Product Innovation

Model 3 displays the coefficients for testing the combination of high industry clustering and high regional-knowledge spillovers on product-enhancement innovations and new product innovations. The interaction term in Model 3 of the new product innovations model reveals a positive but nonsignificant relationship between the interaction and new product innovations. The interaction term in Model 3 of the product-enhancement innovations model reveals a large, positive, and significant relationship ($p < 0.05$). The nonlinear Wald test to assess whether the interaction term of the knowledge spillovers and industry-clustering variables differentially affected new and enhanced product innovations confirmed significant differences ($p < 0.01$). As suspected, small firms in locations with higher industry clustering and higher regional-knowledge spillovers were significantly more likely to be engaging in higher levels of product-enhancement innovations than in new product innovations.

As figure 8.2 shows, the relationship between industry clustering and product-enhancement innovations is positive for firms receiving high levels of regional-knowledge spillovers. As would be expected of firms exhibiting an increased focus on product-enhancement innovations, the relationship between industry clustering and new product innovations for the firms assimilating high levels of regional-knowledge spillovers is negative. Low levels of regional-knowledge spillover assimilation appear to help small firms in clusters to engage in new product innovation activities to a greater extent than product-enhancement innovations. It appears that industry clustering can be beneficial for small firm innovations; however, the receipt of high levels of regional knowledge from the region can be problematic.

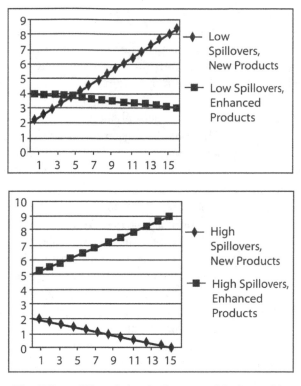

FIGURE 8.2 The Effect of Knowledge Spillovers and Industry Clustering by Type of Product Innovations

WHAT THE FINDINGS MEAN

The higher levels of innovation activity observed for firms that operate from industry clusters are often attributed to the knowledge spillovers that cluster firms receive.[88] However, as Feser found, knowledge spillovers are not solely confined to regions with industry clustering.[89] Thus, our analysis illustrates how a geographic cluster location and the regional-knowledge spillovers that small technology ventures assimilate into their operations influence the venture's new and product-enhancement innovations. Our theoretical development led us to expect a stronger relationship between industry clustering and product-enhancement innovations and a stronger relationship between regional-knowledge spillovers and new product innovations. We further expected to find that the interaction of industry clustering and regional-knowledge spillovers would result in more product-enhancement innovations than new product innovations. Our findings were mostly consistent with our expectations.

We argued that industry clustering provides small firms with the human capital and input providers that are needed to develop their innovation capabilities. However, we also suggested that the close proximity to related firms pushes new cluster ventures to intensify their innovation efforts in response to competitors' product launches and to maintain legitimacy and competitiveness within the industry.[90] The results confirm that industry clustering positively and significantly predicts product-enhancement innovations but not new product innovations. These results suggest that the pressures that exist within industry clusters propel cluster firms to base their product-innovation activities around established routines and may reduce the venture's motivation to pursue new innovations.

Also supporting our arguments are results suggesting that regional-knowledge spillovers provide the pulse of new trends within the industry, as Brown and Duguid argued.[91] These results further suggest that regional-knowledge spillovers contribute to a firm's ability to create new product innovations.[92] Regional-knowledge spillovers had a positive and significant relationship with new product innovations. However, the effect of regional-knowledge spillovers was not significantly different in the new products and product-enhancements models. This finding suggests that the new knowledge that comes from regional-knowledge spillovers has the potential to contribute to new product innovation capabilities but may not be entirely consistent with the small firm's existing knowledge. The clear exception to this rule was for firms that operate from regions with industry clustering that also assimilate high volumes of regional knowledge into their operations. Because industry clusters develop competencies that are unique to that region[93] and firms operating within them develop shared mental models,[94] knowledge flowing within regions with industry clustering is similar to the cluster firms' current knowledge base. Because of higher competition within regions with industry clustering, small firms and especially those that are young may be forced into a cycle of innovation that pushes them to incorporate regional knowledge into existing products rather than to use that knowledge to broaden their product portfolio.

This study provides empirical confirmation that for small firms that are founded in regions with industry clustering and that also assimilated regional knowledge into their operations, the knowledge is generally used for existing innovations rather than for creating new products. Interestingly, at higher concentrations of industry clustering, firms assimilating low levels of regional-knowledge spillovers introduced the most new products and also reflected a decreasing tendency to enhance existing products. Clearly, for small technology firms, operating from a region with industry clustering provides resources that enhance innovation capabilities; however, assimilating high levels of knowledge from the region can adversely affect the firm's new product-innovation activities.

Prior research shows that high levels of product-enhancement innovations can contribute to the demise of new firms,[95] while new product innovations are important for firm survival and growth.[96] In the short term, a cluster firm's focus on product-enhancement innovations may be necessary for maintaining a share of the marketplace,[97] but in the long term, this emphasis has the potential to render the firm incapable of creating new products for the market. By extension, these results suggest, as some have argued, that continued assimilation of regional knowledge by small and young cluster firms can limit their ability to adapt as the industry's technological context changes and may also limit their ability to continue growing the operation.[98] Thus, the finding that cluster firms were more attentive to enhancing existing products than to developing new products provides empirical validity for theoretical arguments that the long-term technological competitiveness of cluster firms will be challenged when knowledge from the region is used for enhancing existing innovations.[99]

AVOIDING THE TRAP

Start-ups are commonly the driving force behind the success of industry clusters.[100] If small firms focus on enhancing existing product lines, over time, their technologies will become obsolete.[101] Because industry cluster competencies are based on the activities of its firms, a similar result could become true for the industry cluster surrounding the small firms. Without an ability to incorporate new knowledge into the operations and generate new innovations, Pouder and St. John have suggested that an industry cluster will face eventual demise.[102] This would also increase difficulties for small firms that rely on cluster resources to sustain their operations. An influx of new knowledge into the region will be essential for sustaining cluster innovativeness.[103] Strategies such as technology-transfer programs with entities that operate from other geographic regions can ensure a region is imbued with new knowledge. Moreover, favorable policies toward direct investments into the region (whether by firms from other U.S. regions or those from other countries) can position the region to evolve with the technological trends of the broader industry context.[104]

From the entrepreneurs' perspective, these results suggest that founding a venture within an industry cluster can be useful for innovation objectives. Regions with industry clustering provide the human, financial, and competency resources needed to develop the requisite innovation orientation. However, the challenge for cluster entrepreneurs to continue benefiting from these advantages is to minimize the use of knowledge from the region. One strategy for achieving this objective may be to hire more employees from outside the region rather than from within the region.[105] Naturally, this strategy would increase the costs incurred for recruiting and relocating employees from other geographic regions, yet it would provide the venture with a mechanism for receiving new knowledge into the operations and aid the venture's ability to recognize opportunities for new product innovations.[106] Another strategy may involve relocating the innovation function of the firm to a more remote location and empowering the subsidiary to source knowledge from the new location to share with the parent firm.[107]

To small business owners, our results highlight the importance of mindful consideration of the constraints and opportunities that are associated with their operating region. For those who operate within geographic clusters, the results suggest it is important to reach out for knowledge beyond cluster borders to sustain new product innovation. The results also caution entrepreneurs from overemphasizing product enhancements at the expense of searching for new opportunities. While too much emphasis on existing innovations has the potential to outdate a firm's capabilities, some focus on existing innovations is still needed to appropriate value from investments into those innovations.[108] Therefore, the results validate the importance of finding balance between new product and product-enhancement innovations.

There are several theoretical implications stemming from the results that we have presented in this research. One is the importance of understanding how industry clustering in a geographic region influences total product development activities. Examining new product innovations alone would have led us to conclude that there is no effect of industry clustering on small technology firm innovation behavior when, in fact, the effect is on product enhancements. Joint consideration of both forms of innovation enabled us to provide a broader understanding of the implications of industry cluster regions for small firm innovation.

The second is the fact that because small firms face considerable consumer and technological uncertainty,[109] which requires constant changes to their innovations to resolve imperfections in design,[110] industry clustering may be useful for helping small firms to strengthen the competitiveness of their product-line offering. In particular, when considering the knowledge spillovers from the region, small firms operating from regions with industry clustering likely have better understanding of user preferences, the technological means of satisfying those preferences, and access to the resources that are needed to effectively implement the necessary changes to the operations.[111]

Given that a natural shifting occurs from product to process innovations as the venture and industry grows, small firms must maintain their ability to introduce new applications to meet market demands.[112] Without a deliberate attempt to source new knowledge into the operations, a small firm within an industry cluster region may continue to innovate around its existing product lines to its eventual demise. Clearly, these arguments suggest that the roles that industry clustering and knowledge spillovers play for small technology firm innovations may change with the stage of the firm and quite likely also with the industry's development.[113] It is important for future research to consider how such factors influence the outcomes that can be expected when firms operate from regions with industry clustering.

BUILDING DEEPER UNDERSTANDING OF INDUSTRY CLUSTERING AND SMALL FIRM INNOVATION

While the results mostly confirm our expectations regarding the influence of industry clustering and regional-knowledge spillovers on small firm innovations, there are several factors that limit the generalizability of this research. The first limitation is that we focused on a sample of young, small firms that undertook an IPO. IPO firms represent an exceptional group of firms, and when undertaken by young ventures, it makes for an especially elite sample. Even so, not all firms in our sample were successful at introducing new products or enhancing existing products during the time period under consideration. While the rate at which these firms innovate may be higher than is true of the general population of small software firms, our sample demonstrated noteworthy variance in firm product-innovation capabilities. Moreover, as our primary research question was to consider how industry clusters and knowledge spillovers impact small technology firm innovations, a sample of innovating firms such as we drew was imperative. Future research will need to explore what the effect is on a broader sample, specifically of private small firms and older, more mature firms.

Our use of software firms restricted our ability to conduct a longitudinal analysis of the effect of industry clustering and knowledge spillovers. Software firms often sell niche products and are commonly acquired by other firms to complete the acquirer's product-line offerings. This characteristic of these industries not only limited the number of firms we could use for analysis but also restricted the number of data years available for this sample of firms. Use of an industry with lower acquisition activity may enable researchers to examine the effects over a longer period of time. There is also a need to examine the product innovations generated over a longer period of time to determine whether there are long-term effects of industry clustering or knowledge spillovers on a firm's ability to introduce products to the marketplace.

The time period from which we drew the sample of firms was a unique period of time—the onset of the Internet revolution and height of the Internet bubble. Although we believe this unusual time period may have resulted in more firms of average capabilities undertaking an IPO than might be true under more normal circumstances, we acknowledge the need for future research to validate these results on firms operating under more traditional IPO environments. Another limitation is our use of patent citations, a coarse measure of knowledge spillovers, as an indicator of knowledge-spillover assimilation. Our measure attempts to capture the extent to which firms assimilate knowledge from regional firms into their technologies, but we recognize there are many other sources of spillovers that should be considered for their influence. Employee turnover, alliances, or customer-supplier relationships can all be sources of spillovers for firms. We encourage future research to consider finer-grained measures of knowledge spillovers and their influence on product innovations.

CONCLUSION

This research provides a greater understanding of the impact of regional-knowledge spillovers and industry clusters on the new product and product-enhancement innovations of small technology firms. By examining product innovations along these two dimensions, our results lead us to conclude that the higher innovation activity for some cluster firms is attributed to the attention they give to enhancing existing products. For these firms, the receipt of knowledge from within the industry cluster exacerbated this behavior. Entrepreneurs operating from industry clusters must decrease their use of regional knowledge to avoid becoming trapped in a cycle whereby attention is given to existing products at the expense of new products. For this reason, it is imperative for future research to continue exploring the interconnections of regions, knowledge spillovers, and small firm innovations.

ACKNOWLEDGMENTS

This research was funded in part by a grant from the Ewing Marion Kauffman Foundation and the Robinson College of Business at Georgia State University. The contents of this manuscript are solely the responsibility of Brett Anitra Gilbert and Mika Tatum Kusar. The authors would like to thank Jeff Covin, Susan Houghton, Erik Monsen, Caron St. John, and Zuoquan Zhan for their comments on earlier versions of this work. The authors accept full responsibilities for any errors in this research.

NOTES

1. Rui Baptista and Peter Swann, "Do Firms in Clusters Innovate More?," *Research Policy* 27 (1998): 525–540.

2. Edward J. Malecki, "Industrial Location and Corporate Organization in High Technology Industries," *Economic Geography* 61 (1985): 345–369.

3. Alfred Marshall, *Principles of Economics* (London: MacMillan, 1920); Michael E. Porter, *On Competition* (Cambridge, MA: Harvard Business School Publishing, 1998).

4. E.g., David B. Audrestch and Maryann P. Feldman, "R&D Spillovers and the Geography of Innovation and Production," *The American Economic Review* 86, 3 (1996): 630–640; Donna Marie Decarolis and David L. Deeds, "The Impact of Stocks and Flows of Organizational Knowledge on Firm Performance: An Empirical Investigation of the Biotechnology Industry," *Strategic Management Journal* 20, 10 (1999): 953–968; Brett Antira Gilbert, Patricia P. McDougall, and David B. Audretsch, "Clusters, Knowledge Spillovers and New Venture Performance: An Empirical Examination," *Journal of Business Venturing* 23, 4 (2008): 405–422; AnnaLee Saxenian, "Regional Networks and the Resurgence of Silicon Valley," *California Management Review* 33 (1990): 89–111.

5. Lynne G. Zucker, Michael R. Darby, and Jeff Armstrong, "Geographically Localized Knowledge: Spillovers or Markets?," *Economic Inquiry* 36, 1 (1998): 65–86.

6. Andaç T. Arikan, "Interfirm Knowledge Exchanges and the Knowledge Creation Capability of Clusters," *Academy of Management Review* 34, 4 (2009): 658–676; Bin Guo and Jing-Jing Guo, "Patterns of Technological Learning within the Knowledge Systems of Industrial Clusters in Emerging Economies: Evidence from China," *Technovation*, 31, 2 (2011): 87–104; Anders Malmberg and Dominic Power, "(How) Do (Firms in) Clusters Create Knowledge?" *Industry and Innovation* 12 (2005): 409–431; Ann Markusen, "Sticky Places in Slippery Space: A Typology of Industrial Districts," *Economic Geography* 72 (1996): 292–313; Patrick Ronde and Caroline Hussler, "Innovation in Regions: What Does Really Matter?," *Research Policy* 34 (2005): 1150–1172.

7. Adam B. Jaffe, Manuel Trajtenberg, and Rebecca Henderson, "Geographic Localization of Knowledge Spillovers as Evidenced by Patent Citations," *Quarterly Journal of Economics* 63 (1993): 577–598.

8. Edward J. Feser, "Tracing the Sources of Local External Economies," *Urban Studies* 39 (2002): 2485–2506.

9. Peter Maskell, "Towards a Knowledge-based Theory of the Geographical Cluster," *Industrial and Corporate Change* 10 (2001): 921–943.

10. Anna Lee Saxenian, "Regional Networks: Industrial Adaptation in Silicon Valley and Route 128," *Cityscape: A Journal of Policy Development and Research* 2, 2 (1994): 41–60; Stephen Tallman, M. Jenkins, N. Henry, and S. Pinch, "Knowledge, Clusters, and Competitive Advantage," *Academy of Management Review* 29, 2 (2004): 258–271.

11. Michael W. Lawless and Philip C. Anderson, "Generational Technological Change: Effects of Innovation and Local Rivalry on Performance," *Academy of Management Journal* 39 (1996): 1185–1217.

12. Daniel A. Levinthal and James G. March, "The Myopia of Learning," *Strategic Management Journal* 14 (1993): 95–113.

13. Jesper B. Sorenson and Toby E. Stuart, "Aging, Obsolescence, and Organizational Innovation," *Administrative Science Quarterly* 45 (2000): 81–112.

14. Steven Klepper, "Entry, Exit, Growth and Innovation over the Product Life Cycle," *The American Economic Review* 86 (1996): 562–583.

15. Oliver E. Williamson, *Markets and Hierarchies: Analysis and Antitrust Implications* (New York: The Free Press, 1975).

16. Klepper, "Entry, Exit, Growth and Innovation."

17. Paul Strebel, "Organizing for Innovation over an Industry Cycle," *Strategic Management Journal* 8 (1987): 117–124.

18. Sorenson and Stuart, "Aging, Obsolescence, and Organizational Innovation."

19. David J. Teece, Gary Pisano, and Amy Shuen, "Dynamic Capabilities and Strategic Management," *Strategic Management Journal* 18 (1997): 509–533.

20. Marshall, *Principles of Economics*.

21. Alfred Weber, *Theory of the Location of Industries*, trans. Carl J. Friedrich (Chicago: University of Chicago Press, 1929).

22. J. V. Henderson, "The Sizes and Types of Cities," *American Economic Review* 64 (1974): 640–656.

23. Maryann P. Feldman and Richard Florida, "The Geographic Sources of Innovation: Technological Infrastructure and Product Innovation in the United States," *Annals of the Association of American Geographers* 8 (1994): 210–229; Marshall, *Principles of Economics*; Jorge Niosi and Tomas G. Bas, "The Competencies of Regions—Canada's Clusters in Biotechnology," *Small Business Economics* 17 (2001): 31–42.

24. Alex F. De Noble and Craig S. Galbraith, "Competitive Strategy and High Technology Regional/Site Location Decisions: A Cross-country Study of Mexican and U.S. Electronic Component Firms," *Journal of High Technology Management Research* 3 (1992): 19–37; Edward L. Glaeser, "The New Economics of Urban and Regional Growth," in *The Oxford Handbook of Economic Geography*, ed. Gordon L. Clark, Maryann P. Feldman, and Meric S. Gertler (New York: Oxford University Press, 2000): 83–92; Niosi and Bas, "The Competencies of Regions."

25. Michael E. Porter, "The Economic Performance of Regions," *Regional Studies* 37 (2003): 549–578; Saxenian, "Regional Networks and the Resurgence of Silicon Valley."

26. Elaine Romanelli and Claudia Bird Schoonhoven, "The Local Origins of New Firms," in *The Entrepreneurship Dynamic*, ed. Claudia Bird Schoonhoven and Elaine Romanelli (Stanford, CA: Stanford University Press, 2001): 40–67.

27. John Seely Brown and Paul Duguid, "Mysteries of the Region: Knowledge Dynamics in Silicon Valley," in *The Silicon Valley Edge: A Habitat for Innovation and Entrepreneurship*, ed. Chong Moon Lee et al. (Stanford, CA: Stanford University Press, 2000): 16–39; Gilbert, McDougall, and Audretsch, "Clusters, Knowledge Spillovers and New Venture Performance."

28. Zucker, Darby, and Armstrong, "Geographically Localized Knowledge."

29. Scott J. Wallsten, "An Empirical Test of Geographic Knowledge Spillovers Using Geographic Information Systems and Firm-level Data," *Regional Science and Urban Economics* 31 (2001): 571–599.

30. Brown and Duguid, "Mysteries of the Region."

31. Maskell, "Towards a Knowledge-based Theory of the Geographical Cluster."

32. Paul Almeida, "Knowledge Sourcing by Foreign Multinationals: Patent Citations Analysis in the U.S. Semiconductor Industry," *Strategic Management Journal* 17, special issue (1996): 155–165; Tony S. Frost, "The Geographic Sources of Foreign Subsidiaries' Innovations," *Strategic Management Journal* 22 (2001): 101–123; Baptista and Swann, "Do Firms in Clusters Innovate More?"; Decarolis and Deeds, "The Impact of Stocks and Flows of Organizational Knowledge on Firm Performance"; Keld Laursen, Francesca Masciarelli, and Andrea Prencipe, "Regions Matter: How Localized Social Capital Affects Innovation and External Knowledge Acquisition," *Organization Science* 23 (2012): 177–193; David B. Audretsch, "Agglomeration and the Location of Innovative Activity," *Oxford Review of Economic Policy* 14, 2 (1998): 18–29.

33. Tom Cottrell and Barrie R. Nault, "Product Variety and Firm Survival in the Microcomputer Software Industry," *Strategic Management Journal* 25 (2004): 1005–1025; Riitta Katila and Gautam Ahuja, "Something Old, Something New: A Longitudinal Study of Search Behavior and New Product Introduction," *Academy of Management Journal* 45 (2002): 1183–1194.

34. Guo and Guo, "Patterns of Technological Learning."

35. James G. March, "Exploration and Exploitation in Organizational Learning," *Organization Science* 2 (1991): 71–88.

36. Zi-Lin He and Poh-Kam Wong, "Exploration vs. Exploitative: An Empirical Test of the Ambidexterity Hypothesis," *Organization Science* 15 (2004): 481–494; Andrew D. Henderson, "Firm Strategy and Age Dependence: A Contingent View of the Liabilities of Newness, Adolescence, and Obsolescence," *Administrative Science Quarterly* 44 (1999): 281–314.

37. March, "Exploration and Exploitation in Organizational Learning"; Sorenson and Stuart, "Aging, Obsolescence, and Organizational Innovation."

38. Catherine M. Banbury and Will Mitchell, "The Effect of Introducing Important Incremental Innovations on Market Share and Business Survival," *Strategic Management Journal* 16, special issue (1995): 161–182; Thomas J. Prusa and James A. Schmitz Jr., "Can Companies Maintain Their Initial Innovative Thrust? A Study of the PC Software Industry," *The Review of Economics and Statistics* 76 (1994): 523–540.

39. March, "Exploration and Exploitation in Organizational Learning."

40. Levinthal and March, "The Myopia of Learning."

41. Porter, *On Competition*; Saxenian, "Regional Networks and the Resurgence of Silicon Valley."

42. Joel A. C. Baum and Paul Ingram, "Survival-enhancing Learning in the Manhattan Hotel Industry, 1898–1980," *Management Science* 44, 7 (1998): 996–1117; Guo and Guo, "Patterns of Technological Learning."

43. Timothy Bresnahan, Alfonso Gambardella, and Annalee Saxenian, "Old Economy Inputs for New Economy Outcomes: Cluster Formation in the New Silicon

Valleys," *Industrial and Corporate Change* 10, 4 (2001): 835–860; Niosi and Bas, "The Competencies of Regions."

44. Jeffrey L. Furman, "Location and Organizing Strategy: Exploring the Influence of Location on the Organization of Pharmaceutical Research," *Advances in Strategic Management* 20 (2003): 49–88; Romanelli and Schoonhoven, "The Local Origins of New Firms."

45. William J. Abernathy and Kim B. Clark, "Innovation: Mapping the Winds of Creative Destruction," *Research Policy* 14 (1985): 3–22; Tallman et al., "Knowledge, Clusters, and Competitive Advantage."

46. Mary M. Crossan, Henry W. Lane, and Roderick E. White, "An Organizational Learning Framework: From Intuition to Institution," *Academy of Management Review* 24 (1999): 522–537; Guo and Guo, "Patterns of Technological Learning."

47. Sorenson and Stuart, "Aging, Obsolescence, and Organizational Innovation."

48. Eric Abrahamson and Lori Rosenkopf, "Institutional and Competitive Bandwagons: Using Mathematical Modeling as a Tool to Explore Innovation Diffusion," *Academy of Management Review* 18 (1993): 487–517.

49. Guo and Guo, "Patterns of Technological Learning."

50. Furman, "Location and Organizing Strategy."

51. Brown and Duguid, "Mysteries of the Region"; Andrew Hargadon and Robert I. Sutton, "Technology Brokering and Innovation in a Product Development Firm," *Administrative Science Quarterly* 42 (1997): 716–749; Zucker, Darby, and Armstrong, "Geographically Localized Knowledge."

52. Jaffe, Trajtenberg, and Henderson, "Geographic Localization of Knowledge Spillovers."

53. Feser, "Tracing the Sources of Local External Economies."

54. Julian Birkenshaw and Neil Hood, "Characteristics of Foreign Subsidiaries in Industry Clusters," *Journal of International Business Studies* 31, 1 (2000): 141–154; Frost, "The Geographic Sources of Foreign Subsidiaries' Innovations."

55. Ikujiro Nonaka, "A Dynamic Theory of Knowledge Creation," *Organization Science* 5 (1994): 14–37.

56. Laursen, Masciarelli, and Prencipe, "Regions Matter."

57. Gilbert, McDougall, and Audretsch, "Clusters, Knowledge Spillovers and New Venture Performance"; Maskell, "Towards a Knowledge-based Theory of the Geographical Cluster."

58. Toby E. Stuart, "Network Positions and Propensities to Collaboration: An Investigation of Strategic Alliance Formation in a High-technology Industry," *Administrative Science Quarterly* 43 (1998): 668–698; Wesley M. Cohen and David A. Levinthal, "Absorptive Capacity: A New Perspective on Learning and Innovation," *Industrial and Corporate Change* 35 (1990): 128–152.

59. Saxenian, "Regional Networks and the Resurgence of Silicon Valley."

60. Guo and Guo, "Patterns of Technological Learning."

61. Richard Pouder and Caron H. St. John, "Hot Spots and Blind Spots: Geographical Clusters of Firms and Innovation," *Academy of Management Review* 21 (1996): 1192–1225.

62. Hargadon and Sutton, "Technology Brokering and Innovation"; Katila and Ahuja, "Something Old, Something New"; Laursen, Masciarelli, and Prencipe, "Regions Matter"; Joseph F. Porac, Howard Thomas, and Charles Baden-Fuller, "Competitive Groups as Cognitive Communities: The Case of the Scottish Knitwear Manufacturers," *Journal of Management Studies* 26 (1989): 397–416.

63. Romanelli and Schoonhoven, "The Local Origins of New Firms"; Tallman et al., "Knowledge, Clusters, and Competitive Advantage."

64. Lori Rosenkopf and Atul Nerkar, "Beyond Local Search: Boundary-spanning, Exploration and Impact in the Optical Disc Industry," *Strategic Management Journal* 22 (2001): 287–306.

65. Lawless and Anderson, "Generational Technological Change."

66. Cohen and Levinthal, "Absorptive Capacity."

67. Cottrell and Nault, "Product Variety and Firm Survival," 1005.

68. E. Ralph Biggadike, *Corporate Diversification: Entry, Strategy and Performance*, (Cambridge, MA: Division of Research, Graduate School of Business Administration, Harvard University, 1976).

69. Porter, "The Economic Performance of Regions"; Audrestch and Feldman, "R&D Spillovers and the Geography of Innovation and Production."

70. Almeida, "Knowledge Sourcing by Foreign Multinationals"; Frost, "The Geographic Sources of Foreign Subsidiaries' Innovations."

71. Jaffe, Trajtenberg, and Henderson, "Geographic Localization of Knowledge Spillovers."

72. Nonaka, "A Dynamic Theory of Knowledge Creation."

73. Frost, "The Geographic Sources of Foreign Subsidiaries' Innovations"; Jaffe, Trajtenberg, and Henderson, "Geographic Localization of Knowledge Spillovers."

74. Luc Anselin, Attila Varga, and Zoltan Acs, "Local Geographic Spillovers between University Research and High Technology Innovations," *Journal of Urban Economics* 42 (1997): 422–448.

75. Jeffrey A. Timmons, *New Venture Creation*, 4th ed. (Homewood, IL: Richard D. Irwin Press, 1994).

76. Zvi Griliches, *R&D, Patents and Productivity* (Chicago: NBER, 1984).

77. Jaffe, Trajtenberg, and Henderson, "Geographic Localization of Knowledge Spillovers."

78. Douglas H. McQueen and Henrik Olsson, "Growth of Embedded Software Related Patents," *Technovation* 23 (2003): 533–544.

79. E.g., Jaffe, Trajtenberg, and Henderson, "Geographic Localization of Knowledge Spillovers."

80. Christopher Marquis, "The Pressure of the Past: Network Imprinting in Intercorporate Communities," *Administrative Science Quarterly* 48 (2003): 655–689.

81. Cluster Mapping Project, Institute for Strategy and Competitiveness, Harvard Business School.

82. See, Porter, "The Economic Performance of Regions." *Regional Studies* 37: 549–578.

83. Leona S. Aiken and Stephen G. West, *Multiple Regression: Testing and Interpreting Interactions* (Newbury Park, CA: Sage Publications, 1991).

84. Sorenson and Stuart, "Aging, Obsolescence, and Organizational Innovation."

85. Paul Almeida and Bruce Kogut, "Localization of Knowledge and the Mobility of Engineers in Regional Networks," *Management Science* 45, 7 (1999): 905–918.

86. Cottrell and Nault, "Product Variety and Firm Survival."

87. Shaker A. Zahra and Gerard George, "Absorptive Capacity: A Review, Reconceptualization, and Extension," *Academy of Management Review* 27, 2 (2002): 185–203.

88. David L. Deeds, Donna Marie Decarolis, and Joseph E. Coombs, "The Impact of Stocks and Flows of Organizational Knowledge on Firm Performance: An Empirical Investigation of the Biotechnology Industry," *Strategic Management Journal* 20 (1997): 953–968; Gilbert, McDougall, and Audretsch, "Clusters, Knowledge Spillovers and New Venture Performance."

89. Feser, "Tracing the Sources of Local External Economies."

90. Abrahamson and Rosenkopf, "Institutional and Competitive Bandwagons"; Lawless and Anderson, "Generational Technological Change"; Porter, *On Competition.*

91. Brown and Duguid, "Mysteries of the Region."

92. C.f., Bruce Kogut and Udo Zander, "Knowledge of the Firm, Combinative Capabilities, and the Replication of Technology," *Organization Science* 3 (1992): 383–397.

93. Feldman and Florida, "The Geographic Sources of Innovation"; Niosi and Bas, "The Competencies of Regions."

94. C.f., Pouder and St. John, "Hot Spots and Blind Spots."

95. Banbury and Mitchell, "The Effect of Introducing Important Incremental Innovations"; Cottrell and Nault, "Product Variety and Firm Survival."

96. C.f., Kathleen M. Eisenhardt and Claudia Bird Schoonhoven, "Organizational Growth: Linking Founding Team, Strategy, Environment, and Growth among U.S. Semiconductor Ventures, 1978–1988," *Administrative Science Quarterly* 35 (1990): 504–529; Henderson, "Firm Strategy and Age Dependence"; Cottrell and Nault, "Product Variety and Firm Survival."

97. C.f., Banbury and Mitchell, "The Effect of Introducing Important Incremental Innovations."

98. E.g., Pouder and St. John, "Hot Spots and Blind Spots"; Sorenson and Stuart, "Aging, Obsolescence, and Organizational Innovation."

99. C.f., Pouder and St. John, "Hot Spots and Blind Spots."

100. Malecki, "Industrial Location and Corporate Organization."

101. Rosenkopf and Nerkar, "Beyond Local Search."

102. Pouder and St. John, "Hot Spots and Blind Spots."

103. Arikan, "Interfirm Knowledge Exchanges."

104. Crossan, Lane, and White, "An Organizational Learning Framework."

105. Levinthal and March, "The Myopia of Learning."

106. Hargadon and Sutton, "Technology Brokering and Innovation."

107. Frost, "The Geographic Sources of Foreign Subsidiaries' Innovations."

108. March, "Exploration and Exploitation in Organizational Learning."

109. Klepper, "Entry, Exit, Growth and Innovation."

110. Williamson, *Markets and Hierarchies*.

111. Brown and Duguid, "Mysteries of the Region"; Klepper, "Entry, Exit, Growth and Innovation."

112. Strebel, "Organizing for Innovation"; Williamson, *Markets and Hierarchies*.

113. Audrestch and Feldman, "R&D Spillovers and the Geography of Innovation and Production."

9

Institutional Impact on Small Venture Exporting: Differences between Developed and Emerging Market Economies

Joseph LiPuma and Christiane Prange

Business does not occur independent of its environment. The context in which business is transacted, in which activities are developed and implemented, deeply affects the nature of strategies employed and the ability of those strategies to improve performance. Contexts for business can be temporal, economic, cultural, political, industrial, and institutional, among others. For example, strategies by companies in the 1950s may be quite different than those in the current era, in which information technology and social networks affect the pace and interconnectedness with which business is executed. Similarly, economic conditions pre- and post–Internet bubble (2000) and pre- and post–economic crisis (2008), combined with global economic integration and trade, created contexts that affected young and old, small and large companies alike.

The past 25 years have seen a remarkable redrawing of the world's economic landscape and its context. Emerging market economies, such as the BRICS (Brazil, Russia, India, China, and South Africa), along with other countries, have moved from factor-driven (based on industries such as agriculture and extraction that rely heavily on labor and natural resources) to efficiency-driven (industrialized with an increased reliance on economies of scale) phases dominated by capital-intensive large organizations. The economies of the more developed countries are based on innovation, in which businesses are increasingly knowledge intensive, with a greater reliance on the service sector. In each of these types of economies, the institutional environment encompassing the system of formal laws, regulations, and procedures and informal conventions, customs, and norms provides the frame within which companies perform, and the nature of this institutional environment affects firm performance.

However, the relationship between institutional context and firm performance is not always clear or linear. While the context of emerging market countries has often been considered detrimental to firm performance, emerging countries are catching up and improving contextual factors. For instance, in 2011, China's patent office received more patent applications than any other country in the same year (followed by Japan, the Unites States, Great Britain, Germany, and France), supported by a more favorable institutional environment. For developing countries, the relationship between context and performance is no longer obvious. The United Arab Emirates, for example, encountered structural problems when Dubai World, a large government-controlled investment firm, announced that it could no longer repay its debts, thereby threatening to bring down the entire economy. This flashy property frenzy, during which government-controlled developers piled up debt, was fostered by financial and cultural institutions.

What are the differences between emerging and developed market economies? An *emerging market economy* is a country that has a rapid pace of economic development and government policies favoring economic liberalization and the adoption of a free-market system.[1] The term "emerging market" was coined by the International Finance Corporation (IFC) in 1981 and was initially used to describe stock markets in developing countries that are considered either low or middle income as defined by the World Bank or that have low investable market capitalization relative to GDP.[2] Today, emerging markets have come to represent entire countries rather than stock markets and, in particular, those countries that hold the promise of high rates of economic growth. While various definitions exist, a *developed market economy* refers to countries that have sound, well-established economies and are therefore thought to offer safer, more stable investment opportunities than emerging market economies. Countries that are part of the OECD (Organization for Economic Co-operation and Development) are considered developed market economies.[3]

It is commonly argued that the institutional environment, which includes financial, regulatory, and judicial systems, and the like, matters more in emerging market countries than in developed market countries. For instance, countries may differ in the development of banking and investment systems (financial), company registration and labor laws (regulatory), and the ability of courts to adjudicate disputes (judicial). McMillan notes that when markets work smoothly in developed economies, the market-supporting institutions are almost invisible, but when markets work poorly in emerging economies, the absence of strong formal institutions is conspicuous.[4] But we are still largely ignorant about which institutions matter most in these different sets of countries. Although governments of emerging economies have long recognized the important role that small firms play in national export performance as an indicator of a nation's overall economic health, little research to date has examined the exaggerated effect that institutional quality has on the export performance of small firms in emerging economies as compared to their counterparts in developed economies.[5] For small firms, a better understanding of the drivers and impediments of export performance is important because exporting improves utilization of productive capacity, enhances financial performance and competitive edge, and provides a foundation for future international expansion.[6] At the national level, exporting enhances the accumulation of foreign-exchange reserves, improves employment levels and productivity, and drives economic growth.[7]

In addition, there is a lack of practical guidance on how to deal with different institutional contexts, as the complex interplay of institutional forces often makes it difficult to classify and quantify differences.[8] In this chapter, we seek to address this gap by defining institutional environments, discussing institutional differences between developed and emerging economies, analyzing how these differences specifically affect small companies and their export performance, and presenting managerial implications.[9]

INSTITUTIONAL ENVIRONMENTS

Institutional theory emphasizes the influence of the systems surrounding organizations that shape social and organizational behavior.[10] Institutional context can be defined as the environment around concrete social forms of the economy and political system, created and refined by the actors who use them, and carried forward by a shared meaning.[11] Institutional contexts may vary on a number of dimensions, such as social, political, economic, cultural, and historical.[12] Along these dimensions, both formal and informal institutions provide the context for competition and are considered the "rules of the game" that are "the humanly devised constraints that structure human interaction."[13] Organizations (such as companies) are the players bounded by those formal and informal rules, and institutional forces affect their processes and decision making.

The role of institutions in an economy is to reduce both transaction and information costs by mitigating uncertainty and establishing a stable structure that facilitates interaction between organizations. Institutions do this by defining what is appropriate in an objective sense and thus rendering other actions unacceptable or even beyond consideration.[14] Institutions simultaneously constrain and enable firms by guiding actions and posing limits on behavior and informing the choices that firms make while constraining the way that they construct knowledge.[15] Nonetheless, firms can react to institutional constraints and can work to take active roles in shaping these constraints.[16] Large firms, in particular, such as Microsoft or Walmart, can shape institutional constraints by lobbying or by internalizing markets for intermediary goods, thereby circumventing potential regulatory constraints across national borders. Small firms have less ability to choose higher commitment or higher control forms of foreign-market entry (e.g., establishing a subsidiary) and thus depend more on exporting than most large firms. Given their lower resource endowment and restricted power in dealing with governments, small firms often depend on the goodwill of such institutional actors as banks and governments to ease institutional constraints.

Despite the potential influence of firms and their ability to change institutional norms, institutional stability, consistency, and predictability are critical for the functioning and growth of economic systems. Environments that demonstrate these characteristics have a well-specified legal system, a clearly defined and impartial judiciary to enforce property rights and adjudicate disputes, and attitudes toward business that encourage people to engage in transactions at low costs.[17] Such institutions tend to be more robust in developed countries and are often underdeveloped in emerging ones, resulting in macroeconomic volatility that reduces economic growth and increases indirect welfare costs to society.[18] This was demonstrated in the early 1990s by stagnant or declining small firm sectors in many emerging economies, compared to growth and productivity in small firms in most developed economies.[19]

Institutions further govern societal transactions in the areas of politics, law, society, and culture. As regards politics, institutions address issues such as corruption and transparency, antidumping, and corporate governance. In terms of law, institutions deal with economic liberalization and the regulatory regime that governs business practices. The societal dimension of institutional governance considers such aspects as ethical norms and attitudes toward business, such as society's view of entrepreneurs and entrepreneurship. Finally, culture plays a part in the institutional framework through such various cultural dimensions as uncertainty avoidance or time orientation, as described by Hofstede, Hofstede, and Minkov.[20]

For business, it is often institutions that provide the framework—both enabling and constraining—for companies formulating and implementing strategies to achieve competitive advantage.[21] Three pillars of the institutional framework, the "regulative, normative, and cognitive structures and activities that provide stability and meaning to social behavior," offer a broad basis to differentiate aspects of countries' institutional profiles.[22] The *regulatory pillar* establishes the ground rules for doing business, reflecting a country's laws and regulations and the extent to which these rules are effectively monitored and enforced. The *cognitive pillar* rests on the widely shared social knowledge and cognitive categories in a society and thus determines much of the informal way of doing business that firms need to consider. The *normative pillar* consists of beliefs, values, and norms that define expected behavior in a society. The regulatory pillar provides the focus for the empirical analyses in this chapter.

Characteristics of Institutional Environments in Developed and Emerging Market Economies

Developed economies have institutional environments that are presumed to be stable, with well-established laws and enforcement of property rights, reliable courts, and well-functioning financial systems. They are generally characterized as having less corruption and more transparency. Transparency International defines corruption as "the abuse of entrusted power for private gains."[23] Corruption inhibits business growth. Expectations of corrupt behavior by government officials discourage the formation and growth of small businesses by delivering an unfavorable signal to managers, as fairness of rules of the game could be omitted by one party, increasing the level of uncertainty and decreasing company gains.[24]

Other difficulties for business involve the length of time or the complexity of addressing legal requirements, such as obtaining certificates or following bureaucratic procedures. For instance, business regulations in different countries require that it take between four (United States) and 97 days (Russia) to register a business.[25] The Ease of Doing Business international studies also note that one of the big issues for governments around the world is to focus their reform efforts on reducing the complexity and the cost of regulatory processes rather than concentrating only on the legal institutions.[26]

Emerging market economies often lack certain institutional features, exhibiting a shortage of skilled labor, thin capital markets, and inconsistent infrastructure and having political and economic instability, with public suspicion of foreign firms.[27] Such market economies often fall short of well-defined property rights and a strong legal framework, permitting opportunism, rent shifting, bribery, and corruption.[28] For example, China's complicated institutional frameworks lead to bribery and a general ignoring of institutions to get things done, from payment for expediting import or export of components or finished goods to moving registration procedures to Hong Kong and reimporting products to avoid many of the hassles that companies face in Mainland China. The institutional quality in emerging market economies is more important for small firms than for their large counterparts for export performance.[29] In particular, in emerging markets, the export performance of small firms is more strongly related to improvements in the court system and the transparency of financial markets than is the case for large firms.

These differences in the institutional frameworks between emerging economies and developed economies provide relevant ground for scholarly study. In addition, these differences force the managers who operate in these respective economies to adapt from using textbook strategies to using practical guidelines. These guidelines should be diversified from one economic region to another (e.g., from an emerging economy to a developed economy) and should help to develop an understanding of the ways in which the institutional environment differentially affects small businesses in each context. Finally, guidelines should help to avoid unexpected institutional deficits and circumvent issues that firms encounter when moving between economic regions.

WHY INSTITUTIONS AFFECT SMALL COMPANIES IN DIFFERENT WAYS THAN LARGE COMPANIES

The dynamics that small firms face play an important role in shaping their dependence on institutional quality. Because of limited resource endowments, small firms often lack the means to engage in resource exchanges or to insure themselves against default in exchanges in which they participate.[30] Local institutions often favor larger firms because of their relationships with them or the market power that larger firms wield. Researchers expect and find that firms are forced to create internal markets for capital, labor, and products in the absence of well-functioning formal institutions that protect property rights and provide incentives for risk taking. These actions are a result of the failure of the institutional environment to provide the necessary political and institutional infrastructure. However, small firms generally lack the tangible or intangible resources necessary to effectively construct or access these informal networks and must rely primarily on the publicly available markets, no matter how insufficient or underdeveloped, resulting in higher than average transaction costs and thereby placing them at a distinct disadvantage to large firms.[31]

In the absence of property rights protection, investments in innovation, for example, may be easily appropriated by competitors, robbing small firms of the benefits of those sunk costs, thereby hindering market entry.[32] This situation is particularly challenging for small firms with few slack resources or little political clout.[33] Ensuring rights to property involves both passing required legislation and its consistent and fair application, allowing entrepreneurship to thrive. The rule of law in emerging economies tends to be particularly unreliable, thereby limiting enforcement of legislation and creating a hostile environment for small, resource-poor firms.

Emerging economies also exhibit high degrees of bureaucracy and government regulation, corruption and bribery, legal complexity, and taxation, coupled with the lack of legal protection afforded to firms. Small firms often do not possess the financial and human capital required to overcome such barriers; small firms that receive both monetary and managerial resources are more likely to survive, to grow, to compete, and to innovate (see table 9.1 for examples of institutional effects on small companies).

While innovation enables firms both large and small to exploit international market opportunities, small firms have long been observed to be more innovative than large firms. A system of enforceable property rights, via laws and fair courts for enforcement, enabling small firms to leverage this innovation advantage, is essential to their ability to grow via exporting. Growing a firm's exports is costly given the necessary investments in market research, channel development, product adaptation, and institutional knowledge. The resource constraints faced by small firms to growing exports can be overcome in high-quality institutional environments where access to finance is fair and unbiased, and presumably fewer regulations and taxes are associated with exporting. However, if small firms are unable to build their own internal markets for capital as large firms can, export costs for small firms will likely be insurmountable. Even if small firms are able to access financing, a low-quality regulatory structure characterized by burdensome taxes and bureaucratic red tape may limit small firms' ability to dedicate capital directly to export-related investments.

TABLE 9.1 Examples of Effects of Institutions on Small Firms

Institutional Dimension	Application	Examples of Effect on Small Companies
Governmental	An impartial governmental body	Equitable support for small firms levels the playing field.
Legal	A well-specified legal system	Stable laws facilitate entrepreneurial entry and safeguards individuals' property rights.
Financial	A highly developed capital market	Ability to access both debt and equity capital provides needed resources.
Regulatory	A regulatory framework that facilitates commerce among individuals and organizations	Positive impact on company formation time and speed to internationalization facilitates growth.

INSTITUTIONAL DIFFERENCES BETWEEN DEVELOPED AND EMERGING ECONOMIES: AN EMPIRICAL ANALYSIS

The above strongly suggests that the effect of institutions on businesses differs from developed to emerging economies and that these differences affect small and large businesses in varied ways. To test this view, we examined data from the World Bank's World Business Environment Survey (WBES), administered by the World Bank's Investment Climate and Institute Units from late 1998 to early 2000, with the intent of providing insight into the quality of the investment climate as shaped by the regulatory institutional context that includes public policy, legislation, public and private institutions, and the like.[34] WBES data were collected through interviews of managers in more than 10,000 firms in 81 developed and emerging economies in six geographic regions—Africa, Middle East/Northern Africa, Central/Eastern Europe, East Asia, South Asia, and Latin America—and the OECD. Our analyses utilized data obtained from the 10,032 enterprises that responded to the core questionnaire. We exclude data on firms from sub-Saharan African countries because of low response rates and differences in how data was collected. As a result, the sample size is 7,989 firms operating in 56 countries.

In each country, the WBES sampling targeted industry composition, size, ownership, exporters, and location to ensure adequate representation of firms. It is noteworthy that roughly 40 percent of the sample firms are small (employ 50 or fewer employees).[35] Overall, small firms are consistently less involved in manufacturing than large firms and are more involved in services and commerce.

Exporting is an important firm-level performance measure that contributes to country-level development.[36] Consistent with our examination of the relationships between institutional factors and the export performance of small ventures, we operationalize our dependent variable as the percentage of the firm's total sales that it exports, a commonly used measure. We measure the institutional quality of an emerging economy along four dimensions: impartial governmental body, a well-specified legal system, a highly developed capital market, and a regulatory framework that facilitates commerce among individuals and organizations. We constructed these variables from survey results.

The WBES asked respondents to indicate the frequency with which the government interferes with their firm's decisions regarding investment, employment, sales, pricing, dividends, wages, and mergers and acquisitions. Government intervention may, in some cases, reduce uncertainty and thus assist firms, although the survey specifically identified aspects of intervention generally perceived as inhibiting or destructive to business. Similarly, the WBES asked respondents to comment on the host country's court system according to their perception of its fairness, impartiality, honesty, expediency, affordability, consistency, and enforceability. The WBES also asked respondents to comment on the degree to which their firms face obstacles in obtaining finance because of issues of collateral, bureaucracy, interest rates, necessity of connections, availability of capital, corruption, access to foreign banks, access to nonbank capital, and access to lease finance and credit. Lastly, the WBES asked respondents to assess the degree to which government regulations, such as those pertaining to licensing, customs, labor, currency exchange, environment, safety, and taxes, impinge on the firm's operation and growth.

We control for effects at the firm-level, industry-level, and country-level that might affect firm exports. Regarding *firm-level effects*, we control for firm age and firm size, each of which can affect the ability of firms to intensify their foreign activities because of the scale, resource, and legitimacy challenges they present. Regarding *industry-level effects*, we control for the industry sectors in which WBES respondents indicated that their firms competed: service, manufacturing, agriculture, construction, or other. We also control for the manner in which the practices of a firm's competitors presented obstacles to fair competition, such as avoiding paying taxes or duties or violating copyrights, patents, or trademarks, and the like. Regarding *country-level effects*, we control for macroeconomic factors, including currency strength and trade and FDI policies, given that they may also affect export growth. We include dummy variables for each country in the sample to control for additional country-level effects not captured by the variables described above.

Utilizing the multi-item scales in the WBES measuring institutional quality and fairness of competition, we conducted an exploratory factor analysis to create indices to assess the multidimensionality of these constructs. Three institutional constructs relating to competition, financial markets, and regulations yielded two factors each, suggesting a finer-grained measure than initially inferred from the survey data. Specifically, the construct "competition" yielded factors for both legal and business dimensions of competition. The construct "financial" yielded factors for access to capital (i.e., availability of capital) along with the process associated for obtaining capital. Finally, the construct "regulations" yielded factors for both tax regulations and general business regulations. We operationalize all institutional variables with the regression scores obtained from this analysis.

Overall, more than one-quarter of the firms in the sample exported, averaging nearly one-third (32 percent) in foreign sales. More than 41 percent of the companies were small enterprises, slightly less than the percentage (42 percent) that was seven or fewer years old. Manufacturing represents

27 percent in OECD and 36 percent in emerging economies, services 61 percent and 48 percent, respectively. Slightly more than one-sixth of companies have some foreign ownership.

EMPIRICAL ANALYSIS RESULTS

Not all ventures export. Managers select their geographic strategy, requiring use of a Heckman two-stage procedure to model this self-selection for accuracy and generalizability of the results.[37] This first stage of the procedure estimates the likelihood of a firm's exporting based on a set of characteristics, and the second stage evaluates how specific factors relate to export performance for only those firms that export (hence the sample is not random, thus requiring the first stage), controlling for factors that may also relate to the intensity of exporting.

While the focus of our analysis is on export performance, per se, the results of the first-stage model (probability of exporting) provide insights into exporting differences between OECD and emerging market economies. (The results of the Heckman analyses are provided in tables 9.2 and 9.3.) In both types of economies, small companies are less likely to export, while manufacturing firms are more likely to export, as are firms with some foreign ownership, suggesting that foreign investors can facilitate exporting opportunity identification or enactment. In emerging markets, young companies are less likely to export. Agricultural firms in OECD countries are more likely to export, whereas service firms in emerging markets are more likely to export, as compared to firms in the omitted category, "Other Industries" (i.e., firms that are nonmanufacturing, nonservice, nonagricultural, and nonconstruction). In OECD countries, firms facing competitive obstacles based on legal circumvention (e.g., avoiding taxes, not paying duties, violating patents, and illegal domestic and foreign price setting) are more likely to export, while firms facing competitive obstacles based on shady business practices (receiving subsidies, colluding, or gaining favored access to credit) are less likely to export.

Parameters from the first stage that examines the likelihood to export for all firms are entered into an equation that describes the export intensity of only the firms that export. Several interesting results emerge from the second-stage analyses that, though only indirectly related to our research question, provide a more general view of factors that affect firms' export intensity in emerging and developed markets. For instance, in emerging markets (Models 1–3 in table 9.2), young firms have higher export intensity and manufacturing and agriculture firms have higher export intensity than firms in "Other

Industries" (the omitted category), and that high inflation relates to higher export intensity. Exporting manufactured goods and agricultural outputs is easier and quicker because of the ability to separate their production from consumption. In addition, for people-bound services, personnel need to be trained and adjusted to the new institutional context, which is cost and time intensive.

As exporting is the least costly and least committing form of internationalization, young firms may utilize exporting more than other high-control forms, such as joint ventures, to sell to foreign markets. High inflation may push ventures to more rapidly sell goods abroad while the value of the good is at its highest level, thereby stimulating high-export intensity. In emerging economies, competitive obstacles related to laws (e.g., avoiding taxes, not paying duties, violating patents, and price fixing) relate positively to export intensity, whereas business-related competitive obstacles (e.g., revenue subsidies, favored access to credit, and credit collusion) are negatively associated with export intensity (Models 2 and 3 in table 9.2). As the prevalence of law-based competitive obstacles increases, firms in violation of these laws may more easily export (if avoiding taxes or duties), whereas those not in violation may be forced to export rather than compete domestically with the violators. Tax regulations relate positively to export intensity, suggesting that either the regulations constrain domestic sales, pushing companies to export a higher percentage of their goods, or that business regulations facilitate exporting, allowing companies to more easily export, thereby increasing the overall percentage of goods exported.

There are further insights on the differential effect of institutions on small versus large companies in emerging economies (Model 3, table 9.2). We find that for small companies, government intervention negatively affects small businesses' export intensity as compared to larger firms, but a good court system positively affects export intensity. A good finance process helps small firms' export intensity more than it helps larger firms.

In OECD countries, we observe some differences in institutional effects as compared to emerging economies (Models 5 and 6 in table 9.2). Inflation is significantly and negatively related to firm-export intensity. As prices increase in the domestic market, sales of goods internationally is less attractive, decreasing international intensity. Government intervention is negatively related to export intensity; as business perception of government intervention increases, export intensity decreases. Competitive obstacles related to law are negatively related to export intensity, in contrast to the positive relationship found in emerging economies. Small firms are more positively affected by government intervention and business regulations in developed countries than are large firms (Model 6, table 9.2).

TABLE 9.2 Heckman Analysis Results—Second Stage: Intensity of Exporting

	Emerging Economies			Developed Economies		
	(1)	(2)	(3)	(4)	(5)	(6)
Age 7 years or less	7.768***	6.784***	6.610***	-1.103	0.437	-1.094
Small enterprise	0.362	-0.681	0.524	-0.377	-1.465	14.29**
Industry—Manufacturing	10.300***	11.300***	11.280***	-5.373	-8.886	-8.762
Industry—Construction	9.330**	9.085*	8.716*	-6.140	-8.406	-7.298
Industry—Agriculture	16.350***	15.990***	15.800***	-5.432	-10.840	-8.695
Industry—Service	6.406*	5.889	5.808*	-4.940	-7.012	-7.22
Inflation percentage	0.081**	0.085**	0.090**	-7.835*	-9.329**	-10.370**
Trade Openness average 1997–99	0.228*	0.182	0.198	-0.089	-0.177	-0.195
Government Intervention		0.366	0.965		-5.280*	-8.376**
Quality of Courts		0.005	-0.687		-1.355	-1.964
Competition Obstacles—Legal		3.675***	3.831***		-5.090**	-4.481**
Competition Obstacles—Business		-1.159	-1.662		-0.949	-3.515
Finance—Access		-0.594	-1.065		-2.415	-3.114
Finance—Process		0.756	0.003		-1.067	-0.096
Regulations—General		1.190	0.996		-1.920	-2.905
Regulations—Tax		1.684**	1.841**		-0.708	-0.547
Small x Government Intervention			-2.742*			11.96**
Small x Quality of Courts			2.991*			2.789
Small x Competition Obstacles—Legal			-0.317			-4.755
Small x Competition Obstacles—Business			2.097			9.606**

	(1)	(2)	(3)	(4)	(5)	(6)
Small x Finance—Access			2.179			6.358
Small x Finance—Process			3.703			–4.411
Small x Regulations—General			0.564			2.202
Small x Regulations—Tax			–0.584			0.374
Constant	2.507	5.962	3.235	58.59	69.66	68.32
Observations	7128	7128	7128	7128	7128	7128
Observations censored	4902	4902	4902	4902	4902	4902
Observations uncensored	2226	2226	2226	2226	2226	2226
Wald chi2	542.38	594.90	613.29	25.49	38.09	50.62
Prob > chi2	0.0000	0.0000	0.0000	0.0300	0.0179	0.0107
Log Likelihood	–14467.41	–14447.38	–14440.2	–1870.28	–1864.3	–1858.9
Prob indep of equations	0.0000	0.0002	0.0003	0.0011	0.0002	0.0002

***p < 0.01; **p < 0.05; *p < 0.1

Data source: WBES.

INSTITUTIONAL ENVIRONMENTAL EFFECTS ON SMALL COMPANIES: COMPARING DEVELOPED VERSUS EMERGING ECONOMIES

First, our analytic approach provides some insights regarding firms' propensity to export. Firms in manufacturing and agricultural sectors seem to be more likely to export, on average, than those in other sectors, consistent with prior research regarding industries with high usage of machinery and domestic inputs.[38] Second, firms with some foreign ownership are also more likely to export, which is also consistent with prior research.[39] Third, small firms and young firms are less likely to export than larger and better-established firms in emerging economies, consistent with our earlier arguments regarding the obstacles to be overcome to export, and with the fact that new and small firms are less equipped to meet those challenges.[40] Finally, competitive obstacles affect the propensity to export for OECD companies but not emerging economy companies. The nature of the effect is different, based on the type of competitive obstacle: business or legal.

More broadly, despite some similarities between the results of the propensity to export models (table 9.3) and our analyses predicting export intensity (table 9.2), it appears that the factors that contribute to whether firms export at all may be different than those related to the firm-level performance of that exporting activity.

We observe that, across our models, emerging economy firms in the manufacturing and agricultural sectors export more as a percent of sales than firms in other industries. For OECD companies, both manufacturing and agriculture firms are more likely to export, but for those that do export, there is no difference in export intensity as compared to companies in other industrial sectors. This difference between emerging economy and OECD companies may underscore the respective stages of development: OECD countries are more knowledge based with a greater service sector.

Institutional Factors and Export Intensity: Main Effects

Before presenting the findings related to different effects of institutions on small firms in emerging versus developed economies, we briefly summarize the main effects of the institutional factors related to export intensity as presented in table 9.4.

Regarding the effect of institutional factors on export intensity, we find that government intervention, competitive obstacles—legal, competitive obstacles—and business and tax regulations differentially affect firms in emerging economies and OECD countries.

TABLE 9.3 Heckman Analyses Results—First Stage: Probability of Exporting

	Emerging Economies			Developed Economies		
	(1)	(2)	(3)	(4)	(5)	(6)
Age 7 years or less	-0.302***	-0.299***	-0.299***	-0.126	-0.13	-0.128
Small enterprise	-0.484***	-0.485***	-0.485***	-0.446***	-0.434***	-0.442***
Industry—Manufacturing	0.96 ***	0.962***	0.962***	1.048***	1.072***	1.074***
Industry—Construction	0.001	0.005	0.005	0.306	0.333	0.333
Industry—Agriculture	0.140	0.147	0.147	1.186**	1.231**	1.246**
Industry—Service	0.142**	0.147**	0.147**	0.145	0.165	0.167
Foreign ownership dummy	0.643***	0.644***	0.643***	0.777***	0.782***	0.782***
Competition Obstacles—Legal	-0.017	-0.002	-0.001	0.125***	0.161***	0.161***
Competition Obstacles—Business	0.018	0.023	0.023	-0.142***	-0.139**	-0.139**

*** p < 0.01; ** p < 0.05; * p < 0.1

Data source: WBES.

TABLE 9.4 Institutional Effects on Firms' Export Intensity

	Emerging Economies		Developed Economies	
	All Firms	Small vs. Large Firms	All Firms	Small vs. Large Firms
Government intervention		Negative effect smaller for small firms than for large firms	Negative	Negative effect greater for small firms than for large firms
Quality of courts		Positive for small firms	-	
Competitive obstacles—legal	Positive		Negative	
Competive obstacles—business	Negative			Positive for small firms
Finance—access				
Finance—process		Positive for small firms		
Regulations—general				
Regulations—tax	Positive			

Government Intervention

In emerging economies, government intervention is not found to be related to export performance of firms, whereas in the developed OECD economies, government intervention is negatively related to firms' exporting. This indicates that as the perception of government interference in business decisions increases, export performance decreases for exporting companies.

Competitive Obstacles (Legal Factors)

For emerging economy companies, competitive-legal factors are significantly and positively related to the average export performance of firms. These results suggest that certain higher-quality institutions are associated with the increased export performance of firms in emerging economies. Specifically, it seems that firm export performance will be highest in countries where competitive-legal factors tend to facilitate rather than impede commerce. In contrast, competitive-legal obstacles pose more of a barrier to OECD firms' exporting intensity.

Competitive Obstacles (Business Factors)

For companies in emerging economies, the perceived presence of competitive obstacles related to business practices, such as taxes and tax administration, is related to firms' export performance. Firm export performance will be lower in countries where the perception of tax-related competitive obstacles is highest. No such relationship exists between such business-related competitive obstacles and export performance in developed economies.

Regulations: Tax

Higher-quality tax regulation regimes are associated with greater export intensity in emerging economies. When tax administration is not onerous and the tax burden is not excessively high, firms in emerging economies are more able to export, and more intensively.

Institutional Factors and Export Intensity: Effects on Small Businesses

Our comparative analyses of small versus large firms in emerging and developed countries adds richness to our broad understanding of institutional quality on export performance by suggesting that the relationship of institutional quality to export performance differs somewhat based on firm size and economic context, as seen in table 9.4.

Government Intervention

A finding worthy of discussion is the effect of government intervention on small firms in the two different economies. In developed countries, small firms may use government intervention programs to their benefit, as such programs are designed to assist in financing and training for small businesses and to assist in navigating the process for exporting. In emerging market environments, such government intervention could support small firms' ability to grow and penetrate foreign markets through their economic development, trade promotion, and related services. This is a role that may be especially important for small firms that lack the slack resources and legitimacy that the government might otherwise provide that are necessary to export. For example, government-subsidized training, R&D, and export-support programs, as well as trade agreements (e.g., WTO) would likely all have an important bearing on the growth of exports among small firms. In emerging economies that often lack such programs, government intervention may solely take the form of interference and red tape intended to extract additional taxes or other payments.

Quality of Courts

Our findings suggest that a high-quality court system has a greater positive effect on the export performance of small firms than on larger firms in emerging economies. This result suggests that small firm export performance in emerging economies is especially vulnerable to insufficient court systems and that improvements in the fairness, impartiality, honesty, expediency, affordability, consistency, and enforceability of such a system may disproportionately benefit small firms. This result is consistent with the hypothesis that small firms do not have resources or connections to manage certain deficiencies in the institutional environment and are more exposed to those institutional conditions than larger firms.

Exporting requires the use of various public and private intermediaries, such as customs authorities, customs brokers, and freight forwarders. The overall court system logically affects small firms' confidence in these intermediaries and the enforceability of contracts that they enter into with them, as small firms lack resources to devote to petitioning unfair and biased court systems subject to corruption or other uneven application of the law. Larger firms may be able to influence the court system by deploying resources or exploiting connections, or they may internalize some functions that small firms must contract out because of their lack of slack resources.[41] For small firms lacking resources to devote to managing the court system, illegal (e.g., bribes) or legal (e.g., lawsuits) improvement in such systems would enable greater focus on operational issues that could improve export performance.

Competitive Obstacles (Business Factors)

There is no evidence that the export performance of small companies in emerging economies is more or less affected than larger firms by the perceived presence of competitive obstacles related to business practices. However, in developed countries, small firms are more impacted by such competitive obstacles. The enforcement of tax regulations may be more uniform in developed economies, and small firms may have fewer resources to find tax loopholes or other legal means to pay a lower effective tax rate, further straining their financial resources. Export taxes may disproportionately affect such small firms.

Finance: Process

In addition, our findings suggest that, for emerging economies, a reduction in the bureaucracy needed to obtain financial capital has a greater positive effect on the export performance of small firms. This result suggests that small firm export performance is especially vulnerable to unfair requirements and expectations regarding capital markets. Small firms must often rely on the publicly available financial markets, no matter how bureaucratic and opaque they might be, as they lack the resources, prestige, and connections of their larger counterparts, who are able to access private, informal capital markets.[42] This is evidenced by the persistence of large business groups in many parts of the emerging world, which feature interlocking cross-ownership among multiple businesses, including banks, and effectively self-finance operations.[43] For example, Malaysia has become the most important country for Islamic finance. Over one-fifth of the country's banking system, by assets, is sharia compliant; the average for Muslim countries is more like 12 percent, and often less. Two institutions, the International Centre for Education in Islamic Finance (INCEIF) and the Islamic Banking and Finance Institute of Malaysia (IBFIM), have played a major role in this development in concentrating on vocational training, disseminating acceptable rules for Islamic finance, and acting as a consultancy to banks.

MANAGERIAL IMPLICATIONS

This chapter provides several insights that are important for managers of small firms when considering exporting to foreign countries. While there is an abundance of research that focuses on the institutional context in emerging markets, only a few studies have investigated the role of context in developed economies or have engaged in comparative analysis associated with internationalizing new ventures in emerging economies.[44] We will first discuss some implications for small business managers in emerging market economies, then look at implications for small business managers in developed countries, and finally suggest implications for small businesses seeking to export from one institutional context to the other. Complementing existing literature, we highlight exporting from emerging economies to developing economies as "the other way around," which is tremendously challenging, especially for small ventures.[45]

Implications for managers of small businesses in emerging economies are manifold. The principal challenge is to cope with competitive-legal and business-related obstacles. Trying to benefit from the positive influence of courts and the legal system in general, small business managers may join trade associations to initiate and accelerate specific interventions. In general, though, they may be less able to lobby to promote supportive government intervention or push back on destructive government intervention, or may be less able to "grease the skids" or resist requests for bribes. To prepare themselves for higher competitiveness, they may initially prefer to select countries where competition is stringently regulated by law and enforced by respective courts.

Working to overcome business-related obstacles, it seems timely to lobby to influence the development of higher-quality institutions. Small firm owners may also choose those emerging market countries where taxes are favorable to their exporting intention. As government intervention is seen as less negative in emerging market economies, small business managers should proactively work with government to implement policy frameworks that further support domestic firms. These strategies should enhance their competitiveness and enable them to compete effectively in the global arena. Small emerging market firms can usually operate more successfully in the domestic market than abroad because they have competitive advantages that are created or reinforced by governmental support.

Finally, small companies are generally more resource constrained and may need letters of credit and quick access to capital to export, thus an efficient and transparent finance process may be more important to small firms than to larger firms. Small business managers should be aware of clear structures, guidelines, and time frames as to where, how, and when to organize their financial strategies. This involves selecting banks as well as negotiating mutual objectives to avoid interruptions in the process.

Managers of small businesses in developed economies seeking to establish subsidiaries in emerging economies would be wise to consider the institutional benefits and impediments associated with these economies. These relate predominantly to established financial markets and the finance process and to high-quality court systems. If the goal of internationalization is to provide a regional foothold from which the firm can export to multiple countries, the firm would be subject to the same court system, government intervention, regulatory, and competitive factors as host country firms.

Finally, we look at implications for small firms in particular when exporting to countries at different levels of economic development. Emerging market contexts bring institutional pressures for developed economy firms as much as developed market contexts pose difficulties for emerging market firms. Given that emerging economy institutions are often plagued by underdeveloped law enforcement, weak labor protection, and a lack of transparency, developed economy firms will have difficulty responding. In turn, multinational enterprises from emerging economies need to understand institutional norms in developed markets that are alien to them to successfully enter those markets. Many of the contexts, both formal and informal, will pose challenges and encourage a greater emphasis on experimenting with and developing indigenous approaches to solving problems.[46]

While using well-informed procedures, guidelines, and frameworks in their home markets, developed firm managers may realize that doing business in emerging markets is largely a matter of complexity, with different elements of the institutional context intermingling—some favorably, some less favorably. Managers may first aim to improve their institutional context by reducing the complexity and cost of regulatory processes. In cooperating with local governments, they may later move on to reforms that strengthen legal institutions relevant to business regulation (in such areas as getting credit).

For small firms from both emerging and developed countries, we argue that they need to be especially aware of developing and adapting strategies to local contexts. However, in formulating their strategies, they may face contradictory challenges: they may be more flexible in their ability to deal with institutional voids, while lacking the resource endowments of larger firms, and they may be quicker in adaptation because of informal communication and decision-making procedure but also lack the deeply rooted internal structures, processes, and routines to deal with new environments and to incorporate foreign knowledge. Finally, a developed institutional context with overly restrictive regulations can hamper their founding,[47] while an inadequate institutional environment can complicate their development.[48] Overall, both the existence and the absence of formal institutions can impede economic growth,[49] whereas informal institutions, such as building ties with the government, can be helpful but also costly and may further hamper the venture's development.[50]

Beyond an understanding of the economic contexts, guidelines will have to take into account that strategies often follow a "both/and" rather than an "either/or" approach, emphasizing a need to balance and reconcile different elements of the institutional context. For example, government intervention may be both beneficial and detrimental, and managers need to balance conflicting effects: if local players are too flexible in circumventing legal contexts, engaging with partners bound by internationally accepted guidelines may help. In turn, dealing with an overregulated context may be countered by adopting less complex procedures successfully operated by local firms. These adaptation or balancing strategies have been described from the theoretical angle of ambidexterity theory.[51] We suggest here that dealing with institutional contexts requires ambidextrous strategies, for example, dealing with various trade-offs. Four different trade-offs can be described that are valid for firms in both emerging and developed markets (table 9.5).

First, small firm managers should decide how much to change their own organization to fit the new institutional context. While these changes may be mostly cosmetic to please governments or consumers (e.g., utilizing new labels or sizes or investing more in quality), they may also affect the essence of

TABLE 9.5 Adaptation Strategies to Various Institutional Contexts

Adaptation Layer	Trade-off	Strategy for Cross-entry
Change	Cosmetic vs. wholesale	Adopt technological requirements but only as long as core competence can be maintained.
Relationships	Local actors' specific standards vs. international standards	Collaborate with local actors through institutional brokering while investing in market education.
Adoption	Ignorance of local context vs. nonmarket entry	Carry outward signaling of adoption forward into implementation.
Reformation	Change of local context vs. nonmarket entry	Promote or reinforce new institutional norms and redefine behaviors.

a company (e.g., variation of technology base or source of competitive advantage). As a guideline, companies may only engage in change if it does not risk destructing their core competence. That is, if companies need to change the core processes (e.g., high quality) or competences (e.g., miniaturization associated with premium products) on which their competitive advantage is built, market entry into a new country may be postponed or abandoned as too risky.

Second, companies may investigate the degree of potential and desired relationships in the market and whether they want to adopt local players' prescriptions or impose their own institutional standards. For example, Tracy and Phillips talk about "institutional brokering," where entrepreneurs found ventures or new organizational forms to reduce institutional uncertainty and adjust to the local context.[52] The creation of "havala" or "hundi" money transfer in South Asia is such an example of a new organizational form created to build on local standards and raise them to higher levels of international acceptance that reinforce findings on the positive impact of finance processes.[53] As a guideline, companies may find markets favorable if they can collaborate with partners and improve standards. This may work in two ways, that is, educating players in process optimization to lower the costs of operations (in which emerging market players are experts) or focusing on brand and product innovation (in which developed market players are experts). That is, adaptation is contingent on the upgrading of the firms' skills in the respective market environment.

Third, there may be markets with rather inflexible institutional contexts (overregulated or underregulated), and small firm managers need to first check whether they can potentially ignore these contexts and move to more informal or formal ways of doing business or whether they would rather refrain from entering the respective markets. If there are only a few commonly accepted business practices or standards, small business managers need to engage in high degrees of ambiguity and risk. That is, they can pretend to comply with norms and standards while working on factual circumvention. For instance, China does not allow foreign publishing on its grounds, but moving the headquarters to Hong Kong and importing foreign press products is a tolerated strategy.

Finally, companies may be convinced to radically change a foreign institutional context by introducing lasting improvements that enhance business conditions. This is reflected in the fact that institutions themselves are not entirely exogenous but are affected by economic actors. These strategies are typically adopted when investment is conditional on the acceptance of formal guidelines (i.e., formal schooling, official elections, or antinepotism laws). Authors such as North have argued that economic actors not only adapt to given institutions but aim to shape institutions—at least over longer periods of time.[54] For most companies entering emerging markets, these reforms relate to efficient financial systems and the reduction of corruption and bribery. If actors do not believe this to be possible, they should rather refrain from entering the market. For instance, small firms reflecting on corruption issues may use Transparency International's corruption score to identify "no-go" markets. In addition, as firms cross borders, they do not need to enter every country in which they wish to sell, but consider increasing exporting on a region level.

Overall, one of the basic questions of succeeding in different institutional contexts relates to the choice between acceptance, ignorance, and the attempt to change.[55] In most institutional contexts, whether developed or emerging, there are nonlinear choices that require the reconciliation of conflicting strategies. For all the elements of the institutional context that we mentioned in this article, firms need to decide how much they expect them to influence their business.

CONCLUSIONS

In this chapter, we discussed the importance of the institutional environment on small firms in both emerging and developed economies. Based on data from the World Bank's World Business Environment Survey (WBES) from late 1998 to early 2000, we investigated both the export propensity and the export intensity of small firms in both economic contexts. One of the major results pertains to the fact that the institutional environment, and especially the regulatory pillar, differentially affects small businesses. Business-related competitive obstacles are favorable to small firms' exports in developed economies, and government intervention affects them negatively. In emerging markets, efficient court systems and a functioning financial process support the export intensity of small firms, while government interventions—like in developed countries—affect them negatively. As a consequence of the differential impact, firms that move between institutional contexts need to be able to balance their enabling function and reconcile their detrimental effects. This calls for fine-grained adaptation strategies, which we introduced as change, relationships, adoption, and reformation layers. Taken collectively, our study offers insights for managers of small firms in both emerging and developed economies to better understand and manage the institutional context of their respective counterpart.

NOTES

1. Robert E. Hoskisson, Lorraine Eden, Chung Ming Lau, and Mike Wright, "Strategy in Emerging Economies," *Academy of Management Journal* 43, 3 (2000): 249–267.

2. International Finance Corporation, *Emerging Markets Factbook and Database* (Washington, D.C.: International Finance Corporation, 1999).

3. The 34 OECD countries as of 2013 are Australia, Austria, Belgium, Canada, Chile, Czech Republic, Denmark, Estonia, Finland, France, Germany, Greece, Hungary, Iceland, Ireland, Israel, Italy, Japan, Korea, Luxembourg, Mexico, the Netherlands, New Zealand, Norway, Poland, Portugal, Slovak Republic, Slovenia, Spain, Sweden, Switzerland, Turkey, the United Kingdom, and the United States.

4. John McMillan, "Market Institutions," in *The New Palgrave Dictionary of Economics*, 2nd ed., ed. Lawrence E. Blume and Steven N. Durlauf (London: Palgrave, 2007).

5. Tulus Tambunan, "The Role of Small Firms in Indonesia," *Small Business Economics* 4 (1992): 59–77.

6. Jane W. Lu and Paul W. Beamish, "The Internationalization and Performance of SMEs," *Strategic Management Journal* 22 (2001): 565–586.

7. Tulin Ural, "The Effects of Relationship Quality on Export Performance: A Classification of Small and Medium-sized Turkish Exporting Firms Operating in Single Export-market Ventures," *European Journal of Marketing* 43 (2009): 139–168.

8. Farzad H. Alvi and Peter J. Williamson, "Operationalising the Adaptation of Strategies to the Institutional Context of Emerging Markets," *Cambridge University Working Paper Series* 1 (2012): 1–29.

9. What categorizes a firm as small or large depends mainly on the country's stage of economic development. While it is customary to define small firms as those with fewer than either 500 (see Janet Marta, Anusorn Singhapakdi, and Kenneth Kraft,

"Personal Characteristics Underlying Ethical Decisions in Marketing Situations: A Survey of Small Business Managers," *Journal of Small Business Management* 46 (2008): 589–606) or 100 (see Anne M. Knott, "Induced Discrimination and Firm Size: Information vs. Incentive Effects," *Small Business Economics* 25 (2005): 393–405) employees, the European Union (EU) defines small firms as having 50 or fewer employees (European Commission, 2003).

10. W. Richard Scott, *Institutions and Organizations* (Thousand Oaks, CA: Foundation for Organizational Science, a Sage Publications Series, 1995).

11. Neil Fligstein, *The Architecture of Markets: An Economic Sociology of Twenty-first-century Capitalist Societies* (Princeton, NJ: Princeton University Press, 2001).

12. Alvi and Williamson, "Operationalising the Adaptation of Strategies to the Institutional Context of Emerging Markets."

13. Douglas C. North, *Institutions, Institutional Change and Economic Performance* (Cambridge, U.K.: Cambridge University Press, 1990).

14. Paul J. DiMaggio and Walter W. Powell, eds., *The New Institutionalism in Organizational Analysis* (Chicago: Chicago University Press, 1991), 1–38.

15. Scott, *Institutions and Organizations*.

16. Christine Oliver, "Strategic Responses to Institutional Processes," *The Academy of Management Review* 16 (1991): 145–179.

17. Douglas C. North, "The New Institutional Economics," *Journal of Institutional and Theoretical Economics* 142 (1986): 230–237; Douglas C. North, "Institutions and Credible Commitment," *Journal of Institutional and Theoretical Economics* 149 (1993): 11–23.

18. Viktoria Hnatkovska and Norman Loayza, "Volatility and Growth," in *Managing Economic Volatility and Crises: A Practitioner's Guide*, ed. Joshua Aizenman and Brian Pinto (Cambridge, U.K.: Cambridge University Press, 2005).

19. Zoltan Acs and David Audretsch, *Small Firms and Entrepreneurship: An East-West Perspective* (Cambridge, U.K.: Cambridge University Press, 1993).

20. Geert Hofstede, Gert Jan Hofstede, and Michael Minkov, *Cultures and Organizations: Software of the Mind*, 3rd ed. (New York: McGraw-Hill, 2010).

21. Paul Ingram and Brian S. Silverman, "The New Institutionalism in Strategic Management," in *Advances in Strategic Management*, ed. Paul Ingram and Brian S. Silverman (Greenwich, CT: JAI Press, 2002): 1–32.

22. Scott, *Institutions and Organizations*, 33.

23. Transparency International, 2011. Corruption Perception Index, www.transparency.org/cpi2011.

24. Ruta Aidis and Tomasz Mickiewicz, "Entrepreneurs, Expectations and Business Expansion: Lessons from Lithuania," *Europe-Asia Studies* 58 (2006): 855–880.

25. Gary D. Bruton, David Ahlstrom, and Han-Lin Li, "Institutional Theory and Entrepreneurship: Where Are We Now and Where Do We Need to Move in the Future?," *Entrepreneurship Theory & Practice* 34 (2010): 421–440.

26. International Finance Corporation (IFC), *Doing Business 2013* (Washington, D.C.: The World Bank, 2013), www.doingbusiness.org/~/media/GIAWB/Doing%20 Business/Documents/Annual-Reports/English/DB13-full-report.pdf.

27. Hoskisson et al., "Strategy in Emerging Economies."

28. Joan M. Nelson, Charles Tilley, and Lee Walker, *Transforming Post-Communist Political Economies: Task Force on Economies in Transition* (Washington, D.C.: National Academy Press, 1998).

29. Joseph A. LiPuma, Scott L. Newbert, and Jonathan P. Doh, "The Effect of Institutional Quality on Firm Export Performance in Emerging Economies: A Contingency Model of Firm Age and Size," *Small Business Economics* 40 (2013): 817–841.

30. Arthur Stinchcombe, "Social Structure and Social Organization," in *The Handbook of Organizations*, ed. James G. March (Chicago: Rand McNally, 1965): 142–193.

31. Lauretta C. Frederking, "A Cross-national Study of Culture, Organization and Entrepreneurship in Three Neighbourhoods," *Entrepreneurship & Regional Development* 16 (2004): 197–215.

32. Sheila Puffer, Daniel McCarthy, and Max Boisot, "Entrepreneurship in Russia and China: The Impact of Formal Institutional Voids," *Entrepreneurship Theory & Practice* 34 (2010): 441–467.

33. Zoltan Acs et al., "The Internationalization of Small and Medium-sized Enterprises: A Policy Perspective," *Small Business Economics* 9 (1997): 7–20.

34. Scott, *Institutions and Organizations*.

35. We use the European Union cutoff of 50 employees as our definition of small firm size (see note 8).

36. Tambunan, "The Role of Small Firms in Indonesia."

37. Heckman's two-stage least square method is widely used in econometrics to investigate parameters in systems of linear simultaneous equations and to solve problems of omitted variable-bias in single-equation estimation. James J. Heckman, "Sample Selection Bias as a Specification Error," *Econometrica* 47 (1979):153–161.

38. Jan Ter Wengel and Edgard Rodriguez, "SME Export Performance in Indonesia after the Crisis," *Small Business Economics* 26 (2006): 25–37.

39. Andrew J. Bernard et al., "Firms in International Trade," *The Journal of Economic Perspectives* 21 (2007): 105–130.

40. Mark Roberts and James Tybout, "An Empirical Model of Sunk Costs and the Decision to Export," *American Economic Review* 87 (1997): 545–64.

41. Tarun Khanna and Krishna Palepu, "Why Focused Strategies May Be Wrong for Emerging Markets," *Harvard Business Review* 75 (1997): 41–51.

42. Stinchcombe, "Social Structure and Social Organization."

43. Tarun Khanna and Krishna Palepu, "Is Group Affiliation Profitable in Emerging Markets? An Analysis of Diversified Indian Business Groups," *Journal of Finance* 55 (2000): 867–891.

44. Yasuhiro Yamakawa, Mike W. Peng, and David L. Deeds, "What Drives New Ventures to Internationalize from Emerging to Developed Economies?," *Entrepreneurship Theory and Practice* 32 (2008): 59–82.

45. Harry J. Sapienza et al., "A Capabilities Perspective on the Effects of Early Internationalization on Firm Survival and Growth," *Academy of Management Review* 31 (2006): 914–933.

46. Neil Fligstein and Jianjun Zhang, "A New Agenda for Research on the Trajectory of Chinese Capitalism," *Management and Organization Review* 7 (2001): 39–62.

47. Hernando de Soto, *The Mystery of Capital: Why Capitalism Triumphs in the West and Fails Everywhere Else* (New York: Basic Books, 2000).

48. William J. Baumol, Robert E. Litan, and Carl J. Schramm, *Good Capitalism, Bad Capitalism, and the Economics of Growth and Prosperity* (New Haven, CT: Yale University Press, 2009).

49. Harry G. Broadman et al., *Building Market Institutions in South Eastern Europe: Comparative Prospects for Investment and Private Sector Development* (Washington, D.C.: World Bank Publications, 2004).

50. Yasheng Huang, *Capitalism with Chinese Characteristics: Entrepreneurship and the State* (New York: Cambridge University Press, 2008).

51. Zi-Lin He and Poh-KamWong, "Exploration vs. Exploitation: An Empirical Test of the Ambidexterity Hypothesis," *Organization Science* 15 (2004): 481–494.

52. Paul Tracey and Nelson Phillips, "Entrepreneurship in Emerging Markets: Strategies for New Venture Creation in Uncertain Institutional Contexts," *Management International Review* 51 (2011): 23–39.

53. Leonides Buencamino and Sergei Gorbunov, "Informal Money Transfer Systems: Opportunities and Challenges for Development Finance" (discussion paper of the United Nations Department of Economic and Social Affairs (DESA), no. 26, 2006): 1–19, www.un.org/esa/esa02dp26.pdf.

54. North, *Institutions, Institutional Change and Economic Performance*.

55. Tarun Khanna, Krishna Palepu, and Richard Bullock, *Winning in Emerging Markets: A Road Map for Strategy and Execution* (Boston: Harvard Business Press, 2010).

10

Regional Banking Development and Small Business Growth: Evidence from China

Iftekhar Hasan, Haizhi Wang, and Mingming Zhou

The past few decades have witnessed a revaluation of the important role of small businesses in economic development.[1] During the process of small business formation, acquisition of resources, especially financial resources, is crucial for small business owners to pursue their entrepreneurial vision and bring their innovative ideas into reality. Banks not only accumulate financial capital but also channel scarce resources to support the growth of small firms. Difficulty in accessing external financial resources and lack of support from creditors have resulted in the high failure rate of small firms. Therefore, the development of a banking sector in the financial system is particularly important to small firms, which are often highly dependent on credit provided by local banking systems to support their start, survival, and continuous growth. (Using the data from 1993 National Survey of Small Business Finance, Cole et al. report that banks provide more than 60 percent of small business credit.)[2]

Most of the existing research that investigates the effect of financial development or of banking systems on the formation and growth of small businesses focuses exclusively on countries in North America and Europe.[3] The exploration of related domains outside of these two developed economic regions remains extremely limited. Among the existing studies, cross-country samples are usually used to pursue this line of inquiry. However, such an approach falls short, as the systematic differences between markedly different economies could be the hidden factors that drive the results. We argue that a research design that focuses on intracountry information rather than cross-country samples avoids this cross-country idiosyncrasy and ensures "data comparability and functional equivalence."[4]

We believe that China provides a unique environment for us to examine how financial development, especially in the banking sector, affects the growth of small businesses. First, compared to developed economies, banking institutions in emerging countries are usually much more strictly regulated, and their lending practices are heavily government directed, with different levels of government intervention.[5] By focusing on provincial-level data, we can largely ignore the uniform institutional settings at the country level but retain sufficient variation in banking development at the regional (provincial) level to explain the growth of small businesses. Second, lending to small businesses requires banks to rely more heavily on "soft information" to make decisions because "hard information" is difficult to collect because of an inadequate historical récord or a lack of audited financial reports for the small firms.[6] Because of the lack of security of property rights, rule of law, and disclosure of accounting information, banks play an even more important role in producing information about borrowers and assume a monitoring role in the lending process in emerging economies.[7] Therefore, in this chapter, we attempt to contribute to the literature and provide new evidence on the relation between the development of banking institutions in the local markets and the growth of small businesses in China, one of the largest and fastest-growing transitional and emerging economies in the world.

In this chapter, we collect data from different regions in a single emerging economy and form a panel of 30 provinces in China over the period from 1998 to 2008 to ensure that we have sufficient variations in both cross-sectional and time-series dimensions. From various sources, we obtain information on both the number and output of small businesses, and we construct two measures to capture the growth of small businesses in local areas. Further, we measure regional banking development from different aspects based on related theoretical underpinnings to examine the role played by financial intermediations in fostering small business growth. We also control for the regional economic environment and for demographic information in the regression analysis. Our empirical analysis yields novel evidence and sheds further light on the relation between development of the financial sector and small business in an emerging and transitional country. Specifically, we find that the presence of large banks has a negative effect on small business growth, which is consistent with the view that large banks have an informational disadvantage in making loans to small business.

This negative relation is mainly driven by large banks' participation in the short-term debt market. When we control for the market concentration and explore the contingent effect of large banks, we find that in concentrated markets, large banks can significantly facilitate the growth of small businesses. It is noteworthy that almost all of the financial liberalization that we observed happened in rural areas. Therefore, we also examine the role played by rural financial institutions in the growth of small business. We document a significantly positive relation between credit supplied by rural credit unions and small business growth. In addition, consistent with existing literature, our study confirms the positive impact of financial deepening, trained human capital, and personal wealth level on nurturing entrepreneurship in local markets.

LITERATURE REVIEW

Built on a large body of literature that dates back to Joseph Schumpeter, research has highlighted the influence of a country's financial development on the economic growth.[8] Banking institutions are essential for economic development in that they play a crucial role in screening potential borrowers and allocating financial and real resources in an efficient way.[9] Small businesses are extremely reliant on external financing to support their survival and long-term growth.[10] The relation between the banking sector and small business financing has received great attention in developed countries, and the causal relationship has been well established in the literature.[11] Given the importance of small business in economic development, we intend to investigate the effect of the banking sector on small business growth in an emerging country and provide further evidence.[12]

Small firms are known to be subject to "the liability of smallness."[13] According to Aldrich and Auster, the liability of smallness emerges from a lack of financial resources as well as a lack of strong support from creditors.[14] Small firms cannot buffer themselves from market contractions. It often requires special efforts for small firms to get access to external financial resources that are available in their environment and to establish a stable exchange relationship with creditors.[15]

In this chapter, we explore some important aspects of banking sector development in facilitating the growth of small business. For example, Stein points out that the key distinguishing characteristic of small business lending is the "softness" of the information used in the decision making compared to large banks that rely more heavily on "hard" information.[16] This suggests that large banks may shy away from relationship-based lending, preferring transaction-based lending, and that they are less likely to extend credit to small businesses, especially to small firms with almost no history. Empirical evidence has confirmed that larger banks have a lower fraction of small business lending in their lending portfolio.[17] Therefore, we intend to examine how the presence of large banks in the loan market may affect the growth of small businesses.[18]

Traditional banking theory, which treats borrowers as a homogenous group, suggests that all borrowers will be better off with increased banking competition because banks in relatively highly competitive environments are forced to be more efficient and to do a better job in loan screening and monitoring to survive.[19] However, bank competition is less favorable to new firms who suffer greater information asymmetries in general.[20] In particular, a highly competitive banking market gives more opportunities for small businesses to switch across different lenders, thus reducing the incentives for an average bank to make costly efforts to acquire soft information to mitigate the greater information asymmetry of their small borrowers.[21] Consequently, banks in competitive markets make lending decisions on a period-by-period basis and are less likely to extend credit to small firms associated with large information asymmetries. Therefore, a concentrated banking market is more likely to benefit small firms, and we expect that the effects of regional banking development on small business growth depend on local market concentration.

The current banking structure in China could be traced back to the late 1940s, when a new socialist banking system was established following the model from the Soviet Union. The central bank, the People's Bank of China, was founded in 1948 and took responsibility for currency issue and monetary control. The banking system was dominated by four very large state-owned banks, which controlled about three-fourths of banking assets until the 1990s.[22] Competition in the banking sector was limited because banks lacked sufficient incentives to make profits out of real business lending.

In the early 1990s, the central government began to reform the financial system in a fundamental way. The 1995 Commercial Bank Law of China officially specified the role of state-owned banks as commercial banks in accordance with market principles instead of in accordance with policy requirements. Additional changes were implemented after China's entry into the WTO, in 2001, including the liberalization of interest rates and a relaxation of restrictions on equity ownership. In more recent years, the Chinese government has taken cautious actions to partially privatize its banks by selling shares to both domestic and foreign investors, and the gradual reform of the banking system in China and various regulatory changes have significantly increased competition among banks and bank efficiency.[23] However, while a flourishing private sector has been significant to the economic development of China, the role of the banking sector in fostering small business growth is still inconclusive in existing literature.[24] Given the size of the banking sector in China, it would be interesting to examine the development of the banking sector in local markets and its effects on small business growth.

In China, banking institutions play a particularly important role in shaping the development of small firms for the following reasons. First, with China's underdeveloped capital market, most small firms are largely precluded from raising funds from such public resources as equity financing and public debt. Banks, therefore, are the main source of funding for small business owners in China. We argue that there is a dynamic interaction between small firms and banking institutions. Given the limited resources for which small firms are competing, small businesses' funding tends to be rationed, and small businesses are subject to a screen for credit worthiness and for future prospects by banking institutions.[25] Banks have an informational advantage in identifying potential borrowers and thus can nurture lending relationships with small firms.[26] As both insider lenders and delegated monitors, banks have access to small firms' information from the onset of a loan application, as well as to information from previous lending relationships, and so they are able to provide more effective monitoring at a lower cost.[27]

Second, it has been documented that China has grown by relying on unique, context-specific local institutional innovations, while the conventional mechanisms of growth, such as private ownership, protection of property rights, and reforms of political institutions, are not of central importance to China's growth story.[28] Given the unique institutional and political environment, the lack of organizational legitimacy increases the probability of failure of small firms. Organizations overcome the liability of smallness by establishing relationships with banking institutions, the major players in the economy, some of which are owned or partially owned by the government. In other words, banks function in the economic system as a certification of the quality and viability of small firms and increase the firms' probability of successful commercialization of innovations.[29]

In addition, it is important to recognize "the existence of two Chinas— an entrepreneurial rural China and a state-controlled urban China," which largely explains the success of the Chinese economy.[30] The changing structure of traditional rural industries and the impact of those changes on rural communities have been the driving forces behind the revitalization of rural areas.[31] The growth of small business in rural areas can promote local economic development by increasing employment, stabilizing the local environment, and transforming rural industries.[32] Consequently, rural banking institutions (e.g., rural credit unions) may provide crucial financial support to rural small firms that leads to regional economic development. In this chapter, we empirically examine the development of regional banking in China, and we formally test the following hypotheses based on our earlier discussions. First, we hypothesize that small banks (proxied by rural credit unions) play a bigger role than large banks in fostering the growth of small businesses. Second, we hypothesize that long-term loans are associated with greater small business growth than short-term loans. Third, we hypothesize that the link between bank lending and small business growth depends on the level of bank concentration.

DATA AND METHOD

In a standard cross-country setting, it is very difficult to observe and control for the set of social and cultural variables that potentially play an important role in affecting financial intermediations. Therefore, researchers are often forced to compare a large number of countries that possess dramatically different legal systems and institutional settings, which play an important role in shaping the practice of financial institutions.[33] For example, a bank's ability to force repayment and the cost of contract enforcement can vary widely across sample countries. Consequently, cross-country comparisons are subject to "data comparability and functional equivalence."[34] To reduce the sample biases, we examine the role of bank financing in explaining small business growth using provincial data in China, which is one of the largest and fastest-growing transitional and emerging economies in the world. By using the subnational-level data, we are able to focus on the regional development of the banking sector and to largely avoid the data comparability issue in cross-nation studies because many institutional factors—such as diversity in historical experiences and cultural norms—are homogeneous for our sample regions.[35] As a result, we construct a panel of 30 provinces (including four municipalities) in mainland China from 1998 to 2008.[36]

Measures of Small Business Growth

The National Bureau of Statistics of China (NBSC) provides various statistics on the number of firms in different size categories at the provincial level in their yearbooks. However, before 1997, the industrial statistics were based on types of ownership, and it is not until 1998 that the calibration of industrial statistics was changed from the types of ownership to the sizes of enterprises. Therefore, we are able to obtain aggregate information at the provincial level with a consistent definition of small business from 1998 onward.

The efficient operations of banking institutions require a careful screen of the credit worthiness and future growth prospect of small firms. Moreover, lending to small business is highly regulated by certain quotas set by the government in China, as dominating megabanks are state owned. This practice of the banking sector in China implies that banks have to shift their lending portfolios to allocate scarce financial resources to the most promising borrowers, which will further intensify the competition for bank loans by small firms. Given that environmental resources set a limit on population density, the growth rates of small business vary substantially within local markets because the number of organizations competing for the same pool of resources is constrained. We thereby use the growth rate of small business to investigate the effects of regional banking sector development.[37] We define growth rate of small business as the percent change in the total number of small businesses (defined as firms with fewer than 300 employees):

$$\text{Growth rate of small business}_{it} = \frac{N_{it} - N_{it-1}}{N_{it-1}} \times 100\% \qquad (1)$$

where N represents the number of small businesses.

And we collect the information at the end of each year, denoted as t, for each province, denoted as i.

To validate our measure of small business growth, we construct an alternative output-based measure that emphasizes the gross domestic product (GDP) attributable to small businesses, which is calculated as the percent change in total output of small businesses:

$$\text{Growth in output of small business}_{it} = \frac{P_{it} - P_{it-1}}{P_{it-1}} \times 100\% \qquad (2)$$

where P represents the output of small businesses.

We recognize that these measures are not perfect and are subject to sample errors, but they are the best available proxies to our knowledge.

Measures of Regional Banking Development

We obtain the regional banking loans data from the annual issues of the *Almanac of China's Finance and Banking* (ACFB) and collect GDP data from the annual issues of *China Statistical Yearbook*. Building on existing literature, we use several measures to capture regional banking development. Big Four loans/total loans is defined as the ratio of total loans made by the Big Four (China Construction Bank, Bank of China, Industrial and Commercial Bank of China, and Agricultural Bank of China) to total loans by all banking institutions (including credit unions). We use this variable to capture the presence of large banks in local markets, which are believed to have informational disadvantages in making loans to small businesses.[38] The pecking order hypothesis indicates that firms have a preference order for financing choices, with great information asymmetry leading to more reliance on internally generated funds and external debt relative to equity issuance.[39]

Evidence has shown that small firms seek short-term secured loans rather than longer-term debt to satisfy their financing needs because of the existence of great information asymmetry and their inability to secure long-term debt at low cost.[40] We thereby make a distinction between short-term debt and long-term debt and define two additional variables. Big Four's ST loans/total ST loans is defined as the ratio of total short-term loans made by the Big Four to total short-term loans made by all banking institutions. Big Four's LT loans/total LT loans is defined as the ratio of total long-term loans made by the Big Four to total long-term loans made by all banking institutions. As there is no nationwide credit score system in China, fund suppliers are generally lending to geographically proximate small businesses. More importantly, as rural small business growth is key to the success of China's economic growth, we measure the ratio of loans made by all rural credit unions to total loans by all banking institutions as an additional explanatory variable capturing the regional banking development.[41]

Other Control Variables

The ratio of total bank loans to GDP is commonly used in the banking literature as a proxy for banking-sector depth, which measures the role and importance of financial intermediation in the economy.[42] Following existing literature, we measure the quantity of bank lending as the ratio of total loans outstanding at the end of the year in the balance sheet of all banking institutions to total GDP in the region (termed as "total bank loans/GDP"). Moreover, taking asymmetric information into consideration, Petersen and Rajan argue that a concentrated market can foster entrepreneurship because banks are willing to subsidize entrepreneurial firms initially and recoup their cost in the long run.[43] Therefore, we construct a Herfindahl-Hirschman Index (HHI) based on bank loan information to measure the competition at the local markets through summing up squared market shares for each bank. When there is only a single bank in a particular province, the HHI is equal to one. For a perfectly atomistic market, HHI will be quite close to zero.

We collect province-level information about GDP, education, and FDI data from the annual issues of the *Statistics Yearbook of China*. The real GDP growth per capita is defined as the percentage change of real GDP per capita, with price level adjusted to year 1990, and we use this variable at year $t - 1$ to control for regional economic development momentum and local business environment. In addition, real GDP per capita also serves as an indicator of personal wealth level, which signifies the personal commitments of small business owners in operating their firms.[44]

Foreign direct investment (FDI) can encourage small business development.[45] It is also plausible that FDI may crowd out domestic small firms.[46] Despite the ambiguous effect of FDI on small business growth, we measure the ratio of foreign direct investment to GDP as an additional control variable.

Armington and Acs document the positive relationship between college graduates and the number of newly formed small firms.[47] Therefore, following their method, we calculate the proportion of the population with college degrees and use this as a proxy for the availability of trained human capital in the local area. The inclusion of these control variables is based on the natural link between broader economic development and small business growth discussed earlier.

Table 10.1 presents the summary statistics, and table 10.2 reports the pairwise correlation matrix of the variables used in the regression analysis. We find that the average growth rate of small business is 7.4 percent, with a standard deviation of 14.8 percent, while the average growth rate in output

TABLE 10.1 Descriptive Statistics

	Variable Names	Obs	Mean	Median	Std. Dev.	Minimum	Maximum
(1)	Growth in number of small businesses	310	0.074	0.059	0.148	–0.562	0.639
(2)	Growth in output of small businesses	310	0.217	0.221	0.205	–0.438	0.752
(3)	Big Four loans/total loans	390	0.595	0.597	0.114	0.299	0.960
(4)	Big Four's ST loans/total ST loans	390	0.669	0.676	0.208	0.137	0.991
(5)	Big Four's LT loans/total LT loans	390	0.595	0.558	0.176	0.274	0.982
(6)	Rural credit union's loans/total loans	390	0.104	0.103	0.052	0.011	0.289
(7)	Concentration Index	390	0.209	0.199	0.041	0.151	0.392
(8)	Insurance premium/GDP	372	0.020	0.018	0.011	0.000	0.099
(9)	Bank loans/GDP	399	1.084	1.009	0.510	0.086	8.425
(10)	Real GDP growth per capita	371	0.100	0.095	0.049	–0.070	0.327
(11)	FDI/GDP	357	0.029	0.015	0.032	0.000	0.169
(12)	College-degree holders/ population	372	0.052	0.041	0.043	0.001	0.301

Table 10.1 presents the descriptive statistics of all variables used in the regression analysis. *Growth in number of small businesses* is calculated as the percent changes in total number of small businesses (defined as firms with fewer than 300 employees). *Growth in output of small businesses* is calculated as the percent changes in total output of small businesses. *Big Four loans/total loans* is defined as the ratio of total loans made by the Big Four (China Construction Bank, Bank of China, Industrial and Commercial Bank of China, and Agricultural Bank of China) to total loans made by all banking institutions (including credit unions). *Big Four's ST loans/total ST loans* is defined as the ratio of total short-term loans made by the Big Four to total short-term loans made by all banking institutions. *Big Four's LT loans/total LT loans* is defined as the total long-term loans made by the Big Four to total long-term loans made by all banking institutions. *Rural credit union's loans/total loans* is defined as the total loans made by all rural credit unions to total loans by all banking institutions. *Bank loans/GDP* is defined as the ratio of total loans by all banking institutions to total GDP. *Real GDP growth per capita* is defined as the real-term GDP growth per capita. *FDI/GDP* is defined as the ratio of foreign direct investment to GDP. *College-degree holders/population* is defined as the proportion of the population with a college degree or higher education to the total population above age six. All of the variables are measured at province-year level.

TABLE 10.2 Correlation Matrix

	Variable Name	(1)	(2)	(3)	(4)	(5)	(6)	(7)	(8)	(9)	(10)	(11)	(12)
(1)	Growth in number of small businesses	1											
(2)	Growth in output of small businesses	0.5348*	1										
(3)	Big Four loans/total loans	−0.1943*	−0.0611	1									
(4)	Big Four's ST loans/total ST loans	−0.3029*	−0.1855	0.7420*	1								
(5)	Big Four's LT loans/total LT loans	0.0433	−0.0254	0.4238*	0.2764*	1							
(6)	Rural credit unions' loans/ total loans	0.2360*	0.2566*	−0.1741*	−0.1419	0.0588	1						
(7)	Concentration index	0.2052*	0.1009*	−0.1689	−0.3021*	−0.1648	−0.3942*	1					
(8)	Insurance premium/GDP	0.1505	0.0254	−0.1297*	−0.1156	−0.2673*	0.1526*	0.5112*	1				
(9)	Bank loans/GDP	−0.0295	−0.0914	−0.0185	0.0569	−0.1031	−0.3372*	0.3714*	0.403	1			
(10)	Real GDP growth per capita	0.2308*	0.2865*	−0.2087*	−0.2774*	−0.1546	0.2473*	0.0133	0.1633	−0.0103	1		
(11)	FDI/GDP	0.1021	−0.0399	0.0008	−0.0319	0.2596*	−0.1816*	0.2950*	0.0792	0.1104	−0.1201	1	
(12)	College-degree holders/ population	0.1336	0.0965	−0.0739	−0.1819*	−0.1333	−0.3162*	0.7221*	0.7967	0.4424*	0.1528	0.2142*	1

Table 10.2 presents the pairwise correlation coefficients between each pair of variables used in the regressions with Bonferroni-adjusted significance levels. Coefficients that are associated with 5% significance levels (or lower) are indicated by *. See table 10.1 for the definitions of variables.

of small business is 21.7 percent, with a standard deviation of 20.5 percent during our sample period. It is noteworthy that the two measures capturing small business growth in local markets are strongly correlated with a correlation coefficient of 0.54 ($p < 0.01$).

EMPIRICAL FINDINGS

While correlation analysis reveals certain patterns relating measures of regional banking development to small business growth, these results do not take into account potentially significant differences in economic environment and other demographic characteristics among the local markets. Therefore, we intend to uncover the relationship through regression analysis by controlling for a set of variables that capture various economic and demographic conditions in different provinces.

Fixed-Effects Panel Regressions

Table 10.3 presents regression results relating the growth rate of small business to various measures of regional banking development. It is plausible that unobserved characteristics in different provinces may be correlated to our variables of interest but are omitted from the regression model, which would in turn result in biased estimation based on pooled ordinary least squares (OLS). Therefore, we include province-fixed effects to control for the time-invariant heterogeneity at the province level. Indeed, the F-test of the null hypothesis that the constant term is equal across units leads to a rejection of the null hypothesis ($p < 0.01$), which suggests that there are significant individual (province-level) effects, and fixed effects models are thereby better specified than pooled OLS.

In column 1 of table 10.3, we enter our measure of Big Four loans to total loans, and the result indicates that the presence of large banks in local markets is negatively correlated with the growth rate of small business. The technology of lending to small firms differs fundamentally from the technology of lending to large, matured firms in the sense that loans to small firms are often made primarily on the basis of soft information generated from daily relationships.[48] Large firms with established track records may have access to the public debt market, and they tend to borrow based on hard information. Moreover, small business loans may require tighter control and oversight because there is no nationwide credit score system to analyze the credit worthiness of small firms that are potential borrowers. As a consequence, the complex hierarchy in large banks increases the cost of relationship loans and,

TABLE 10.3 Fixed-Effects Regressions of Growth in Number of Small Businesses

	Dependent Variable: Growth in Number of Small Businesses					
	(1)	(2)	(3)	(4)	(5)	(6)
Constant	−0.280**	−0.232**	−0.027	−0.149	−0.141	−0.324
	[−2.46]	[−2.21]	[−0.13]	[−1.01]	[−0.68]	[−1.69]
Big Four loans/total loans	−0.178*		−0.639**		−0.620*	
	[−1.86]		[−2.10]		[−2.02]	
(Big Four loans/total loans) × Concentration index			2.154**		2.067**	
			[2.25]		[2.40]	
Big Four's ST loans/total ST loans		−0.086**		−0.292*		−0.369**
		[−2.17]		[−1.92]		[−2.15]
(Big Four's ST loans/total ST loans) × Concentration index				1.013*		1.349*
				[1.86]		[1.80]
Big Four's LT loans/total LT loans		−0.105		−0.076		−0.041
		[−1.55]		[−0.21]		[−0.11]
(Big Four's LT loans/total LT loans) × Concentration index				−0.123		−0.321
				[−0.09]		[−0.22]
Rural credit unions' loans/total loans	1.348***	1.353***	1.260***	1.266**	2.441*	3.521*
	[3.12]	[3.11]	[2.94]	[2.60]	[1.85]	[1.97]
(Rural credit unions' loans/total loans) × Concentration index					−5.489	−10.626
					[−0.75]	[−1.28]
Concentration index	0.839**	0.751*	0.357	0.350	0.174**	1.236
	[2.05]	[1.77]	[0.38]	[0.49]	[2.17]	[1.29]
Total loans/GDP	0.019**	0.021***	0.022***	0.022***	0.021***	0.021***
	[2.73]	[3.22]	[2.82]	[3.42]	[2.85]	[3.57]
GDP per capita, real	0.437***	0.386***	0.415***	0.379**	0.421***	0.383**
	[3.13]	[2.90]	[2.77]	[2.75]	[2.80]	[2.66]
FDI/GDP	0.461	0.523	0.388	0.481	0.305	0.333
	[0.80]	[1.09]	[0.70]	[1.04]	[0.55]	[0.69]
College-degree holders/population	1.248**	0.969*	1.512**	1.090*	1.444**	0.936
	[2.14]	[1.97]	[2.40]	[1.95]	[2.31]	[1.67]
Observations	296	296	296	296	296	296
R-squared: Adjusted:	0.264	0.273	0.266	0.270	0.265	0.272
Within:	0.282	0.292	0.286	0.294	0.287	0.299

	Dependent Variable: Growth in Number of Small Businesses					
	(1)	(2)	(3)	(4)	(5)	(6)
Between:	0.072	0.053	0.035	0.028	0.040	0.034
Overall:	0.168	0.184	0.139	0.163	0.139	0.160
F-statistic	28.106	40.656	33.267	43.120	36.553	57.865
rho	0.299	0.273	0.362	0.309	0.368	0.329
Corr(u_i, Xb)	−0.558	−0.487	−0.632	−0.538	−0.642	−0.573

Table 10.3 presents the fixed-effects panel regression results where the dependent variable is the growth in the number of new small businesses. The main regressors of interest are the banking market variables regarding the lending activities by the Big Four and rural credit unions and the concentration in the banking industry in each province. All of the regressions control for GDP per capital growth in real terms, FDI to GDP ratio, and proportion of population with college degrees among the total population over 6 years old. All right-hand-side variables enter the regressions in the one-year lagged term. Standard errors are clustered at the provincial level and are robust to misspecification of (i.e., allow for) intragroup correlation. The t-statistics are reported in brackets. Asterisks (*, **, ***) indicate significance levels of 10%, 5%, and 1%, respectively. See table 10.1 for the definitions of variables.

in turn, results in organizational diseconomies associated with small business lending. Our finding thereby is consistent with evidence documented in developed countries.[49]

In column 2 of table 10.3, we further make a distinction between short-term and long-term loans made by Big Four because of the inability of small firms to secure long-term debt and their high dependence on short-term debt.[50] Note that an important characteristic of Chinese banking is that the majority of the loans were directed by the government toward large and state-owned enterprises, which suffer from soft-budget constraints because of a lack of efficient corporate governance.[51] Our finding points out that the short-term loans made by the Big Four is the driving force of the negative relationship between large bank presence and small business growth.

There has been a long debate regarding the effects of bank competition and concentration on economic activities.[52] A competitive banking market should benefit all borrowers, providing more loanable funds and lower interest rates. An important feature of small business lending is that small firms prefer to concentrate their borrowing at a single bank and strive to establish a long-term relationship.[53] Relationship banking facilitates the collection of private information on the credit worthiness of small firms. However, fostering long-term relationships may not be easy in a competitive market because small firms have low switching cost to other banks. In other words, small firms moving on from their current lenders can switch to other banks with the established loan records. Therefore, in the first place, banks are unwilling to extend credit to small firms in competitive markets because there may be little public information available. Taking into consideration asymmetric information, Petersen and Rajan argue that, in a concentrated market, banks are willing to subsidize small business in the short run because they are able to recoup the cost in the long run.[54] Therefore, we interact our measures of large bank presence with an HHI capturing the market concentration based on loan amount in columns 3 and 4 of table 10.3. Strikingly, we find consistent results that in highly concentrated markets, the participation of large banks helps to nourish small business growth significantly, which is supportive of the view of intertemporal rent sharing between banking institutions and small firms.

In the history of banking sector development in China, financial reforms in the rural areas were substantial, and the Chinese banking system has channeled a surprisingly high level of credit to the private sector since the 1990s.[55] Rural financial reforms along with credit provisions to the private sector have helped to alleviate credit constraints on rural small business growth. We measure the credit supplied by rural financial institutions and report in table 10.3 a positive effect of rural credit unions on the growth rate of small business across all model specifications, regardless of market concentration.

Now we turn to other control variables. Continuous regulatory changes have been implemented gradually to promote a sound and competitive banking system. Major changes in the banking sector began with China's entry into the WTO, in 2001, which was accompanied by the liberalization of interest rates, decreased restrictions on ownership, and increased operational freedom.[56] Given that the credit markets in China are relatively large, we measure the ratio of total loans to GDP as an indicator of financial deepening. We document a significantly positive relationship between regional small business growth and financial deepening, which adds additional evidence to the Schumpeterian view.[57]

In this chapter, we use real GDP per capita to capture the average personal wealth at the provincial level. It is common practice in small business lending that owners of small firms use their own assets to guarantee borrowings and are personally liable for business debts.[58] In addition, personal wealth (as represented by real GDP per capita) also serves as a commitment device to mitigate the loan loss exposure of lenders. Consequently, a higher level of personal wealth allows small business owners to negotiate better terms and thus plays a key role in determining the allocation of credit to small firms and their ultimate survival. Therefore, it is not surprising that real GDP per capita is significantly and positively associated with the new venture formation.

Without sufficient physical assets, the growth of small business is foremost a matter of human development. Human capital is composed of the body of knowledge and skill sets that reside within individuals. Abundant theoretical and empirical studies have shown the importance of knowledge and experience in enabling firms to successfully implement and adapt to changes in technology.[59] In China, government strives to eliminate adult illiteracy by promoting basic education, especially in rural areas. The accumulation of human capital has been a significant source of small business development.[60] In this chapter, consistent with the vital role of trained human capital, we find that small businesses are more active and more successful in areas where the average citizen is relatively more educated.

To test the robustness of our main findings, we use an alternative measure based on the GDP generated by small business. Using the output-based measure of small business growth, we replicate our analysis in table10.3 and report generally consistent results in table 10.4. We believe that this additional analysis further validates our findings reported in table 10.3.

TABLE 10.4 Fixed-Effects Regressions of Growth in Output of Small Businesses

	Dependent Variable: Growth in Output of Small Businesses					
	(1)	(2)	(3)	(4)	(5)	(6)
Constant	−0.339**	−0.226*	0.124	0.031	0.378	0.159
	[−2.12]	[−1.84]	[0.44]	[0.17]	[1.19]	[0.59]
Big Four loans/total loans	−0.118*		−0.964**		−1.007**	
	[−1.84]		[−2.08]		[−2.21]	
(Big Four loans/ total loans) × Concentration index			3.951*		4.143**	
			[1.96]		[2.14]	
Big Four's ST loans/ total ST loans		−0.132*		−0.363*		−0.307*
		[−1.79]		[−1.74]		[−1.88]
(Big Four's ST loans/ total ST loans) × Concentration index				1.250**		1.006**
				[2.15]		[2.39]
Big Four's LT loans/ total LT loans		−0.055		−0.322		−0.347
		[−0.58]		[−0.72]		[−0.72]

(Continued)

TABLE 10.4 Fixed-Effects Regressions of Growth in Output of Small Businesses (*Continued*)

	Dependent Variable: Growth in Output of Small Businesses					
	(1)	(2)	(3)	(4)	(5)	(6)
(Big Four's LT loans/ total LT loans) × Concentration index				1.275 [0.62]		1.419 [0.62]
Rural credit unions' loans/total loans	1.676*** [3.19]	1.694*** [3.24]	1.514*** [2.87]	1.588** [2.70]	−1.119 [−0.59]	−0.052 [−0.02]
(Rural credit unions' loans/total loans) × Concentration index					12.235 [1.45]	7.731 [0.72]
Concentration Index	0.896** [2.40]	0.675* [1.76]	−1.298 [−1.09]	−0.697 [−0.74]	−2.483 [−1.52]	−1.341 [−0.90]
Total loans/GDP	0.002 [0.20]	0.003 [0.25]	0.008 [0.78]	0.007 [0.79]	0.009 [0.88]	0.008 [0.85]
GDP per capita, real	1.189*** [4.88]	1.109*** [4.91]	1.149*** [4.54]	1.075*** [4.69]	1.136*** [4.54]	1.072*** [4.73]
FDI/GDP	0.638 [0.68]	0.796 [0.91]	0.505 [0.57]	0.655 [0.80]	0.689 [0.81]	0.762 [0.90]
College-degree holders/population	2.141* [1.93]	1.842 [1.68]	2.625** [2.22]	2.312* [1.94]	2.776** [2.36]	2.424* [1.99]
Observations	296	296	296	296	296	296
R-squared: Adjusted:	0.297	0.301	0.300	0.300	0.301	0.298
Within:	0.313	0.320	0.319	0.324	0.322	0.325
Between:	0.023	0.016	0.040	0.033	0.047	0.037
Overall:	0.132	0.151	0.102	0.124	0.103	0.126
F-statistic	21.031	17.509	20.202	20.061	20.104	20.622
rho	0.347	0.321	0.424	0.379	0.421	0.372
Corr(u_i, Xb)	−0.606	−0.567	−0.688	−0.636	−0.681	−0.627

Table 10.4 presents the fixed-effects panel regression results where the dependent variable is the growth in output of new small businesses. The main regressors of interest are the banking market variables regarding the lending activities by the Big Four and by rural credit unions and the concentration in the banking industry in each province. All of the regressions control for GDP per capita growth in real terms, FDI to GDP ratio, and the proportion of the population with college degrees among the total population over 6 years old. All right-hand-side variables enter the regressions in the one-year lagged term. Standard errors are clustered at the provincial level and are robust to misspecification of (i.e., allow for) intragroup correlation. The t-statistics are reported in brackets. Asterisks (*, **, ***) indicate significance levels of 10%, 5%, and 1%, respectively. See table 10.1 for the definitions of variables.

IV Panel Estimation: A Robustness Check

One potential issue in our empirical tests is the endogeneity of loan ratios. To be specific, it is arguable that the proportion of Big Four loans to total loans, or the proportion of rural credit union's loans to total loans, could be reversely affected by small new business growth. In the presence of an endogenous independent variable, neither OLS nor fixed-effects models could yield unbiased and consistent estimates because of the reverse-causality problem. Therefore, we use the instrumental variables (IV) approach to address this issue and obtain more consistent and unbiased parameter estimates.

As it is well understood, the efficiency and consistency of an IV estimator crucially depend on the selection of the instrument(s). A good instrumental variable in our study, ideally, would be strongly correlated with the independent variable to be instrumented (i.e., the loan proportions made by the Big Four or by rural credit unions) and uncorrelated with small business growth except through the role of bank loans. We use the ratio of total insurance premiums to GDP to instrument the loans made by the Big Four (or by rural credit unions) as a proportion of total loans by all banks. The reason that we believe this is valid IV is because it is well documented that the ratio of insurance premiums to GDP, which measures the relative size of the insurance industry in an economy, is in general highly correlated with popular indicators of financial depth or development[61] and therefore should be highly correlated with the proportionate loans made by Big Four (or rural credit unions) in the banking system (the negative correlation between the financial depth in China and the proportionate loans made by Big Four has been well documented by studies, including Berger et al. and Hasan et al.).[62] On the other hand, it is unlikely that the small business growth by itself will affect the increases in the insurance premiums in China.

Table 10.5 and table 10.6 report the two-step IV panel regressions (with fixed effects) of small business growth on various loan ratios and their interaction terms. Loan ratios such as the Big Four's loans to total loans, the Big Four's short-term loans to total short-term loans, the Big Four's long-term loans to total long-term loans, and rural credit unions' loans to total loans are all instrumented by the insurance premium to total GDP respectively in the IV regressions. In addition, the interaction terms between each of these loan ratios and the concentration index are instrumented by the interaction terms between insurance premium/GDP and the concentration index. Taken together, the IV estimations show largely consistent results with the fixed-effects estimations.

We also report some important specification tests for the IV estimators. In particular, because the p-values of the overidentification test (i.e., Hansen's J

TABLE 10.5 IV Panel Regressions of Growth of Number of Small Businesses

		Dependent Variable: Growth in Number of Small Businesses						
	(1)	(2)	(3)	(4)	(5)	(6)	(7)	(8)
Big Four loans/total loans, *instrumented*	-1.608* [-1.84]	-8.041* [-1.74]						
(Big Four loans/total loans, *instrumented*) × Concentration index		39.916* [1.83]						
Big Four's ST loans/total ST loans			-0.538* [-1.92]	-0.440* [-1.80]				
(Big Four's ST loans/total ST loans, *instrumented*) × Concentration index				4.132* [1.84]				
Big Four's LT loans/total LT loans, *instrumented*					0.117 [0.40]	-1.178 [-1.59]		
(Big Four's LT loans/total LT loans, *instrumented*) × Concentration index						5.725 [1.63]		
Rural credit union's loans/total loans, *instrumented*							3.328* [1.92]	0.619* [2.05]
(Rural credit union's loans/total loans, *instrumented*) × Concentration index								26.446 [0.66]
Concentration Index	1.582* [1.88]	-20.853 [1.57]	1.827* [1.85]	1.612 [1.61]	0.630* [1.77]	-3.100 [-1.23]	1.410* [1.90]	-0.511 [-0.12]
Total loans/GDP	0.044 [0.50]	0.091 [0.70]	0.021 [1.11]	0.004 [0.16]	0.015 [1.49]	0.027** [2.31]	0.031 [0.85]	0.040 [1.02]
GDP per capita, real	0.800** [2.25]	0.069* [2.06]	0.965* [1.80]	0.466** [2.17]	0.646*** [3.31]	0.478*** [2.95]	0.203** [2.25]	0.041* [2.08]

FDI/GDP	-1.598	-1.764	-0.599	1.325*	0.242	0.148	0.037	0.267
	[-0.26]	[-0.37]	[-0.19]	[1.77]	[0.36]	[0.21]	[0.04]	[0.22]
College-degree holders/population	4.861	7.264*	3.194*	0.685**	2.454**	3.223**	0.921	0.642**
	[1.58]	[1.84]	[2.04]	[2.19]	[2.28]	[2.15]	[1.42]	[2.37]
Observations	296	296	296	296	296	296	296	296
Number of id	30	30	30	30	30	30	30	30
F statistic	28.526	25.625	23.798	25.996	24.041	28.875	27.869	24.06
Adjusted R-squared	0.149	0.180	0.180	0.151	0.179	0.149	0.120	0.180
Hansen J statistic of overidentification test	0.090	0.100	0.120	0.110	0.080	0.130	0.120	0.110
Underidentification test (p-value)	0.021	0.018	0.032	0.025	0.016	0.028	0.029	0.039
Weak IV test (K-P rk Wald F statistic)	20.548	25.198	27.476	20.672	18.630	19.576	23.872	25.098

Table 10.5 presents the IV/GMM estimation of the fixed-effects panel data models with possibly endogenous regressors, where the dependent variable is the growth in the number of new small businesses. The lending variables (which are entered into regression one at a time) are assumed endogenous and are instrumented by the ratio of insurance industry premiums to GDP. Correspondingly, the interaction terms of each one of the lending variables and the concentration index are instrumented by the interaction term between the insurance premium to GDP ratio and the concentration index. All of the regressions control for GDP per capita growth in real terms, FDI to GDP ratio, and the proportion of the population with college degrees among the total population over 6 years old. All right-hand-side variables (including the instrumental variable) enter the regressions in the one-year lagged term. Standard errors are clustered at the provincial level and are robust to misspecification of (i.e., allow for) intragroup correlation. The t-statistics are reported in brackets. Asterisks (*, **, ***) indicate significance levels of 10%, 5%, and 1%, respectively. See table 10.1 for the definitions of variables.

TABLE 10.6 IV Panel Regressions of Growth of Output of Small Businesses

	Dependent Variable: Growth in Output of Small Businesses							
	(1)	(2)	(3)	(4)	(5)	(6)	(7)	(8)
Big Four loans/total loans, *instrumented*	-3.020* [-1.88]	-10.201* [-1.92]						
(Big Four loans/total loans, *instrumented*) × Concentration index		54.694* [1.86]						
Big Four's ST Loans/total ST loans, *instrumented*			-1.010* [-1.94]	-0.851* [-1.77]				
(Big Four's ST loans/total ST loans, *instrumented*) × Concentration index				6.679* [1.77]				
Big Four's LT Loans/total LT loans, *instrumented*					-0.22 [-0.54]	1.461 [1.03]		
(Big Four's LT Loans/total LT loans, *instrumented*) × Concentration index						-7.43 [-1.14]		
Rural credit union's loans/total loans, *instrumented*							6.250* [1.88]	2.924 [0.16]
(Rural credit union's loans/total loans, *instrumented*) × Concentration index								22.283 [0.34]
Concentration index	2.365* [1.77]	-28.377 [-0.50]	2.825* [1.81]	2.478 [0.60]	0.578* [2.06]	-4.263 [-0.95]	2.043* [2.02]	0.425 [0.07]
Total loans/GDP	0.049 [0.44]	0.114 [0.63]	0.007 [0.30]	-0.021 [-0.54]	-0.004 [-0.20]	0.012 [0.58]	0.025 [0.44]	0.033 [0.60]
GDP per capita, real	1.738** [2.05]	0.736 [0.42]	2.049 [1.24]	1.242*** [3.70]	1.448*** [5.33]	1.231*** [4.75]	0.617 [0.50]	0.411 [0.51]

FDI/GDP	-3.053	-3.280	-1.176	1.934	0.403	0.282	0.019	0.212
	[-0.38]	[-0.49]	[-0.27]	[1.19]	[0.40]	[0.29]	[0.01]	[0.13]
College-degree holders/population	8.265*	11.557*	5.133	1.078**	3.744*	4.743*	0.865	0.630
	[1.72]	[1.95]	[1.19]	[2.29]	[1.94]	[1.94]	[0.31]	[0.28]
Observations	296	296	296	296	296	296	296	296
Number of id	30	30	30	30	30	30	30	30
F-statistic	27.801	20.465	21.011	27.782	23.112	22.494	22.253	20.066
Adjusted R-squared	0.123	0.137	0.146	0.150	0.142	0.139	0.146	0.180
Hansen J statistic of overidentification. test	0.140	0.150	0.130	0.110	0.090	0.080	0.100	0.110
Underidentification test (p-value)	0.029	0.021	0.039	0.027	0.014	0.019	0.012	0.015
Weak IV test (K-P rk Wald F statistic)	19.935	23.829	29.716	21.580	17.095	20.903	21.539	23.368

Table 10.6 presents the IV/GMM estimation of the fixed-effects panel data models with possibly endogenous regressors, where the dependent variable is the growth in output of new small businesses. The lending variables (which are entered into the regression one at a time) are assumed endogenous and are instrumented by the ratio of insurance industry premiums to GDP. Correspondingly, the interaction terms of each one of the lending variables and the concentration index are instrumented by the interaction term between the insurance premium to GDP ratio and the concentration index. All of the regressions control for GDP per capita growth in real terms, FDI to GDP ratio, and the proportion of the population with college degrees among the total population over 6 years old. All right-hand-side variables (including the instrumental variable) enter the regressions in the one-year lagged term. Standard errors are clustered at the provincial level and are robust to misspecification of (i.e., allow for) intragroup correlation. The t-statistics are reported in brackets. Asterisks (*, **, ***) indicate significance levels of 10%, 5%, and 1%, respectively. See table 10.1 for the definitions of variables.

statistic) are larger than 0.05, we cannot reject the null hypothesis that the excluded instruments are valid instruments, suggesting that the instruments are valid. In addition, given that the p-values of the underidentification test (i.e., Kleibergen-Paap rk statistic)[63] are less than 0.05, we reject the null hypothesis that the excluded instruments are not correlated with the endogenous variables. We also report a heteroskedasticity-robust Kleibergen-Paap Wald rk F-statistic and draw conclusions regarding the weak identification hypothesis by comparing the F-statistic to the Stock-Yogo IV critical values at a 5 percent significance level.[64] Given that the reported F-statistics across all regressions are larger than the 10 percent maximal IV size bias critical value, we reject the weak identification null hypothesis at a 5 percent significance level and conclude that our IV estimators have a maximum relative size distortion of 10 percent.

DISCUSSION AND CONCLUSIONS

Banking institutions play an important role in channeling financial resources to small businesses and fostering lending relationships. This is particularly true in emerging countries, where small firms are generally financially constrained and have limited access to various sources of external financing because of a lack of track records or of assets-in-place to serve as collateral.

In this chapter, building on existing literature, we focus on a single emerging country, China, and use a panel of provincial-level data covering 30 provinces in China from 1998 to 2008 to investigate the effects of banking system development on regional small business growth. For this purpose, we construct various measures of regional banking development. We find that the proportion of large banks in the credit market (especially short-term loans) has a negative effect on small business growth. Our finding suggests that the dominance of large banks is associated with an unfavorable environment for small business growth, which is consistent with the view that large banks have an informational disadvantage in making lending decisions for small businesses. However, in highly concentrated markets, large banks are able to help finance small firms because they can subsidize and lock in small borrowers. In addition, we find that lending activities by rural credit unions greatly facilitate the growth of small firms. Our results also confirm the importance to small business growth of financial deepening, the availability of trained human capital, and the overall personal wealth level. In summary, our findings provide further evidence from an emerging and transitional country and establish a robust link between financial-sector development and small business growth.

Our findings and analysis in this chapter also provide important impli-cations for policy makers and small business owners in China and beyond. They establish the crucial role of smaller financial intermediaries and argue that any future consolidation plans in favor of economies of scale and scope arguments associated with larger institutions may be counterproductive. The benefits associated with small banks and their local development focus out-weigh any other alternative arguments.

NOTES

1. Bruce A. Kirchhoff, *Entrepreneurship and Dynamic Capitalism: The Economics of Business Firm Formation and Growth* (Westport, CT: Praeger, 1994).

2. Luigi Guiso, Paola Sapienza, and Luigi Zingales, "Does Local Financial Devel-opment Matter?," *Quarterly Journal of Economics* 119 (2004): 929–969; Rebel A. Cole, John D. Wolken, and R. Louise Woodburn, "Bank and Nonbank Competi-tion for Small Business Credit: Evidence from the 1987 and 1993 National Survey of Small Business Finances," *Federal Reserve Bulletin* 82 (1996): 983–995.

3. Sandra E. Black and Philip E. Strahan, "Entrepreneurship and Bank Credit Availability," *The Journal of Finance* 57 (2002): 2807–2833; Martin R. Blinks and Christine T. Ennew, "The Relationship between U.K. Banks and Their Small Busi-ness Customers," *Small Business Economics* 9 (1997): 167–178; Garry D. Bruton, David Ahlstrom, and Krzysztof Obloj, "Entrepreneurship in Emerging Economies: Where Are We Today and Where Should the Research Go in the Future?," *Entrepreneurship Theory and Practice* 32 (2008): 1–14; William Kerr and Ramana Nanda, "Democra-tizing Entry: Banking Deregulations, Financing Constraints and Entrepreneurship," *Journal of Financial Economics* 94 (2009): 124–149; Howard J. Wall, "Entrepreneur-ship and the Deregulation of Banking," *Economic Letter* 82 (2004): 333–339.

4. Uma Sekaran, "Methodological and Theoretical Issues and Advancements in Cross-cultural Research," *Journal of International Business Studies* 14 (1983): 61–73.

5. Tatiana S. Manolova, Rangamohan V. Eunni, and Bojidar S. Gyoshev, "Insti-tutional Environments for Entrepreneurship: Evidence from Emerging Economies in Eastern Europe," *Entrepreneurship Theory and Practice* 32 (2008): 203–218.

6. Howard E. Aldrich and Ellen Auster, "Even Dwarfs Started Small: Liabilities of Size and Age and Their Strategic Implications," *Research in Organizational Behavior* 8 (1986): 165–198; Jitendra V. Singh, David J. Tucker, and Robert J. House, "Orga-nizational Legitimacy and Liability of Newness," *Administrative Science Quarterly* 31 (1986): 171–193; Jeremy C. Stein, "Information Production and Capital Alloca-tion: Decentralized versus Hierarchical Firms," *The Journal of Finance* 57, 5 (2002): 1891–1921.

7. Because small businesses do not have sufficient physical assets as well as human capital to use as collateral, they experience difficulty in gaining support from external resource providers. Small businesses have to overcome such challenges (liabilities) to ensure long-term survival and growth.

8. Joseph A. Schumpeter, *The Theory of Economic Development* (Cambridge, MA: Harvard University Press, 1934); Robert G. King and Ross Levine, "Finance and Growth: Schumpeter Might Be Right," *Quarterly Journal of Economics* 108 (1993): 717–737.

9. Douglas W. Diamond, "Monitoring and Reputation: The Choice between Bank Loans and Direct Placed Debt," *Journal of Political Economy* 99 (1991): 689–721.

10. Pietro Alessandrini, Andrea Filippo Presbitero, and Alberto Zazzaro, "Bank Size or Distance: What Hampers Innovation Adoption by SMEs?," *Journal of Economic Geography* 9 (2009): 22–42.

11. Black and Strahan, "Entrepreneurship and Bank Credit Availability"; Bill Francis, Iftekhar Hasan, and Haizhi Wang, "Bank Consolidation and New Business Formation," *Journal of Banking & Finance* 32 (2008): 1958–1612; Kerr and Nanda, "Democratizing Entry"; Wall, "Entrepreneurship and the Deregulation of Banking."

12. Brian Headd and Bruce Kirchhoff, "The Growth, Decline and Survival of Small Businesses: An Exploratory Study of Life Cycles," *Journal of Small Business Management* 47, 4 (2009): 531–550.

13. Aldrich and Auster, "Even Dwarfs Started Small"; Arthur L. Stinchcomber, "Social Structure and Organizations," in *Handbook of Organizations*, ed. James G. March (Chicago: Rand McNally, 1965).

14. Aldrich and Auster, "Even Dwarfs Started Small."

15. Singh, Tucker, and House, "Organizational Legitimacy and Liability of Newness."

16. Stein, "Information Production and Capital Allocation."

17. Joe Peek and Eric S. Rosengren, "Bank Consolidation and Small Business Lending: It's Not Just Bank Size That Matters," *Journal of Banking & Finance* 22 (1998): 799–819.

18. In a somewhat similar study, using a theoretical model followed by empirical findings, Hakenes, Hasan, Molyneux, and Xie investigate the effects of small banks on economic growth in Germany. The study reveals that small banks are more effective in enhancing local economic growth, especially in regions with low access to finance. See Hakenes et al., "Small Banks and Local Economic Development," *Review of Finance* (2014).

19. Marco Pagano, "Financial Markets and Growth: An Overview," *European Economic Review* 37 (1993): 613–622.

20. Emilia Bonacorsi di Patti and Giovanni Dell'Ariccia, "Bank Competition and Firm Creation," *Journal of Money, Credit and Banking* 36, 2 (2004): 225–251.

21. Jin Chen, Yufen Chen, and Wim Vanhaverbeke, "The Influence of Scope, Depth, and Orientation of External Technology Sources on the Innovative Performance of Chinese Firms," *Technovation* 31 (2011): 362–373; Mitchell A. Petersen and Raghuram G. Rajan, "The Effect of Credit Market Competition on Lending Relationships," *The Quarterly Journal of Economics* 110 (1995): 407–443.

22. The "Big Four" are Bank of China (established in 1912), China Construction Bank (established in 19544), Agricultural Bank of China (established in 1979), and Industrial and Commercial Bank of China (established in 1984).

23. See, Allen N. Berger, Iftekhar Hasan, and Mingming Zhou, "Bank Ownership and Efficiency in China: What Will Happen in the World's Largest Nation?," *Journal of Banking and Finance* 33, 1 (2009): 113–130.

24. Iftekhar Hasan, Paul Wachtel, and Mingming Zhou, "Institutional Development, Financial Deepening and Economic Growth: Evidence from China," *Journal of Banking & Finance* 33 (2009): 157–170.

25. Howard E. Aldrich, "Using an Ecological Perspective to Study Organizational Founding Rates," *Entrepreneurship Theory and Practice* 14, 3 (1990): 7–24.

26. Allen N. Berger et al., "Does Function Follow Organization Form? Evidence from the Lending Practices of Large and Small Banks," *Journal of Financial Economics* 76 (2005): 237–269.

27. Douglas W. Diamond, "Financial Intermediation and Delegated Monitoring," *Review of Economic Studies* 51 (1984): 393–414; Diamond, "Monitoring and Reputation"; Gordon Roberts and Lianzeng Yuan, "Does Institutional Ownership Affect the Cost of Bank Borrowing?," *Journal of Economics and Business* 60 (2010): 604–626.

28. Hasan, Wachtel, and Zhou, "Institutional Development, Financial Deepening and Economic Growth," *Journal of Banking & Finance*, 33 (2009): 157–170; Jiahua Che and Yingyi Qian, "Insecure Property Rights and Government Ownership of Firms," *The Quarterly Journal of Economics* 113 (1998): 467–496.

29. Riccardo Lucchetti, Luca Papi, and Alberto Zazzaro, "Bank's Inefficiency and Economic Growth: A Micro-macro Approach," *Scottish Journal of Political Economy* 48 (2001): 400–424; Basil J. Moore, *Horizontalists and Verticalists: The Macroeconomics of Credit Money* (Cambridge, U.K.: Cambridge University Press, 1988).

30. Yasheng Huang, *Capitalism with Chinese Characteristics: Entrepreneurship and the State* (Cambridge, U.K.: Cambridge University Press, 2008).

31. C.H. Gladwin et al., "Rural Entrepreneurship: One Key to Rural Revitalization," *American Journal of Agricultural Economics* 71 (1989): 1305–1314.

32. Stephan J. Goetz et al., "Evaluating US Rural Entrepreneurship Policy," *Journal of Regional Analysis and Policy* 40 (2010): 20–33.

33. Manolova, Eunni, and Gyoshev, "Institutional Environments for Entrepreneurship."

34. Sekaran, "Methodological and Theoretical Issues and Advancements in Cross-cultural Research."

35. Hasan, Wachtel, and Zhou, "Institutional Development, Financial Deepening and Economic Growth."

36. There are 31 provinces (including four municipalities) in China. We have to omit one province (Tibet) because of missing data. In addition, our sample period starts from 1998 because it is since then that China began to report data on small businesses based on consistent definitions, which is discussed in more detail in section 3.1.

37. Francis, Hasan, and Wang, "Bank Consolidation and New Business Formation"; Kirchhoff, *Entrepreneurship and Dynamic Capitalism*; Bruce A. Kirchhoff et al., "The Influence of University R&D Expenditures on New Business Formations and Employment Growth," *Entrepreneurship: Theory & Practice* 31 (2007): 543–559.

38. Cole, Wolken, and Woodburn, "Bank and Nonbank Competition for Small Business Credit"; Stein, "Information Production and Capital Allocation."

39. Stewart C. Myers and Nicolás S. Majluf, "Corporate Financing and Investment Decisions When Firms Have Information that Investors Do Not Have," *Journal of Financial Economics* (1984): 187–221.

40. Gavin Cassar and Scott Holmes, "Capital Structure and Financing of SMEs: Australian Evidence," *Accounting and Finance* 43 (2003): 123–147.

41. Goetz et al., "Evaluating US Rural Entrepreneurship Policy"; Huang, *Capitalism with Chinese Characteristics*.

42. Allen N. Berger, Iftekhar Hasan, and Leora F. Klapper, "Further Evidence on the Link between Finance and Growth: An International Analysis of Community Banking and Economic Performance," *Journal of Financial Services Research* 25 (2004): 169–202; King and Levine, "Finance and Growth"; Ross Levine, "Financial Development and Growth," *Journal of Economic Literature* 35 (1997): 688–726; Ross Levine, Norman Loayza, and Thorsten Beck, "Financial Intermediation and Growth: Causality and Causes," *Journal of Monetary Economics* 46, 1 (2000): 31–77.

43. Petersen and Rajan, "The Effect of Credit Market Competition on Lending Relationships."

44. Robert B. Avery, Raphael W. Bostic, and Katherine A. Samolyk, "The Role of Personal Wealth in Small Business Finance," *Journal of Banking & Finance* 22 (1998): 1019–1061.

45. Laura Alfaro et al., "FDI and Economic Growth: The Role of Local Financial Markets," *Journal of International Economics* 64 (2004): 89–112.

46. Koen De Backer and Leo Sleuwaegen, "Does Foreign Direct Investment Crowd Out Domestic Entrepreneurship?," *Review of Industrial Organization* 22 (2003): 67–84.

47. Catherine Armington and Zoltan J. Acs, "The Determinants of Regional Variation in New Firm Formation," *Regional Studies* 36 (2002): 34–35.

48. Stein, "Information Production and Capital Allocation"; Philip E. Strahan and James P. Weston, "Small Business Lending and the Changing Structure of the Banking Industry," *Journal of Banking & Finance* 22 (1998): 821–845.

49. Peek and Rosengren, "Bank Consolidation and Small Business Lending"; Strahan and Weston, "Small Business Lending and the Changing Structure of the Banking Industry."

50. Cassar and Holmes, "Capital Structure and Financing of SMEs."

51. The term *soft budget constraint* was introduced by Kornai (1979) and illuminates well-documented economic behavior in socialist and transitional economies. See Janós Kornai, "Resource-constrained versus Demand-constrained Systems," *Econometrica* 47, 4 (1979): 801–819, and M. Dewatripont and E. Maskin, "Credit and Efficiency in Centralized and Decentralized Economies," *The Review of Economics and Statistics* 62, 4 (1995): 541–555. More specifically, *soft budget constraint* refers to the slackness that state-owned enterprises suffer from in their capital budgeting and financing activities because they can rely on the government bailout or intervention when there is a deficit. For a detailed discussion of soft budget constraints for Chinese

state-owned enterprises, see Chong-en Bai and Yijiang Wang, "Bureaucratic Control and the Soft Budget Constraint," *Journal of Comparative Economics* 26, 1 (1998): 41–61, and Robert Cull and Lixin Colin Xu, "Who Gets Credit? The Behavior of Bureaucrats and State Banks in Allocating Credit to Chinese State-owned Enterprises," *Journal of Development Economics* 71, 2 (2003): 533–559.

52. J. A. Bikker and K. Haaf, "Competition, Concentration and Their Relationship: An Empirical Analysis of the Bank Industry," *Journal of Banking & Finance* 26 (2002): 2194–2214.

53. Strahan and Weston, "Small Business Lending and the Changing Structure of the Banking Industry."

54. Petersen and Rajan, "The Effect of Credit Market Competition on Lending Relationships."

55. Huang, *Capitalism with Chinese Characteristics*.

56. Iftekhar Hasan, Haizhi Wang, and Mingming Zhou, "Do Better Institutions Improve Bank Efficiency? Evidence from a Transitional Economy," *Managerial Finance* 35 (2009): 107–127.

57. King and Levine, "Finance and Growth"; Joseph Schumpeter, *The Theory of Economic Development* (Oxford, U.K.: Oxford University Press, 1969).

58. Avery, Bostic, and Samolyk, "The Role of Personal Wealth in Small Business Finance."

59. Donald S. Siegel, David A. Waldman, and William E. Youngdahl, "The Adoption of Advanced Manufacturing Technologies: Human Resource Management Implications," *IEEE Transactions on Engineering Management* 44, 3 (1997): 288–298.

60. Armington and Acs, "The Determinants of Regional Variation in New Firm Formation"; Mike Wright et al., "The Role of Human Capital in Technological Entrepreneurship," *Entrepreneurship Theory and Practice* 31, 6 (2007): 791–806.

61. E.g., Robert Cull, Lemma W. Senbet, and Marco Sorge, "The Effect of Deposit Insurance on Financial Depth: A Cross-country Analysis," *Quarterly Review of Economics and Finance* 42 (2002): 673–694.

62. Berger, Hasan, and Zhou, "Bank Ownership and Efficiency in China"; Hasan, Wachtel, and Zhou, "Institutional Development, Financial Deepening and Economic Growth."

63. Frank Kleibergen and Richard Paap, "Generalized Reduced Rank Tests Using the Singular Value Decomposition," *Journal of Econometrics* 133 (2006): 97–126.

64. Based on Stock-Yogo (2005), Stock-Yogo weak ID test critical values for Cragg-Donald F-statistic and i.i.d. errors are the following: 10% maximal IV size: 19.93; 15% maximal IV size: 11.59; 20% maximal IV size: 8.75; 25% maximal IV size: 7.25; James H. Stock and Motohiro Yogo, "Testing for Weak Instruments in Linear IV Regression," in *Identification and Inference for Econometric Models: Essays in Honor of Thomas Rothenberg*, ed. Donald W. K. Andrews and James H. Stock (Cambridge, U.K.: Cambridge University Press, 2005): 80–108.

11

Small Firms in Transition Economies: Challenges and Opportunities

David Smallbone

This chapter is concerned with small firms in countries whose economies have recently emerged from central planning. This means that, in most cases, private business was actually an illegal activity, for example, in all former Soviet republics and some Central and Eastern European countries. Over the last 20 years or so, running one's own business has increasingly become a global phenomenon, with some countries that were previously operating under central planning now embracing private business to varying degrees. As a result, an approach that ignores more fragile, and in some cases hostile, environments for small business is essential if we are to analyze the world as it is. This is important because the study of small business in transition conditions can be linked much more directly than it is into the mainstream of theory, which must be sufficiently robust to be able to form a basis for the analysis of the variety of conditions.

During the early years after the process of transition began, the study of small business in transition economies was viewed by many researchers as rather eccentric, partly because the empirical reality did not fit well with existing theories and also because some argued that the empirical data gathered at the time was often dubious. In addition, in the early years, the official statistical data on enterprises was far from perfect. One feature, for example, was the inclusion of a large number of businesses that were not trading and in many cases had never traded. This was a feature of the early transition conditions where some people registered businesses but actually never got them off the ground.

In addition, the collection of primary data was far from easy because of the hostility of officials and governments toward private business in some countries. Researching the topic was almost a clandestine activity. More importantly perhaps, there were questions about the reliability of some of the survey data, in particular its representativeness, given the absence or limitations of existing databases that could be used as a basis for a sampling frame.[1]

But this was a long time ago, and in recent years there has been a growing recognition of the need to pay more explicit attention to the context in which small business develops.[2] This is not a new phenomenon, but it is certainly a new emphasis, given that some of the theories that were used in the past were rather devoid of context and tended to implicitly assume that external conditions were those of mature market economies. Small businesses are now developing in a variety of external conditions, which researchers cannot ignore.

It is also important to recognize that the term *transition* is potentially misleading because it implies that a country is shifting from one known state to another, specifically from central planning to a market-based system, whereas in reality some countries (e.g., Belarus) have not really moved toward a market system. The variety of transition contexts may be summarized in a simple threefold typology: first, countries that are republics of the former Soviet Union; second, countries that previously operated under central planning but are now members of the European Union (EU); and, third, China. Hence, a key theme running through the chapter will be the distinctiveness of the operating environment of small business in these three types of location. Of course, the distinctiveness of small business in transition conditions is not solely a result of the characteristics of the external environment; it is also affected by the characteristics and background of the population and of the entrepreneurs who emerge from that population.

THE TRANSITION CONTEXT

One of the main sources of the distinctiveness of small businesses in transition conditions is the nature of the external environment, particularly in the initial stages of transition, when instability and rapid change present particular challenges to the small business manager. Indeed, all business development results from an interaction between the internal characteristics of the business and of the small business owner on the one side and characteristics of the external environment on the other. But in countries that have emerged from socialism, it is the nature of the external environment that is the dominant influence, which explains why a growing number of researchers studying these countries have been attracted to institutional theory.[3] Although there is a variety of external conditions in so-called transition economies, there are nevertheless a number of common features that they share. In some cases, privately owned businesses were illegal during the socialist period. In some countries this was absolute, while in others, such as Poland and Hungary, certain types of non-state-owned economic activity were tolerated. In Poland, for example, agriculture remained in private hands throughout the socialist period, and small craft businesses were also tolerated as long as they remained very small. This contrasted with the former Soviet republics and also with China, where all economic activity was publicly owned.

The centrally planned model included price setting, an absence of private property ownership, and a model of resource allocation based on administrative decisions rather than market forces. As a consequence, prices remained low while shortages of certain products were part of everyday life. Another shared feature between these countries can be found in the role of government, which, during Soviet times in the former Soviet Union and its satellites, involved government as dominant in every walk of life, as a financier and decision maker with regards to economic activity. This presented many challenges when the collapse of the Berlin Wall contributed to a process of change that resulted in a much more central role for the market, leaving government to change its role to that of a facilitator of economic development and of a regulator to ensure fair competition and a balance within society between economic and social policy objectives.

Other sources of distinctiveness include the characteristics and experiences of small business managers themselves, which typically involved a period of management in large state-owned companies (leading to the comment that this is perhaps not the best preparation for small business ownership), and the characteristics of the businesses, which initially were predominantly service businesses, with many of those in retail. This was partly because of the absence of many personal services during Soviet times, but it was also a reflection of the low barriers to entry for these types of activities.

One feature of small business development in transition economies, particularly in the former Soviet republics and in China, is the tendency for enterprises to evolve through different legal forms. For example, in the late 1980s, Russia and the former Soviet republics saw the toleration of cooperatives as a nonstate form of enterprise. This reflects what is politically acceptable at a given moment in time and may be more determined by local policy than national.

Another feature of the transition context is that a high proportion of businesses are started out of necessity and, it is often assumed, do not develop into much more than one- or two-person microenterprises. People who say that they started their business because of a lack of alternatives are categorized by the Global Entrepreneurship Monitor (GEM) as "necessity entrepreneurs," which are distinguished from "opportunity entrepreneurs." GEM is a database of the entrepreneurial activity, aspirations, and attitudes of individuals across a wide range of countries. It can be argued that the concept of necessity entrepreneurship is a weak one. There is no problem if its use is confined to the point when a business is actually created, but to go beyond that is potentially very misleading for a number of reasons. For example, empirical evidence shows that some people in transition economies who start businesses for necessity-driven reasons actually become very entrepreneurial as new opportunities present themselves. So the issue is more about the lack of opportunities when they start-up rather than their own motives. Some people learn, which means that the experience of running a business for one or two years may result in business owners raising their expectations above those that they had when they first started their businesses.

Moreover, particularly in the early stages of transition, the environment itself can change very rapidly. As a consequence, regardless of the reason that an entrepreneur started a business, changes in the external environment can result in new business opportunities presenting themselves. Not surprisingly, therefore, case study evidence shows that some of the people who say that they started their business out of necessity become opportunity driven as external conditions improve.[4]

SMALL FIRMS IN THE FORMER SOVIET REPUBLICS

In this section, we deal with countries where the environment for small business is typically difficult, where government either has little interest in promoting and supporting small businesses or does not have the technical knowledge and capacity to provide the framework conditions to facilitate business ownership. While not confining discussions to a single country, we will feature the Russian Federation as the largest economy in this group of nations. Although it is not the most hostile environment for private business among the former Soviet republics, Russia may be used to illustrate many of the issues facing this group of countries.

A Low Level of Small Business Activity

The difficult environment for small business is reflected in low rates of new business start-up and low levels of business ownership, both of which are well below those countries in the other two groups. It has to be kept in mind that until the collapse of the former Soviet Union, in all Soviet republics, private business was illegal because the law protected the state-owned monopolies. As a consequence, there are still large sections of the population in these countries who view small business ownership as a criminal activity and not something to be supported. But alongside such attitudes are entrepreneurial people interested in responding to the opportunities for starting and running a business in the new economic systems in their countries.

Figure 11.1 illustrates the size structure of enterprises in the Russian Federation and in other selected countries and highlights the higher proportion of economic activity still in large companies compared with new member states of the European Union and mature market economies.

Unlike in Central and Eastern European countries that have emerged from central planning to show many of the characteristics of market-based economies, the pace of privatization of state-owned companies in the former Soviet republics has been slow. This has implications for the development of small business, where a degree of crowding out may be identified, particularly in some of the less prosperous regions. At the same time, data drawn from a 2011 study by GEM suggests there is a considerable latent supply of people interested in starting and running their own businesses. However, one of the barriers to actually achieving this lies in the need for upskilling those people with a desire to start their own businesses to equip them for the day-to-day operational issues that they will face. At the same time, there is a feeling that these Russian potential entrepreneurs have an inflated view of the skills and resources available to people starting up their own businesses in mature market economies.

According to the census of small and medium enterprises (SMEs) in 2011, SMEs in Russia (including individual entrepreneurs) employ a total of

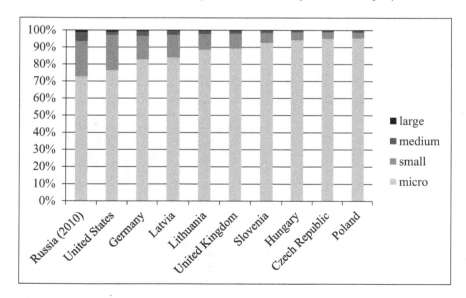

FIGURE 11.1 Enterprises by Size Class, 2008 or Latest Available Year
Note: These size classes used in the figure above are those normally distinguished in the European Union. In terms of the number of employees: micro 1–9 employees, small 10–49 employees, medium 50–249 employees, and large 250+ employees.
Source: Adapted from data available in OECD (2012) and Rosstat (2011).

19 million people, including working family members, partners, and employees.[5] While 19 million jobs make a significant contribution to job generation in the Russian economy, it appears modest when compared with other countries. In the United Kingdom, for example, 4.5 million SMEs employ an estimated 23.4 million people with an estimated combined annual turnover of 31.5 billion pounds. In addition, data from the GEM study suggests that there is a low involvement of Russians in creating businesses. In other words, not only is there a lower level of small business activity but many of the businesses that are created employ few, if any, people, and they are fairly marginal and of low viability.

Just as with the rates of business start-up and business ownership, Russia also has a very low rate of self-employment. As figure 11.2 shows, only 7.3 percent of workers in Russia were self-employed in 2008, compared to an average of 15.8 percent of all OECD (Organization for Economic Co-operation and Development) countries. At the same time, starting from this low base, unlike most OECD countries, Russia has experienced a recent growth in self-employment, which is partly a survival strategy of people who cannot find any other means of earning income, although it does also demonstrate a degree of entrepreneurship. The survey referred to above shows more similarities than differences between attitudes toward self-employment in Russia and those within EU countries.[6] For example, when asked if they would prefer to be self-employed rather than employed, 39 percent of respondents in Russia

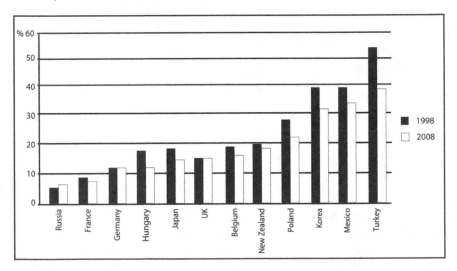

FIGURE 11.2 Self-Employment in Russia and Selected Countries
Source: Adapted from data available in World Bank, World Development Indicators Database.

answered in the affirmative compared with 37 percent in EU countries. Similarly, when asked why this was so, 60 percent of the Russian respondents said they wanted personal independence or self-fulfillment, which was very similar to the 62 percent reported in the European Union.

Where there was a greater difference between Russian and EU respondents, however, was with regards to whether self-employment was seen as a desirable option; in this case, 43 percent of Russian respondents suggested that it was, including 16 percent who saw it as very desirable. This compared with response in the EU countries, where just 32 percent saw self-employment as desirable, including 11 percent who saw it as very desirable. Clearly the pattern of response is affected by alternative job opportunities, but it also reflects the fact that Russian people have only relatively recently been able to participate in the self-employment option. One of the implications of this pattern of response is the need to explain why more people in Russia did not go ahead and actually become self-employed. In Russia, this was explained mainly in terms of the risk of bankruptcy and the associated risk of losing one's home as a result of failure. In Russia, 53 percent of respondents gave this as the reason that they did not go ahead, compared with the lower 43 percent within the EU countries. Russians also saw more practical problems, which they tended to associate with their own lack of skills—in other words, a doubt as to whether they would be able to succeed in such a venture.

Finally, some 25 years after the collapse of the former Soviet Union and the start of the transition process, survey evidence from the GEM study provides a picture of attitudes toward small business activity in the population.[7] Among those members of the adult population surveyed who were not currently small business owners, two-thirds stated that they did not have sufficient knowledge and experience to undertake entrepreneurial activity, and 81 percent were very pessimistic about the conditions for starting a business. These results are not encouraging, particularly given the low levels of new business creation in these countries, but they point toward a need to improve the external environment for small business, particularly with regard to the institutional frame and the behavior of institutions within it.

A Challenging Environment for Small Business

The Russian business owner faces many deficiencies in the external environment for entrepreneurial activity. In some cases, the deficiencies reflect the absence of key institutions, but more typically, they represent behavioral characteristics of these institutions. Passing legislation to provide a legal basis for institutional change is in many ways the easy part; much more difficult is to get these institutions to behave in a market-oriented way when a high proportion of the staff have no experience in working with private business and many of them have very negative views about entrepreneurial activity, which are inherited from the past when such forms of small business owner-ship was actually illegal.

Evidence of the barriers that Russian business owners consider to be the main constraints that they face can be drawn from the 2012 International Finance Corporation (IFC) Enterprise Survey.[8] The results show that out of the 15 areas of the business environment identified in the survey, private businesses in Russian cities identified tax rates as the biggest obstacle, fol-lowed by access to finance, and then corruption. More than 36 percent of respondents reported tax rates as their biggest obstacle, compared to around 10 percent of firms in other countries surveyed; 15 percent ranked it as the biggest obstacle, and more than 8 percent decided corruption was their big-gest obstacle in their business environment.

Another feature of the environment for small businesses in Russia is the size and scope of the informal economy. Russia has one of the largest informal sectors in the world. It is one aspect that is inherited from the former Soviet times and which has been exacerbated by high levels of taxation and, more importantly in the early years, by frequent changes in the tax regime, which has made it difficult for firms and entrepreneurs to comply with the law while making a profit. This would force many entrepreneurs to operate, at least partly, in the black economy to survive. So, although a business might be registered and declare some of its revenue for taxation, its reporting would be partial, and it would typically employ between a quarter and one-fifth of its workforce non declared.

The informal economy is important for a number of reasons. On the one hand, the informal economy can be a breeding ground for entrepreneurs by increasing social inclusion, but on the other hand, it is illegal and runs the risk of undermining the survivability of businesses that are fully compliant with the law. Reducing the size of the informal economy is difficult because it involves increasing the policing of existing regulations, which is a challenging exercise because of the scale, location, and ease of entry of informal markets. Informality is a regular feature of economic activity in transition economies, although the distinction between formal and informal can be rather blurred. For example, a business may be registered and may be compliant with registration require-ments yet be forced to operate at least partly informally to have any possibility of generating profits. Legal registration combined with noncompliance with tax laws is a regular feature. According to a study undertaken by the Inter-national Labour Organization (ILO) in 2011, Russia had 7.78 million jobs in the informal economy, which represented 12 percent of total nonagricultural employment; so, it made a significant contribution to the country's economy.[9]

Not surprisingly, perhaps, one of the findings of the ILO study was that informal employment tends to be negatively correlated with income per capita and positively correlated with poverty. This is not a feature confined to Russia but much more generally. What it means is that informal economic activity is important in poorer countries because it contributes to social and economic inclusion. Hence, from a policy point of view, it is not advisable for the authorities to adopt an entirely negative stance toward the informal economy because an approach focused on policing it out of existence will result in even more poverty. Strategies for reducing informal economic activity need to be balanced and not to be simply a policing exercise.

Given the enormity of the institutional change required as economies shift from central planning toward market-based systems, it is hardly surprising that institutional deficiencies are a common phenomenon. Together with behavioral patterns inherited from the past, this often contributes to a high level of corruption. A simple example is deficiency in the drafting of legislation, which can leave too much discretionary power to those responsible for interpreting it. A large amount of discretionary power inevitably breeds corruption. Evidence drawn from IFC surveys of enterprises in Russia, together with Russia's position in the Index of Economic Freedom, suggests that corruption is endemic in the country, but, at the same time, Russia is far from the worst country in this regard. For example, in the context of the Index of Economic Freedom (which is based on a scale of 0 to 100; 0 meaning that the country is perceived as highly corrupt and 100 meaning that the country is perceived as being very clean), Russia has a score of 51 against a global average of 59.6 and is ranked 133 out of 177 countries on the 2013 index.

As well as establishing the basic framework conditions for private business activity, government also has an important role in providing a framework for a specialist infrastructure to encourage and support innovative activity. Indeed, one of the current policy priorities of the Russian government is the promotion of innovation, recognizing the importance of innovation and the competitiveness of firms and also, of course, the innovative performance of the Russian economy as a whole. As far as SMEs are concerned, the innovative performance is hampered by the absence of a market-oriented innovation system. In common with other former centrally planned economies, building in a market-oriented innovation system is necessary because the innovation system that existed before was not one that focused on individual firms but rather on emphasizing national military effort with an associated concentration of expenditure on research, development, and innovation resting with state-owned research organizations and in state-owned companies. In other words, one of the key characteristics of the environment for business in contemporary Russia is an underdeveloped innovation system. Another

TABLE 11.1 Doing Business and Starting a Business in 2014

	Russia	Poland	China
Doing business rank	92	48	96
Starting a business rank	88	116	158
Procedures (number)	7	4	13
Time (days)	15	30	33
Cost (% of income per capita)	1.3	14.3	2
Paid-in min. capital (% of income per capita)	1.2	12.6	78.2

Source: Table compiled by the author on data supplied by the World Bank's *Doing Business 2014.*

indicator of innovation drawn from the GEM study is the level of involvement of SMEs in high-technology sectors, which in Russia is low.

To summarize, placed in an international context, small business ownership in Russia is underdeveloped, which is reflected in low business densities per head and little sign of any major shift in attitudes toward small
business ownership on the part of the population at large. The low level of
small business activity, with a corresponding larger share of medium and large
enterprises than in many other countries, reflects a relatively slow pace of
structural reform. During Soviet times, the economy was dominated by large
state-owned entities, and in comparison with most Central European countries, the pace of privatization and reform of these large state-owned companies has tended to be relatively slow.

Even in Russia, there are some signs of change. For example, as table 11.1
shows, while Russia scores poorly on the ease of doing business index overall
and significantly worse than both Poland and China, the environment for
new business start-up is more facilitating, involving less time and money.

SMALL FIRMS IN THE NEW MEMBER STATES OF THE EUROPEAN UNION

In this section, the focus is on countries that previously operated under
central planning but are now members of the European Union. These are
mainly located in Central and Eastern Europe, including Poland, Hungary,
Czech Republic, Slovakia, Slovenia, Bulgaria, and Romania, but they also
include the three Baltic states that were previously Soviet republics. While
sharing a contemporary EU context, the conditions in the countries somewhat varied when their transitions started in 1989–1990, and the transformation processes that have been adopted, such as in the privatization models,
have also differed. There are also some differences between these countries

in what was tolerated during the Soviet period. In most cases, as in former Soviet republics, private business activity was illegal, leaving state-owned companies holding monopoly power.

In cases such as Poland, however, there were forms of private enterprise that were tolerated during the Soviet period. The whole of agriculture, for example, was in private hands rather than those of the state, as it predominantly was in other countries. In Poland, small craft firms were also tolerated during the Soviet period. *Craft* is defined as a type of economic activity in which the craftsman (owner of the firm) participated directly, performing the same operations as the employees that he hired.[10] However, these businesses were tiny. They were typically manufacturing firms in sectors such as engineering and only employed two or three people. As one would expect, the pace of transformation and market reform has been faster in these countries where some private enterprise already existed than in those former Soviet republics where it did not. This is particularly reflected in a more rapid process of institutional change, reflecting the EU influence, bearing in mind the influence of institutions on entrepreneurial behavior.

Rising Levels of Small Business Activity

As in the case of the former Soviet republics, a single country will be used to illustrate wider issues. In this case, the country is Poland. In Poland, the process of administrative reform, which made private enterprise legal, began in 1981 (some years ahead of when the process started in former Soviet republics). As already mentioned, there was also some private enterprise that was tolerated during Soviet times. In addition, the large expatriate Polish community, particularly in the United States, became a source of finance, which therefore gave Poland certain advantages compared to other former centrally planned economies. The result is that Poland saw very rapid growth in the number of small firms during the 1990s, although the period between 1991 and 1993 saw the real explosion. It is important to stress that this was not directly a result of government policy but rather that there was an initial take-up of opportunities in personal services that were neglected during Soviet times. These were also typically activities with low entry barriers, although as the number of firms entering these markets contributed to increasing competition, the number of new businesses in these economic activities began to decline.

The number of registered enterprises in Poland grew rapidly after 1991, when the administrative reforms, which made private business legal in Poland, were complete. In fact, between 1991 and 2007, the number of registered firms almost tripled to 3.68 million. But, at the same time, these data include some inactive enterprises, which have been a misleading aspect of the official data in former centrally planned economies. Although not as large in scale, part of the environment for business in Poland is informal, or gray sector, business. The Polish Statistical Office estimated that in 2007 the gray economy in Poland represented 14.7 percent of gross domestic product (GDP), although estimates produced by Schneider et al. were approximately twice this level.[11] However, as official documents do not refer to the number of informal enterprises, it is not clear as to precisely what the size of this activity is. Sectors where informal activity is most prominent are in construction, small restaurants, retailing, and food processing. In Poland, there is a clear need to develop small business activity because of the difficult labor market conditions and the consistently high level of unemployment, which, as in most countries, affects some regions worse than others.

Encouragingly, in Poland, courses and modules in entrepreneurship were introduced as mandatory elements of the education system at the secondary and vocational levels back in 2004. This means that the idea of small business ownership as a career option is systematically introduced to young people through the education system.

Table 11.2 shows the size structure of enterprises in Poland. Poland is often presented as a success story in terms of the rapid growth of small private companies in the period since transformation began. As a consequence, SMEs in Poland contribute 69 percent of employment, nearly 60 percent of sales turnover, and 56 percent of value added in the Polish economy.[12] High entry and exit rates suggest considerable dynamism, which has contributed to the diversification of the Polish economy since the collapse of central planning; nevertheless, the SME sector appears weak in many respects. As in many other transition and developing countries, Poland suffers from the missing middle, with the SME sector mainly comprising microenterprises.

TABLE 11.2 Distribution of Active Enterprises in Poland, 2007

Size Class	Number of Enterprises	Percentage of Total Enterprises
Micro (0–9)	1,713,194	96.4%
Small (10–49)	45,184	2.5%
Medium (50–249)	15,452	0.9%
Subtotal	*1,773,830*	*99.8%*
Large	3,256	0.2%
Total	*1,777,086*	*100%*

Note: Employment figures from CSO enterprise survey data differ from Labor Force Survey figures.
Source: Data supplied by PARP 2008 from CSO figures.

The relatively small number of firms in the 10–49 employee class is a sign of weakness and may reflect growth constraints facing firms that are currently in the microenterprise category. An OECD (forthcoming) report, "Review of SME and Entrepreneurship Issues and Policies in Russia," refers to survey evidence that shows a lack of strategic thinking and of professional management in SMEs, which contributes to the weaknesses described. At the same time, this comment may be applied in many countries where these characteristics are viewed as typical of the SME sector.[13] From the perspective of SME owners and managers, EU membership offers some new market opportunities, although many face the prospect of higher levels of competition in the domestic market. But, in view of the fact that most of Poland has some form of EU-assisted area status, the combination of finance and financial and technical assistance referred to above is potentially an important mechanism for facilitating economic change. The picture painted by the OECD is one of poor management quality across the sector, with the majority of SMEs focused on survival rather than growth.

An Improving Business Environment

A key element in the improving business environment is EU membership, although it is not a magic wand. On the one hand, it presents new market opportunities for some SMEs (which no longer have to cross tariff barriers to sell into other EU markets), but on the other, it means that Polish companies, which during Soviet times were protected against most sources of competition, no longer have this protection. The real benefit of EU membership is that it gives access to funds that can be used for modernization and restructuring. It also gives access to technical advice and assistance. One of the features of EU-funded restructuring, capacity-building, and modernization projects is that they typically involve international teams. This is potentially significant in a context where the development models that are used in individual EU countries are varied and can therefore be used to demonstrate the heterogeneity of market-based systems.

Various changes, which specifically result from World Trade Organization membership and, in some cases, from EU participation, have been made to improve the business environment through the transformation period. At the same time, there are ways in which EU membership makes life more difficult for small business owners. For example, while the European Union has encouraged member states, including Poland, to initiate administrative simplification and an improvement in the regulatory burden, at the same time, countries joining the European Union have been required to meet new regulatory standards, which has resulted in new regulations. But overall the environment is one that is facilitating small businesses, particularly for those owned and managed by people who have ambitions to develop their business.

As one might expect, new members of the European Union, such as Poland, look more like mature market economies every day, particularly with regards to the pace of privatization, the removal of price controls, and a general freeing up of the supply side of the economy. But, at the same time, there are some aspects of the reform process that are particularly challenging. One is the need, shared with other transition economies, to build market-oriented innovation systems in which the firm is the focus of innovative effort. At the same time, a cautious path needs to be followed because one cannot expect countries that are still engaged in such major restructuring processes to operate entirely on market-based principles. While the more established mature market economies may no longer favor the use of financial grants to businesses because of market distortion effects, in countries that are still engaged in such major transformations, this is likely to remain a necessity, at least in the short term.

Since the collapse of the Soviet Union and the beginning of the transition to a market economy, the Polish economy has been significantly transformed. The main elements of a market economy are in place; most economic activities are carried out by private businesses or individuals through membership in the European Union and World Trade Organization. Not surprisingly, however, Poland still lags behind most of its EU and OECD partners. Income levels are low, and there is a desperate need for ongoing improvements in the country's infrastructure. Nevertheless, EU membership offers resources to address these issues. Moreover, the growth of the small business sector has been one of the sources of dynamism during the transformation period. Apart from East Germany, Poland is the largest of the former centrally planned new member states. As a result, its allocation of structural funds represent approximately one-fifth of the EU total.

Unlike Russia, countries such as Poland and their new EU member counterparts have successfully installed the basic framework conditions for small business, which include such institutions as courts of law, banks (as suppliers of finance for business), regulatory bodies, and representative organizations of entrepreneurs and businesspeople. One of the main differences between the new member states of the European Union and the former Soviet republics that have remained outside it is with respect to framework conditions, and in this regard Russia is not the worst example. Basic framework conditions are based on the policies that allow private business to legally exist. They may include private property rights, market-based institutions, a commercial banking system, company and business law, a code of business ethics, a liberal trade regime, and market-based supply of inputs goods and services.[14]

Certain framework conditions are particularly relevant to small business development. These include straightforward and inexpensive procedures for licensing and regulation, a transparent tax system, stable legislation (which means that the parameters are not continually changing), and a business support system (which includes professionally managed development agencies as well as self-governing organizations such as chambers of commerce). Both groups of countries may have chambers of commerce, but in the former Soviet republics, these are often still primarily arms of government rather than independent representative organizations in the way that the Western democracy has tried to promote them. Clearly, the difference impacts whose interests are being promoted.

The difference between former Soviet republics and EU member countries is not completely black and white. For example, as table 11.1 shows, while Poland is significantly more favorably ranked on the overall ease of doing business index, it lags behind Russia in the rankings for ease of starting a new business. The public sector in Poland is very bureaucratic, and the rank of 116 reflects the fact that it takes 30 days on average to complete the start-up process, which is almost as long as in China and is almost three times as long as the OECD average. Starting a business is also an expensive process in Poland in comparison with the OECD average. So, while Poland represents a reasonably facilitating environment for small business development in many respects, as far as start-ups are concerned, there is some way to go to meet the standard of a modern market economy.

In Poland, there is a multiplicity of organizations involved in business support of different kinds. One estimate suggested that it reached 3,000. As a consequence, most of these organizations are seriously underresourced, which clearly influences their effectiveness. Another example relates to the lobbying function, which in market economies is an important way in which business interests are represented with public authorities. The lobbying function is something that needs to be learned and for which people need to be trained, and it has taken time for this to develop in the country.

Clearly, as a member state of the European Union, Poland has access to EU markets as well as to resources to enable businesses to modernize with a view to improving their competitiveness. In this regard, countries such as Poland have an advantage over those former Soviet republics. It also needs to be recognized that SMEs in Poland have many weaknesses. These include a need to modernize equipment as well as the skills and attitudes of the staff managing the businesses. One problem that both new member states of the European Union and other former Soviet republics share is the need to build a market-oriented innovation system in the larger countries at a regional as well as a national level. In the case of Russia, the need is recognized, although so far little has been done to facilitate improvement. In the case of most of the EU member states, this is an ongoing policy priority.

The case of Łódź in Central Poland can be used to illustrate this point. Łódź is a long-established clothing manufacturing city in desperate need of restructuring. One of the local universities in Łódź has been responsible for attracting some 12 million euros of EU funds into the city and for leading the business community toward a restructuring plan. In the case of Russia, access to supranational resources does not exist, neither in terms of finance nor in terms of technical knowledge. In this respect, although the former Soviet republics and new member states of the European Union share a common problem, their ability to respond to it is not the same. So, while the SME sector in Poland and other new member countries have many weaknesses, they also have the advantage of having access to resources to enable them to change this.

Rogut and Piaseski identify not only a number of key barriers to starting a business that potential small business owners face but also barriers to subsequent business development.[15] The former include complex tax laws, which lack clarity in terms of what business owners are expected to pay, and a variety of administrative barriers, making the life of a potential entrepreneur more difficult. Barriers to subsequent business development include market-related constraints associated with poor management quality and a continuation of regulatory gaps and distortions.

Nevertheless, despite these constraints, Polish people have demonstrated considerable entrepreneurial flair as the start-up rate in Poland is not significantly different from that in the rest of the European Union. The case described by Rogut and Piaseski illustrates well this skill in small business development. Unlike Russian people, the Polish appear to feel much less constrained by a lack of technical management knowledge and skill, instead making the ideal of learning by doing explicit in their actions.[16] Of course, Poland has the previously mentioned advantage that when it began its transition, it had more of a tradition of private enterprise, including some that was tolerated during the centrally planned period. Russia, in contrast, had never been through such conditions, having moved from feudalism into socialism with the 1917 revolution, so private business activity had been largely ignored.

SMALL FIRMS IN THE PEOPLE'S REPUBLIC OF CHINA (PRC)

The third category in our classification of different types of transition economy only has one country in it: China. The identification of this category is justified by the fact that although China shares some features with other transition economies, there are also major differences that lead some people to talk of the Chinese way to the market.

China's gradual and controlled way to the market may be illustrated with reference to a number of characteristics of the process of SME development in the country. As a consequence, an important part of the context for small business development in China is the gradualist approach used by the Chinese government to introduce market mechanisms into the economy. In the first place, legislative changes came several years after Deng Xiaoping made his famous speech in 1978 that left the door open for private-sector development. This meant that if things had not worked out satisfactorily from the Communist Party's perspective, it would have pulled back, as it had the ability to do so. One of the key features of the historic development of non-state-owned enterprises in China, which illustrates the step-by-step approach favored by the Chinese Communist Party, is the experience with the Township and Village Enterprises (TVEs).

TVEs are market-oriented public enterprises under the influence of local governments based in townships and villages in China. At one point in time, they were the main way in which nonstate small business was being introduced to the Chinese economy. In the period between 1978 and 2003, the number of TVEs is reported to have increased by around 20 percent per annum, to reach 21.85 million in number, employing 135.7 million people and contributing 30 percent of national GDP.[17] However, contrary to what some observers seem to think, the days of the TVE are over, and the vast majority of them are now restructured into conventional private companies.

An Explosion of Private Business Activity

As shown by figure 11.3, the growth in the number of non-state-owned enterprises in China is impressive by any standards. Between 1990 and 2006, the number of private enterprises increased by 50 times, from 98,000 in 1990 to approximately 4.95 million in 2006. Furthermore, between 1990 and 2006, the number of people employed by private enterprises increased by almost 38 times, from approximately 1.7 million in 1990 to approximately 64 million in 2006. This can be legitimately described as an explosion by any standards.

The explosion of private business activity in China is impressive. The GEM monitor enables us to capture some data that describes the attitudes of the population toward entrepreneurship and business ownership. Because Poland and Russia were also participants in the GEM project, it is possible to compare China with the other two countries featured in this chapter. As table 11.3 shows, a much higher percentage of Chinese people saw opportunities for business ownership, almost twice as many as in Russia and more than in Poland. About one-third were confident that they had the capabilities

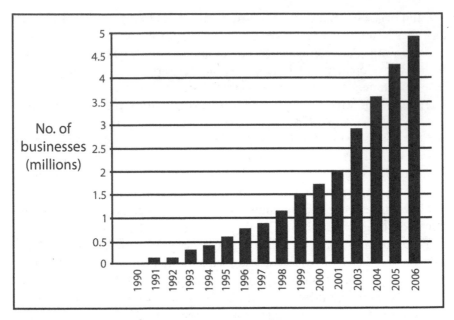

FIGURE 11.3 Growth of Enterprises in China, 1990–2006
Source: China Statistical Yearbook (2000–2006)

TABLE 11.3 Entrepreneurial Attitudes and Perceptions in 2012

	Perceived Opportunities	Perceived Capabilities	Fear of Failure	Entrepreneurial Intentions	Small Business Ownership as a Good Career Choice	High Status to Successful Small Business Owners	Media Attention to Successful Business Ownership
Russia	18	28	29	3	66	68	49
Poland	26	52	47	17	67	60	59
China	33	36	34	14	70	74	71

Source: GEM Global Report 2014.

to start and run their own business, which was significantly lower than in Poland but more than in Russia.

The GEM study also included indicators of the population's attitudes toward private business.[18] Almost three-quarters (70 percent) of Chinese respondents to the survey viewed small business ownership as a good career choice. While the Chinese results were the highest in this regard, small business ownership as a career choice was viewed positively by respondents in all three countries. The

TABLE 11.4 Entrepreneurial Activity, 2014

	Level of Activity, Nascent Entrepreneur	Level of Activity, New Business Owners	Index of Early-Stage Entrepreneurial Activity	Level of Activity, Established Entrepreneurs	Level of Business Discontinuation
Russia	2.4	2.3	4.6	2.8	1.5
Poland	6.0	3.1	9.0	5.0	4.2
China	10.1	14.2	24.0	12.7	5.3

Source: GEM Global Report 2014.

final indicator refers to the nature and extent of media attention to business ownership and entrepreneurship. In China, 71 percent of respondents viewed media attention in this regard as positive, compared to 59 percent of Polish respondents and 49 percent of Russian respondents. As a consequence, the results overall show China in a more positive light than the other two countries in terms of the attitudes toward small business ownership and entrepreneurship and also the emphasis placed by the media on successful business owners.

We have also drawn on the GEM study for indicators of entrepreneurial activity. Once again, because Russia, Poland, and China are all included in the GEM 2014 report, it is possible to use the report to make some comparisons among the three countries. Table 11.4 describes four indicators of entrepreneurial activity. First, the level of nascent entrepreneurship, which refers to the percentage of the population between 18 and 64 years old that is currently involved in starting a business, either as owners or co-owners. The table shows that China has significantly more than both Russia and Poland in this category. The second indicator is the level of new business activity, which describes the percentage of the population of adult age that are currently business owners. Once again, China reports a significantly higher proportion than either of the other two countries. The third indicator, and the key one as far as the GEM project is concerned, is the level of total entrepreneurial activity (TEA). As in the first two cases, China again shows a significantly stronger performance on this indicator than the other two countries. Finally, the fourth indicator describes the level of entrepreneurial activity in established businesses. Here, too, China shows the strongest performance. So the overall conclusion from this comparison of entrepreneurial attitudes and entrepreneurial activity in the three countries is that China consistently shows a higher level of entrepreneurship.

One of the most distinctive characteristics of small business development in China is that the size of small and medium-sized firms is much greater in employment terms than in their counterparts in Western Europe. The employment size definition also varies. The criteria for SMEs varies, but those published by the Ministry of Industry and Information Technology (MIIT), in 2011, define SMEs as industrial enterprises meeting one or both of the following two criteria: (1) number of employees below 1,000 (with small enterprises having 300 or less employees and medium enterprises having between 300 and 1000 employees) and (2) total revenue below RMB 400 million per year (with small enterprises having a total revenue below RMB 20 million and medium enterprises having a total revenue between RMB 20 and 400 million).[19]

Although this definitional difference may be partly explained by the higher labor intensity in China than in European transition economies, the main explanation lies in the cost of labor in relation to the cost of capital, although this is slowly changing. In some sectors small firms can go up to 1,000 employees and medium-sized firms to substantially more. Hence, an important part of the Chinese context is that the Chinese concept of small and medium-sized companies includes companies that employ substantially more people than those that are considered small and medium sized in more developed countries. One consequence is the different nature of the challenges that these businesses face, which includes the way that they use labor. One of the main management areas for which Chinese SMEs seek help from consultants is human resource management. The problems in this area are greatest in firms managed by families or extended families. These are not family businesses with 20 employees; they are family businesses with 250 employees.

In Russia and its satellites, the trigger for the development of small and medium companies was systems collapse. In China, once the external pressure for change was built up, the changes that occurred (gradual as they were) were initiated and controlled by the Chinese Communist Party. As a consequence, small businesses in China have been particularly promoted in the technology-based sectors, which are seen as potential economic motors, although alongside these there are also an enormous number of petty traders and small restaurants, cafes, and similar establishments that are dominated by a small number of companies.

Other distinctive features of small business development in China are associated with wider features of China's economic development. The first is that non-state-owned enterprise development started in China before it began in the Central European and former Soviet republics. It began in China in 1978, following speeches by Deng Xiaoping and other Communist Party leaders, who made it clear that they saw a place for individualism. Since that time, the growth of nonstate enterprise has been a major contributor to economic development in the country, but it has been a more measured and consistent growth. On the other hand, in the Central European countries and former Soviet territories, after an initial explosion of small business activity in the early 1990s, the growth was much reduced as competition within the economy intensified.

The Business Environment

Corruption is a huge issue in China as well as the Russian Federation, and allegedly part of everyday life at all levels within society. This means that in most regions of China, it is very difficult for individuals to become really successful in business unless they have appropriate contacts within the administration. This raises the question of why China has developed so rapidly while Russia and its satellites have not, when corruption is rife in both. One contributory factor is that in China the leaders at a national level are seeking to encourage private business development. If a local official takes a bribe from a budding small business owner or one who wants to expand and develop their business further, they may well receive two benefits. One is the obvious receipt of the money in their pocket, but the second is that they will probably be praised by the local party members because they are contributing to national policy objectives. And if they are doing this frequently and significantly enough, it is likely to enhance their career prospects within the Communist Party.

As in other respects, there is an East-West contrast with regard to the level, extent, and role of corrupt practices. Essentially, as one moves westward, the control of the party increases. It is the eastern seaboard of the country where entrepreneurs, some years ago, laid the foundations of a more independent private ownership. Finally, there is considerable variation across the country in the support offered through public policy. It is suggested that this geographical pattern not only applies to the ability of local city authorities to raise finances for small business support but also extends into the regulatory area.

The IFC survey enables us to view the corruption issue through the eyes of small business owners.[20] The survey evidence shows that, on average, businesses in China are solicited for bribe payments or gifts less frequently than in most countries that have been surveyed, although there is a significant variation between locations. According to the survey, the cities where the corrupt practices are greatest are in Zhengzhou, Jinan, and Guangzhou. So as in other areas, spatial variations in the need to pay bribes is a characteristic. But overall the picture is that corruption is less widely reported than is popularly thought.

An important part of the environment for SME development in China is the influence of major regional variations in economic activity, which is reflected in the density of small and medium companies. East China accounted for 67.3 percent of all private firms in 2005 and 65.5 percent of private-sector employment.[21] These regional differences in SME development reflect the geographical distribution of markets but have also been affected by differences in the behavior of the Communist Party, specifically its involvement in private-sector development. This in turn has been influenced by individuals and groups of individuals who have been described as institutional entrepreneurs who have demonstrated entrepreneurial qualities in shaping the environment for private business.

China is a very large country with 1.4 billion people in total. As a consequence, the domestic market offers many opportunities to SMEs, which means the more challenging export-focused market development does not appeal to many Chinese companies. Hence, in a survey of 500 businesses in three Chinese cities undertaken in 2008 by Smallbone and Jianzhong, only a handful of the businesses were even selling outside of the city in which they were located, let alone exporting.[22] In some other respects, many problems faced by small business owners in China are similar to those faced by SME owners in other countries of the world. One example is access to finance, which in most countries is a difficult area for small businesses, particularly at the start-up stage when the business has no track record and the lending decision depends as much on the bank manager's judgment as on economic logic.

China needs small business development because it needs to create jobs for a very large population, which currently is not in balance because the western part of the country is much less developed than the eastern seaboard, although the state has been stimulating economic development in cities such as Chonquing to bridge the gap between the levels of development in the west and east. This applies to economic development in general, but there is a high correlation between the distribution of small business activity in the country and levels of economic development. At the same time, we must be cautious about drawing direct causal links because these levels are likely to be interactive; in other words, small business development can stimulate economic development, and economic development can also stimulate small business activity (not least through the demand that it generates for materials and other supplies).

But perhaps the most distinctive feature of small business ownership in China is simply the scale of it. Small business in China shares some characteristics with the former Soviet republics in particular, such as the high level of informality and the level of corruption, for example; but scale is so much greater, and the national policy context is more benign than it is in Russia or Belarus, for example. Furthermore, although the formerly centrally planned economies that are now EU members may have some advantages, particularly with regard to access to various forms of development aid, China nevertheless is a dynamic entrepreneurial environment.

What does all this mean for SME managers on the ground? One thing it means in China is that the "know who" is at least as important as the "know what." In other words, connections open doors and are a route to favors. If entrepreneurs wish to be successful, they cannot ignore these aspects of their environment. Keming Yang, a Chinese researcher undertaking a PhD in the United Kingdom, has developed a concept of "double entrepreneurship," where he suggests that in China the successful entrepreneurs need two key qualities.[23] One is the usual set of abilities to recognize and exploit economic opportunities, and the other is the ability to take advantage of connections with officials, without which successful development of business at a local level is almost impossible.

THE ROLE OF GOVERNMENT

A Variety of Transition Contexts

This chapter has shown that there is considerable variation in the conditions for private business between most of the former Soviet republics, Central and East European countries that are now members of the European Union, and China. One of the key factors influencing this distinction is the role of government. While starting a business results from the creative acts, determination, and skills of individuals and groups of individuals, rather than as a result of government action, governments are nevertheless key players that shape and influence the environment in which business operates. This can be enabling in some instances and constraining in others. It is fair to say that many of the things that we take for granted about the business environment in mature market economies ultimately come down to the role of government, but in these instances it is much more hidden than it is in developing or transition economies, where government is typically at the heart of the change, or lack of change, that occurs. Hence, in this instance, we have countries such as the Russian Federation and Belarus, the latter of which is one of the most hostile environments for private business in the world.

Alongside these are Central and Eastern European countries, where the path to EU membership and the subsequent development within the European Union has presented many opportunities for small business and, in general, a facilitating environment. Central to this is a process of institutional change that combines the supranational (i.e., European) with the national and regional levels. In addition, we find China, where government means something rather different than within the European Union. Indeed, if one asked the question, "What constitutes policy?" in China, it largely emanates from the speeches and pronouncements of leading party officials that are translated into statutes somewhat later. Therefore, a key factor shaping the threefold distinction used in this chapter, which contains contrasting environmental conditions, is the role of government.

A Broad View of What Constitutes Policy

At the same time, to capture this influence, we need to take a broadly based view of what constitutes policy. In EU countries, this generally results from a democratic process, although the political systems may differ among member states. And the policy normally would take on some written form. In former Soviet republics, there are still many instances where policies are set by presidential decree (Belarus is a good example of this), but there is typically an implementation gap, that is, between the policy pronouncements and what actually happens in practice.

The procedures that are used within the European Union to link budgets to action plans, and in turn to strategy, are not found within the centrally planned model. So when we speak of the role of government, we need to take a broadly based view that takes into account the policies and, in particular, the actions of government, in so far as they affect small and medium businesses. This means that we cannot confine our attention simply to those policies that are specifically targeted at small business. For example, start-up support, entrepreneurship education, and schemes to promote and develop venture capital are all potentially important, but in most transition economies, they are of secondary importance alongside the government's stance toward SMEs and the actions that it takes to further this. In some cases, these indirect effects are unforeseen. In other words, the policy and policy changes are not sufficiently thought through, and the impact on entrepreneurs or subsets of them may not be on the minds of the legislators at the time that the policy is being created.

From an SME's point of view, continual changes in tax laws, which make it very difficult for them to even know what they are supposed to do to be compliant, may not be the result of government trying to make life more difficult for entrepreneurs but may nevertheless do so. It may be argued that in mature market economies, the current interest and focus on regulatory reform is an example of this, and in most transition countries, it goes much deeper and cuts across so many areas of government. So when we consider the role of government in relation to small business development, we need to look to include not just entrepreneurship and small business policies narrowly defined, but government actions across the board in terms of how they affect entrepreneurs.

Varying Levels of Commitment to Supporting Small Business

In countries such as Belarus, and to a lesser extent Russia, government tends to view small business as a source of tax revenue, and in extremist accounts have been milked. There is also, in some of these countries, an ongoing commitment to large enterprise and to economies of scale, which may have some theoretical justification but often is linked to self-interest and the ability of these large companies to be more generous with the bribes that they offer. The European Union provides a more facilitating environment for small business development because, based on the so-called Lisbon agenda, a dual role is seen for it; first, driving the competitiveness of the European economy and, second, being the basis for increasing social inclusion. This is particularly important with regard to some disadvantaged and excluded groups as well as the people of poorer regions.

In China, the role of government, or more specifically the role of the Communist Party, has been to seek to increase the competitiveness, and indeed the creativity, of the economy by putting greater emphasis on individuals than in the past, which is interpreted to mean more private ownership. At the same time, there are many ways in which the state retains tight control over the small businesses that develop. For example, the main banks are still in public-sector hands, and at the local level it is very difficult for entrepreneurs to obtain the licenses and permissions that they need without strong political support. In this context, one might suggest that entrepreneurs face considerable constraints, as the results show.

Changing Role for Government in a Market-Based System

So as small business ownership has increasingly become a global phenomenon, so the context in which it occurs is almost inevitably becoming more varied. As we have seen, even the term *transition environment* covers some very different situations in different countries. The result is reflected in the level of new venture creation per capita and in the level of growth of the SME sector and its contribution to employment and economic development. It must be recognized that even in cases where the state supports small business development (viewing it as central to the country's economic development), there remain major challenges that need to be faced if the potential contribution of entrepreneurs to economic social development is to be fulfilled.

This is particularly the case in the countries that are now new members of the European Union, not least because the state has been required to change its role in the economy and the society away from that of an entrepreneur, an investor, and an owner of business. Its role in the postsocialist period has moved away from that of a central planner to that of a facilitator of small business in which the regulatory role is a key one. It also has a potential role in identifying and plugging gaps in the market and areas where market forces need to be strengthened.

The Challenge of Institutional Change

One of the biggest challenges faced within the EU countries is institutional development. Others include developing an SME-friendly, market-oriented innovation system, which in larger countries needs to have a regional as well as a national dimension, and increasing the real cooperation between institutions of higher education and business. These are all important areas yet very challenging ones. Developing a governance model that encourages SME owners to participate in consultations and representative activity is another issue. However, in Russia and the former Soviet republics, the policy priorities are rather more basic, focusing on the framework conditions for small business, which Central European countries have largely pushed through. China has a similar problem, although in China the sheer size of the country results in a patchwork at a regional level. Some regions are very highly developed, with small businesses expanding incredibly rapidly, whereas in western provinces there is still considerable poverty, underdeveloped entrepreneurship, and a highly bureaucratic approach to public administration, which can be a major constraint on small business development.

CONCLUSIONS

The collapse of the former Soviet Union was a major event by any standards, with implications throughout the globe. Essentially, it represented a systems collapse and, as a consequence, created conditions that social scientists of different persuasions view almost as a laboratory for analyzing social and economic change. Small business development is very much a part of that because in most of the countries in the former Soviet republics and most of the Central and Eastern European states, private enterprise was an illegal activity under communism. From a scientific point of view, the effect has been to increase the countries in the world where small business activity occurs, although the context and the conditions of this are really quite different from those in mature market economies such as the United States and the United Kingdom.

The implications of this are that the concepts that we use and the theories that we develop must be robust enough to incorporate and explain small business in a wide variety of local conditions. This chapter has demonstrated that some 25 years after the commencement of transformation there is considerable variation between former socialist countries in the nature and pace of private-sector development. As a consequence, it is no longer adequate to aggregate such a wide group of countries into a single category.

This chapter has illustrated some of the distinctive characteristics of small business in postsocialist environments. In some cases, the distinctiveness includes much lower numbers and densities of private businesses compared with mature market economies. This can be explained in terms of attitudes, cultural norms, and the effect of recent development paths on contemporary behaviors. Central to the explanation of these characteristics are institutions that, drawing on Douglass North, include both formal and informal institutions.[24] In the formal case, experience has shown that the creation of new institutions or passing new laws for existing institutions is relatively easy. What is more difficult is to translate this into behavioral change, which has implications for the way that entrepreneurs are treated. Informal institutions also take a long time to change because they include the attitudes of people toward small business ownership, which during Soviet times was an illegal activity and was viewed as an antisocial activity because of the illegality. Informal business activity is a regular feature in these countries that partly reflects a somewhat casual approach to the rule of law, but it is also influenced by the past where workers in large state-owned companies often made use of the equipment of these firms for their own purposes.

In addition, in circumstances where regular employment was hard to come by, many people turned to self-employment or business ownership as a survival strategy; although as we have seen in circumstances where human capital is strong, so-called "necessity push" into small business ownership may soon be replaced by the identification and exploitation of opportunities. As an observer and analyst of these changes, they are best described as exciting and innovative. They are exciting because we can see people gain self-fulfillment through creating and running their own businesses, when their parents and grandparents were legally barred from engaging in this type of activity. It is easy to become enthused by the positive attitudes of the entrepreneurs.

One of the highly distinctive features of transition environments is the role of government, which in mature market economies is often forgotten. Perhaps this is because government adopts a "softly, softly" approach with regard to business, but it is also because the level of intervention is typically low. It is important to stress that small business ownership is the creative act of individuals and groups of individuals that reflect their drive and determination rather than being a result of government action. At the same time, government has had to redefine its role in the society and economy to that of a facilitator and regulator rather than a prime mover. In this context, it is hardly surprising that some countries appear to have lost their way.

The inclusion of China adds a whole new dimension and an environment for small business development that is sufficiently different from those in Central and East Europe and the former Soviet Union to be considered unique. China also demonstrates how government policy can take different forms, not just in terms of its breadth but also in terms of the degree of formality, as the Chinese approach to policy often involves a high level of informality at the outset, allowing for a degree of policy experimentation.

NOTES

1. David Smallbone and Friederike Welter, *Entrepreneurship and Small Business Development in Post-socialist Economies* (Oxon, U.K.: Routledge, 2009).

2. Friederike Welter, "Contextualizing Entrepreneurship: Conceptual Challenges and Ways Forward," *Entrepreneurship Theory and Practice* 35, 1 (2011): 165–184.

3. Ruta Aidis, "By Law and by Custom: Factors Affecting Small- and Medium-sized Enterprises during the Transition in Lithuania" (PhD dissertation, Tinbergen Institute, 2003); David Smallbone and Friederike Welter, "Entrepreneurship in Transition Economies: Necessity or Opportunity Driven?" (paper presented at the Babson College-Kaufmann Foundation Entrepreneurship Research Conference, Babson College, MA, June 2003).

4. Smallbone and Welter, "Entrepreneurship in Transition Economies"; Peter J. Rosa, Sarath Kodithuwakku, and Waswa Balunywa, "Entrepreneurial Motivation in Developing Countries: What Does 'Necessity' and 'Opportunity' Entrepreneurship Really Mean?" *Frontiers of Entrepreneurship Research* 26, 20 (2007).

5. GEM, *High-impact Entrepreneurship Global Entrepreneurship Report* (Global Entrepreneurship Monitor and Ernst & Young, 2011).

6. European Commission, "Entrepreneurship in the EU and Beyond," *Flash Barometer* 354 (2012).

7. GEM, *High-impact Entrepreneurship Global Entrepreneurship Report.*

8. IFC/The World Bank, *Enterprise Survey* (Washington, D.C.: The World Bank, 2012).

9. ILO, *Statistical Update on Employment in the Informal Economy* (ILO Department of Statistics, 2011).

10. Smallbone and Welter, *Entrepreneurship and Small Business Development in Post-socialist Economies.*

11. Friedrich Schneider, Andreas Buehn, and Claudio Montenegro, "New Estimates for the Shadow Economies All over the World," *International Economic Journal* 24, 4 (2010): 443–461.

12. OECD, *SMEs and Entrepreneurship in Poland* (OECD Publishing, 2010).

13. OECD, *Review of SME and Entrepreneurship Issues and Policies in Russia* (LEED, OECD Publishing, forthcoming).

14. OECD, *Fostering Entrepreneurship* (OECD Publishing, 1998).

15. Anna Rogut and Bogdan Piasecki, "Creating a Regional Innovation System: The Case of Lodz in Poland," in *Handbook of Research on Entrepreneurship Policies in Central and Eastern Europe*, ed. Friederike Welter and David Smallbone (Cheltenham, U.K.: Edward Elgar, 2011): 120–140.

16. Ibid.

17. Xue Liang, "The Evolution of Township and Village Enterprises (TVEs) in China," *Journal of Small Business and Enterprise Development* 13 (2006): 235–241.

18. GEM, *Global Report 2013* (Global Entrepreneurship Monitor, 2014).

19. MIIT, *The 12th FYP for Industrial Energy Saving* (Beijing: Ministry of Industry and Information Technology, 2012).

20. IFC/The World Bank, *Enterprise Survey*.

21. David Smallbone and Xiao Jianzhong, "China," in *Handbook of Research on Asian Entrepreneurship*, ed. Leo Paul Dana, Mary Han, Vanessa Ratten, and Isabell Welpe (Cheltenham, U.K.: Edward Elgar, 2009): 67–76.

22. Ibid.

23. Keming Yang, *Entrepreneurship in China* (Hampshire, U.K.: Ashgate Publishing Ltd, 2007).

24. Douglass C. North, *Institutions, Institutional Change and Economic Performance* (Cambridge, U.K.: Cambridge University Press, 1990).

12

Overcoming Hurdles for Commercializing Emerging Technologies: The Harbingers of Schumpeterian Cycles for Superior Economic Rent

Victor A. Chavez, Jonathan D. Linton, Regan Stinnett, and Steven T. Walsh

The commercialization of emerging, often disruptive, technology is the key element in the generation of new Schumpeterian cycles of economic development and gross domestic product improvement.[1] Schumpeterian cycles are initiated by emerging technologies that "creatively destroy" existing industries and create new ones.[2] These emerging technologies do this by either displacing the current technology competencies required to produce an industry standard product or by creating a new technology-product paradigm for a new industry.[3] This Schumpeterian cycle is driven by emerging rather than new technologies—and has occurred five times since 1785. The cycles are: (1) 1785 based on water power, textiles, and iron; (2) 1845 based on steam, rail, and steel; (3) 1900 based on electricity, chemicals, and the internal combustion engine; (4) 1950 based on petrochemicals, electronics, and aviation; and (5) perhaps currently based on nanotechnologies (including biotech), computational science, including the Internet of Things (IOT), and microtechnology.[4]

Each Schumpeterian cycle required new types of technological and business training. Both the National Institute for Nano Engineering (NINE) and University of Twente's regional activities embodied training either for nascent technologists or for entrepreneurial small and medium-sized business commercialization training.[5] Training emphasized nanotechnology as well as business acumen based on the competence-based perspective of the firm rather than on market-based or on resource-based perspectives.[6] The competence-based perspective is the only strategic perspective that is useful in predicting dynamic industrial change and generating new business models that embrace this type of technology based value-added.[7]

Regional activities and training for nascent entrepreneurs, innovators, technologists, inventors, entrepreneurs, and small firms are disproportionately important in the commercialization of emerging technologies because they generate the human capital and organizations that are critically important in the generation of Schumpeterian cycles.[8] Simply stated, small inventors, nascent technologists, innovators, and entrepreneurs are the harbingers of Schumpeterian cycles of differential economic development.[9] If this is so, why does every economic region not disproportionately support emerging technology-based activity for regional economic development?

Perhaps it is because emerging technology commercialization is difficult. There are few commonly agreed upon "best" practices, and appropriate decisions often differ from traditional sustaining business practices. Emerging technology-based solutions are often "bottom-up" solutions that initially seem to be of little value to the traditional market leaders.[10] Other hurdles that cause the disdain of emerging technology commercialization are the lack of clearly identified markets,[11] the unattractiveness of immature product platforms,[12] and the lack of a primary product focus.[13]

Often these emerging technology-based solutions solve critical societal problems in new ways.[14] Products based on microtechnology (micro), nanotechnology (nano), the Internet of Things (IoT), and other creative enterprises often focus on the five major 21st-century world problems or grand challenges. They are; health, food, water, energy, and the environment.[15] Yet many managers never seem comfortable with technology and its importance in the commercial and strategic process of a firm.[16]

Today's managers are even further from technology than managers of decades ago.[17] Yet emerging technology-based management is critical on two dimensions: (1) technology's ability to be strategically important with an ability to disrupt current industry standard competencies and thereby creating exceptional opportunity and (2) the nature of technology and how it pertains to its innovation and general management.[18] Most managers are still focused on theory and concepts relating to assembled physical products and ignore the different management needs and practices associated to materials and service-based business.

Micro, nano, and computational sciences (e.g., the "Internet of Things") are potentially disruptive both singularly and as a group.[19] The first two are materials-based technologies; the third is service related.

Micro- and nano-based technologies are often called *small technologies*. Micro is an extension of semiconductor microfabrication technology that emphasizes the mechanical properties of the base materials, creating small sensing and actuation devices. Applications include micro speakers and cameras for smartphones. These new technical competencies have transformed the industry, disposing of market leaders and generating new ones—regardless of the initial market share and quality of the management team in existing firms. Nano and IoT are trans-industrial technology bases that are not only revolutionizing industries but also creating platforms for new industries.

Nanotechnologies create challenges for traditionally trained managers and, at the same time, they create opportunity for those with more appropriate business training.[20] Along with the IoT, nanotechnology is redefining the practice of developing products in today's pharmaceutical and health care industry.[21] Pharmaceutical therapies are now based on micro, nano, and IoT technology platforms. This is redefining business value statements and redistributing the wealth generated in the industry to favor organizations that have embraced these technologies.

The IoT is poised to redefine our lives by creating a platform for massive sensing and actuation.[22] The embrace of IoT is threatening to flood our current Internet requirements. Forecasts suggest that more than a trillion sensors, interlinked through the IoT, are creating 20+ million new jobs—with new managerial and technological skills. New applications include continuous noninvasive glucose monitoring systems based on the convergence of IoT, micro-, and nano-based technologies.

Solutions for large, important societal problems offer the potential for both job and wealth creation.[23] The new Schumpeterian cycle will favor regions that find a way to support emerging technology-based knowledge workers, innovators, entrepreneurs, and small firms. We consider two attempts to embrace this challenge.

The literature indicates that exceptional economic development in terms of wealth and job creation is underpinned by product development based on emerging technologies.[24] Further, we consider how the next Schumpeterian cycle appears based on micro, nano, and IoT.[25] Now, as in the past, nascent technologists, entrepreneurs, and small entrepreneurial businesses are the first to productize emerging technologies.[26]

Although economic development policy makers recognize the past patterns that are associated with emerging technologies, they have a difficult time accepting that underresourced entrepreneurs can outperform large, experienced firms. Yet experience shows that entrepreneurs are first to commercialize emerging technologies and that their regions benefit economically.[27] This differs from the experience with better understood sustaining technology that stresses support for existing incumbents.[28]

The embrace of emergent technologies by smaller firms is counterintuitive. Emerging technologies are defined as those technologies that are just emerging as solution vectors for new innovations.[29] They are related to, but differ from, *disruptive technologies*, which creatively destroy the competencies that

form the foundation of an industry-standard product for an existing industry and recreate the technology competencies required to make a product
in that industry.[30] Alternatively, disruptive technologies can create entirely
new industries based on new technology paradigms. These technologies differ
from sustaining or traditional technologies.

Sustaining technologies form the foundation of current industry-standard
products. Large market-leading firms, steeped in the current technology-
product paradigm, seek to develop their products through continuous incremental improvement.[31] Traditional technologies are linked to both current
and past products. This is perhaps best illustrated in the pharmaceutical
industry example, where founding firms utilized monomer chemistry solutions based on ink and dye technology.[32]

Many countries and regions are betting heavily on the commercial promise
of such emerging technologies as micro, nano, and IoT technologies—often
in an unsystematic manner.[33] Even so, the education and firm formation
associated with emerging technologies have never been higher.[34] However,
many regions' resource providers and universities find it difficult to embrace
an economy based on emerging technologies. Universities struggle to develop
a new type of professional; a "The T" professional, which is required to fuel
this future.[35] "T" professionals have a deep understanding of one area, such
as nanotechnology or commercial development, but also a background in
other fields that are required for technology commercialization. The depth of
knowledge of other related fields is the *thickness* at the top of the T.

Venture capitalists and other resource providers find emerging-technology-
based enterprises relatively risky and unmanageable compared to conventional firms.[36] Hence, there is a reliance on programs such as the U.S. Small
Business Innovative Research Program (SBIR).[37] Most regions simply cannot rely on their current small business funding sources to assist emerging-
technology-based firm development. Similarly, they cannot rely on the
current education system for their needs relating to emerging technologies
or commercialization.

A model focused on educational development and new firm creation and
based on emerging and disruptive technologies is developed. Science and
technology initiatives, cluster development theories (such as that of the creative class), and the differing roles of participants in that process are considered.[38] This activity is furthered through a discussion of the efficacy of small
firms from the opposing neo-Marshallian and Schumpeterian perspectives.[39]
Finally, micro, nano, and IoT technologies are considered in relation to international and U.S. regional economic development.[40]

This chapter adds to the literature by advancing emerging-technology-
based economic development through a case study approach of two progressive

regional economic development activities based on emerging technology.[41] National Institute for Nano Engineering (NINE) in the United States and entrepreneurial development activities at the University of Twente are the two Case studies considered. The University of Twente has a stated mission of becoming the "Entrepreneurial University" of the Netherlands.[42] Both examples focus on different stages of the economic development process and seek to develop and implement new methods, policies, and support activities to attract, nurture, develop, and retain emerging technologies. An emerging-technology-based economic development model is based on the literature and illustrated by these two exemplars.[43]

LITERATURE REVIEW

A model for emerging technology development that supports the customization of policy to meet the needs of a region's economic development activities is offered.[44] Regions have often overlooked the effect of the individual nascent entrepreneurs, technologists, small businesses, and innovators on the region.[45] If emerging technology commercialization is desirable for economic renewal, and it is led by entrepreneurial activities, then regional policy and action should address the needs of the young, small firms that develop it.[46] The role of emerging technologies and entrepreneurship to Schumpeterian economic development is considered.[47] The development of these nascent or established innovators, technologists, inventors, and entrepreneurs in the emerging technology commercialization process is paramount to future economic and social vitality.[48]

The Role of Emerging Technology in Economic Development

Emerging technologies (nano, micro, and the Internet of Things) are dominating new product development in many industries.[49] These technologies are the "winds of creative destruction," both redefining competition in existing markets and creating entirely new markets.[50] Regional economies that take advantage of these trends will benefit from the shift in wealth and job creation.[51] Yet regional policy makers, managers, educational administrators, and funders are often reluctant or unable to provide the resources required to foster this sort of development.[52]

One challenge is that emerging technology is extremely fluid, and planning efforts based on current assumptions cannot anticipate future scientific developments or the direction that a technology may take.[53] Another challenge is the lack of agreement on basic definitions of the technologies involved and the need for nontraditional road-mapping processes to advance these technologies.[54] Is it any wonder that most managers, venture professionals, and policy makers are uncomfortable with emerging technologies?[55]

The risk of not embracing and fostering the use of emerging technologies to eliminate large societal problems is recognized by many national and international leaders.[56] For example, former Swedish Prime Minister Goran Presson sought to embrace emerging technologies for economic development and as a solution to societal problems. Prime Minister Presson suggested that he is *"not scared of utilizing new (emerging) technologies to solve 21st century problems but is terrified of the continued use of traditional technologies to solve the 21st century problems that their use created."*[57] A challenge is quantifying the risk of the inaction of policy makers, managers, and funding sources.

The Role of Microtechnology (Micro), Nanotechnology (Nano), and the Internet of Things (IoT) as 21st-Century Emerging Technologies

As stated previously, micro- and nanotechnologies combined with computational sciences in the form of the Internet of Things (IoT) appear to be the next Schumpeterian economic cycle.[58] These technologies are expected to be the primary engines of economic growth for the next several decades, taking the role that semiconductors and steam engines took in the past. As these technology platforms are important for enabling innovation,[59] many countries and regions are investing in small technologies and computational sciences.[60]

Dr. Feynman's discussion of plenty of room at the bottom initiated interest in small technology[61] or Nanosystems and Microsystems. The Internet of Things (IoT) is considered the other pillar in this new Schumpeterian cycle.[62] The *Things* (in IoT) includes sensor application becoming so ubiquitous that it overloads the current Internet infrastructure many times over—for example, the Trillion Sensor (TSensor) systems road-mapping efforts.[63] In TSensor's case, this involves having sensors harvest data from the environment and, ultimately, their having the ability to interpret and act upon it.[64] TSensors will require a tremendous boost in the efficiency of the Internet and of big-data analysis to become a reality. These requirements create great opportunity for incumbent and new firms. Other IoT concepts are the "cloud" and Cisco's "Fog"—an evolution of the Internet into a network of interconnected things.

Tierney found that micro- and nanotechnology-based products often have TRL levels barely into the product development range (TRL 5–7).[65] For commercialization, a level of 9 needs to be obtained. The primary challenge to IoT is not readiness, but radical vision and architectural adjustments to the existing systems and infrastructure.[66] Another challenge to development and commercialization is that many small-tech solutions are increasingly being asked to meet the precautionary principle.

The precautionary principle was first utilized in the European Union to regulate genetically modified foods.[67] Later, it was applied to nanotechnology-based solutions. The principle places the responsibility for safety, as well as any societal issues resulting from its use—including disposal and exposure to the technology in the firm. Such an approach encourages firms to use innovation to optimize societal solutions (in health care, water, food, energy, and the environment) rather than creating profit at the expense of optimization of societal solutions.[68] This requirement is a basic commercialization hurdle for many emerging-technology-based firms seeking funding from traditional venture-funding sources.

Cluster Perspectives and Economic Development

The greatest development since the early 20th century in the theory of regional economic development that has resulted from Schumpeterian business cycles is cluster theory.[69] Consequently, four different cluster theories are considered below, including consideration of how they are bounded by political realities.[70] As regional decision making interacts with politics, decisions are often bounded by the election cycle or the term limits of regional politicians who champion a policy. Even though economic development based on developing technologies is longer than this cycle, it often dominates policy development, with policy makers and politicians eager to find methods to accelerate the commercialization of products, thereby demonstrating the success of the policy.[71]

The four popular cluster development approaches to economic development are similar, but place emphasis on different elements of similar packages of activities. The four—market-based, entrepreneurial-based, Triple-Helix, and creative class—are now briefly considered.

The Porter or Market-Based Cluster Theory

Porter defines a *cluster* as a geographically proximate group of interconnected companies and associated institutions in a particular field, linked by commonalities and complementarities.[72] A cluster can be a city, region, state, or span nearby or neighboring countries (e.g., southern Germany and German-speaking Switzerland). The efficacy of a cluster depends on the distance over which information can travel and transactions, incentives, and other efficiencies can occur. This model emphasizes regional markets as drivers of economic development efforts.

Clusters often encompass an array of linked industries and other entities important to competition. They include; suppliers of specialized inputs such as components, machinery, and services as well as providers of specialized infrastructure. Clusters often extend downstream to customers, laterally to manufacturers of complementary products, and to companies utilizing common skills, technologies, or inputs. Many clusters include governments and other institutions (universities, think tanks, vocational-training providers, standards-setting agencies, and trade associations) that provide specialized training, education, information, research, and technical support. Many clusters include trade associations and other collective bodies. Finally, nonregional, or foreign, firms can be and are part of clusters, but only if they invest in a significant local presence.[73]

Entrepreneurial- and Small Business–Based Regional Economic Development

The entrepreneurial model is based on Schumpeter's ideas,[74] and it has been advocated by the U.S. Small Business Administration (SBA).[75] The fundamental concept is that new and small firms' success in commercializing emerging technologies generates the majority of net new jobs. This perspective takes advantage of small firm capabilities in idea generation, professional development, and willingness to commercially embrace new technology-based product platforms that can transform the regions and industries. The theory emphasizes development activities such as expeditionary marketing[76] and research value added[77] rather than taking the market-focused approach proposed by Porter.[78]

The Triple Helix Cluster Theory

The Triple Helix concept is a model that calls for the interaction of (1) academe, (2) industry, and (3) government to develop a region.[79] These three components are used to generate social benefits through regional knowledge translation. This three-legged stool provides support for this cluster perspective on economic development.

The Triple Helix concept focuses on gaining maximum social benefit from knowledge generation and is compatible with the patience required to develop emerging-technology-based products.[80] Most economic development professionals whom we have interviewed believe this model is a piece of their economic development strategy rather than an economic development model or plan on its own.

The Creative Class Cluster Theory

Creative class theory considers the need to attract innovative people, a tactic emphasized in the "Rise of the Creative Class."[81] It focuses on precursors to economic development by emphasizing talent, technology, and tolerance. A region's ability to obtain an exceptional position in these three areas attracts innovators—the creative class—who then produce economic prosperity. This method has been used to rank the future prospects of a number of cities and regions. The creative class concept is equally applicable to sustaining and fostering industry-based models for an improved economy. The theory suggests, though, that the creative class is distinct from others and is attracted to a region through a constant and definable set of attributes. Having introduced the main theories of cluster development, we now consider methodology.

METHODOLOGY

The case method is utilized to consider the activities in two regions.[82] Our two cases were chosen because they represent extremes in entrepreneurial-support activity. Kennispark (Dutch for "Knowledge Park") is located on the University of Twente's grounds and acts as the central hub for commercialization activities at this and other regional universities, incubators, and conferences in the surrounding region. Assistance to developing and developed firms based on emerging small technologies is an area in which Kennispark focuses. The National Institute for Nano Engineering (NINE) program in the United States focuses on potential nascent innovators, inventors, and entrepreneurs.

The NINE Programs

The National Institute for Nano Engineering (NINE) is a response to the need to improve technological competencies, managerial capabilities, and relevant professional training in the United States for emerging technologies.[83] Over the last eight years, NINE's focus has been on the emergent technology base of nanotechnology and on mentoring nascent graduate and undergraduate researchers to ensure that their inventive researcher and innovator capabilities improve. This is accomplished by combining leading-edge technical knowledge with a basic understanding of the important business issues for commercialization. The goal is to improve retention of engineers and scientists in the field as researchers, inventors, and innovators. Students were selected from research institutions across the country to be mentored by Sandia National Laboratory researchers on nanotechnology-based projects on-site for one or more summers. Sandia National Laboratories was chosen for this purpose because it is a national center of excellence for nanotechnology and microtechnology research, cyber security, development, and engineering.

The NINE program utilized Sandia National Laboratories' principal investigators and *knowledge entrepreneurs* to involve participants with large industrial firms and research universities on cutting-edge, industry-relevant research projects deemed important to the nation.[84] The selected students, or nascent *knowledge entrepreneurs, innovators,* and *technologists,* interacted with senior members of Sandia's technical staff, innovation management researchers, serial entrepreneurs, and engineers and managers of Fortune 500 firms.

The students were developed through a series of presentations and experiences in elements of the research and the innovation process related to the emergent technology base of nanotechnology. As with our other case study, the aim was to focus students on innovation, technology, and entrepreneurship. Participants were surveyed, postparticipation. Of the initial 120 surveys sent out, 30.1 percent were returned. Over 30 percent of respondents continued their work after graduation with a national laboratory, nearly 70 percent worked in technical positions, and almost 10 percent in entrepreneurial positions. The surveys also offer insight into the overall program and its efficacy. The case study method reveals which techniques the students were exposed to, educated in, and mentored on.

University of Twente and Surrounding Region

The University of Twente's mission is to be the Netherland's Entrepreneurial University. The university is supposed to create entrepreneurial renewal in a region of the Netherlands devastated by the loss of their traditional industry. Founded in the 1960s as a technological university, it is now recognized as one of the four top universities in the Netherlands. It has a leading role in small-technology research, development, and entrepreneurial activity. Over 800 firms have been spun out from the research activities in both technological and entrepreneurial research centers.

The University of Twente MESA+ research center is one of Europe's top nanotechnology and microtechnology research facilities.[85] The information technology center is also recognized as a center of excellence. Moreover, Kennispark, and the associated university, city, and province, is recognized as a leading European science and technology park. Finally, the Nikos entrepreneurial research center at the University of Twente is one of the leading entrepreneurship research groups in Europe. Over 40 nanotechnology-based firms have been launched in the last 10 years in the region.

DIFFERING REGIONAL USE OF CLUSTER THEORIES

Both cases have utilized aspects of all four of the cluster models. For example, both cases benefit from synergies between industry, academe, and government as proposed by the Triple Helix model. However, what if a region were devoid of one or more of the *legs* of the three-legged Triple Helix stool? Perhaps another path, one that depends on community resources, would suffice.

Therefore, the region's actions are incorporated with cluster perspectives to develop a fuller model. For NINE, the focus was on the development of nascent emerging technology professionals, enabling them to become inventors, innovators, or entrepreneurs. While for Kennispark, the focus is on assisting entrepreneurial firm and team formation and progression. The implications of the differences are considered from the perspective of the differing cluster theories. For this purpose, innovative action is considered as three separate stages.

CATEGORIZING THE STAGES OF SMALL BUSINESS COMMERCIALIZATION

The type of resource needed by any small firm, personnel in the firm, or technologists, is affected by both knowledge base and business maturity. Small firms are often viewed from the perspective of a five-stage maturity continuum: pre-seed, seed, start-up, series A, and series B. Funders specialize in firms at specific stages and the associated monetary requirements of the selected stage.[86] Consequently, a firm's team and development stage affects the type of funders that it attracts. For example, venture capitalists rarely invest in pre-seed, seed, or even start-up small firms. Financial support is overwhelmingly provided by angel funders in these early stages.[87]

The NINE program, however, focuses on professional development and education of nascent innovators, inventors, small business owners, and entrepreneurs. The University of Twente focuses on entrepreneurs who are either in the process of developing a firm or are with a fully developed firm. Both approaches are very useful in generating positive economic results.

Small Firm Value Proposition

Differing value propositions result in different resource requirements. The opportunity and related entrepreneurial value proposition for each firm are often different. Classifying entrepreneurial business models into three generic categories can be helpful:[88] (1) the entrepreneur's ability to recognize and capitalize on Schumpeterian technology change,[89] (2) the entrepreneur's ability to recognize market gaps,[90] and (3) the ability to decrease transaction cost.[91]

While one may generate value in any one of these three categories alone, the combination of two or more in a value statement is preferred. However, the type and focus of resources differ for each of these three generic-value propositions. This categorization of value proposition helps economic development personnel to better provide appropriate and customized assistance to emerging-technology-based firms.[92] It is critical for economic development specialists to define the type(s) of assistance that are most applicable based on the firm's value statement.

Small Firm Personnel Competency and Capability Alignment

Economic development professionals must use their limited resources to make decisions on how, what, and whom to fund. The factors determining what to nurture differ among regions; this decision is often based on a combination of the idea, management team, and the proposed technology-product platform. Common tools for evaluating the business-value statements include team evaluations and normative methods such as SWOT,[93] as well as quantitative decomposition approaches.[94] The Strategic Technology Firm Fit Audit (STFFA) is provided as a new guide to opportunity assessment.[95]

STFFA is a multidimensional decomposition model for evaluating the appropriateness of an opportunity to its entrepreneurial team.[96] It ignores the question, "Is this a good opportunity?" and helps with the more important question, "Is this a good opportunity for the entrepreneurial team?" STFFA supports internal product innovation, merger, and acquisition decisions. *Open innovation* decisions on joint ventures, precompetitive collaborations, and strategic supply chain partnerships can also be supported with this technique. The STFFA supports evaluation of the potential of new ventures by economic development professionals, entrepreneurial teams, institutional investors, and venture capitalists.

The STFFA views business opportunities based on the managerial, technological, and product history of the firm and its founders; this is a competency-based theoretical perspective.[97] This decomposition model uses an objective review of a firm's personnel and products to align technological, competency, and managerial capabilities inherent in a firm to those required by the opportunity under consideration.[98] The elements included are generic and specific technological knowledge, specific operational knowledge, specific product-type experience, and industry-specific experience. The results to date have shown that the more aligned that a small firm and its founders are in these areas to the requirements of an opportunity, the more likely a success is to occur. The elements of the tool are summarized in table 12.1.

TABLE 12.1 Generic Strategic Technology Firm Fit Audit

Managerial Capabilities	Opp.	P1	P2	Pn
Tier 1: Opp. type				
Physical product type				
Service product type				
Tier II: Managerial emphasis				
Complexity				
Innovation type				
Technology competencies				
Tier III: Generic engineering				
Tier IV: Specific technologies				

CASE STUDY RESULTS

Having introduced the STFFA, attention is now given to the types of activities provided by the two programs to develop entrepreneurial action. After considering the assistance provided by the NINE program to hundreds of knowledge and commercial entrepreneurs, the more extensive activities on nascent and ongoing entrepreneurial activities at the University of Twente is discussed.

NINE Activities

As stated earlier, the NINE program provides students with education, exposure, and mentorship on relevant subjects. NINE emphasizes technical research in micro- and nanotechnology areas with support from academic and industry partners with hands-on training at Sandia National Laboratories. These activities supplement ongoing guidance from the students' faculty advisers from more than 20 top U.S. universities, such as Rensselaer Polytechnic Institute, the University of Florida, and the University of Texas. Several Fortune 500 firms helped to select projects that are considered both commercially interesting and also important to the nation's interests. NINE brought in experts from entrepreneurial high-tech firms and industry as well as academic leaders in commercialization and innovation to inspire and inform the student researchers as part of its Innovation Training Program. NINE used Sandia National Laboratories as the hub for a variety of activities summarized in table 12.2.

As the goal of NINE is to develop the next generation of engineers and scientists by providing them with exposure to the mechanics of

TABLE 12.2 NINE Activities

Activity	Education	Mentorship	Exposure
Undergraduate education	Universities		
Graduate education	Universities		
Research work		SNL	
Technology readiness levels			SNL
Ethics and emerging technology			SNL/Experts
Attributes of a principal investigator			SNL/Experts
Innovation versus invention			Experts
Research choice		SNL/Firms	
Business of nanotechnology			Experts
Nanotechnology and society			Experts
Intellectual property			Experts
Innovation in small firms			Local firms
Market focused versus market developed			Experts/SNL
Learning from failure			Experts
Sales and communications			Experts
Industry partner research presentations		Firms	
The process of innovation			Experts/SNL

commercializing emerging technologies to fuel entrepreneurial spirit and improve the likelihood of excellence in innovation and entrepreneurship, students were exposed to the elements of both scientific investigation and commercial innovation. The vast majority of the 200 plus graduate and undergraduate students have excelled in their work after their NINE experiences.

University of Twente Regional Activities

The University of Twente's entrepreneurial climate has grown considerably over the past 20 years. Initiatives have moved from the technological research community to include policy, management, and entrepreneurial centers of excellence. Kennispark is a centerpiece that, over the past 10 years, has grown to be a model research park in Europe. In addition to Kennispark, two university centers of excellence are considered: MESA plus and Nikos.

A summary of regional efforts are shown in table 12.3, categorizing both types and origins of the regional effort. The activities are designed with the goal of creating ambitious firms focused on emerging-technology-based value propositions. Both cases meet their goals, but have very different aims. NINE

TABLE 12.3 Twente Regional Activities

Activity	Education	Mentorship	Exposure	Infrastructure
Undergraduate education	Twente			
Graduate education	Twente			
Research centers	Twente			Twente
Business development efforts		Kennispark		
Ethics and emerging technology	Twente		Experts	
Valorization grants	Government	Government		
Innovation versus invention	Twente		Experts	
Top early-stage funding		Kennispark Twente		
Business of nanotechnology		Kennispark Twente	Experts	
Nanotechnology and society	Twente			
Intellectual property		Kennispark		
Incubation		Twente Kennispark		Twente Kinnespark
Market focused versus developed		Experts		
Angel (hero funding) funding		Kennispark Government	Experts	
Early-stage venture capital		Kennispark Government		
Industry partner research presentations		Twente Kennispark		
The process of innovation			Experts	
Nano-manufacturing facility				Twente Government
Micro and NanoNed partnerships				Twente
Facilities rotating fund				Twente Government
International networking		Twente Government Kennispark		

seeks to develop the next generation of technologists, innovators, and entrepreneurs, and University of Twente seeks to generate firms. Both could benefit from better alignment between economic policy research and opportunity team fit to allow for the focus of precious but limited resources. Consequently, the proposed approach is applied to the funds that were focused on early-stage investment for specific emerging-technology-based firm types.

MODEL DEVELOPMENT

Neither case had formal methods for recognizing the type of value proposition that candidates had. Nor was there a formal process for evaluating presence or absence of fit between the team focusing on a particular opportunity in terms of appropriate competencies and capabilities. These functions have been added to the STFFA model table 12.4).

The model focuses on assisting economic development decision makers throughout the value chain. A four-step process is used to assist regions in developing better ways to embrace and support translation of emerging technologies. Our model is a four-step process. First, economic development decision makers identify elements of cluster theories that best fit the knowledge base and economic climate of their region. Next, the state of a region's nascent and developed activity is quantified. In step three, an STFFA is completed to consider whether support of the applicant is a good opportunity for

TABLE 12.4 Emerging Technology Regional Economic Development Model

Cluster Type	Porter theory Small firm model	Triple Helix Creative class	Step 1

| | **Small Firm Focus** | | |
	Transaction	Technology Gap	Market Gap	
Nascent	NINE	NINE	NINE	Step 2
Scope of Activity	UT	UT	UT	
Developed				

Managerial Capabilities	Opp.	P1	P2	Pn	
Tier 1: Opp. type					
Physical product type					
Service product type					
Tier II: Managerial emphasis					
Complexity					Step 3
Innovation type					
Technology competencies					
Tier III: Generic engineering					
Tier IV: Specific technologies					

Emerging Technology Funding Review	Step 4

the region. Finally, early-stage funding and resources are provided to each innovation and team, if the opportunity fits the regional strategic goals and is within budgeted funds. The fund involves government, university, and industrial sponsorship for emerging technology firms.

DISCUSSIONS AND FURTHER RESEARCH

This chapter offers a model for emerging-technology-based regional economic development. The literature review provided the importance of emerging-technology-based firms in regional economic development, and the case studies considered two regions' responses to developing programs for emerging technology translation.

In both cases, funding portions of the emerging technology commercialization process was difficult. Surprisingly, some pervasive techniques were utilized with little overall commonality in the ways that regions assisted firms. In both cases, cluster theories were known, but neither group felt that any singular theory provided much value. However, there was a feeling that improvement and value could be obtained through a combination of elements from multiple theoretical models.

The pervasive use of exposure to experts in the NINE program, for example, is somewhat reflected in the approach at University of Twente. However, many of the exposure activities provided by the NINE programs have been moved to mentorship programs. Mentorship programs were noted as often requiring infrastructure development. There are large differences in the type and intensity of assistance between the NINE programs and the programs in the University of Twente area. In the NINE program, the infrastructure was primarily developed for the internal needs of Sandia National Laboratories. In the case of University of Twente, new facilities were constructed with the needs of spin-out firms as a major consideration in infrastructure development. Future research will expand on the number of cases and quantification of the research area and model.

NOTES

1. Robert M. Solow, "Technical Change and the Aggregate Production Function," *Review of Economics and Statistics* 39 (1957): 312–330; Nikolai D. Kondratief, "Long Waves in Economic Life," *Lloyds Bank Review* (1978): 1937; Steven T. Walsh and Aard J. Groen, "Introduction to the Field of Creative Enterprise," *Technological Forecasting and Social Change* 80, 2 (2013): 187–190.

2. William J. Abernathy and James M. Utterback, "Patterns of Industrial Innovation," *Technology Review* 50, 7 (1978): 40–47.

3. Steven T. Walsh, "Portfolio Management for the Commercialization of Advanced Technologies," *Engineering Management Journal* 13, 1 (2001): 33–37.

4. Steven T. Walsh, *Let Failure Be Your Guide: Becoming a Relevant Researcher for Industrial Renewal* (Enschede, Netherlands: University of Twente Press, 2013): 28

5. Regan W. Stinnett and Steven T. Walsh, "National Lab-centered Innovation Institutes for Creating the Next Generation of Innovation Leaders" (paper presented at the Commercialization of Micro Nano Systems Conference, Enchede, Netherlands, August 25–28, 2013).

6. C. K. Prahalad and Gary Hamel, "Corporate Imagination and Expeditionary Marketing," *Harvard Business Review* 69, 4, (1991): 81–92; Michael E. Porter, "Location, Competition, and Economic Development: Local Clusters in a Global Economy," *Economic Development Quarterly* 14, 1 (2000): 15–18; T. A. Wise, "IBM's $5,000,000,000 Gamble," in *Readings in the Management of Innovation*, 2nd ed., ed. Michael L. Tushman and William L. Moore (Pensacola, FL: Ballinger, 1982): 45–54.

7. Steven Walsh and Jonathan Linton, "The Competence Pyramid: A Framework for Identifying and Analyzing Firm and Industry Competence," *Technology Analysis & Strategic Management* 13, 2 (2001): 165–177.

8. Steven Walsh, Bruce Kirchhoff, and David Tolfree, "Roadmapping Nanotechnology," in *Commercialization of Micro and Nanotechnology Products*, ed. David Tolfree and Mark J. Jackson (Boca Raton, FL: Taylor Francis Group, 2008): 51–70.

9. Steven Walsh and Bruce Kirchhoff, "Entrepreneurs' Opportunities in Technology-based Markets," in *Technological Entrepreneurship*, ed. Philip H. Phan (Charlotte, NC: Information Age Publishing, 2002): 17–30.

10. Clayton M. Christensen, *The Innovators Dilemma* (Boston: Harvard Business School Press, 1997).

11. Michael E. Porter, *Competitive Advantage* (New York: The Free Press, 1985); Porter, "Location, Competition, and Economic Development."

12. Robert Tierney, Wahid Hermina, and Steven T. Walsh, "The Pharmaceutical Technology Landscape: A New Form of Technology Roadmapping," *Technological Forecasting and Social Change* 80, 3 (2013): 194–211.

13. Scott L. Newbert, Steven T. Walsh, Bruce A. Kirchhoff, and Victor A. Chavez,"Technology-driven Entrepreneurship: Muddling through and Succeeding with the Second Product," in *Entrepreneurship: The Engine of Growth*, vol. 2, ed. Maria Minniti (New York: Praeger, 2006): 291–312.

14. Scott L. Newbert, Bruce A. Kirchhoff, and Steven T. Walsh, "Defining the Relation among Founding Resources, Strategies, and Performance in Technology-intensive New Ventures: Evidence from the Semiconductor Silicon Industry," *Journal of Small Business Management* 45, 4 (2007): 438–46.

15. K. Eric Drexler, "Nanotechnology: From Feynman to Funding," *Bulletin of Science Technology Society* 24, 1 (2004): 21–27; Aard J. Groen and Steven T. Walsh, "Introduction to the Field of Creative Enterprise," *Technological Forecasting and Social Change* 80, 2 (2013): 187–190.

16. Christensen, *The Innovators Dilemma.*

17. Mario Yanez, Tarek Khalil, and Steven T. Walsh, "IAMOT and Education: Defining a Technology and Innovation Management (TIM) Body-of-knowledge (BoK) for Graduate Education (TIM BoK)," *Technovation* 30, 7–8 (2010): 389–400.

18. Jonathan D. Linton and Steven T. Walsh, "From Bench to Business," *Nature Materials* 2 (2003): 287–289.

19. Tierney, Hermina, and Walsh, "The Pharmaceutical Technology Landscape."

20. K. Eric Drexler, *Engines of Creation: The Coming Era of Nanotechnology* (New York: Anchor Doubleday, 1986).

21. Tierney, Hermina, and Walsh, "The Pharmaceutical Technology Landscape."

22. J. Bryzek and Steven Walsh, "MEMS 'Inside the Tornado'; Real Job and Wealth Creation for the Second Decade of the 21st Century," *Commercial Micro Manufacturing North America* 4, 8, (2011): 25–27.

23. Steven Walsh and Jonathan Linton, "Infrastructure for Emerging Markets Based on Discontinuous Innovations," *Engineering Management Journal* 12, 2 (2000): 23–31.

24. Bruce A. Kirchhoff, Jonathan D. Linton, and Steven T. Walsh, "Neo-Marshellian Equilibrium versus Schumpeterian Creative Destruction: Its Impact on Business Research and Economic Policy," *Journal of Small Business Management* 51, 2 (2013): 159–166; Kondratief, "Long Waves in Economic Life"; Joseph A. Schumpeter, *The Theory of Economic Development: An Inquiry into Profits, Capital, Credit, Interest, and the Business Cycle* (New Brunswick, NJ: Transaction Books, 1934).

25. Kevin Ashton, "That 'Internet of Things' Thing: In the Real World Things Matter More Than Ideas," *RFID Journal* (2009): 1.

26. Mihail C. Roco, "Broader Societal Issues of Nanotechnology," *Journal of Nanopartical Research* 5, 3–4 (2003): 181–189; Mihail C. Roco, "International Perspective on Government Nanotechnology Funding," *Journal of Nanoparticle Research* 7, 6 (2005): 707–712.

27. Walsh and Kirchhoff, "Entrepreneurs' Opportunities."

28. Douglas Robinson, Arie Rip, and Vincent Mangematin, "Technological Agglomeration and the Emergence of Clusters and Networks in Nanotechnology," *Research Policy* 36, 6 (2007): 871–879.

29. R. Gouvea, J. Linton, M. Montoya, and S. Walsh, "Emerging Technology and Ethics: A Race to the Top or a Race to the Bottom," *Journal of Business Ethics* 109, 4 (2012): 553–567; M. F. Said, K. A. Adham, K.A. Abdullah, S. Hänninen, and S. T. Walsh, "Incubators and Government Policy for IT Industry and Regional Development in Emerging Economies," *Asian Academy of Management Journal* 17, 1 (2012): 65–96; Jonathan D. Linton and Steven Walsh, "Acceleration and Extension of Opportunity Recognition for Nanotechnologies and Other Emerging Technologies," *International Small Business Journal* 26 (2008): 83–99.

30. Walsh, Kirchhoff, and Tolfree, "Roadmapping Nanotechnology."

31. Ibid.

32. Tierney, Hermina, and Walsh, "The Pharmaceutical Technology Landscape."

33. Minna Allarakhia and Steven T. Walsh, "Analyzing and Organizing Nanotechnology Development: Application of the Institutional Analysis Development Framework to Nanotechnology Consortia," *Technovation* 32, 3–4 (2012): 216–226.

34. Minna Allarakhia and Steven T. Walsh, "Managing Knowledge Assets under Conditions of Radical Change: The Case of the Pharmaceutical Industry," *Technovation* 31, 2–3 (2011): 105–117.

35. Jonathan Linton and Steven Walsh, "A Theory of Innovation for Process-based Innovations Such as Nanotechnology," *Technological Forecasting and Social Change* 75, 5 (2008): 583–594.

36. Jonathan D. Linton and Steven T. Walsh, "Extracting Value from Learning Curves: Integrating Theory and Practice," *Creativity and Innovation Management* 22, 1 (2012): 10–25.

37. Bruce A. Kirchhoff, *Entrepreneurship and Dynamic Capitalism: The Economics of Business Firm Formation and Growth* (Westport, CT: Praeger, 1994).

38. Richard Florida, *The Rise of the Creative Class: And How It's Transforming Work, Leisure, Community and Everyday Life* (New York: Basic Books, 2002).

39. Alfred Marshall, *Principles of Economics* (London: Macmillan and Co., 1890); Aron S. Spencer, Bruce A. Kirchhoff, and Craig White, "Entrepreneurship, Innovation, and Wealth Distribution: The Essence of Creative Destruction," *International Small Business, Journal* 26, 1 (2008): 9–26.

40. Norman Augustine, "Rising above the Gathering Storm: Energizing and Employing America for a Brighter Economic Future," Technical Report (Washington, D.C.: National Academies Press, 1999); Matthias Kautt, Steven Walsh, and Klaus Bittner, "Global Distribution of Micro–nano Technology and Fabrication Centers: A Portfolio Analysis Approach," *Technology Forecasting and Social Change* 74, 9 (2007): 1697–1717.

41. Kathleen M. Eisenhardt, "Building Theories from Case Study Research," *Academy of Management Review* 14, 4 (1989): 532–550; Robert K. Yin, *Case Study Research: Design and Methods* (Thousand Oaks, CA: Sage Publications, 2009); Krsto Pandza, Terry A. Wilkins, and Eva A. Alfoldi, "Collaborative Diversity in a Nanotechnology Innovation System: Evidence from the EU Framework Programme," *Technovation* 31, 9 (2011): 476–489.

42. Kees Eijkel, Erik Knol, and Steven Walsh, "Architectural Innovation in Perspective," in *Converging Technologies: Innovation Patterns and Impacts on Society*, ed. Maurits Doorn (The Hague: Study Centre for Technology Trends, 2006): 244–265.

43. Steven T. Walsh and Aard J. Groen, "Introduction to the Field of Emerging Technology Management," *Creativity and Innovation Management Journal* 22, 1 (2013): 1–5.

44. Richard A. Bendis, "Technology Based Economic Development," in *Defence Related SMEs*, NATO Science Series, Series V: Science and Technology Policy, vol. 43, ed. F. D. Carvalho (Amsterdam: IOS Press, 2004): 1–9.

45. Stephen Appold, "The Control of High-skill Labor and Entrepreneurship in the Early US Semiconductor Industry," *Environment and Planning*, A 32 (2000): 2133–2160; Ron A. Boschma and Jan G. Lambooy, "Evolutionary Economics and Economic Geography," *Journal of Evolutionary Economics* 9 (1999): 411–429.

46. Steven Walsh, "An Introduction to Nanotechnology Policy: Opportunities and Constraints for Emerging and Established Economies," *Technological Forecasting and Social Change* 74 (2007): 1634–1642; Schumpeter, *The Theory of Economic Development*; Bruce Kirchhoff and Steven Walsh, "Entrepreneurship's Role in Commercializing Micro and Nano Technology Products," in *Commercialization of Micro and Nanotechnology Products*, ed. David Tolfree and Mark J. Jackson (Boca Raton, FL: Taylor Francis Group, 2008): 29–50.

47. Tatyana P. Soubbotina, *Beyond Economic Growth: An Introduction to Sustainable Development* (Washington, D.C.: The World Bank, 2004), 133, www.worldbank. org/depweb/english/beyond/global/glossary.html#19.

48. Suleiman K. Kassicieh et al., "The Role of Small Firms in the Transfer of Disruptive Technologies," *Technovation* 22 (2002): 667–674; Steven Walsh, Bruce Kirchhoff, and Scott Newbert, "Differentiating Market Strategies for Disruptive Technologies," *IEEE Transactions on Engineering Management* 49, 4 (2002): 341–351; Edwin Mansfield, *The Economics of Technological Change* (New York: W.W. Norton, 1968).

49. Richard Feynman, "There's Plenty of Room at the Bottom," *Engineering and Science* 23 (1960): 22–36; Kirchhoff and Walsh, "Entrepreneurship's Role in Commercializing Micro and Nano Technology Products."

50. Abernathy and Utterback, "Patterns of Industrial Innovation"; Inderpreet Thukral et al., "Entrepreneurship, Emerging Technologies, Emerging Markets," *International Small Business Journal* 26, 1 (2008): 101–116.

51. Jonathan D. Linton and Steven T. Walsh, "Road Mapping: From Sustaining to Disruptive Technologies," *Technological Forecasting and Social Change* 71, 1 (2004): 1–3; Jonathan D. Linton and Steven T. Walsh, "Integrating Innovation and Learning Curve Theory: An Enabler for Moving Nanotechnologies and Other Emerging Process Technologies into Production," *R&D Management* 34, 5 (2004): 513–522.

52. Vincent Mangematin and Steve Walsh, "The Future of Nanotechnologies," *Technovation* 32, 3–4 (2012): 157–160.

53. Jan G. Lambooy and Ron A. Boschma, "Evolutionary Economics and Regional Policy," *Annals of Regional Science* 35 (2001): 113–131.

54. Marc Saner and Anna Stoklosa, "Reducing Ambiguity to Increase Emerging Technology Commercial Potential: The Case of Nanomaterials," *Creativity and Innovation Management* 22, 1 (2013): 26–36.

55. Christensen, *The Innovators Dilemma*.

56. Pandza, Wilkins, and Alfoldi, "Collaborative Diversity in a Nanotechnology Innovation System"; Thukral et al., "Entrepreneurship, Emerging Technologies, Emerging Markets."

57. Kees Eijkel, G. Rogers, and Steven Walsh, "The State of Small Tech Based Startups," *Commercial Micro Manufacturing International* 5, 4 (2012): 50.

58. Linton and Walsh, "Acceleration and Extension of Opportunity Recognition."

59. I. Thukral, J Von Ehr, S. Walsh, A. Greon, P. Van de Sijde, and K. A. Adham, "Entrepreneurship, Emerging Technologies, Emerging Markets," *International Small Business Journal*, 26 (2008): 101–116.

60. Tuomo Nikulainen and Christopher Palmberg, "Transferring Science-based Technologies to Industry—Does Nanotechnology Make a Difference?" *Technovation* 30, 1 (2010): 3–11; Jayavardhana Gubbi et al., "Internet of Things (IoT): A Vision, Architectural Elements, and Future Direction," *Future Generation Computer Systems* 29, 7 (2013): 1645–1660.

61. Feynman, "There's Plenty of Room at the Bottom"; Steven Walsh, "Road-mapping a Disruptive Technology: A Case Study—The Emerging Microsystems and Top-down Nanosystems Industry," *Technological Forecasting and Social Change* 71, 1 (2004) 161–185; Yasuyuki Motoyama and Matthew N. Eisler, "Bibliometry and Nanotechnology: A Meta-analysis," *Technological Forecasting and Social Change* 78, 7 (2011): 1174–1182.

62. Gubbi et al., "Internet of Things."

63. Christensen, *The Innovators Dilemma.*

64. Ibid.

65. Tierney, Hermina, and Walsh, "The Pharmaceutical Technology Landscape."

66. Gubbi et al., "Internet of Things."

67. Tierney, Hermina, and Walsh, "The Pharmaceutical Technology Landscape."

68. Ibid.

69. Kondratief, "Long Waves in Economic Life."

70. Maryann P. Feldman, Johanna Francis, and Janet Bercovitz, "Creating a Cluster while Building a Firm: Entrepreneurs and the Formation of Industrial Clusters," *Regional Studies* 39, 1 (2005): 129–141.

71. Harold A. Linstone, "Three Eras of Technology Foresight," *Technovation* 31 (2011): 69–76; Jonathan Linton and Steven Walsh, "Acceleration and Extension of Opportunity Recognition for Nanotechnologies and Other Emerging Technologies," *International Small Business Journal* 26 (2006): 83–99; Linton and Walsh, "From Bench to Business."

72. Michael E. Porter, *Competitive Advantage* (New York: The Free Press, 1985); Porter, "Location, Competition, and Economic Development."

73. Ibid.

74. Schumpeter, *The Theory of Economic Development.*

75. David L. Birch, *Job Creation in America: How Our Smallest Companies Put the Most People to Work* (New York: Free Press, 1987).

76. Prahalad and Hamel, "Corporate Imagination and Expeditionary Marketing."

77. Walsh and Linton, "The Competence Pyramid."

78. Porter, "Location, Competition, and Economic Development."

79. Henry Etzkowitz and Loet Leydesdorff, eds., *Universities in the Global Economy: A Triple Helix of University-industry-government Relations* (London: Cassell Academic, 1997).

80. Eric Von Hippel, "Lead Users: A Source of Novel Product Concepts," *Management Science* 32, 7 (1986): 791–805.

81. Florida, *The Rise of the Creative Class.*

82. Yin, *Case Study Research*; Eisenhardt, "Building Theories from Case Study Research"; Eisenhardt and Graebner, "Theory Building from Cases."

83. Augustine, "Rising above the Gathering Storm."

84. Donna K. Kidwell, "Principal Investigators as Knowledge Brokers: A Multiple Case Study of the Creative Actions of PIs in Entrepreneurial Science," *Technological Forecasting and Social Change* 80, 2 (2013): 212–220.

85. Job Elders, Vincent Speiring, and Steve Walsh, "Microsystems Technology (MST) and MEMS Applications: An Overview," *MRS Bulletin* 26, 4 (2001): 312–318.

86. Kirchhoff, *Entrepreneurship and Dynamic Capitalism*.

87. Ibid.

88. Scott Newbert et al., "Technology-driven Entrepreneurship"; Spencer, Kirchhoff, and White, "Entrepreneurship, Innovation, and Wealth Distribution."

89. Schumpeter, *The Theory of Economic Development*.

90. Israel Kirzner, *Perception, Opportunity and Profit: Studies in the Theory of Entrepreneurship* (Chicago: University of Chicago, Press, 1979).

91. Oliver E. Williamson, "Transaction Cost Economic and Business Administration," *Scandinavian Journal of Management* 21, 1 (2005): 19–40.

92. Ibid.

93. T. A. Wise, "IBM's $5,000,000,000 Gamble," in *Readings in the Management of Innovation*, 2nd ed., ed. Michael L. Tushman and William L. Moore (Pensacola, FL: Ballinger, 1982): 45–54.

94. Alan R. Fusfeld, "How to Put Technology into Corporate Planning," *Technology Review* 80, 6 (1978): 63–74.

95. Steven Walsh and Jonathan Linton, "The Strategy-technology Firm Fit Audit: A Guide to Opportunity Assessment and Selection," *Technological Forecasting and Social Change* 78, 2 (2011): 199–216.

96. Ibid.

97. Prahalad and Hamel, "Corporate Imagination and Expeditionary Marketing."

98. Walsh and Linton, "The Strategy-technology Firm Fit Audit."

13

Public Policy Assistance for American Small Business: Promoting Supports and Reducing Impediments

William J. Dennis Jr.

The term *public policy* has no generally accepted definition. Many variants on the same theme are put forward for one, some more detailed and subtle, others less so. However, for present purposes, a useful way to think of the term is that public policy is "action taken by government to address a particular public issue."[1]

This chapter focuses on public policy undertaken to purposefully assist small business to overcome the problems that it faces. Perspective is important in this regard. Most public policy is not purposefully designed to affect smaller firms and their owners, though it often does, and sometimes adversely. These nonspecific small business policies are considerably more important to small business owners as a general rule than are those specifically intended for them. Think of policies that affect the banking system. Policy specifically designed to regulate commercial banks is likely to have a greater impact on the availability of small business loans than is any public program specifically designed to provide them. Further, the problems that small business–specific policies address are not necessarily problems common to all small enterprises, nor do the small business–specific policies that have been implemented address all of the problems that small business owners face. This chapter, therefore, is narrow, even in the context of small business and public policy.

Small business policy is traditionally presented as a menu of subsidized support programs that small business owners can use to aid their businesses.[2] Such programs indeed must occupy a substantial share of any discussion on the topic. However, there is more to consider; particularly important are the policies and programs designed to eliminate barriers and unnecessary costs for small business entry and operation. They, too, can be public policy activities supporting smaller enterprise; the most thoughtful would argue that they are even more important than support programs. Subsidized programs and barrier elimination represent two quite different approaches to small business policy, though they are not mutually exclusive and both have the same overall objective. Throughout the following discussion, the former is referred to as "policy supports" or "supports" and the latter as "impediment reductions" or "barrier reductions."

SMALL BUSINESS IN THE POLICY CONTEXT

Virtually every politician and legal jurisdiction of which the writer is aware claims to support small business. There are many reasons for them to do so. Small businesses are plentiful: they include 5.75 million employing enterprises,[3] there are almost 14 million people whose principal employment in a year is working for themselves,[4] and 31 million tax returns are filed with business income on them.[5] Small businesses and their owners make important economic and community contributions: they create almost two-thirds of the net new jobs,[6] are responsible for a disproportionate share of innovation,[7] commonly participate in and lead community activities,[8] and provide a wide variety of goods and services. Small business ownership is part of American history and tradition;[9] Alexis de Tocqueville observed on his tour of the United States in the early 1830s that "what most astonishes me in the United States is not so much the marvelous grandeur of some undertakings as the innumerable multitude of small ones."[10] Small business owners are the good guys in popular opinion, the ones who wear the white hats. Gallup reports that small business is consistently among those segments of society held in highest regard by the American public.[11] Given this context, it is only natural that policy makers want to associate themselves with small businesses and offer them support, both in words and actions.

The specific public policies discussed here are typically conducted by the federal government. The most important reason for the limitation is the vast number of governmental jurisdictions in the United States. They number about 90,000.[12] Though there are almost 20,000 municipalities, the most numerous kind of public authority is the special district, which includes divisions such as school districts, transportation districts, water districts, and fire districts, entities that can cross traditional municipal, county, and even state boundaries. Many have the authority to tax and purchase goods or services, and some have authority to regulate commerce and land use. These activities have the potential to affect small business. A thorough analysis of small business support policies emanating from them would fill volumes. Therefore, to keep the discussion manageable, this chapter focuses on the single jurisdiction that is common to all readers. Concentrating on the federal government does not denigrate the importance or relevance of states and localities. They, too, have extensive small business support policies, many of which parallel and coordinate with those coming out of Washington.[13]

POLICY SUPPORTS

Supports in the current context are government activities that directly or indirectly subsidize individual small businesses or small business owners. To be clear, a subsidy is assistance financed by government that is provided to a person or business. Subsides can be direct or indirect. Direct subsidies tend to be transparent and indirect subsidies opaque. A direct subsidy can be an outright grant, a "free" service, or a loan with a below-market interest rate. An indirect subsidy can be a loan guarantee, an infrastructure project, or a curb on the number of eligible competitors. The federal government likely has well over 100 subsidy programs for small business, as will be discussed below, though there appears to be no complete count. The dollar amount involved is also not known, but it is well into the tens of billions of dollars annually, if not substantially more.

Federal small business support programs have several implications for small business owners in addition to the taxes that they must pay to help finance them. The first is that they are numerous but often fragmented, duplicative, and overlapping. Second, they tend to fall into three program types: finance, advice, and procurement. And, third, they tend be inadequately evaluated, thereby making it difficult to determine how well they work compared to their objectives and to complementary activities.

Programs, Programs, Programs

There is a plethora of federal small business support programs, and they are located throughout government. A Catalogue of Federal Assistance Domestic Programs appears on the Internet, listing and describing 2,225 programs in the various federal agencies, with 577 making reference to small business.[14] Many of the 577 are narrowly drawn or thinly related. A more practical number, in the sense that a reasonable amount of small businesses might directly benefit, is somewhat over 100 programs,[15] not counting the procurement targets that virtually every department and agency must meet. The U.S. Small Business Administration (SBA) has about two dozen programs, depending on the classification of programs and subprograms, as does the Department of Agriculture (USDA), assuming farms and ranches qualify as small businesses. Even if they do not, the USDA maintains multiple programs that support rural small businesses. The Department of Housing and Urban Development

(HUD) and, to a lesser extent, the Department of Commerce (DOC) also have several. Those four entities alone administer 52 programs for small businesses.[16] The Departments of the Treasury, Energy, Interior, Labor, Health and Human Services, Defense, Education, Veterans Affairs, and so on also have at least a few. So do the Environmental Protection Agency (EPA) and the Overseas Private Investment Corporation (OPIC), among others. Many of these programs fall directly under the authority of agencies within departments, such as the Economic Development Administration (EDA) and the Minority Business Development Agency (MBDA), both of which fall under the umbrella of the Department of Commerce.

Every agency with contracting (purchasing) authority must have an Office of Small and Disadvantaged Business Utilization (OSDBU) within it to provide maximum practicable contracting opportunities to small, small disadvantaged, and women-owned businesses. The requirement extends to participation as subcontractors in contracts awarded for large projects, such as prime aerospace contracts.[17] These offices exclusively handle federal contracting issues and are not what many would term ombudsmen, which are people who handle more general small business problems with agencies and act as advocates for the owner(s).

Many, if not most, support programs offer indirect assistance to small business. They are designed to finance public and private entities, which in turn offer assistance to small business owner clients. Advice and technical assistance programs are virtually all of this nature. The Small Business Development Center program provides an illustration of this type of program. It receives well over $100 million from the SBA (and obtains additional resources from state and local governments and private sources) to provide information, training, and counseling to nascent and operating small business owners.

Consequences of Multiple Programs

The corollary of multiple support programs is the absence of coordination among many federal small business support activities. No overall small business strategy or policy exists. Fragmentation, duplication, and overlap abound. For example, the Government Accountability Office (GAO) reports,

Federal efforts to support entrepreneurs are fragmented—including among the 52 programs at the Department of Agriculture (USDA), Commerce, and Housing and Urban Development (HUD) and the Small Business Administration (SBA). All overlap with at least one other program in terms of the type of assistance they are authorized to offer, such as financial (grants and loans) and technical (training and counseling), and the type of entrepreneur they are authorized to serve.[18]

The same situation occurs with export promotion services. The SBA and five other agencies, including the Department of Commerce and the Export-Import Bank, engage in such activities as outreach, training and counseling, and finance.[19] Much of the overlap involves programs that support socially disadvantaged business owners and economically distressed areas.[20] GAO notes, "Commerce's Economic Development/Technical Assistance program and SBA's 7(j) Technical Assistance Program are among the 33 programs that assist businesses located in economically distressed areas," among the several similar examples cited.[21] The lines of demarcation between the Minority Business Development Agency's (Department of Commerce) programs for minorities and the disadvantaged and those of the SBA are frequently murky, leading to overlap in assistance for minority small business owners.

There are other organizational issues. At times, supports are located in what may not appear to be logical places. Help for incubators is located in the Departments of Commerce, Energy, Health and Human Services, Housing and Urban Development, and Interior, but not in the Small Business Administration. Administrative rivalries among competing agencies can also create problems for small business owners seeking help. In one hopefully extreme case, two large agencies signed a Memorandum of Understanding (MOU) mandating that employees of each agency advise individuals/businesses ineligible for its program of similar programs in the other agency for which the client may be eligible.[22]

Different federal support programs have different eligibility standards. Part of the reason for this variation is that the federal government has no single definition of *small business*. It has multiple definitions, each of which is an operating definition instituted for programmatic purposes.[23] The SBA's definitions for its programs, which are arbitrarily drawn, principally use an industry-based system.[24] Depending on which of more than a thousand industries they fall into, firms have a size cap of either the average annual number of employees or the average gross receipts over the prior three-year period, but not both. In a few very specific cases, criteria other than employees or gross receipts will be used. Asset size distinguishes a large bank from a small one, for example. The classification method sorts businesses into small and large; there is no middle ground, nor are there classes or divisions among small firms. The SBA's small business definitions change periodically, but as a general rule, more capital-intensive small businesses are larger and use the employment criterion and less capital-intensive firms are smaller and use the receipts criterion.

The SBA's size definitions not only apply to the agency's programs; they also govern eligibility for small business procurement activities (which will be subsequently discussed). However, they do not apply to most other business support programs. These programs possess other eligibility criteria. For example, the Department of Agriculture's Business & Industry Guaranteed Loan program is restricted to firms in rural areas, defined as areas having a population of less than 50,000.[25] The program's application contains no information that would allow a determination of a firm's size. Similarly, small firms are eligible for Trade Adjustment Assistance from the Department of Commerce (or, if they are farmers, from the Department of Agriculture) if they have been damaged by imported products. Size has no bearing on the aid.

Implications for Small Business Owners

The federal government offers considerable help to small business and small business owners, though much of it is located among third-party delivery entities. The assistance may not always be the right type for an individual situation, and it may not be useful for reasons associated with the business. But after reviewing the number of supports and their variety (the next section), small business owners have much to choose from.

Besides waste and less effective delivery (the section after next), the primary concern that overlap and duplication creates is confusion for small business owners attempting to access support programs. Which program fits best? Which program is delivered most efficiently? How do programs work together, if at all? Where are they found? Computer technology has reduced the search problem substantially over the years, or at least has made it more manageable. Every agency has a Web site with a more or less functioning search engine. The sites typically provide a useful description of the support available, and, more importantly, they provide the application forms, which usually reveal more about the program in question than the site's description. Sites also list telephone numbers, e-mail addresses, and, where applicable, local offices. Still, the small business owner must interact with a great variety of federal agencies at a large number of entry points to locate the desired help.

The search problem intensifies when states and local opportunities, often overlapping or paralleling those of the federal government, are thrown into the mix. And once an individual finds a suitable state or local program, he or she will also often find that there are jurisdictional attachment standards. For example, a state usually requires that the business be physically situated in the jurisdiction. That is typically not a problem for a small business, but it can be when the firm has more than a single location. Further, state's and local government's definitions of small business usually cap business size at fewer employees or lower revenues than the federal government's. A larger small business, therefore, may be eligible for a federal program but too large for a similar state or local program.

Types of Support Programs

Small business supports typically fall into three groups: finance programs, advice programs, and procurement programs. While there are also hybrids, these three generic types represent the overwhelming bulk of federal small business support activities.

Participation in support programs is often based on individual application and approval. The number of approvals is subject to a legislative cap or ceiling usually tied to legislative appropriations (money allocated). This is particularly characteristic of finance programs. There are exceptions, however, the most prominent being tax expenditures (discussed later) and certain information programs that are generally open to all.

Finance Programs

Finance programs are the ones most commonly associated with government support for small business. The most prominent of these are loans or loan guarantees. The trend in loan programs over the last several years has been toward loan guarantees, the two most conspicuous reasons for this being avoidance of duplicative administrative structures and the ability to leverage private funds. Direct government lending, in contrast to government guarantees, requires a structure to take loan applications, evaluate them, service them, and so on. That administrative apparatus replicates the activities of the country's more than 7,500 existing private financial institutions. If a very small number of highly specialized loans constituted the financial support program, a single centralized lender may be cost-effective. But when thousands of relatively modest small business loans, scattered across the country, are at stake, it makes more sense to piggyback them on an established and experienced structure that reaches into local communities and neighborhoods.

The second reason for the trend toward loan guarantees is that guarantees leverage multiples in private money. The actual amount of additional money leveraged depends on the amount of the guarantee, default rate, and salvage values on loan losses. However, the SBA expects to guarantee $15 billion in new private small business loans in FY 2013 for an outlay of about $200 million.[26] The accounting is significantly more complex than the previous sentence suggests, but it exemplifies the leverage obtained through guarantees.

Besides guaranteed and direct lending, the federal government also invests; provides grants; subsidizes insurance, such as flood insurance; and guarantees surety bonds for smaller firms. Finance programs provide direct payments to some, but far from all, farmers and growers. Less frequently, indirect financial subsidies finance classes of small businesses through tariffs and other trade barriers; quotas, including the number of operating licenses; and even minimum price levels, such as certain state or local rules on gasoline and milk. The financial benefit in these latter cases derives from limiting supply and putting a floor under prices. However, the trend is to phase out these latter types of subsidies.

The SBA's (7)a Loan Guarantee Program

The most visible publicly supported small business finance activity is the SBA's 7(a) loan guarantee program, the agency's flagship finance activity. Its size has oscillated over the last decade with the run-up to the Great Recession, the Great Recession dip, and its aftermath. In FY 2012, about 40,000 7(a) guaranteed loans were made, with a dollar volume for new approvals of approximately $15 billion, excluding paybacks and disbursements on approved credit lines.[27] Though comparative numbers are difficult to come by, approximately seven-tenths of 1 percent of the nation's small employers obtained a 7(a) guaranteed loan in FY 2011,[28] amounting to about 2.9 percent of the total small business loans (commercial and industrial) approved and 1.8 percent of the small business loan market.[29]

Not all small businesses are eligible for 7(a) guarantees. The critical consideration is that the applicant must be creditworthy (and able to repay the loan) but not able to access credit elsewhere on reasonable terms or at reasonable rates. The program is therefore premised on either the proposition that small business credit markets are not operating properly or that certain businesses need to be subsidized in order to obtain a loan (or to obtain one with "reasonable" interest rate and terms). During the mid-2000s, a concerted and successful effort was made to eliminate the direct subsidy from the program, but it was restored with the onset of the Great Recession.

A 7(a) guaranteed loan can be used for most business purposes. One recent study found that loan proceeds were most likely used to purchase or install new equipment, finance working capital, or acquire a new business, though several loans were used to purchase, build, or rehab buildings and land.[30] The maximum amount of a loan is currently $5 million, though the average loan in FY 2012 was $337,730 and the median much smaller.[31]

About 3,500 financial institutions participate in the 7(a) program,[32] including most of the larger ones.[33] A prospective small business borrower should approach an SBA-certified lender, generally a commercial bank, to obtain a loan guarantee.

Small Business Lending Fund

The Small Business Lending Fund (SBLF) is a different type of small business finance program because it provides capital to community banks and community development loan funds (CDLF) that in turn make conventional loans to their small business customers. A child of the Great Recession (the Small Business Jobs Act of 2010), the fund's purpose was to *temporarily* support small businesses financially by supporting community banks, themselves small businesses. The actual mechanism to get money to the banks proved rather arcane, but it worked so that the more money that a bank lent to small businesses, the lower the rate the bank paid the government for its capital.

Faulty assumptions underlying the program's creation meant that it produced only modest positive returns. The Department of the Treasury sent just $3.9 billion of the allocated $30 billion to 281 out of approximately 7,000 community banks.[34] Still, the Small Business Lending Fund is an example of a support program with an indirect subsidy. Small business owners who obtained loans because of the fund probably had no idea that they were beneficiaries of a small business support program. They likely saw the transaction as receipt of a normal loan from their community bank. And, from all outward appearances, that was exactly what it was.

Tax Expenditures and the Small Business Health Insurance Tax Credit

Taxes can be classified as a small business support or a small business impediment. The classification largely depends on what public finance people call a "tax expenditure." While the term is not precise, tax expenditures can be regarded as "revenue losses attributable to Federal tax laws which allow a special exclusion, exemption or deduction from gross income or which provide a special credit, a preferential rate of tax or a deferral of tax liability."[35] Effectively, it is government spending through the tax code, which implies use of the code to advance policy objectives not directly related to the primary objective of taxation, that is, raising revenues to finance government.

The federal tax code is riddled with tax expenditures that benefit both individuals and businesses, including small businesses.[36] For example, small businesses benefit from the ability to expense rather than depreciate certain investments (Sec. 179 of the Internal Revenue Code); the tax rate is reduced on the first $10 million of taxable corporate (C-corporations) income; and, small businesses can generally use the cash method of accounting for tax purposes. However, the largest tax expenditures often directly benefit individuals rather than businesses. Businesses, including small business, benefit from them indirectly through increased demand for their goods and services. Perhaps the best example is the home mortgage interest deduction, which amounts to a $364 billion revenue loss over five years,[37] but it helps to boost sales for the small business–intensive construction industry.

An example of a tax-related finance support is the small business health insurance tax credit that became law as part of the 2010 Patient Protection and Affordable Care Act, also known as Obamacare. The tax credit was instituted to provide an incentive for very small businesses to purchase employee health insurance, though it more often proved to be a windfall to those already purchasing insurance. The law laid out four criteria for small business owners to be eligible for the credit: they had to offer employees a minimum level of health insurance, they had to pay a minimum of 50 percent of the insurance premium, they could employ no more than 10 people to receive the full credit and no more than 25 to receive a partial credit, and average earnings for covered employees could be no more than $25,000 for the full credit and $50,000 for the partial credit. The number of years that eligible businesses could take the credit was capped.

The health insurance credit typifies many of the small business support programs operated through the tax code. Note that this credit is highly focused, targeted on the smallest and poorest paying small businesses. And, it is temporary.

Despite a narrow, moving target, small business owners should take advantage of the credit and similar tax supports when they are able. The same is true for tax supports at the state and local levels. The problem is that few owners can stay abreast of all of the federal, state, and local tax-related opportunities, though it is easier to do so in states that piggyback on the federal tax code (known as conforming states)[38] than in others. As a consequence, most owners are wise to use a tax professional to help them with their taxes, as almost 90 percent of small employers currently do.[39]

Advice (and Information) Programs

Small business owners continuously solicit and absorb information relevant to their businesses. Some do it more consciously and actively than others, but all do it to some degree. Advice (or counsel) is a subset of information that is focused on decisions and choice. And it tends to be supplied one-on-one rather than wholesale, making it more tailored but also more costly.

About three in four small employers solicit advice when a critical business decision confronts them.[40] A larger percentage (83 percent) do so on a continuing basis, with accountants, insurance agents or brokers, colleagues (other business owners), suppliers, bankers, lawyers, and computer and software specialists being the prime sources of advice.[41] There is in fact a huge industry in the private sector that provides business-advisory services to smaller firms. The Bureau of the Census, for example, counts 108,000 management-consulting businesses in the United States and another 141,000 management, scientific, and technical consulting firms.[42]

In the midst of a large and functioning private market of business information and advice suppliers, government has established a number of advice and information programs. Three factors explain that apparent anomaly. First, government imposes business-entry and operational requirements. Some are straightforward and intuitive, such as filing for an Employer Identification Number (EIN); others are arcane and widely disbursed across governments and agencies, such as zoning and land-use rules. The more complex the requirements, the more likely inadvertent errors will be made, creating problems for both government and business. It is in government's administrative best interest, in addition to small businesses', to establish information hubs, or one-stop shops, that consolidate business requirements and associated information in one readily identifiable place.

Second, the private sector charges for its services. Even when the charge is indirect, that is, wound in with a purchase price of a related good or service, there is typically a cost. Owners of new and marginal businesses often have little cash to spare. Arguably, if information and advice are not free or heavily discounted, these business owners will not seek it, which will decrease the viability of their enterprises.

Third, owners of nascent and marginal businesses often do not know where to go for the business information they need and waste considerable time and money chasing down readily available material. Often, these owners also do not know what they do not know. When an owner cannot ask the right question, he or she cannot hope to get the right answer. Nascent and new business owners gravitate toward public programs, while more established firms do so much less frequently on a relative basis.[43] Many of these of resources, therefore, appear to be consumed by those who have not yet entered the market.

The federal government's largest small business advice initiative is the Small Business Development Center (SBDC) program, a loosely affiliated group of 63 lead centers in the 50 states and territories with more than 900 locations.[44] Patterning the program after the Department of Agriculture's Cooperative Agriculture Extension Service, the SBA funded a handful of university-based centers in the late 1970s to provide management-consulting services to smaller businesses. The number of centers grew rapidly and, over time, broadened their resource base, though not altering their small business focus. The program added new funding sources, primarily from state and local governments, but also from the private sector. It also withdrew somewhat from its university underpinnings, as some of the program's state headquarters are now located off-campus and many of its personnel are no longer university employees or students.

Centers provide a variety of information services to their small business owner and prospective-owner clients. They offer training and one-on-one counseling. Their counseling services are usually extended at no cost to the client. In FY 2012, SBDCs provided 62,000 clients with long-term (5+ hours) counseling but offered assistance to almost 1 million individuals, about three-quarters face-to-face and one-quarter online.[45]

In addition to the information conveyed, SBDCs offer four primary benefits to prospective clients and consumers. First they are generally accessible, as there is an average of between 15 and 20 locations per state. A nearby location can be found quickly on the Internet. Second, free is always nice, and their services are often free. Third, the affiliations that most have with universities allow them to direct a client in need of technical services to someone in the university who may know how to help. And, fourth, SBDCs will often hold sessions that provide networking opportunities. Those opportunities are particularly valuable for individuals who have not been in business before.

Procurement Programs

The federal government is the world's largest purchaser of goods and services, awarding about $500 billion in contracts every year.[46] Long-standing policy targets a small business share of 23 percent of prime contracts awarded and 40 percent of subcontracts. A running controversy about contract counts obfuscates the precise number of contracts and dollars channeled to small businesses.[47] Still, the "official" figures show that, in total, small businesses procured $89.9 billion in FY 2012, with an inclusive $16.2 billion directed to women-owned businesses, $32.3 billion to small disadvantaged businesses, $12.3 billion to service-disabled veteran-owned small businesses, and $8.1 billion to HUBZones, that is, to businesses in depressed areas.[48]

The procurement contracts won by small businesses may or may not be small business support programs as earlier defined. This depends on whether they are won in open competition against any and all bidders or whether they are won in a sheltered competition, that is, in competition limited to only small businesses or in the case of so-called 8(a) contracts, small minority-owned businesses. If a small business wins an open competition, and small business wins about $49 billion that way,[49] it is not a support program, and vice versa.

Federal agencies engage in small business "set-asides." Acquisition rules define a set-aside as reserving "an acquisition exclusively for participation by small business concerns."[50] All contracts valued at between $3,000 and $100,000 are automatically set aside when there are at least two qualified small business bidders that are "competitive in terms of market prices, quality, and delivery."[51] Contracts above $100,000 can be set aside if the federal contracting officer has a reasonable expectation that two or more responsible small businesses can compete to provide the acquisition at fair-market prices. In other words, though the competitive bidders are sheltered, they cannot offer unreasonable prices or terms as determined by a procurement official. It is these contracts that allow a procurement activity to be considered a support.

Small business owners must register their firms with the System of Award Management (SAM), the federal government's primary database of eligible vendors, to be eligible for federal contracting.[52] This process requires interested owners to complete a certification that is a bit like creating resumes for their businesses, including information about the business's size, experience, location, and so on. While contracting agencies use SAM as a source to locate eligible vendors, government contracting is not a spectator sport. Interested owners should actively search for government business by locating contracts for which they are able to compete rather than waiting to be contacted about bidding.[53]

Subcontracting is different from contracting because the government does not make the contract award; the prime contractor does. Every federal prime contractor with a substantial award must develop a plan to provide subcontracting opportunities for small businesses.[54] However, the prime contractor goals are not rigid. They are goals, not fixed rules. There are penalties for noncompliance, but it has been difficult to find examples of penalty assessments.[55]

About one in five employing small businesses have won a government contract over the prior three years and a nonmutually exclusive 15 percent recognize that they have won a contract to provide goods and service to another business that will use their work in sales to a government agency or unit; that is, they provided their goods and services to a business that was subcontracting government work.[56] Those percentages include all governments, not just the federal, and there is some evidence that more small businesses participate at the local level.

There are reasons that some small business owners do not attempt to compete for government contracts. Among the more important are the lack of demand for their product or service, lack of awareness about government contracting opportunities, and the paperwork and hassle involved.[57] There is also a reasonably steep learning curve to obtaining the first contract.

Evaluation

The federal government has many and varied small business support programs that reach a variety of people and groups. The federal government spends billions of dollars every year to fund them. The follow-up question is, how well do these programs work for the money spent on them? The answer to that question requires an evaluation of each program to determine its strengths and weaknesses, its ability to reach stated goals and reach them cost-effectively, and, most importantly, to determine if there exists a *causal* effect between program and outcomes.[58] In other words, we ultimately want to know whether a program actually *causes* a desired outcome rather than to know whether a program is *associated* with a desired outcome. Should the program cause desired outcomes, policy makers rationally would maintain or increase resources for the program, other factors equal; should the program fail to cause desired outcomes, policy makers rationally would reduce or eliminate resources for it, other factors equal.

Current evaluations of small business support programs do not provide policy makers with the necessary information to determine whether they actually cause the outcomes desired. Often no evaluations are conducted, and virtually none of those that are conducted are able to determine whether a causal relationship exists. The GAO reports that 32 of the 52 programs at the four primary agencies with small business support programs lack evaluations altogether or have not had one done in over 10 years.[59] Others evaluations simply employ monitoring rather than actual evaluation. In other words, they count the number who use the program, solicit feedback on recipient satisfaction, or gather opinions about the efficacy of the assistance.[60] They fail to use more sophisticated and helpful techniques such as comparing matched samples and exploring selection bias. A Congressional Research Service (CRS) report concludes that the data that the SBA captures on the economic impact of its training and counseling activities (advice programs), for example, is "somewhat limited" and "subject to methodological challenges," though most small business owner clients think the programs are useful.[61] The Rand Corporation examined 22 peer-reviewed program evaluations on a similar set of programs and found just one that employed the highest standards of methodological rigor.[62] And the SBA's inspector general (IG) asserted that several of the IG's 47 open recommendations involve "establishing meaningful performance metrics and periodically assessing the same."[63]

Most support programs have performance goals, and agencies tend to meet them.[64] But that does not ensure that small business owners obtain the greatest value or assistance for the dollars that legislators have allocated to help them. Nor does it mean that any or all of these programs are valueless in the sense that they do not cause the outcomes intended. It is simply that no one knows. If it is not operating blindly, the government is operating in very dim light.

Change is coming. The Government Performance and Results Act (GPRA), originally passed in 1993 and amended in 2010, now requires the Office of Management and Budget (OMB) to work with the agencies to develop and implement output measures on certain crosscutting activities and report results. Given that most small business support programs crosscut agencies, the evaluation of programs should improve over time.

ELIMINATING IMPEDIMENTS

If one thinks of small business support programs as government assistance to boost small businesses over the barriers and problems that their owners face, one can think of government's removing or eliminating impediments as tearing down those barriers and problems. Most exogenous barriers can be attributed to government itself, but cartels, price fixing, and other anticompetitive activity are barriers that originate in the private sector. Often action to reduce or eliminate government barriers is broadly referenced as "regulatory reform." Most regulatory reform initiatives focus on an industry or on all businesses rather than on small businesses, per se, though affected small businesses still benefit. However, both the federal government and state and local governments have taken steps to specifically assist small business owners to overcome government-generated problems by reducing or eliminating barriers.

Lowering barriers has different implications for small business participation than support programs. The most obvious is that the individual owner does not have to apply to participate or obtain a benefit. There is neither an approval process nor any official who must sign off. Similarly, there is no cap on the number of eligible participants; anyone affected receives the benefit. Further, self-elimination because of an individual's reticence to apply or ignorance of a program's existence is irrelevant to lower barriers. The number of small business owners who benefit from eliminating impediments, therefore, is typically far greater than the number participating in support programs.

Given that the elimination of impediments approach seems so much more attractive from the small business owner's perspective, why is there not more of it (and perhaps less devoted to support programs)? There are two fundamental reasons. The first is that there is typically, but not always, a public purpose for regulations. For example, rules exist to govern storage of food in restaurants. Most people consider those health requirements desirable. Second, even barriers that are unwarranted or counterproductive are in place because someone wants them there. There is often political resistance to eliminating them, and political resistance typically results in a healthy political battle between the initiative's proponents and detractors. That is why it is usually easier to create or expand a support program (lack of opposition) than to eliminate a barrier.

The Regulatory Flexibility Act as Amended

One of the most novel and interesting approaches to eliminating or reducing barriers for small businesses is the federal Regulatory Flexibility Act (RFA) of 1980.[65] The RFA is premised on the idea that regulation has a disproportionate impact on small entities, most of which are small businesses. Regulations create two types of costs, fixed and variable.[66] The former cost is the same whether applied to the local gift store or Walmart, while the latter varies with the number of units sold or produced. Thus, it costs the local gift store more to comply with the same set of rules than it costs Walmart. One recent study found that the relative cost differential between firms with fewer than 20 employees and those with over 500 employees is about 36 percent.[67] These cost differences persist over time; they are not a single event.[68]

There are also instances when regulatory requirements imposed on all businesses make little sense or are even counterproductive. The Bureau of the Census and the Bureau of Labor Statistics, for example, often apply the principle for business data collection. They will survey the largest firms with "certainty," that is, include all large firms, but they will only sample smaller firms because the dollars saved on data collection and processing are enormous and the imposition on small business owners is minimized while data quality remains high. The additional requirements created by Employee Retirement Income Security Act (ERISA) of 1974 actually proved counterproductive for small businesses and their employees.[69] The law was designed to prevent pension plans, particularly in large firms, from financially collapsing and leaving employees and pensioners without promised retirement benefits. ERISA largely accomplished its goals by strengthening large pension plans, but its highly undesirable and unintended consequence was to force a substantial percentage of small employers to eliminate their pension plans altogether.

Regulatory tiering, that is, providing different sets of rules for different sizes of firms, was offered as a way to address the negative effects of disproportionate impacts. The concept was not new with the Regulatory Flexibility Act; rather the act systematized it and introduced a process that made assessment of disproportionate regulatory impacts routine and adjustments for it frequent.[70] The RFA requires virtually all federal departments and agencies to assess their proposed rules and regulations to determine whether they have a disproportionate impact on small businesses. If they do have such an impact, the issuing agency must determine whether there are ways, such as exemption, a lesser or different standard, or a delayed implementation date, that would alleviate those impacts without undermining the intent of the rule making.

RFA effectively institutes a process. No outcome is required. The agencies must only make an analysis, *consider* alternative rules for small firms, and report their findings to the SBA. No further action is necessary. If an agency refuses to comply with the procedure, the SBA can take the offending agency to court, but this is rarely done.

The SBA's Office of Advocacy, which oversees the process, estimates that the act saved small business $2.4 billion in one-time costs in FY 2012,[71] a relatively modest amount compared to the $17 billion saved in FY 2004.[72] Advocacy concluded that even with only modest enforcement capability, "most agencies continued to comply with the requirements of RFA."[73] GAO has been less buoyant about agency response.[74] However, by all accounts, agency compliance with both the letter and spirit of the law has improved over the years.

Forty-five states have followed the federal government's lead and enacted some form of the RFA or an executive order that does much the same thing.[75] However, their performances have been mixed. An enthusiastic executive appears essential for the act to work well, and not all states have one.[76]

The Tax Code and Pass-Throughs

Policy makers help small businesses through the tax code. Earlier in this chapter, the writer cited examples of support-type tax policy, also known as tax expenditures, which are intended to assist smaller firms. But impediment reductions within the federal tax code also occur. One of the most important was enactment of Subchapter S of the Internal Revenue Code,[77] creating a type of corporation (with a corporation's liability protection) that recognizes income earned from it as equivalent to income earned from wages or salaries for income tax purposes.

C-corporations, the legal form used by publicly traded companies and many larger small firms, pay income taxes twice. They pay them on corporate earnings and then individuals who receive dividends (paid to them by C-corporations on after-tax earnings) pay personal income tax on their dividend income. The latter effectively represents a second tax payment on one income stream. In contrast, other legal forms, such as S-corporations, LLCs, partnerships, and proprietorships, which are traditionally small business forms, pay income tax only once. Their business earnings are effectively personal income, which is taxed along with any other income as part of the personal income tax. The latter four legal forms are therefore known as "pass-throughs"; that is, business earnings.are passed directly through the business (without corporate income tax) to its owner(s). Depending on one's definition of "small business," anywhere between 75 percent and 90 percent of small employers are now pass-throughs.[78]

The S-corporation has been growing in popularity, particularly since the favorable tax changes in the mid-1980s, and is currently more common than the C-corporation form.[79] By tax year 2008, there were over 4 million S-corporations filing tax returns, compared to 1.7 million C-corporations.[80]

Lower Entry Barriers

Those who have been in business are familiar with all of the necessary registrations, permits, and processes that government, particularly state and local governments, require to start a business.[81] Low-entry barriers, that is, minimal costs, hassles, and time to complete the legal formalities prior to the start of operations, are generally considered a positive factor in a jurisdiction's business climate because they ease entry and deter fewer potential owners.[82] It typically takes just a few days to complete all of the formalities in the United States, meaning a low-entry barrier. In contrast, it may take months to register a business in many countries.[83] Still, American small business owners are intolerant of excess bureaucracy and paperwork that consume their time and resources. The result is that many American local governments have hired ombudsmen and instituted one-stop shops to reduce the time and hassle required to open a business. Check out the one-stop shop in the City of New Orleans, for example.[84]

SMALL BUSINESS POLICY IN PRACTICE

Most political jurisdictions, at least the substantial ones, if not the vastly more numerous small districts, have different climates or conditions brought on by a blend of small business support and impediment-reduction policies. The distinguishing factor among the jurisdictions is the composition of the blend. Some rely more heavily on one than the other; in a few cases, one or the other is barely visible. Therefore, to understand the small business policy of one jurisdiction compared to another, it is helpful to present a typology that examines policy blends.[85]

Table 13.1 effectively crosses the relative degree of supports and impediments in a jurisdiction. The x-axis presents jurisdictions that have high and low impediments (and presumably the policies that underlie them); the y-axis presents jurisdictions that have high and low supports (and presumably the policies that underlie them). *High* and *low* are relative terms. When comparing jurisdictions, high and low on the axes may be far apart or reasonably close. Typically, they are at their most extreme when comparing conditions across countries and least extreme when comparing conditions across small, contiguous jurisdictions.

The typology in table 13.1 creates four broad policy blends. The first is a policy that allows high (relatively) impediments and enjoys high (relatively) supports. That type of policy is titled "compensating" because a high level of supports is intended to compensate for a high level of barriers. The concept behind the policy is to selectively lift a limited number of small businesses over the hurdles created. The policy thereby favors some owners at the expense of others. The criteria for determining favored firms or owners rest with policy priorities, which can result in preferences toward companies ranging from those that are high growth to those that are export oriented to those that are minority owned. High impediments are barriers that must be surmounted, making new firm entry relatively difficult. At the same time, they constitute a body of policy that shelters incumbents. That outcome may not be the purpose of the impediments; the purpose may be to protect some value considered important to society. But incumbent protection is typically an effect.

The opposite quadrant in the typology consists of low barriers and low supports. It is the most market-oriented policy because it is the most hands-off and

TABLE 13.1 Impediments and Supports: A Typology

		Impediments	
		High	Low
Supports	High	Compensating	Nurturing
	Low	Limiting	Competing

the most likely to encourage competition, and not just among small businesses but among all competitors. It is therefore named "competitive." Entry barriers are low. Because entrepreneurs tend to thrive in a competitive environment, the policy is most conducive for entrepreneurial small businesses, typically more aggressive, growth-oriented firms. Life-style small businesses, the more numerous type of small firm, are not likely to find the policy as endearing. There are no supports, no help. Competitors are left to succeed or fail on their own devices.

The third type is a "nurturing" policy. A nurturing policy involves a high level of supports and a low level of impediments. This generic policy type appears the most favorable to small business, the best of all worlds. It has few barriers, but it also has supports to raise affected firms over the minimal impediments that exist. The question that such a policy raises is whether the policy is too encouraging, in the sense that it nurtures too many weak firms that cannot possibly survive the rigors of the market. The existence of too many weak firms not only pries their owners from more productive activity but may also draw away just enough business from potentially successful firms so that it destroys them as well.

The fourth and last quadrant in the typology appears least favorable to small business. It consists of a high level of impediments and a low level of supports. It is a "limiting" policy. The impediments are high, making it relatively difficult to enter and successfully operate, and there is little public help to assist the owners to surmount them. Thus, the individual is on his own, just as in a competitive policy climate. The difference is that under the limiting policy, the owner must still battle the impediments. A severe climate with no assistance is unlikely to produce crops of thriving small businesses.

The varying combinations of supports and impediments create a varying set of climates for small business. Some combinations appear more conducive than others for the population as a whole, but individual perspectives may differ on which is which. The quandary that many small business owners face is that they have no choice in the matter. They are tied to a location by costs, customers, or family. Relocating to a different, more favorable jurisdiction with a more sympathetic policy climate is simply not practical. They have no choice but to work with what they have. That infers involvement in public policy and the political process, which consumes time and money, but perhaps less of them than the alternative.

CONCLUSION

The text to this point has described several flavors of small business policies that government has employed to help owners enter, survive, and thrive. Still, many policies have been passed over because of space limitations. The programs that attempt to specifically assist socially and economically disadvantaged small business owners are the most notable to receive short shrift, largely because they parallel the policies established for owners in general. The principal difference between them is that participant eligibility for those programs is narrower, confined to women, racial minorities, or, most recently, veterans. But beyond these, there remain more unmentioned support and impediment-reduction policies that individual small business owners will find helpful and worthy of additional investigation.

There is one other policy type that people often forget in the abstract, but that many elected officials and governments perform very well in practice— simple cheerleading. Public encouragement and verbal advocacy for local small business activity is an important element of a supportive culture, one that nurtures small and innovative enterprises and the people who found and operate them. Historically, a supportive culture has been the bedrock on which entrepreneurial and small business activity has grown, and even flourished.[86] This is no less true today. Some public officials are reticent to engage in cheerleading. They believe that it is beneath their dignity or they fear being painted as friendly to self-serving and nonproductive business ventures.[87] Yet, public verbal encouragement of enterprise in general and productive, growing enterprise specifically by public officials provides, at minimal cost, assistance to a broad swath of small business owners, both now and into the future.

NOTES

1. Johns Hopkins School of Public Policy, accessed July 10, 2013, http://ips.jhu.edu/pub/public-policy.

2. Anders Lundström and Lois Stevenson, "Dressing the Emperor: The Fabric of Entrepreneurship Policy," in *Handbook of Research on Entrepreneurship Policy*, ed. David B. Audretsch, Isabel Grilo, and A. Roy Thurik (Cheltenham, U.K.: Edward Elgar, 2007).

3. U.S. Small Business Administration. Office of Advocacy, "Firm Size Data," accessed August 6, 2013, www.sba.gov/advocacy/849/12162.

4. U.S. Department of Labor, Bureau of Labor Statistics, "The Employment Situation," Table A-9, accessed August 6, 2013, www.bls.gov/news.release/pdf/empsit.pdf.

5. U.S. Department of the Treasury, Internal Revenue Service, *Statistics of Income Bulletin*, Tax Stats, Table 12, accessed August 6, 2013, www.irs.gov/uac/SOI-Tax-Stats-Historical-Table-12.

6. U.S. Small Business Administration. Office of Advocacy, Frequently Asked Questions, accessed August 6, 2013, www.sba.gov/sites/default/files/FAQ_Sept_2012.pdf.

7. Ibid., accessed August 6, 2013.

8. William J. Dennis, Jr., ed., "Contributions to Community," *National Small Business Poll*, 4, 6 (Washington, D.C.: NFIB Research Foundation, 2004).

9. Sandra M. Anglund, *Small Business Policy and the American Creed* (Westport, CT: Praeger, 2000).

10. Alexis de Tocqueville, *Democracy in America*, ed. Phillips Bradley (New York: Alford A. Knopf, 1972), 157.

11. Elizabeth Mendes and Joy Wilke, "America's Confidence in Congress Falls to Lowest on Record," *Gallup Political*, June 13, 2013, accessed June 13, 2013, www.gallup.com/poll/163052/americans-confidence-congress-falls-lowest-record.aspx; William J. Dennis Jr., *The Public Reviews Small Business* (Washington, D.C.: NFIB Research Foundation, 2004); William J. Dennis Jr., *The Public Reviews Small Business* (Washington, D.C.: NFIB Research Foundation, 1997).

12. U.S. Department of Commerce, Bureau of the Census, *Statistical Abstract of the United States: 2012* (Washington, D.C.: Government Printing Office, 2012), tables 428 and 429.

13. See for example, National Governors' Association, *"Making" Our Future: What States Are Doing to Encourage Growth in Manufacturing through Innovation, Entrepreneurship and Investment*, accessed August 7, 2013, www.nga.org/files/live/sites/NGA/files/pdf/2013/1301. NGAManufacturingReportWeb.pdf; National Governors Association's Center for Best Practices, "State Strategies to Promote Angel Investment for Economic Growth," Washington, D.C., February 14, 2008. For examples of operating programs used by cities, see the National League of Cities, "Small Business & Entrepreneurship," accessed August 7, 2013, www.nlc.org/find-city-solutions/city-solutions-and-applied-research/economic-development/small-business-and-entrepreneurship.

14. Catalog of Federal Domestic Assistance, www.cfda.gov.

15. House Committee on Small Business (report by Democratic staff), "The Impact of the FY 2007 Budget on Small Business," March 2, 2006.

16. U.S. Government Accountability Office, GAO-12-819, "Entrepreneurial Assistance: Opportunities Exist to Improve Programs' Collaboration, Data-tracking, and Performance Management," William B. Shear, August 2012, 6.

17. Public Law 95-507.

18. U.S. Government Accountability Office, "Entrepreneurial Assistance," p. Highlights.

19. U.S. Government Accountability Office, GAO-13-217, "Small Business Administration Needs to Improve Collaboration to Implement Its Expanded Role," Loren Yeager, January 30, 2013.

20. U.S. Government Accountability Office, "Entrepreneurial Assistance."

21. Ibid., 54.

22. U.S. Government Accountability Office, GAO-12-553. T, "Economic Development: Efficiency and Effectiveness of Fragmented Programs Are Unclear," William B. Shear, March 21, 2012, 6–7.

23. The Patient Protection and Affordable Care Act (Obamacare), for example, uses seven different definitions of small business. See Janemarie Mulvey,

Memorandum: What Is Small? Definition of Small Business in the Patient Protection and Affordable Care Act (Washington, D.C.: Library of Congress, Congressional Research Service, September 27, 2012).

24. U.S. Small Business Administration, Office of Government Contracting & Business Development, Size Standards Division, SBA Size Standards Methodology, April 9, 2009, accessed August 14, 2013, www.sba.gov/sites/default/files/size_standards_methodology.pdf.

25. U.S. Department of Agriculture, Rural Business Cooperative Service, Loan Application Form, accessed August 14, 2013, http://forms.sc.egov.usda.gov/efcommon/eFileServices/eForms/RD4279-1-A.PDF.

26. U.S. Small Business Administration, FY 2014 Congressional Budget Justification and FY2012 Annual Performance Report, 35, accessed July 30, 2013, www.sba.gov/sites/default/files/files/1-508-Compliant-FY-2014-CBJ%20. FY%202012%20 APR.pdf.

27. Ibid.

28. Writer's calculation.

29. Robert Jay Dilger, Small Business Administration's 7(a) Loan Guaranty Program, R41146 (Washington, D.C.: U.S. Library of Congress, Congressional Research Service, November 8, 2011), 12, footnote 47.

30. Christopher Hayes, "An Assessment of Small Business Administration Loan and Investment Performance: Survey of Assisted Businesses" (Washington, D.C.: Urban Institute, 2008), 3, accessed August 7, 2013, www.urban.org/Uploaded-PDF/411599_assisted_business_survey.pdf.

31. U.S. Small Business Administration, Loans & Grants, General Small Business Loans: 7(a), accessed July 30, 2013, www.sba.gov/content/7a-loan-amounts-fees-interest-rates.

32. Hayes, "An Assessment of Small Business Administration Loan and Investment Performance," 7.

33. Lenders, particularly large lenders and lenders who specialize in SBA guarantees, that can climb a steep learning curve and achieve scale economies, find the SBA7(a) loan guarantee program quite attractive for a number of reasons. The loans are guaranteed, up to 85 percent on smaller loans and 75 percent on larger ones. The loans with the guarantee can be sold on a secondary market where they are packaged into securities and sold to private investors. The sales take the loans off the lender's books, except for the small share SBA requires it to retain. The lender services the loans and keeps those fees. In addition, the loans have a positive publicity value. It has been argued that lenders benefit from the program more than borrowers. See, Veronique de Rugy, "Banking on the SBA," *Mercatus on Policy 2* (Arlington, VA: Mercatus Institute, George Mason University, August 2007).

34. The disbursements were as of March 31, 2013, accessed July 30, 2013, www.treasury.gov/resource-cener/sb-programs/Pages/Small-Business-Lending-Fund.aspx.

35. Congressional Budget and Impoundment Control Act of 1974, Pub. L. No. 93–344, § 3, 3 (1974).

36. U.S. Congress, Joint Committee on Taxation, *Estimates of Federal Tax Expenditures for Fiscal Years 2012–2017* (Washington, D.C.: U.S. Government Printing Office, February 1, 2013).

37. Ibid., 33.

38. A "conforming" state uses the federal tax code with minor modifications to establish taxable income. Taxable income is then multiplied by the state rate to obtain state tax liability. Nonconforming states require taxpayers to calculate a second taxable income, different than the federal, and then apply the state rate.

39. William J. Dennis Jr., ed., "Tax Complexity and the IRS," *National Small Business Poll* 6, 6 (Washington, D.C.: NFIB Research Foundation, 2006).

40. William J. Dennis Jr., ed., "Advisors on Critical Decisions," *National Small Business Poll* 12, 1 (Washington, D.C.: NFIB Research Foundation, 2012).

41. Ibid.

42. U.S. Department of Commerce, Bureau of the Census, Statistics of U.S. Businesses, accessed August 2, 2013, www.census.gov/econ/susb.

43. William J. Dennis Jr. and Paul D. Reynolds, "Knowledge and Use of Assistance," *Handbook of Entrepreneurial Dynamics: The Process of Business Creation*, ed. William B. Gartner, Kelly G. Shaver, Nancy M. Carter, and Paul D. Reynolds (Thousand Oaks, CA: Sage Publications, 2004).

44. U.S. Small Business Administration, FY 2014 Congressional Budget Justification and FY2012 Annual Performance Report, 48.

45. Ibid.

46. U.S. Small Business Administration. Contracting, Getting Started, accessed July 31, 2013, www.sba.gov/content/sba%E2%80%99s-role-government-contracting.

47. J. D. Harrison, "Small Business Contracting Numbers Inflated by Errors and Exclusions, Data Show," On Small Business, *Washington Post*, July 29, 2013, accessed July 31, 2013, www.washingtonpost.com/business/on-small-business/small-business-contracting-numbers-inflated-by-errors-and-exclusions-data-show/2013/07/28/7fa2a4fc-f2f6-11e2-8505-bf6f231e77b4_story.html.

48. U.S. Small Business Administration, FY 2012 Small Business Procurement Scorecard, accessed July 31, 2013, www.sba.gov/sites/default/files/files/FY12_Final_Scorecard_Government-Wide_2013-06-20.pdf.

49. U.S. House of Representatives, House Small Business Committee, Majority Staff.

50. Federal Acquisition Regulation, Subpart 19.5—Set-Asides for Small Business, accessed July 31, 2013, www.acquisition.gov/far/html/Subpart%2019_5.html.

51. Ibid., Subpart 19-502-2(a).

52. U.S. Federal Contractor Registration, www.uscontractorregistration.com.

53. See, Federal Business Opportunities, www.fedbizopps.gov.

54. Federal Acquisition Regulation, 5.206.

55. Max V. Kidalov and Keith F. Snider, "US and European Public Procurement Policies for Small and Medium-sized Enterprises (SME): A Comparative Perspective," *Business and Politics* 13, 4 (2011).

56. William J. Dennis Jr., ed., "Contacting Government," *National Small Business Poll* 3, 1 (Washington, D.C.: NFIB Research Foundation, 2003).

57. Ibid.

58. Qian Gu, Lynn A. Karoly, and Julie Zissimopoulos, *Small Business Assistance Programs in the United States: An Analysis of What They Are, How Well They Perform, and How We Can Learn More about Them*, Kauffman-Rand Institute for Entrepreneurship Public Policy Working Paper (Santa Monica, CA: Rand Corporation, September 2008).

59. U.S. Government Accountability Office, "Entrepreneurial Assistance."

60. See, David J. Storey, "Six Steps to Heaven: Evaluating the Impact of Public Policies to Support Small Businesses in Developed Economies," in *The Blackwell Handbook of Entrepreneurship*, ed. Donald Sexton and Hans Landström (Oxford, U.K.: Blackwell Publishers, Ltd., 2000).

61. Robert Jay Dilger, "SBA Assistance to Small Business Startups: Client Experiences and Program Impact," R43083 (Washington, D.C.: U.S. Library of Congress, Congressional Research Service, May 22, 2013).

62. Gu, Karoly, and Zissimopoulos, *Small Business Assistance Programs in the United States*.

63. U.S. House of Representatives, Committee on Small Business, Statement of P. E. Gustafson, Inspector General, Small Business Administration, June 5, 2013, 6.

64. U.S. Government Accountability Office, GAO-12-553. T, "Economic Development," 7.

65. As Amended by Small Business Regulatory Enforcement Fairness Act (SBREFA) (1996) and Executive Order 13272 (2002).

66. C. Steven Bradford, "Does Size Matter? An Economic Analysis of Small Business Exemptions from Regulation," *Journal of Small Emerging Business Law* 8, 1 (2004): 1–37; William A. Brock and David S. Evans, *The Economics of Small Businesses: Their Role and Regulation in the U.S. Economy* (New York: Holmes & Meier, 1986).

67. Nicole V. Crain and W. Mark Crain, *The Impact of Regulatory Costs on Small Business*, U.S. Small Business Administration, Office of Advocacy, SBAHQ-08-M-0466, September 2010.

68. Bradford, "Does Size Matter?"

69. James D. McKevitt, Washington Counsel, National Federation of Independent Business, Statement to the U.S. Senate Judiciary Committee, Administrative Practices Subcommittee, October 7, 1977.

70. William J. Dennis Jr., "Tailoring Regulation to the Regulated: The U.S. Regulatory Flexibility Act," in *Business Regulation and Public Policy: The Cost and Benefits of Compliance*, ed. Andre Nijsen et. al. (New York: Springer, 2007).

71. U.S. Small Business Administration, Office of Advocacy, *Report on the Regulatory Flexibility Act FY2012*, February 2013, i.

72. U.S. Small Business Administration, Office of Advocacy, *Report on the Regulatory Flexibility Act FY2005*, April 2006, 11.

73. U.S. Small Business Administration, Office of Advocacy, *Report on the Regulatory Flexibility Act FY2012*, 30.

74. J. Christopher Mihm, "Regulatory Flexibility Act: Congress Should Revisit and Clarify Elements of the Act to Improve Its Effectiveness," U.S. Government Accountability Office, GAO-06-998. (Washington, D.C.: GAO, July 20, 2006).

75. U.S. Small Business Administration, Office of Advocacy, *Research on State Regulatory Flexibility Acts*. (Washington, D.C.: Microeconomic Applications, Inc., 2013).

76. Ibid.

77. Mirit Eyal-Cohen, *When American Small Business Hit the Jackpot: Taxes, Politics and the History of Organizational Choice in the 1950s*, UCLA School of Law, Law-Econ Research Paper No. 09-04, February 23, 2009.

78. Author's calculations from Statistics of Income (SOI) data published by the Internal Revenue Service.

79. Tom Petska et al., "An Analysis of Business Organizational Structure and Activity from Tax Data," *Statistics of Income Bulletin* (2005), accessed August 25, 2013, www.irs.gov/pub/irs-soi/05petska.pdf.

80. U.S. Department of the Treasury, Internal Revenue Service. SOI Tax Stats, Integrated Data, accessed August 25, 2013, www.irs.gov/uac/SOI-Tax-Stats-Integrated-Business-Data.

81. Registration and permitting are not the only entry barriers for small business. Others can include infrastructure issues, such as a reliable supply of electricity, property rights questions, various incumbent protections that include limiting the supply of competitors, etc.

82. World Bank, "Starting a Business," in *Doing Business in 2014: Understanding Regulations for Small and Medium Enterprises* (Washington, D.C.: World Bank, 2013): 72–76.

83. Ibid., Appendix: Doing Business Indicators.

84. City of New Orleans, One Stop Permits & Licenses, www.nola.gov/onestop.

85. The following discussion is a condensation of that found in William J. Dennis Jr., "Entrepreneurship, Small Business and Public Policy Levers, Part 2," *Journal of Small Business Management* 49, 2 (2011): 149–162.

86. Paul D. Reynolds, "Business Creation: The Impact of National Factors and Individual Attributes," mimeo, 2012; David S. Landes, *The Unbounded Prometheus: Technological Change and Industrial Development in Western Europe from 1750 to the Present*, 2nd ed. (Cambridge, U.K.: Cambridge University Press, 2003); Joel Mokyr, *The Lever to Riches: Technological Creativity and Economic Progress* (Oxford, U.K.: Oxford University Press, 1999); Douglas C. North, *Institutions, Institutional Change, and Economic Progress* (Cambridge, U.K.: Cambridge University Press, 1990).

87. William J. Baumol, "Entrepreneurship: Productive, Unproductive, and Destructive," *Journal of Business Venturing* 11, 1 (1996): 3–22.

About the Editor and Contributors

THE EDITOR

SCOTT L. NEWBERT is an associate professor of management, the Harry Halloran Emerging Scholar in Social Entrepreneurship, and the Anne Quinn Welsh Faculty Fellow in Honors at Villanova University, where he teaches graduate and undergraduate courses on strategy and entrepreneurship at the Villanova School of Business. He received his PhD in strategic management and entrepreneurship from Rutgers University. His research interests include the processes by which existing and nascent firms create value through the entrepreneurial use of resources, the determinants of firm creation, and the socioeconomic impacts of entrepreneurial activity. His research on these and related topics has been published in the top entrepreneurship and management journals, including *Strategic Management Journal*, *Journal of Business Venturing*, *Entrepreneurship Theory and Practice*, *Small Business Economics*, *Journal of Business Ethics*, and *IEEE Transactions on Engineering Management*. He currently serves as a field editor for *Journal of Business Venturing* as well as an editorial review board member for the *Strategic Management Journal*, *Journal of Management Studies*, and the *Journal of Small Business Management* and has previously served as guest editor for special issues of *Journal of Social Entrepreneurship* and *Technovation*. he is an active member of the Academy of Management entrepreneurship and business policy and strategy divisions. In addition to his academic endeavors, he also provides consulting services to nonprofit and for-profit organizations, with clients that include the United States and Dutch governments and Sandia National Laboratories. Prior to obtaining his PhD, he worked in sales for a Fortune 100 company, worked as a collegiate athletics coach, and cofounded a privately owned marketing firm, whose clients include Colgate-Palmolive and McNeil Nutritionals.

THE CONTRIBUTORS

DOUGLAS A. BOSSE is associate professor of strategy and entrepreneurship at the Robins School of Business at University of Richmond. He received his PhD from Fisher College of Business at the Ohio State University. His work appears in *Strategic Management Journal, Journal of Business Venturing, Business Horizons, Technovation, Venture Capital, New Directions in Business Ethics*, and *Stakeholder Theory: Impacts and Prospects*, among others. He is a two-time winner of the International Association for Business and Society's Best Paper Published Award and is on the editorial board of *Stakeholder Theory and Practice*. He is a founding member and associate program chair for the Stakeholder Strategy Interest Group at the Strategic Management Society. His current research examines how firms manage key stakeholder relationships to improve firm-level performance. In addition to teaching at the MBA and undergraduate levels, he delivers leadership development workshops, facilitates strategic planning activities for executive teams, and conducts business-to-business relationship improvement studies for clients in a wide variety of industries. Prior to joining academe, he spent over 10 years in corporate strategy consulting.

VICTOR A. CHAVEZ is currently the principal at Chavez and Associates Consulting. He is utilizing over 40 years of experience working with academic institutions; local, state, and federal government research and development (R&D) agencies and centers; and private industry to engage federal agencies in strategic planning, technology management, and utilization. He retired as the technology transfer coordinator for the USDA/ARS North Atlantic Area (NAA) and was responsible for facilitating technology transfer activities and serving as liaison between ARS and the private sector. Mr. Chavez was the manager of the Supply Chain Resource & Development Department at Sandia National Laboratories, which includes small business development and training, including entrepreneurs; small business assistance; regional economic development; small business advocacy and outreach; supplier relations; and supply chain development programs. He was also responsible for developing and implementing a mentor-protégé program for small business suppliers and partners. He has received numerous awards, including being inducted into the University of New Mexico's Anderson Schools of Management Hall of Fame, the NNSA Administrator's Inaugural Small Business Innovation Award, the DOE Small Business Program Manager of the Year Award, and the SBA Small & Minority Business Advocate of the Year Award. He was also recognized by the Federal Laboratory Consortium for his lifetime achievement by being given the Harold Metcalf Award, which is the highest award given by the FLC.

KEVIN D. CLARK is associate professor and Richard and Barbara Naclerio Emerging Scholar in Strategic Management at the Villanova School of Business (VSB). He received his PhD from the University of Maryland's Robert H. Smith School of Business. His research focuses on the top management team's (TMT) influence on organizational advantage, particularly in knowledge-intensive and entrepreneurial firms. More specifically, he has investigated the impacts of TMT decision-making processes and social networks on outcomes such as innovation, decision speed, and firm performance. Other areas of research interest include social entrepreneurship and ethical decision making, the gender wage gap, and the changing role and composition of boards of directors. Current projects include a study of SME boards of directors in conjunction with the nonprofit Directors' Institute. His work has been published in the *Academy of Management Journal,* the *Journal of Management Studies,* the *Journal of Business Ethics* (forthcoming), *Organizational Dynamics,* and the *Leadership Review.* A VSB faculty member since 2001, he has served as chair of the Management and Organization Department, senior associate dean, and most recently as interim dean. He teaches global strategic management, the MBA global practicum, and an innovative semester abroad program in Urbino, Italy.

JUSTIN B. CRAIG holds a PhD in the field of behavioral science as well as a master of counseling and an honors degree in psychology, all with an intentional focus on entrepreneurial family businesses and those responsible for their stewardship. He is an associate professor of entrepreneurship and innovation at Northeastern University in Boston. Prior to joining Northeastern in 2012, he was an associate professor of entrepreneurship and family business at Bond University in Australia, where he was also codirector of the globally recognized Australian Centre for Family Business, and before that he was an assistant professor of entrepreneurship at Oregon State University. His research has been published in leading international academic journals, including the *Journal of Business Venturing, Entrepreneurship Theory and Practice, Family Business Review, Journal of Business Research, Journal of Small Business Management, Small Business Economics, Journal of Family Business Strategy,* and *Journal of World Business,* among others. He has been an associate editor of *Family Business Review* since 2010.

WILLIAM J. ("DENNY") DENNIS JR. is recently retired from his position as senior research fellow at the National Federation of Independent Business (NFIB) Research Foundation in Washington, D.C., where he directed its activities. He was employed more than 38 years in various research capacities by the NFIB, the nation's largest small business organization. Previously he spent over five years as a professional staff member in the U.S. House of Representatives. He was founder and editor of the National Small Business Poll; president of the International Council for Small Business and its vice-president for research and publications; team leader for the Entrepreneurship Research Consortium; coauthor of *Small Business Economic Trends* (series); member of the Business Research Advisory Committee, U.S. Bureau of Labor Statistics; member and chair of the Commonwealth of Virginia's Board of Professional and Occupational Regulation; and member of two panels for the National Academies of Science. He testified on policy issues before a variety of committees in the U.S. House of Representatives and the U.S. Senate as well as before state legislative bodies. He received the Academy of Management's (entrepreneurship division) Advocate Award for outstanding contributions to the field of entrepreneurship, the U.S. Small Business Administration's Special Advocacy Award for Research, and a lifetime membership from the Babson Entrepreneurship Research Conference.

DAWN R. DeTIENNE is an associate professor of entrepreneurship at Colorado State University in Fort Collins, Colorado. She is a former entrepreneur who successfully exited a venture to return to academics. Her research focuses on entrepreneurial exit, gender and entrepreneurship, family business, and opportunity identification. Her research has appeared in *Academy of Management Learning & Education, Journal of Business Venturing, Entrepreneurship Theory & Practice, Small Business Economics, Journal of High Technology Management,* and *IEEE Transactions on Engineering Management.* She is a six-year dean's scholar and, in 2009, was awarded the Colorado State University College of Business Researcher of the Year. In 2011, she received the Colorado State University Excellence in Teaching Award. She is an associate editor for the *Academy of Management Learning & Education Journal* and serves on the editorial boards of *Entrepreneurship Theory & Practice* and the *Journal of Business Venturing.* In 2013, she received the J. William Fulbright Scholarship to Dublin, Ireland.

PAUL DRNEVICH received his PhD from Purdue University and is an associate professor of strategic management at the University of Alabama and a visiting associate professor with the University of Illinois while on sabbatical for the 2013–2014 academic year. His research interests include examining how organizational capabilities contribute to value creation and appropriation, the effects of environmental uncertainty on their contribution, and the role of information technology (IT) in enhancing these contributions, particularly to innovation and performance in entrepreneurial ventures and small business. He has authored research for the *Academy of Management Learning & Education, Decision Sciences, Journal of Management Studies, Journal of Small Business Management, MIS Quarterly*, and *Strategic Management Journal*. He is a member of the Academy of Management and the Strategic Management Society, serves on the executive committee as treasurer of the Academy's Business Policy and Strategy division, and holds editorial board appointments with AMLE and SMJ.

MANUEL EBERHARD is a member of a third-generation family business in Germany and currently works at General Logistics Systems Holding, an international logistics company based in Amsterdam, Netherlands. Before joining GLS, he was a research associate at the Australian Centre for Family Business and lecturer for international business and entrepreneurship at Bond University, Australia. He received his doctorate from Bond University and held a visiting PhD position at the Wharton School, University of Pennsylvania. His primary research interests are in the area of international management, entrepreneurship, and family business; his research has been published in the *Journal of World Business* and presented at several international conferences. He also serves as an ad hoc reviewer for the *Family Business Review* and the *Journal of Management and Organization*.

BRETT ANITRA GILBERT is an associate professor in the Department of Management and Global Business at Rutgers Business School. She teaches a variety of undergraduate and graduate entrepreneurship courses that range from introductory courses to electives such as technology ventures. Her overarching research interest can be described as seeking to understand the conditions under which new ventures thrive. Her research spans the geographic cluster, alliances, innovation, internationalization, and performance streams of literature, and she is currently published or forthcoming in the *Journal of Business Venturing, Journal of International Business Studies, Journal of Management, Research Policy, Small Business Economics*, and *Strategic Management Journal*. Current projects focus on understanding emerging clean energy technologies and the factors that allow these technologies to enter the market. She is also currently engaged in projects that seek to understand how technology communities emerge within distressed urban regions. This research is focused on Newark, New Jersey, and Johannesburg, South Africa. Originally from Detroit, she comes from an entrepreneurial family, received her PhD in entrepreneurship from Indiana University, and was the first entrepreneurship PhD to graduate from the program. Her BA is in management from Wittenberg University, which not only sparked her love for learning but also for research.

DAVID GRAS is an assistant professor of entrepreneurship and strategy in the Neeley School of Business at Texas Christian University. He holds a PhD in entrepreneurship and emerging enterprises from Syracuse University and an MS in marketing from Clemson University. He has developed and taught courses on entrepreneurship, opportunity generation, assessment and promotion, and strategic management. His research focuses on social entrepreneurship and diversification within new ventures. His work has been published in *Journal of Business Venturing, Journal of Social Entrepreneurship, Small Business Economics, Journal of Business Strategy*, and *Academy of Management Learning and Education*.

JAMES HA is an undergraduate student majoring in management and information systems in the College of Commerce and Business Administration at the University of Alabama. He is a member of the Emerging Scholars program at the University of Alabama and served as a research assistant to Paul Drnevich from 2011 to 2012.

IFTEKHAR HASAN is the E. Gerald Corrigan Professor of Finance at Fordham University and concurrently serves as a scientific adviser to the Central Bank of Finland. He is the managing editor of the *Journal of Financial Stability* and has served as an associate editor in several academic journals. He has over 300 publications in print, including 14 books and edited volumes, and over 175 journal articles in reputed finance, economics, management, and accounting journals.

MIKA TATUM KUSAR is an assistant professor of management in the School of Business at Fort Lewis College in Durango, Colorado. Her research examines how organizations develop new capabilities and adapt existing capabilities to address changing market conditions. Her dissertation, "The Development and Renewal of Strategic Capabilities," examines the impact that a firm's past strategies and experiences have on the firm's ability to develop new capabilities and adapt existing capabilities. Her current research explores how a firm's past experiences with acquisitions and internal development impact the learning processes embedded in the firm's organizational structure and the firm's learning orientation. She received her PhD in management from Georgia State University, her master of healthcare administration from the University of North Carolina at Chapel Hill, and her bachelor of arts in economics from the University of Arkansas.

JONATHAN D. LINTON is the Power Corporation Professor in the Management of Technological Enterprises at the University of Ottawa. He is the editor-in-chief of *Technovation: The International Journal of Technological Innovation, Entrepreneurship and Technology Management*; foreign co-head for Laboratory for Science and Technology Studies, Higher School of Economics, Moscow; and the associate director for the Institute for Science Society and Policy, University of Ottawa. He also is on a number of editorial boards and was formerly on the faculty of Rensselaer Polytechnic Institute and Polytechnic Institute of New York University. He has published over 100 articles in academic and practice-oriented journals. His research focuses on the challenges to operations associated to emerging technologies and innovation. Prior to entering academe, he consulted for a number of years and was an advanced manufacturing engineer at Ford Electronics Manufacturing. He has consulted to a variety of firms and governments in North America and Europe on issues related to the management and integration of technology. While his research and work focuses on management of technology, he is still a registered professional engineer.

JOSEPH LiPUMA currently serves as a part-time senior lecturer at Boston University, and was previously associate professor and director of the International MBA program at EMLYON Business School in France. His research centers on international entrepreneurship, and he has been published in leading academic journals, including *Entrepreneurship Theory & Practice*, *Small Business Economics*, the *International Entrepreneurship and Management Journal*, the *Journal of Business Research*, and *Frontiers of Entrepreneurship Research*. His coauthored book, *Unlocking the Ivory Tower: How Management Research Can Transform Your Business*, makes academic research accessible to managers and businesspeople. He has more than 25 years of business experience, much of it in information technology consulting in the United States, Europe, and the Middle East, prior to his current academic career. He has started businesses in the United States, United Kingdom, Italy, and Saudi Arabia and has held executive management and board-level roles at small and medium-sized companies as well as large enterprises. He holds an MBA from SUNY Buffalo and a DBA in strategy and policy from Boston University; he has taught at both of these schools as well as at Drexel University and St. Joseph's University prior to his position in Lyon, France.

G. T. ("TOM") LUMPKIN is the Chris J. Witting Chair of Entrepreneurship at the Whitman School of Management at Syracuse University in New York. His primary research interests include entrepreneurial orientation, social entrepreneurship, family business, and strategy-making processes. He is a globally recognized scholar whose research has been published in the *Academy of Management Review*, *Academy of Management Journal*, *Strategic*

Entrepreneurship Journal, Entrepreneurship Theory and Practice, Journal of Business Venturing, Journal of Management, and *Strategic Management Journal.* He is a coeditor of *Strategic Entrepreneurship Journal* and serves on the editorial boards of *Journal of Business Venturing, Entrepreneurship Theory and Practice,* and *Family Business Review.* He has won multiple awards for his research, including the prestigious IDEA Awards Foundational Paper award from the Entrepreneurship Division of the Academy of Management. He is the coauthor of a textbook in its seventh edition, *Strategic Management: Creating Competitive Advantages,* with Greg Dess, Alan Eisner, and Gerry McNamara. He received his PhD in business administration from the University of Texas at Arlington and MBA from the University of Southern California.

ROBERT S. NASON is an assistant professor of management in the John Molson School of Business at Concordia University. He received his PhD in entrepreneurship from Syracuse University. His research interests lie at the intersection of strategy and entrepreneurship. He has developed a stream of research on entrepreneurial activity within family firms, and his current endeavors include developing theory on firm growth as a distinct performance outcome. Specifically, he is exploring the heterogeneous rates of growth dimensions within a firm (e.g., sales versus assets) and how the decoupling of growth dimensions affects the boundaries of the firm. He has published his research in several peer-reviewed academic journals, including *Strategic Entrepreneurship Journal, Family Business Review,* and *Entrepreneurship Theory and Practice.* He has presented at leading conferences, including the Academy of Management (AOM), the Babson College Entrepreneurship Research Conference (BCERC), the Family Enterprise Research Conference (FERC), and the European Institute for Advanced Studies in Management (EIASM). In his commitment to research with practical relevance, he has served in leadership roles at the Family Firm Institute and STEP Project for Family Enterprising at Babson College.

PANKAJ C. PATEL is an associate professor of management in the Miller College of Business at Ball State University. He has published articles in journals such as *Academy of Management Journal, Journal of Applied Psychology, Journal of Management, Journal of Operations Management, Production and Operations Management, Organization Science,* and *Strategic Management Journal.* He has also made over 60 presentations at national and international conferences. He currently serves on the editorial review boards of *Academy of Management Journal, Entrepreneurship Theory and Practice, Family Business Review, Journal of Business Venturing,* and *Journal of Management Studies.*

CHRISTIANE PRANGE is a professor of international strategy and management at EMLYON Business School in France and lectures both at the Lyon and the Shanghai campus. She obtained her PhD from Geneva University, Switzerland, and has lectured as a visiting professor in more than 10 countries, including Austria, China, Malaysia, Russia, Romania, the United Kingdom, and Switzerland, among others. Her current research revolves around global strategies and dynamic capabilities, international ambidexterity, and innovative customer functions in the MNC. Before joining academia, she had several years of experience in business development in the e-commerce and digital media industry (interim head of alliance management and business development), as director of consulting (business development and corporate relations), and as international project leader (SAP internal business consulting). She has also conducted research and training programs for major international firms. She has published five books and numerous articles, both in academic and practitioner journals.

DAVID SMALLBONE joined Kingston University in 2004 from Middlesex University. He is also a visiting professor at Hubei School of Economics, Wuhan, China, and at the Centre for Entrepreneurship, Innovation and Regional Development in Ventspils, Latvia. His research on entrepreneurship and SME development dates back to the 1980s, much of it with an applied policy focus. As a leading expert on entrepreneurship in former socialist economies, he was awarded an honorary doctorate by the University of Lodz in Poland for his work in this area. He has numerous publications on entrepreneurship in transition economies. The breadth of his research interests related to entrepreneurship, SMEs and public policy is reflected in his publications, covering high-growth SMEs, enterprise development in rural areas, innovation and innovation policy, internationalization and ethnic minorities, and immigrant entrepreneurship. He has extensive experience in research-based consultancy for a range of national and international clients, including central government departments in different countries, the European Commission, UNDP, and the OECD. He was elected president of the ICSB (2010–2011), having previously served as president of the ECSB (2005–2007). He is an associate editor of the *Journal of Small Business Management* and is on the editorial boards of a number of leading entrepreneurship journals.

REGAN STINNETT received his PhD in plasma physics from the University of Texas at Austin and was hired by Sandia National Laboratories to do research in inertial confinement fusion. In 1987, he was promoted to manage Sandia's intense pulsed ion beam experiments. In 1995, he left Sandia to commercialize a new ion beam surface treatment technology that he coin-vented. To do this, he cofounded Quantum Manufacturing Technologies, serving as president and CEO. In 1999, he returned to Sandia to help intro-duce micro/nano systems technologies to Sandia's business units, establishing the Microsystems and Engineering Sciences Applications Institute to create partnerships with U.S. universities. He also explored incorporation of micro/nano technologies into networked sensors systems for the War on Terrorism as a member of Sandia's Advanced Concepts Group and later as manager of Sandia's Intrusion Detection Technology Department. In 2007, he became program manager for the National Institute for Nano-engineering, with the goal of creating a government/industry/university collaborative research alli-ance to help develop the next generation of nanotechnology innovators. The NINE program supported collaborative nano-engineering research projects, with students from 28 universities. In 2011, he became program manager of Sandia's Materials Aging and Surveillance Program. He also serves on the executive board of the Micro and Nanosystems Commercialization and Education Foundation. Regan has received the U.S. Department of Energy Award of Excellence for contributions to the Nuclear Weapons Program and is the holder of five patents.

LARRY TRIBBLE is a doctoral candidate at the University of Alabama. His research interests include exploring how firms create and capture value in the acquisition of strategic assets, the governance of exchange, and the role of technology in value creation. His research has been presented at conferences that include the *Academy of Management,* the *Strategic Management Society,* and the *Americas Conference on Information Systems.* He is a member of the Academy of Management and the Strategic Management Society.

STEVEN T. WALSH is a distinguished professor and the Regents Professor at the University of New Mexico. He is the Institute Professor of entrepreneur-ial renewal of industry at the University of Twente. Both the MOT program (top 10) and the entrepreneurial program (top 20) at UNM were ranked among the best programs in North America under his tenure. He currently acts as an area editor for two journals and is on the review board of several others. He has many business service awards, including the lifetime achieve-ment award for commercialization of small technology from MANCEF. Most recently, he was recognized as one of top seven researchers worldwide in technology and innovation management in the world over the past 10 years. He has also been named a Tech All Star from the State of New Mexico Economic Development Department. Finally, he is exceptionally proud of the Anderson School of Management Service to the Community Award.

He earned his PhD from RPI. He has also written over 150 archival books, book chapters, academic articles, and practitioner articles. He has won many academic research awards as well. These include the Best Paper of the Year paper in *Technology Forecasting and Social Change*.

HAIZHI WANG is an assistant professor of finance at the IIT Stuart School of Business. His research focuses on corporate finance, financial institutions, and entrepreneurial finance. His research has been published in academic journals that include the *Journal of Banking and Finance*, *Financial Review*, *Journal of Business Research*, *Small Business Economics*, and *Strategic Management Journal*. He has received research grants from multiple organizations, including the Federal Deposit Insurance Corporation (FDIC), Berkley Research Center of the Stern School of Business, and the Kauffman Foundation.

KARL WENNBERG is an associate professor of management at the Stockholm School of Economics and affiliated with the Ratio Institute. His recent research deals with entrepreneurial exit, growth in new ventures, and the relationship between entrepreneurship and economic inequality. This research has appeared in *Management Science*, *Journal of Business Venturing*, *Journal of International Business Studies*, and *Strategic Entrepreneurship Journal*, among other journals.

MINGMING ZHOU is an assistant professor of finance at the University of Colorado at Colorado Springs. Her research focuses on the financial market and institutions in the transitional economies. She has several publications in finance journals that include the *Journal of Banking and Finance*, *Journal of Investing*, *Financial Markets, Institutions & Instruments*, and *Economic Development Quarterly*.

Index